HITLER AND FILM

HITLER
AND FILM
THE FÜHRER'S
HIDDEN PASSION

BILL NIVEN

YALE UNIVERSITY PRESS
NEW HAVEN AND LONDON

For information about this and other Yale University Press publications, please contact:

U.S. Office: sales.press@yale.edu   yalebooks.com
Europe Office: sales@yaleup.co.uk   yalebooks.co.uk

Set in Adobe Garamond Pro by IDSUK (DataConnection) Ltd
Printed in Great Britain by TJ International Ltd, Padstow, Cornwall

Library of Congress Control Number: 2017955406

ISBN 978-0-300-20036-2

A catalogue record for this book is available from the British Library.

10 9 8 7 6 5 4 3 2 1

To my wife Helena, and my sister Ruth,
for your support and encouragement

Contents

Illustrations

10. Hitler and Goebbels at the Babelsberg studios in early 1935, where they were shown the set of Gerhard Lamprecht's film *Barcarole*. BARCH Bild 183-1990-1002-500.

11. Czech actress Lída Baarová. INTERFOTO / Alamy Stock Photo.

12. Still from *Victory in the West* (1941). ullstein bild Dtl / Getty Images.

13. Otto Gebühr as Frederick the Great in Veit Harlan's *The Great King* (1942). ullstein bild Dtl / Getty Images.

14. Ferdinand Marian as the title character in the notorious anti-Semitic feature film *Jew Süss* (1940), directed by Veit Harlan. Photo 12 / Alamy Stock Photo.

15. Advertising for the Nazi 'documentary' *The Eternal Jew* (1940). BARCH Plak 003-020-030.

16. Hitler in the last Nazi newsreel, March 1945. ullstein bild Dtl / Getty Images.

17. Henny Porten with Oskar Messter at the International Film Congress in 1935. BARCH N1275 Bild-349.

Acknowledgements

This book would not have been possible without archives. Several visits to the German Federal Archives in Berlin-Lichterfelde, Freiburg and Koblenz were necessary to be able to trace evidence of Hitler's film viewing and interventions. Denazification files held at the State Archives in Freiburg shed light on Leni Riefenstahl. Material relating to post-war trials of the director of *Jew Süss*, Veit Harlan, held at the State Archives in Hamburg shed light on that film and Harlan's involvement. The Regional Archive of North Rhine-Westphalia proved a useful source of information on Fritz Hippler, responsible for making several Nazi films, including *The Eternal Jew*. Berlin's Regional Archive contains denazification material on a number of Third Reich directors and actors. Invaluable information relating to Hitler's film viewing was also found at the Institute for Contemporary History in Munich. Foreign Office files in Berlin were also consulted, as were the Gerdy Troost papers held at the Library of Congress in Washington, which provided insights into Hitler's involvement with the film company Bavaria. Every one of these archives provided me with all the support I could have wished for, and for this I am truly grateful. Above all I am grateful to Dr Elizabeth Ward, who acted as my research assistant while I was researching the book. She spent as much time in archives as I did, and identified important material. Her interest in the project meant a lot.

Thanks are due also to Heather McCallum of Yale University Press for suggesting the project, and for her patience throughout: I very much appreciate her support of my work over the years. I benefited hugely both from Heather's and Marika Lysandrou's comments on earlier drafts of this book, as well as from those of Yale's external readers. I would also like to thank Nottingham Trent University both for granting me research leave when it was most needed and for providing financial support. Financial support was also generously provided by the Humboldt Foundation in Germany; this enabled me to undertake an important two-week research trip to Berlin.

My wife, Helena, has had to endure my various research topics over the years and, to help me with this book, she sat through several Nazi films that were, to put it mildly, not very entertaining. As often was the case in the past, her observations helped to shape my thoughts. For this, I am more grateful than I can say. Thanks, too, go to Dr Paul Moore of Leicester University for inviting me to speak on the topic of the book, and for the comments made by students and other members of the audience afterwards. They inspired me to think some matters through more thoroughly.

Nottingham, May 2017

Introduction

Hitler's interest in the arts has in key respects been exhaustively documented: there are studies about the books Hitler read,[1] about his preoccupation with architecture,[2] and about his passion for Wagnerian Opera.[3] His personal involvement in the Great German Art Exhibitions between 1937 and 1944 is well known.[4] We know much about his personal taste in art.[5] The interior design of Hitler's domestic space has also been expertly investigated.[6] Much less, however, is known about his interest in film. A typical view can be found in Frederic Spotts' classic study about Hitler's attitude to the arts, which informs us that, while Hitler enjoyed watching movies, he had no interest in film as an art form and 'left it to Joseph Goebbels to exploit cinema for propaganda purposes'.[7] This view is reflected implicitly in the numerous studies of film in the Third Reich. Due consideration has been given by scholars to the crucial role of 'Film Minister' and Propaganda Minister Joseph Goebbels,[8] and of the Propaganda Ministry more generally, in steering the Nazi film industry.[9] In this context, reference is usually made to Hitler's film viewing, his expectations of film and his occasional film censorship.[10] There have also been important publications on the American film industry and its reaction to

1

Nazism, in which mention of Hitler's interest in film is made.[11] But the impression one gains from most books on the Third Reich film industry is that there would be little to be learned by examining Hitler's involvement more closely.[12] This book sets out to show that, in fact, much can be learned from doing so.

My argument is not that Hitler was more important than Goebbels when it came to overseeing film production. I am claiming, however, that Hitler was more than a passive consumer of feature films, watched night after night at his mountain residence, the Berghof. At a number of points during the Third Reich, Hitler directly or indirectly encouraged the creation of Nazi films that promoted his political visions and agendas. Hitler well understood the persuasive power of film. In *My Struggle*, he wrote: 'in a much shorter time, at one stroke I might say, people will understand a pictorial presentation of something which it would take them a long and laborious effort of reading to understand'.[13] More than Goebbels, Hitler believed feature film directors should be given a chance to make documentary films. Real events were to be filmed not just with the right dose of propaganda, but also with the aesthetics and dramatic techniques of feature film so that the political message could be conveyed to maximum effect.

Hitler also stepped in on several occasions to ban films, allow them when a ban was looming, or ask for changes. These interventions, to be sure, were sporadic, and usually occurred because Goebbels consulted with Hitler over controversial films. That they occurred, however, demonstrates that Hitler was the ultimate arbiter in film matters. His decisions for or against films were motivated by a range of considerations: ideological, political, diplomatic and military. This book points to an apparent contrast. Privately, Hitler consumed all manner of films, from the epic to the trivial, and not just German ones. In public, for the most part at least, he wanted to be associated only with films carrying a serious political message. Private film viewings suggest the lazy armchair consumer, his attendance of film showings in public suggests the robust ideologue. At least in the pre-war period, there is evidence that Hitler privately watched and sometimes enjoyed films either made by or starring Jews (or both). Occasionally, he saw to it that certain actors with Jewish spouses or of a Jewish background, actors he admired, were to a degree protected from the effects of Nazi anti-Semitism, even as he was calling for Goebbels to produce more anti-Semitic films. And, while Hitler enjoyed American films in private, and quite probably watched *Gone with the Wind* (1939) after American films had been banned from German cinemas, in public he pronounced a strong dislike of American culture. Film, for Hitler, was trivia and entertainment on the one hand, and a vehicle for supporting Nazi ideology on the other.

Hitler seldom talked about film in his public pronouncements. His speeches on the subject of culture – notably at the Nazi Party rallies – often avoided concrete references to individual cultural products. Instead, he spoke in lofty and vague terms about art, architecture, sculpture, music and theatre, though rarely film. His engagement in the Great German Art Exhibitions, his architectural commissions, not least for the New Reich Chancellery building, and his plans for rebuilding Berlin generally ('Germania') seem to confirm his greater interest in art and architecture. Yet he probably spent as much, if not more time watching films than poring over architectural plans. And in commissioning Leni Riefenstahl's Nazi Party rally films, he had, arguably, more success than he ever did with the German Art Exhibitions. So disappointed was Hitler in the products of Nazi art that 'he could not even bear to have the paintings around him'.[14] Riefenstahl's Nazi-period films were much more to his liking. During the first years of the war, Hitler personally monitored every weekly newsreel before it reached cinema screens. In doing so, he ensured the newsreels showed what he wanted, and were provided with the commentary he considered the most appropriate. But he was not just thinking of the present: the newsreels were to be a lasting document of what he hoped would be the triumph of Nazism. Hitler regarded the representation of Nazism in celluloid as a gift to the future. Nazi art is now largely forgotten; 'Germania' remained a pipe dream, and the New Reich Chancellery was demolished. Riefenstahl's films, however, as well as any number of Nazi weekly newsreels and other Nazi films with which Hitler is associated, are widely available today on the internet or on DVD. No other aspect of Nazism's artistic legacy enjoys the dubious privilege of such wide circulation in the present. It is time, then, to explore the importance of film for Hitler.

The opening chapter begins by looking at Hitler's private film-viewing habits, and by asking to what extent film might have influenced him. It then examines the numerous claims about Hitler's 'favourite film'. One has to tread carefully here, as clear evidence is hard to come by. And, while some candidates for 'favourite film' do seem likelier than others, in the end what matters, perhaps, is not so much Hitler's supposed preference for individual films as the fact of his seemingly limitless consumption of whatever films the Propaganda Ministry was able to provide. The eclecticism of his film tastes is what is striking. While Chapter 1 looks at Hitler as film consumer, the focus of Chapter 2 is on his film politics. It explores his reasons for banning, or resisting the imposition of a ban, on specific films. The second part of the chapter analyses two of Hitler's most significant film interventions: his commissioning of documentary films on the sterilization of the disabled (*Victims of the Past*, 1937) and on the Spanish Civil War (*In Battle against the World Enemy*, 1939). Hitler, then, was centrally involved in the gestation of two important Nazi film projects promoting ideas fundamental to his worldview: the need to 'protect' the Germans against the mentally and physically handicapped, and to resist the global aspirations of Bolshevism. Chapter 2 ends with a discussion of a different kind of intervention: Hitler's commitment to large-scale film-related building projects. The Reich was to have a truly representative film studio and cinema to reflect the status Hitler accorded to film.

Chapters 3 and 4 turn attention towards a much better-known set of film commissions by Hitler: Leni Riefenstahl's Nazi Party rally films *Victory of Faith* (1933) and *Triumph of the Will* (1935), and her film of the 1936

Berlin Olympics, *Olympia* (1938).[15] After the Nazis attained power in January 1933, several feature films depicting the defeat of communism reached German cinema screens. But such films soon outlived their usefulness, as the Nazis consolidated their control over Germany and political conflict became a thing of the past. Hitler personally gave the highest priority to the filming of an event which more than any other was intended to symbolize the end to national strife. The 1933 and 1934 Nuremberg Rallies called for Germans, literally, to rally round the Nazi leader in disciplined formations. Hitler wanted the message of the rallies to be conveyed on cinema screens across the country. As the Riefenstahl chapters show, Hitler arranged for her films to be financed, thereby ensuring she did what he wanted. *Olympia* may appear to be a tribute to the international spirit of world Olympics, but Hitler did not ask Riefenstahl to make it for this reason. Her film was conceived by Hitler as a form of masquerade: it would help to conceal Nazism's real character, its plans for European hegemony and racial war.

Hitler used the cinema in a variety of ways to promote Nazism. Chapter 5 looks at his visits to German cinemas. For the most part, he only showed himself in cinemas when films with politics or political subtexts with which he wished to be associated were running. Such visits conferred an official seal of approval on particular films, and were stage-managed so that the films concerned were explicitly harnessed to the wagon of Nazi propaganda. For Hitler and Goebbels, the cinema was not just about entertainment, it was also a political space. Cinemas became auditoriums for the broadcasting of Hitler's speeches, and Hitler was, of course, shown in weekly newsreels and a variety of documentaries, with figures resembling Hitler in one way or another also being a characteristic of Nazi feature films. While Chapter 5 demonstrates how the cinema was mobilized to immerse audiences in the sight and sound of Hitler, Chapter 6 looks at the way actors were mobilized by Hitler. Actors, especially actresses, were frequent guests at Hitler's private soirées. When Goebbels found the films shown on such occasions dull, he consoled himself with the fact that the company was attractive: 'at the Führer's. Films, as always. Rubbish! But the women were nice!'[16] However, there was more to Hitler's cultivation of actresses than the wish to be surrounded by pretty women.[17] The attention he and Goebbels lavished on actors generally was designed to secure their loyalty, a loyalty they were expected to demonstrate in a variety of ways, from appearing at diplomatic receptions to participating in propaganda films. It is unlikely, however, that Hitler, in contrast to Goebbels, had sexual relations with actresses. The chapter ends with a discussion of Goebbels' relationship with the Czech actress Lída Baarová. Hitler's reaction to Baarová, and to Goebbels' infatuation with her, illustrates the clear difference between him and his propaganda minister when it came to affairs.

This book is divided into two halves. Chapters 1 to 6, with one or two exceptions where developments discussed span the pre-war and war period, focus on the peacetime years of Hitler's rule, 1933–39. The remaining four chapters concentrate on the war years. One reason for this division was practical. Thematic chapters running from 1933 to 1945 would have been impossibly long; and I wanted to spare the reader the effort of having to repeatedly think her or his way back from the end of the war to the beginning of the Third Reich. There is also a conceptual reason for the division into pre-war and wartime chapters. Obviously, life changed fundamentally with the start of the Second World War. It changed in the world of film, too – not least for Hitler himself. As Chapter 7 shows, Hitler radically reduced his private feature film viewing, and stopped watching films in German cinemas, from the day the Nazis invaded Poland. But he kept an eagle eye on the production of German documentaries about the Nazi war effort, notably the films *Campaign in Poland* (1940) and *Victory in the West* (1941). Chapter 8, in turn, shows that he also kept very much in touch with the production of anti-Semitic films, the most notorious of which were the feature film *Jew Süss* (1940) and the Nazi 'documentary' film *The Eternal Jew* (1940). A lot has been written about these films,[18] but Hitler was more central to their creation than is commonly assumed. They reached German cinemas in late 1940, just as the Nazi radicalization of anti-Semitic policy was developing towards genocide. The chapter explores the impact of *Jew Süss* on German and non-German audiences. Its dissemination accompanied Hitler's genocidal programme at each of its stages.

After 1 September 1939, then, Hitler's preoccupation with film became bound up with the Nazi war in one way or another. This is underscored by his regular previewing of the weekly Wochenschau, or newsreel, the focus of Chapter 9. Hitler, as Supreme Commander of the Armed Forces, took it upon himself to personally vet the newsreel coverage of events.[19] After defeat at Stalingrad in February 1943, as it became harder and harder to provide images of German military success, Hitler gradually lost interest in the newsreels.[20] And as his health deteriorated, so he became less and less willing to show himself in them. For years, film footage of Hitler had been an essential part of Nazi documentaries and newsreels, which sought to convey the impression that the Führer was indispensable. Again and again it was stressed that he was committed to defending the Reich against a host of enemies – and that Nazism was about self-defence was a message Hitler encouraged in the film projects in which he was involved. Hitler's withdrawal from the newsreels as of 1943 left some German cinemagoers, at least, feeling abandoned and rudderless.

The final chapter returns to the subject of actors. Convinced of the importance of film for both relaxation and propaganda during a gruelling war, Hitler ensured that many of Germany's leading actors were exempted from military service; they returned the favours bestowed upon them by doing their bit to help prosecute Hitler's war. The current book is not about Nazi film production: there are already several studies on that topic, or key aspects of it.[21] However, the second half of the chapter, like the concluding section of Chapter 5, looks closely at important Nazi propaganda films to demonstrate how they reflected the range of Hitler's ideology and how flexible they could prove, adaptable to the situations in which they were deployed. Right to the end of the war, Goebbels did all he could to keep the film industry going, despite the effects of Allied bombing. On 30 January 1945, Hitler's final speech to the nation on the radio calling for determined resistance against the enemy coincided with the premiere of the final Nazi cinema blockbuster, *Kolberg*, about Germans holding out against the French during the Napoleonic wars. Almost to the very end, Hitler's politics and Nazi film worked together.

Films at the Berghof

HITLER'S HOME CINEMA

Between 1933 and September 1939, Hitler spent a considerable amount of time watching feature films. He watched films in the Reich Chancellery in Berlin, and above all at his Bavarian residence, the Berghof. There is even evidence he planned to have a film projection unit installed in his car by the firm Telefunken.[1] Hitler was, as his bodyguard and courier Rochus Misch put it, a 'film addict'.[2] He watched adventure films, crime thrillers, film dramas, historical epics, musicals, revue films, comedies, romance films, westerns, cartoons – anything. Some of his film preferences we might expect; others are surprising. Hitler the private film-viewer indulged the passive, lazy side of his nature, but he also cultivated international tastes. Ideological reflexes sometimes determined his responses, but often he allowed himself to appreciate film as film. This was a Hitler the German public did not know.

The Evidence

Hitler's film viewing is testified to by those who worked for or knew him. Julius Schaub, Hitler's adjutant and general factotum, writes of the almost incontrovertible routine of Hitler's day, in which film played a central role. Hitler would sleep all morning, getting up in time to greet his guests for lunch. After eating, everyone would walk to the Kleines Teehaus, which lay to the south of the Berghof. During this outing, Hitler would present himself to the public, standing under a specially planted tree on the approach road to the Berghof (he couldn't take the sun). He would shake hands and let himself be photographed. At the Teehaus, after refreshments, there was usually a siesta between 5 p.m. and 6 p.m. Then it was back to the Berghof for the evening meal. Every day until the eve of war, according to Schaub, films were shown after dinner, and Hitler watched every one of them.[3] Schaub once remarked to film director Veit Harlan that he, Harlan, should not imagine that Schaub's life was fun: 'Last night,' Schaub said, 'I had to watch three – yes, three! – films, and this morning another one. And that on an empty stomach. The Führer has got unbelievable stamina when it comes to films. Unfortunately I am not remotely interested in them. Believe me, I'm living in a golden cage, and I will never escape to freedom.'[4] Schaub also had to endure Hitler's passion for Wagner. Christa Schroeder, a personal secretary of Hitler, relates that Hitler's entire entourage fell asleep during a performance of *Tristan and Isolde*. When Hitler's photographer Heinrich Hoffmann began to slump over the balustrade of the proscenium box, Hitler had to wake Schaub to get him to wake Hoffmann; Chief Adjutant Brückner continued snoring in the background.[5]

Ernst Hanfstaengl, Hitler's confidant before he fell out of favour, later recalled that Hitler's favourite evening pastime was watching films.[6] Hitler's valets, Heinz Linge and Karl Wilhelm Krause, make mention of the Führer's extensive film-watching habits in their memoirs,[7] as does Berghof manager Herbert Döhring in his.[8] Schaub was not the only one to suffer under Hitler's obsession. Heinrich Hoffmann bemoaned the fact that Hitler – as with his favourite pieces of music – 'delighted to have endlessly repeated those [films] that had pleased him; and when I was staying with him, I had no option but to watch them too'.[9] Fritz Wiedemann, Hitler's personal adjutant until 1939, had sympathy for Hitler's need for distraction, but why, he later asked in his memoirs, did this have to take the form of films? 'The year has 365 days, and there were not many days on which there were no film showings.'[10] The atmosphere at Hitler's private movie evenings was invariably relaxed. Valet Heinz Linge writes that, in contrast to a public cinema, there was no church-like silence during the viewings: those present made lively comment, and there was often much laughter.[11] According to Albert Speer, Hitler usually sat next to Eva Braun, and to other female guests, with whom he would engage in whispered conversation. Sometimes he would stare broodily into the open fire of the Berghof's Great Hall, where the films were shown. At such moments, everyone else would fall silent so as not to disturb him in his 'significant thoughts'.[12] Unlike Stalin, who liked to issue instructions concerning the Soviet film industry and ideology in general when watching films, Hitler, during the showings themselves at least, refrained from such direct interventions.[13] Speer reports that viewings frequently went on for three to four hours, so at least two films were shown on many occasions. While others emerged stiff and numb from these lengthy sessions, Hitler, remembers Speer, seemed revitalized, and liked to discuss the performances of the actors (or, rather, actresses, while Eva Braun held forth on the male actors) before moving on to other conversation topics.[14]

Stalin watched films with his inner circle in the Kremlin cinema. Hitler preferred the environment of his home or the Reich Chancellery. At the Berghof, the cinema screen was concealed behind a Gobelin tapestry on one side of the Great Hall, while the projection unit was hidden away behind another tapestry on the other side, directly opposite. The hall was known for its massive panorama window, which could be lowered and 'was intended to open up monumental views of the surrounding landscape'.[15] The tapestries, in turn, could be raised to allow the world of artifice and make-believe to enter Hitler's home;[16] afterwards, the tapestries returned to their original positions, and the Great Hall was restored to its function as reception and meeting room. The room's double purpose reflected the two sides to Hitler's life, sides that unfolded in the same physical space, yet were kept separate. The film showings were nevertheless usually a social occasion. Hitler did sometimes watch films alone, or with his adjutants and valets. Karl Wilhelm Krause relates that, when Hitler was in a bad mood, he asked for an amusing film to be shown, such as Gustav Ucicky's 1937 film of Heinrich von Kleist's famous play, *The Broken Jug*.[17] Most of the time, though, the film showings were part of the Berghof's after-dinner social calendar. Hitler would entertain himself and his guests with a film or two of his own choosing. At some point during dinner, Krause would present Hitler with a menu of 'four to six films from Germany and abroad'. This list was often compiled from films just received from the Propaganda Ministry. Hitler then made his choice.[18] If a film displeased him, he had it stopped, and asked for another one (regardless, it seems, of the opinion of the gathering). Among the guests were Nazi leaders and their wives, as well as actors and film directors. The Berghof's staff were also invited to watch the films. In fact, Krause claims it was Hitler's express wish that they attend, both at the Berghof and in Berlin.[19] Hitler clearly believed in the beneficial effects of cinema on those working for him. Therese Linke, Hitler's cook, recalled that a cinema was constructed from wood for the many workers employed around the Berghof; there were free showings three times a week.[20] Anna Plaim, who worked as a maid at the Berghof, also remembers a cinema for the soldiers stationed there. The film showings were organized by the Nazi leisure organization Strength Through Joy.[21]

Goebbels' diaries frequently comment on his film viewings with Hitler, particularly in the years after the Nazis came to power. Mostly, they watched contemporary German films, but American films also featured. In March 1934, for instance, they watched Frank Lloyd's film *Cavalcade* (USA, 1933), a sweeping historical epic covering the 1899–1933 period and addressing events such as the Boer War and the sinking of the *Titanic*. Hitler and Goebbels must have enjoyed it, because they watched it again in May 1934.[22] And, in April 1934, they watched Gregory La Cava's *Gabriel over the White House* (1933). One might have expected Hitler to admire a film depicting the dissolution of Congress and the apparent establishment of a dictatorship in the USA. According to one film scholar,

Gabriel over the White House was 'the first major fascist motion picture'.[23] But Goebbels reports that Hitler did not quite know what to make of it: he found it too 'theoretical' and 'modern', an indication perhaps that Hitler believed the most effective form of political cinema to be one that relied more on image than voice.[24] Further evidence of Hitler's film viewing is provided by the extensive correspondence between Hitler's adjutants and the Propaganda Ministry regarding the sending and return of films. This correspondence was conducted, to judge at least from extant records at Berlin's Federal Archives, between January 1936 and July 1939. Most of the films sent on by the ministry were those that had recently become available, either in Germany or abroad: Hitler kept up to speed with new or forthcoming releases. Occasionally, he explicitly asked for particular films to be acquired. One of these was Carl Lamac's *The Hound of the Baskervilles* (1937), which Hitler wanted to be permanently available at the Berghof.[25] Hitler is known for his dismissal of occult and mystical trends within National Socialism, but this did not stop him admiring *The Hound of the Baskervilles* or Hans Deppe's 1934 film *The Rider on the White Horse*, another film in the Berghof archives. The gloomy supernaturalism of both films clearly appealed to him.

Hitler's Likes and Dislikes

Apart from the occasional reference to Hitler's opinions of films in Goebbels' diaries, the only explicit source we have for these are notes taken by Hitler's adjutants over the 1938–39 period.[26] These were passed on to the Propaganda Ministry in terse, even monosyllabic terms, usually in the form of 'good' or 'bad', or variations thereof. On 24 April 1939, for instance, the ordnance officer Ludwig Bahls informed the ministry that Hitler had found Josef von Báky's light-hearted 1939 film *The Stars of Variety* 'good', and Veit Harlan's *The Immortal Heart* (1939), about the assumed inventor of the watch, Peter Henlein, 'very good'. By contrast, Peter Paul Brauer's comedy *I'll Be Back in a Minute* (1939) was considered 'not particularly good'.

Hitler took strong exception to Paul Martin's romantic comedy *Woman at the Wheel* (1939) starring Lilian Harvey and Willy Fritsch. He dismissed it as 'very bad, disgusting'. He did not like *Tarzan*, either – it was 'bad': whether this was the original 1932 film or a later one is not clear. Bahls also reports that Hitler broke off the showing of a 1934 film, *Prosperity Crooks*, directed by Fritz Kampers, because it was 'bad'.[27] On occasion, Hitler's adjutants report simply that Hitler 'left the room'. Film scholars can only be disappointed by such brief comments. What exactly might have constituted a 'bad' as opposed to a 'very bad' film, for Hitler? Occasionally, at least, Hitler's adjutants do provide reasons why Hitler liked or disliked a film. The reasons are as briefly noted as Hitler's overall assessment, yet they do tell us one thing: Hitler did not always or only judge films by their contents.

On 19 July 1938, after spending part of the day with Unity Mitford, his English admirer, Hitler watched Herbert Selpin's *I Love You* (1938), a comedy starring Viktor de Kowa and Luise Ullrich. In the film, a ladykiller is outsmarted by the woman he wants to seduce. It would be tempting to see in Hitler's choice of evening viewing an indication of romantic interest in Mitford, but all we know for certain is that Hitler liked *I Love You* because it was 'well acted'.[28] And, in fact, this expression of approval occurs several times. On 13 June 1939, Bahls told the Propaganda Ministry that Hitler had found three films 'well acted': Fritz Peter Buch's *Detours to Happiness* (1939), a light comedy about a philandering husband; Carl Boese's *Hello Janine* (1939), a 'Revuefilm' (a musical with dance elements) with Marika Rökk; and the more serious *Border Fire* (1939), a feature film about smuggling, directed by Alois Lippl.[29] Hitler at times distinguished the quality of the acting from that of the film, as in the case of the 1938 German-Spanish production *Nights in Andalusia*, a musical directed by Herbert Maisch, and starring Argentinian actress Imperio Argentina; he praised her performance while dismissing the film as 'bad'.[30] On a typical whim, Hitler, an admirer of Imperio Argentina, ordered the Propaganda Ministry in April 1937 to 'win her over' for the German film industry.[31] She proved a costly acquisition, arriving from Havana complete with car and chauffeur, and posing huge wage demands.[32] Soon, the German film industry was trying to avoid engaging her.[33] Hitler was also a fan of boxer Max Schmeling's actress-wife Anny Ondra. He lamented that Hans Deppe's *Fools in the Snow* (1938) was 'not particularly good' and had made little of Ondra's acting skills.[34] Hitler appreciated good acting and a director's ability to bring out an actor's talents. He had, after all, himself learnt to act. In 1932, he had taken voice training lessons from the singer Paul Devrient.[35] Devrient had also taught Hitler the importance of gesture, rhythm and rhetoric.

Hitler's response to film, then, was often informed by an interest in the effectiveness of performance. Indeed, when he criticized Hans Steinhoff's film *Dance on the Volcano* (1938), it was not because it appeared to call for revolution (albeit in nineteenth-century France), but because he did not like either the directing or Gustaf Gründgens' acting.[36] We cannot always assume that Hitler's dislike of a film was grounded in a rejection of its ideas, narrative or milieu. Other factors may have played a part. On 15 September 1938, British Prime Minister Neville Chamberlain made his way to Germany to meet with Hitler to discuss the Sudetenland crisis. After negotiations at the Berghof, in the course of which Hitler appeared to retreat from his intention to resolve the Sudeten issue if necessary by means of violence,[37] Hitler relaxed by watching the film *Four Apprentices* (1938). It was directed by Carl Froelich, one of Hitler's favourite directors, and starred the young and talented Ingrid Bergman. Yet Hitler did not like the film.[38] His mood may not have been the best after the discussions with Chamberlain. Perhaps he disliked it because it depicts the attempt by four women to prove that their function in life is not simply to serve as housewives, but then, at the end, they all end up hitched. On 16 September, Hitler continued to discuss the Sudetenland, this time with Konrad Henlein, the leader of the Sudeten German Party, and German Foreign Minister Ribbentrop. In the evening, he sat down to watch Robert Stemmle's *By a Silken Thread* (1938), a German film about a prisoner of war who returns to Germany from Japanese internment after the First World War and invests in the production of artificial silk. One would have expected such a theme to appeal to Hitler, who, after all, had committed the National Socialists to an economic programme of autarky. But Hitler found *By a Silken Thread* 'not good'.[39] Perhaps, then, the Sudeten crisis was indeed clouding his mood. But he could still appreciate the 1932 German romantic comedy *Cheeky Devil*, directed by Carl Boese, which he watched on 17 September.[40] Interpreting his reactions as noted by his adjutants remains a difficult task.

Surviving lists of films kept at the Berghof do tell us something about Hitler's film tastes, which, on this evidence, are both predictable and surprising. Some of the listed films conform completely to Hitler's ideological expectations. In December 1937, Goebbels gave Hitler a present of thirty-two films 'from the last four years' of German (and Austrian) film production.[41] If anyone knew Hitler's film preferences well, it was Goebbels, and he will have been sure to give Hitler films the latter admired. The titles found their way into a 'List of Archive Films'.[42] One of the films was the feature film *The Higher Command* (1935, directed by Gerhard Lamprecht), about an attempt by an English lord to forge a treaty between Austria, England and Poland against Napoleonic France. It could be read as providing historical support for Hitler's post-1933 diplomacy, which aimed at isolating France and forming alliances (e.g. the 1934 German–Polish Non-Aggression Pact) to undermine its interests. Goebbels also gave Hitler a copy of Veit Harlan's *The Ruler* (1937), celebrating an autocratic industrialist, and of Carl Froelich's schoolteacher drama *The Dreamer* (1936). *The Dreamer* ends with a call to youth to 'steel and overcome themselves' for the future, a message of which Hitler would have approved. A second list of films kept at the Berghof, the 'List of Permanent Stock' from 1935,[43] contains a number of Frederick the Great films, one of which, Hans Steinhoff's *The Old and the Young King* (1935), was also on Goebbels' list. From the mid-1930s, Hitler could regularly draw, at home, on filmic representations of Frederick whenever he needed to reinforce his sense of identification with him.[44] At such moments, it must have seemed to Hitler as if these Frederick films had been made just for his own private consumption, allowing him privileged historical access. The 'List of Permanent Stock' also includes Nazi classics such as Franz Seitz's *Storm Trooper Brand* (1933), depicting the SA's (the Nazi Storm Troopers') fight against communism, and Hans Steinhoff's *Mother and Child* (1934), centring on the triumph of the maternal bond.

Other films kept at the Berghof, however, suggest a more unbuttoned Hitler. When Goebbels gave Hitler his present of films in 1937, it was supplemented with twelve Walt Disney *Mickey Mouse* films: 'He is delighted,' Goebbels confided to his diary: 'he is so happy about this treasure, which, I hope, will give him much joy and help him to relax.'[45] Goebbels also included in his present a copy of Willi Forst's *Masquerade* (1934), which he knew Hitler liked.[46] *Masquerade* was an Austrian operetta film, the plot of which turned around the question of who acted as a model for a near-nude portrait. Set in 1905, the film simultaneously celebrates and gently satirizes the decadence of fin-de-siècle middle-class Vienna. Hitler could react allergically to films that celebrated Austrianness.[47] But he clearly admired *Masquerade*. The 'List of Permanent Stock' also contains surprises. Among the films listed are several Weimar Republic films, such as F.W. Murnau's silent classics *Faust* (1926) and *Tabu* (1931), a semi-documentary film set on the South Sea island of Bora Bora. Leontine Sagan's 1931 film *Girls in Uniform* is the biggest surprise. Set in a girls' boarding school run in accordance with a strict regimen, its lesbian undertones and critique of the Prussian education system led to it being banned in the Third Reich, but not from the Berghof. Hitler admired films about Frederick the Great, yet could also appreciate *Girls in Uniform*, in which the autocratic and unpleasant school director, with her walking stick, is clearly meant to embody a female equivalent of Frederick. Hitler's interest in Weimar Republic film is a recurring theme. When the Reich Chancellery in Berlin sent on a list of films to the Berghof in the summer of 1937, Hitler's secretary Bormann wrote back to say Hitler did not want a list of films currently running, but of films 'from the earlier period, that is to say from the time between the end of the war until about 1932'.[48] The

Chancellery duly obliged, and Bormann requested seventeen films presumably at Hitler's bidding.[49] The majority of these were German, and mostly lighter fare, such as Kurt Gerron's *A Mad Idea* (1932), about a Munich painter, or Hanns Schwarz's film operetta *Monte Carlo Madness* (1931), starring Hans Albers and Heinz Rühmann.[50]

For all his public dismissal of the culture of the Weimar Republic, in private, Hitler consumed the Republic's film production constantly. There are other discrepancies. He admired *Masquerade* despite the fact that it starred Adolf Wohlbrück. Wohlbrück left Austria in the course of the 1930s; he was an anti-Nazi, a homosexual and would have been classified by the Nazis as 'half-Jewish'. Hitler's public condemnation of the supposed dominance of Jews in German culture did not stop him appreciating their artistic gifts, or ordering up films directed by Jews. Kurt Gerron was Jewish; he fled the Nazis in 1933, only to be murdered in Auschwitz in 1944.[51] The Austrian-Hungarian director Leontine Sagan was of Jewish descent. Billy Wilder, a Jew who fled the Nazis 1933, wrote the script for *Emil and the Detectives* (1931), another of the films on the 'Permanent Stock' list. Hitler's pronounced anti-Americanism was similarly shelved when it came to private film viewing. We can be sure he watched the twelve *Mickey Mouse* films Goebbels gave him in December 1937. In fact, Hitler had already ordered up five *Mickey Mouse* films for the Berghof through his chief adjutant Brückner in July 1937.[52] There is no clear record of whether Hitler watched any Charlie Chaplin films. But he was a fan of Laurel and Hardy. Hitler's adjutants record at least three viewings of Laurel and Hardy films: in June 1938, Hitler watched and enjoyed *Way Out West* (1937, directed by James W. Horne) and *Swiss Miss* (1938, directed by John G. Blystone), and, in November 1938, Hitler viewed and appreciated *Block-Heads* (1938, also directed by John Blystone).[53] *Block-Heads* he found good because of its 'nice ideas and funny jokes'.[54] One can imagine Hitler sympathizing with its opening scene, in which we see Stan Laurel still patrolling a First World War trench twenty years after the war has finished. The message here – that, for some, the war has never ended – is one Hitler would have well understood.[55] Hitler's appreciation of Laurel and Hardy demonstrates his approval of strongly *visual* cinema, cinema still rooted in the pre-talkies era – which the three films cited certainly are, for all their dialogue. His appreciation of German-made films from the pre-1933 era, many of them silent, stems from the same approval, and his seeming dislike of dialogue.

Hitler's Favourite Film

It is tempting to try to identify, among the films Hitler watched, the one he liked the most. That would make it possible, in theory, to get a sense of exactly what he expected film, in an ideal scenario, to achieve. It might also make it possible to gain some deeper insight into Hitler's psychology, if one accepts – and this is a big if – that one film can somehow explain Hitler. Accordingly, various suggestions have been made as to what Hitler's 'favourite film' was. Unfortunately, none of these is really convincing. One candidate, according to a quick search on Google, is the Walt Disney production *Snow White and the Seven Dwarfs* (1937). This suggestion may have something to do with the influence of Kate Atkinson's 2013 novel *Life after Life*, where Hitler is a fan of *Snow White*: he sees himself 'as the saviour of Germany, and poor Germany, his *Schneewittchen*, would be saved by him whether she wanted it or not'.[56] In 2008, the director of a Norwegian Museum claimed to have discovered cartoons showing characters from *Snow White* that had been drawn by Hitler during the Second World War.[57] This turned out, not surprisingly, to be a hoax,[58] but the claim nevertheless helped to sustain the notion that *Snow White* had some kind of special meaning for Hitler. *Snow White*, with its death potion and notions of magical rebirth, is certainly close to the Wagnerian world Hitler inhabited, and it tells a tale of jealousy and wickedness confronting true beauty, corresponding perhaps to Hitler's understanding of post-Versailles Germany as a country beleaguered by the hostility of inner and outer enemies. Yet we have no clear evidence Hitler ever saw *Snow White*. It was ordered for the Berghof in February 1938 and was expected to arrive in two or three weeks, but we cannot assume from this that it did. And even then, we have no trustworthy record of what Hitler thought of it.[59]

Precisely the same constellation of speculation and lack of evidence obtains in the case of another film that was rumoured to be Hitler's favourite: Merian C. Cooper's *King Kong* (1933). In his 1970 autobiography, Ernst Hanfstaengl, once a friend of Hitler, wrote: 'one of Hitler's favourite films was *King Kong*, as we all know the story of a giant ape who falls in love with a woman no bigger than his hand and goes berserk over her. A terrible story, but Hitler was fascinated by it. Hitler often talked about it and watched it often.'[60] In 2015, the German historian Volker Koop published a book called *Why Hitler Loved King Kong but Banned Mickey Mouse*. King Kong stares menacingly at the reader from its cover.[61] Koop speculates as to why Hitler loved *King Kong*. Was it because of the film's superb use of trick photography? Did the attractive Fay Wray appeal to him in the role of the helpless victim? Or did the melodramatic downfall of King Kong move him?[62] The Bavarian writer Herbert Rosendorfer – perhaps tongue-in-cheek – even claims that Hitler saw *King Kong* at least 300 times, the last time being in the Reich Chancellery in April 1945.[63] Yet, as with *Snow White*, we have no reliable evidence that Hitler ever saw *King Kong*, nor has his opinion of it been passed down if he did. Given his massive grudge against Hitler, Hanfstaengl is not the most trustworthy of witnesses. In February 1937, fed up with Hanfstaengl's proneness to exaggeration and with his negative comments about the German troops fighting for Franco in the Spanish Civil War, Goebbels and Hitler played a practical joke on him by making him believe he was to be dropped behind enemy lines in Spain. Hanfstaengl thought he had fallen prey to an assassination attempt.[64] His autobiography takes revenge by, among other details, associating Hitler with a film about a monster ape.

It is possible, of course, that Hitler watched *King Kong*. It is possible he saw in the threatened purity of Ann Darrow an analogy with Germany or with the German race. Hitler was a self-declared animal-lover.[65] Hans Baur,

Hitler's pilot, recalls that Hitler would cover up his eyes when films showing animal hunting were being shown, asking to be told 'when it was all over'. Then again, the ostensibly squeamish Hitler liked films sent to him by a 'friendly Maharajah' that showed 'men being torn to pieces by the animals they had set out to hunt'.[66] This suggests a liking on Hitler's part for that moment when the hunted becomes the hunter, the victim the aggressor, where the captive goes berserk – themes in *King Kong*, and leit-motifs in Hitler's understanding of Germany's relationship with its neighbours, who had imposed upon it the 'shackles' of the Versailles Treaty. But it is worth stressing that the German censors at the time objected to *King Kong* on the grounds that it violated 'German racial sentiment' by portraying the love of a gorilla for a white-skinned woman.[67] In the end, that *Snow White* and *King Kong* should be thought of as Hitler's favourites tells us more about us than Hitler. Behind these suppositions is a desire to find the answer to Hitler in an archetypal fairy story about innocence and evil, or a morality tale about the danger posed to civilization by its failure to control destructive primordial energies. Psychohistorian Robert Waite tells of an 'experienced analyst' who, in connection with Hitler's supposed admiration for *King Kong*, claimed it was 'easy to read Hitler as the huge gorilla – but he was only that in part. He was also, at the same time, the helpless sweet little blonde.'[68] Hitler's obsession with the film, in other words, can be traced to a psychopathic sadomasochism. To say this is drawing rather large conclusions from very little evidence would be an understatement.

Of all the films thought to be Hitler's favourite, the most serious candidate is surely the silent two-part epic *The Nibelungs* (1924). Hitler's photographer, Heinrich Hoffmann, claimed to have seen this film with Hitler 'at least 20 times'.[69] Goebbels describes Hitler as being deeply impressed by *The Nibelungs*.[70] Given Hitler's passion for Wagner's *Ring* cycle, this is perhaps not surprising. Hitler, in *My Struggle*, draws comparisons between recent historical events and the Nibelung saga. He accuses 'Jewish world finance' of more or less mobilizing an international army against 'the horned Siegfried' Germany in the First World War.[71] At another point, Hitler credits himself, following one of his early Nazi Party speeches in 1920, with having 'stoked a fire' in whose 'flames the sword would be forged that would restore freedom' to the 'Germanic Siegfried', and 'give life again to the German nation'. 'I felt the goddess of inexorable vengeance getting ready to seek redress for the perjury of 9 November 1918.'[72] For Hitler, Siegfried was the victim of betrayal – he had been speared in the back just as the German army had been 'stabbed in the back' in 1918 by left-wing politicians. But he was also the hero who would revive Germany. After Hitler came to power, the new German Reich was identified with the heroic and triumphant Siegfried, while productions of Wagner's *Ring* presented Alberich and Mime as scheming Jews. The director of *The Nibelungs*, Fritz Lang, had a Jewish mother, and when Goebbels first saw the film in 1924 he dismissed it as a 'typically Jewish concoction', though feeling obliged to recognize that 'the Jew knows how to direct'.[73] But he changed his mind, and by 1929 was calling Lang's film 'the pinnacle of German achievement'.[74] The answer to this volte-face may be found in Goebbels' belief that 'the Jew has the fateful mission to help the sick Aryan race recover its sense of self'.[75] In the Third Reich, the Nibelung saga generally came to stand for the struggle between Judaism and Germanic strength.

Lang emigrated in 1933. Although his film was reshown shortly after the Nazis came to power,[76] Goebbels and Hitler set about initiating the production of a new film about the Nibelungs.[77] Goebbels refers to conversations he had with Lang's former wife and scriptwriter of the original film, Thea von Harbou, and to what must have been a first draft of the script.[78] According to Goebbels, Hitler wanted the new film to be a sound film (despite his distrust of film dialogue), and it was to be 'really monumental. Educational material for schools. The definitive work.'[79] Hitler returned to the idea in September 1940, again telling Goebbels he wanted 'a truly grand and monumental film about the Nibelungs'. The director Veit Harlan seemed enthusiastic about the project when Goebbels spoke to him about it,[80] but, in the end, nothing came of it. In frustration, Hitler

even suggested synchronizing the old Fritz Lang film, at least for schools
– whether he was thinking here of music, or music and words, is not clear.
Nothing came of this either.[81] One commentator has suggested that any
new Nibelungs film would have involved too much economic risk.[82] But
the more likely reason the project never got off the ground is because a
story about treachery and revenge lost its relevance once the Nazis had
overcome the 'shameful' legacies of the First World War and the Weimar
Republic. Goebbels' propaganda machine tried to convince the German
people in February 1943 that the battle of Stalingrad had been comparable
with the self-sacrificial struggle of the Nibelungs at Etzel's court (where
they were massacred to a man) or the Battle of Thermopylae. According to
a Security Service report, the Germans, while open to such comparisons,
wanted there to be more 'reticence' in the use of terms such as heroism,
martyrdom and sacrifice.[83] So, even if Goebbels was able to draw on the
Nibelung notion of heroic collective martyrdom as of 1943, there was
clearly a limit to how much he could do so without exhausting the patience
of his audience.

Hitler, like most of us, probably had several favourite films. This,
certainly, would seem to have been Goebbels' view. In April 1939, he
prompted the German film industry to give Hitler a special gift: an album
made from parchment paper containing the titles of Hitler's favourite films
along with facsimile signatures from participating actors.[84] Unfortunately,
I was unable to trace it.

The Influence of Film

Hitler's admiration for particular films tells us little about how they might
have influenced him, and, while the archives provide us with the dates films
were sent to the Berghof, rarely do they indicate which days he watched
them on. In a few cases, however, they do, so that one can explore, to a
limited extent, possible correlations between viewings and Hitler's other
activities. On 19 June 1938, for instance, Hitler sat down to watch an

American film directed by Louis King about a group of gangsters who hold up freight trucks to steal merchandise – *Tip-Off Girls* (1938). A few days later, he signed off a law which made setting road blocks with intention to rob punishable by death. *Daily Mail* journalist Craig Brown recently took film historian Ben Urwand to task for suggesting that *Tip-Off Girls* might have influenced Hitler to pass this law.[85] According to Brown, this represents a 'bogus shackling of cause (Hitler watching a film) and effect (Hitler issuing a new order)'.[86] Brown has a point. For a start, Hitler did not appear interested in *Tip-Off Girls*: he stopped the showing.[87] Besides, there is no evidence for Urwand's claim that Hitler requested the film from the Propaganda Ministry (at least not in the sources Urwand cites).[88] And Brown is right that Hitler would have signed the law anyway, especially in view of the murderous car-robbery exploits of the Götze brothers, whose trial was under way in Berlin at the time. Urwand implies that Hitler came up with this law. It was more likely the brainchild of the Ministry of Justice, which was keen to ensure there was a legal basis for executing the Götzes. Nevertheless, that watching (what he did of) *Tip-Off Girls* might have reinforced Hitler's support for the law is not a completely unreasonable claim.[89] Nor would it be unreasonable to suggest that his support for it was bolstered by his viewing of *Nights in Andalusia* (1938) a mere matter of hours before signing off the law. In *Nights in Andalusia*, prisoners being transported for forced labour purposes are set free in an ambush.[90]

Hitler did not always choose films from a list presented to him, but sometimes asked for a specific film to be shown from one of the various Berghof archives. This was the case on 29 June 1938, when he watched the German film *Mazurka* (1935), directed by Willi Forst and starring Pola Negri, one of the films given to him as a present by Goebbels. *Mazurka* premiered in mid-November 1935, and Hitler first viewed it about the same time; according to Goebbels, Hitler was enthusiastic.[91] Negri later claimed that Hitler had *Mazurka* screened 'during his bouts of chronic insomnia'. He would, so she wrote, 'demand my picture in the early hours of the morning', often two or three times a week. Negri surmises that its 'story of mother love' reduced him to tears.[92] Whatever the appeal of the film's sentimentality to Hitler, he may have requested it on 29 June for another reason. Earlier in the day, Hitler had confirmed the death sentence for the Götze brothers. *Mazurka* is about a singer called Vera who takes justice into her own hands to prevent the composer Michailow abusing her daughter in the same way he abused her: Vera shoots Michailow spectacularly in a theatre. In the end, she receives a mild sentence, with the prospect of amnesty, from an understanding court. *Mazurka*, in other words, demonstrates the importance of preventing a repeat offence – which is precisely what was achieved by executing the Götzes. Hitler's adjutant noted that Hitler's response to the film, predictably, was positive.[93] Hitler's choice of *Mazurka* as evening viewing helped to confirm his own sense of the need for drastic preventative action.

On 28 September 1938, in the midst of the Sudetenland crisis, Hitler watched Léo Joannon's *Alert in the Mediterranean* (1938), a French film.[94] His reaction to it was not recorded. In *Alert in the Mediterranean*, the captains of British, French and German ships unite to rescue passengers from a boat in danger of being engulfed in poisonous smoke. Hitler had threatened to attack Czechoslovakia unless the Czechs ceded the Sudetenland, and the morning of 28 September was taken up with feverish diplomatic activity as the British, French and Italians tried to get Hitler to back down. He agreed to delay the threat of hostilities for twenty-four hours. It is, to say the least, a remarkable coincidence that Hitler should watch a film about French–German–British collaboration on the eve of negotiations with France, Britain and Italy over the future of the Sudetenland.[95] That *Alert in the Mediterranean* put Hitler in a less aggressive mood for these negotiations is conceivable. Of course, Hitler's mood largely depended on a sense of having outmanoeuvred France and Britain, who, in the early hours of 30 September, agreed to the cession of the Sudetenland. Soon, however, as Hitler biographer Ian Kershaw has argued, any pleasure Hitler might have got out of the Munich Agreement had evaporated.[96] Cheated of his chance to seize the Sudetenland by force, he made up for his disappointment by invading the rest of Czechoslovakia six months later. It may be going too far to claim that Hitler's true motivation for watching films was to allow himself to be seduced by them.[97] But watching them certainly enabled him to play out possible scenarios in his mind, and they were a way of providing confirmation of his view of the world, or of his sentiments at any given time. On 3 October 1938 – the Sudetenland had been occupied on 1 and 2 October – Hitler and Goebbels watched part of a film financed by Mussolini, Carmine Gallone's *Scipio Africanus* (1937), a heroic epic celebrating Scipio's victories against Hannibal in the Second Punic War. The film was designed as propaganda in support of Mussolini's colonial aspirations in Africa. Hitler and Goebbels no doubt saw in it confirmation of their own colonial ambitions, this time directed towards Eastern Europe.[98]

It was not just feature films that could provide confirmation. Leni Riefenstahl recalls an occasion at the Berghof in August 1939 when the evening's cinematic fare consisted of newsreels. One showed Stalin reviewing the troops in Moscow. The close-up shots of Stalin in profile seemed to preoccupy Hitler: he kept leaning forward and scrutinizing them. After the viewing, he asked for the reel to be shown again. When Stalin's face reappeared, Hitler could be heard saying: 'This man has good features – it surely must be possible to negotiate with him.' Riefenstahl goes on to remark that German Foreign Minister Joachim von Ribbentrop was dispatched to Moscow two days later; three days on, the non-aggression pact between the Soviet Union and Germany was signed, paving the way for Hitler's attack on Poland.[99] This tale sounds apocryphal, but Christabel Bielenberg, the British wife of Peter Bielenberg, an opponent of National Socialism, heard a similar account from Walther Hewel, Ribbentrop's liaison officer to Hitler in the Foreign Office. Hewel spoke to her about Hitler's 'uncanny intuitions' before citing the Hitler–Stalin Pact as a key example:

I was privileged to be there in the Berghof, when the seed of that masterstroke was sown in the Führer's mind. We were watching films

– the Führer finds his sole recreation in watching films – and we were watching a news reel of Stalin reviewing the Russian troops on May Day. The Führer insisted that the film should be run through again and again, and each time, when the close-up appeared of Stalin's face, he ordered that the film should be stopped. STALIN – HALT! Stalin – Halt! It was most dramatic. After about the tenth run-through, the Führer held up his hand. 'Enough,' he said, 'enough, that is a real man; with him I will make a Pact.'[100]

Goebbels also reports that Hitler had 'seen Stalin in a film, and he immediately liked him. That was really the moment where the German-Russian coalition began.'[101] Does this prove that the Hitler–Stalin Pact resulted from Hitler's viewing of a newsreel? Or would this be a 'bogus shackling of cause and effect'? At the very least it proves that Hitler found in the newsreel visual corroboration of his sense that he could do business with Stalin – a confirmation theatrically staged to his audience as a moment of intuition. But visual corroboration is significant. Viewing films and newsreels *had* an influence on Hitler, even if it would be rash to suggest that political action flowed directly from it.

Film viewing may also have influenced Hitler's views of other countries, reinforcing existing prejudices. Hollywood was not free of blame when it came to Hitler's 'complete misrecognition' of the USA and its inhabitants, writes Hitler's former adjutant Fritz Wiedemann: 'the many gangster films made in the USA, a great number of which Hitler watched, encouraged in him a view that might be valid in relation to some characteristics of the Americans, but does not hold true in general'.[102] According to historian Klaus Fischer, Hitler regarded the USA as a '"mongrel nation", as racially polluted as it was decadent and materialistic'.[103] Gangster films will have confirmed this view. Yet, as Fischer also points out, Hitler admired America for its 'powerful industrial capacity and its creative Nordic stock'.[104] Similarly, he did not just draw sustenance for prejudice from American films, he genuinely admired some of them; he would hardly have consumed so many – westerns, comedies, cartoons, as well as gang-ster films – had this not been the case. Such was Hitler's interest in English-language films that he watched them in the original when they had not yet been dubbed. In early May 1936, the Berghof was sent two American film comedies, Clarence Brown's *Wife vs. Secretary* (1936), starring Clark Gable and Jean Harlow, and Fred Guiol's *Breakfast in Bed* (1930) – in the original English. Included in the same package was a 1935 French film, Marcel L'Herbier's *Sacrifice of Honour*, with German subtitles.[105] Other films in the original English sent to Hitler's home over the 1936 period include the Shirley Temple films *Captain January* (1936, directed by David Butler) and *Now and Forever* (1934, directed by Henry Hathaway). They also include William Wellman's *Robin Hood of El Dorado* (1936), Fritz Lang's *Fury* (1936), King Vidor's *So Red the Rose* (1935), Sidney Franklin's *The Dark Angel* (1935), George Archainbaud's *The Return of Sophie Lang* (1936), and Charles Barton's *And Sudden Death* (1936), a drama about an heiress who falls in love with a traffic policeman.

Hitler watched films in a variety of foreign languages apart from English. On 31 January 1936, for instance, the Propaganda Ministry sent *Walpurgis Night* (1935) in the original Swedish.[106] Propaganda Ministry dispatches to the Berghof in 1936 included French films such as Vladimir Strizhevsky's *Volga Boatmen* (1936), Claude Heymann's *The Brighton Twins* (1936), Maurice Tourneur's *Samson* (1936) and Léo Joannon's *Mad Girl* (1935). Hitler was presented with a summary of the plots of films during dinner.[107] Given his at best rudimentary grasp of English and French, this was usually the only orientation he received. According to his doctor Hanskarl von Hasselbach, however, it was actually through watching films in French and English that he improved his knowledge of these languages.[108] That Hitler watched foreign films that had not been dubbed or subtitled indicates the Propaganda Ministry was not always able to satisfy his appetite; sometimes, there were just not enough German films available. Hitler does not seem to have been concerned about not understanding all the detail of films in a foreign language (although sometimes the ministry provided translations of the dialogue). This again confirms his rootedness in the pre-talkies world, his interest in the movement and power of images, one of the reasons he chose Leni Riefenstahl as his personal director.[109] It bears out the argument of a recent book by Wolfgang Pyta which focuses on the importance of visuality to Hitler.[110]

The Other Hitler

German newspaper-readers in the Third Reich would have known Hitler watched films. The Nazi *Film-Kurier* celebrated Hitler's approaching fiftieth birthday by praising Hitler's services to the film industry. There is no other statesman in the world, we read, who watches as many films as the Führer. 'As long as the Führer watches films and gives them awards, the people will want to see them too.'[111] Two days later, the *Film-Kurier* reported on a present of films made to Hitler 'designed for the Führer's film collection'.[112] In one of photographer Heinrich Hoffmann's various picture books about Hitler, Hitler's chief adjutant Wilhelm Brückner wrote that Hitler found time 'between the pressing questions of the day' to watch German and foreign films in the Reich Chancellery.[113] What the Germans did not know was that film viewing took up most of Hitler's evenings, and that it acquired an obsessive quality from the mid-1930s through to the start of the war. It would have surprised Germans, too, to learn of Hitler's limitless appetite for musicals, revue films and comedies, many of them made in Hollywood. Hitler was careful to avoid any hint reaching the German public that his film watching was anything other than serious-minded. Nazi newspapers did report on his liking for certain films from the Weimar Republic, but that he consumed all manner of films made in the Republic was also not common knowledge. Nor was it known that he watched films with Jewish directors and actors. In *My Struggle*, Hitler had railed against the Jews as the 'intellectual creators' of 'dreadful' and 'shoddy' films and plays: 'that was pestilence, worse than the Black Death'.[114] He had stressed the need to 'purify our theatres, art, literature and press from the manifestations of a rotting world and place them in the service of a morally principled idea of state and culture'.[115] This need 'to purify' does not seem to have applied to his private film viewing habits.

While some Hollywood films produced or directed by Jews, or starring Jewish actors, were banned in pre-war Nazi Germany, others were shown and enjoyed. On occasion, Hitler himself decided whether they were to be shown in German cinemas. This was the case with *Camille* (1936), for instance, starring Greta Garbo, whom Hitler much admired. The director, George Cukor, was of Jewish background, but Hitler decided *Camille* should run in Germany nonetheless.[116] One wonders at what point Hitler might have considered a film simply 'too' Jewish, although the Polish film *The Young Forest* came into this category: Hitler banned it because there were Jews involved in writing the script, directing the film, playing the music and acting in it.[117] There is evidence Hitler sometimes broke off watching films which featured Jewish actors or had been directed by Jews, such as Louis Friedlander's *Stormy* (1935),[118] and Charles Vidor's *The Great Gambini* (1937).[119] But he could have broken these films off for any number of reasons. He watched and enjoyed the Laurel and Hardy film *Swiss Miss*, even though the lead female role was played by Grete Natzler (Della Lind), who had left Nazi Germany in 1933 because of her Jewish background. The ambivalence of National Socialism towards American culture, which was rejected on ideological and often racial grounds but was standard fare in German cinemas, can be traced to Hitler himself. The public, political Hitler denounced supposed trivialization through Hollywood, but indulged in it privately at the Berghof. Goebbels was no less Janus-faced. Hitler's film viewing confronts us with an apparent paradox. Hitler's anti-Semitism, anti-Americanism and his rejection of the Weimar Republic 'system' were deep beliefs, passionately held doctrines. But his response to film was not always determined by ideological or racist preconceptions. For the private Hitler, films could transcend the – for him – problematic circumstances of their production.

2

From Bans to Commissions

HITLER INTERVENES IN THE FILM INDUSTRY

Prior to the outbreak of the Second World War, Hitler endeavoured to watch *every* German and foreign feature film released in Germany. He also decided on the fate of films when the Propaganda Ministry was unable to make up its mind whether to pass them or not.[1] Aesthetic considerations usually played little if any part in Hitler's interventions. They were mostly informed by a mixture of ideological principle and sensitivity to the immediate political situation. Moreover, Hitler played a central role in commissioning not only Riefenstahl's Nazi Party rally films, but also films promoting eugenicist and anti-Bolshevist policies. That film mattered to him as a political tool is amply demonstrated by his various building projects.

Banning Films

On 13 November 1933, Goebbels called on Hitler at midnight. They discussed – and may have watched – a feature film called *Abel with the Mouth Organ*, a seemingly harmless tale, directed by Erich Waschneck, about a balloon and a sailing boat on the North Sea. The main female character, Corinna, falls in love with an American she calls 'Hurry'. Abel falls unhappily in love with Corinna, but at the end sets sail with his two male friends. Goebbels described the film as 'terrible tasteless shit', and Hitler was furious.[2] He clearly perceived in its imagery and narrative a celebration of the male body, male bonding and homosexuality. Matters were presumably not helped by the fact that one of the male characters was played by a homosexual actor, Hans Brausewetter; in 1936, Brausewetter was sent to a concentration camp on account of his sexuality. Goebbels banned the film,[3] and used the ban as an excuse to begin a restructuring of the German film company Ufa.[4] The ban did not affect showings abroad, however. The exiled German writer Thomas Mann saw *Abel with the Mouth Organ* in Zurich in February 1934. He liked it for the same reasons that Goebbels and Hitler disliked it. In his diary, Mann wrote: 'from the cinema, I went into the café near the hotel feeling satisfied, indeed delighted after seeing [. . .] "beautiful" young bodies'. Mann's response can be read as an indication of his own homosexual leanings,[5] that of Goebbels and Hitler as an indication of their homophobia. Hitler would have disliked *Abel with the Mouth Organ* no matter when he saw it. But political circumstances were not without influence. On 12 November 1933, the Germans had gone to the polls to vote in the first Reichstag elections held in what was now a one-party state. Over 90 per cent of those who voted approved the Nazi list. Hitler and Goebbels, buoyed by the results, reacted to the innocuous *Abel with the Mouth Organ* with particular moral self-righteousness.

About a month later, Hitler was confronted with the first potential diplomatic difficulty caused by a Nazi film. The film was Gustav Ucicky's adventure drama *Refugees* (1933). Quite in keeping with Nazi Germany's negative attitude towards the Soviet Union, it portrayed the Bolshevist persecution of Volga Germans, who are rescued from their plight by a heroic German modelled on Hitler – played by cinema heart-throb Hans Albers. *Refugees* was due to be premiered in early December, just as Soviet Commissar for Foreign Affairs Maxim Litvinov was visiting Berlin.

German–Soviet relations were at a low ebb, and Litvinov had been pushing for a military alliance with France following Germany's departure from the League of Nations and World Disarmament Conference in October. Banning *Refugees* might have done something (if not much) to defuse German–Soviet tensions, but Hitler decided against a ban.[6] Instead, he delayed the premiere by a day or two; *Refugees* was first shown, behind Litvinov's departing back, on 8 December 1933. The minimal postponement was Hitler's way of appearing to make a concession without really making one. By contrast, when it suited him, he opted to intensify a diplomatic spat over a film. In 1937, Chinese leader Chiang Kai-shek protested to Werner von Blomberg, Germany's minister of war, about Herbert Selpin's adventure film *Alarm in Peking* (1937). Set in 1900 during the Boxer Rebellion, it portrayed the Europeans as noble and condemned the violence of the Chinese. Goebbels wanted the film banned,[7] but, on 30 June 1937, Hitler refused. Goebbels, dutifully changing his mind, wrote in his diary: 'where would it lead if we allowed historical films to be vetted by the countries portrayed?'[8] Hitler made Goebbels write a detailed letter to the Chinese ambassador explaining the decision not to ban the film. Even when the Chinese threatened a protest demonstration, Hitler would not give way.[9] Relations between Germany and China had been deteriorating, with China moving closer to the Soviet Union, and Germany to Japan. When Japan declared war on China on 7 July 1937, Hitler expressed full support for his ally in the Anti-Comintern Pact. Refusing to ban *Alarm in Peking* was a clear statement by Hitler of his disregard for the Chinese.

Anti-communist considerations were never far from Hitler's mind, and they could induce him to impose as well as refuse bans. This was the case with *White Slaves* (1937), a historical epic directed by Karl Anton and starring Camilla Horn, one of Germany's truly international film stars.[10] *White Slaves* was set in Sebastopol at the time of the Bolshevik revolution, and depicted the violence of the revolutionaries. 'Führer has banned it,' Goebbels wrote in mid-October 1936: 'realistic, taken from Bolshevism. Very borderline.'[11] When speaking to Horn about the ban, Goebbels maintained that Hitler had found the film *pro*-communist.[12] Goebbels imposed on Horn to convey demands for changes to the director, Anton.[13] Goebbels personally oversaw the reworking of the film: 'I myself have revised the manuscript. Now, it has a profile.'[14] On 18 December 1936, he proudly noted that Hitler had lifted the ban.[15] In June 1937, Goebbels complained about another Nazi film focusing on the Bolshevik revolution, Herbert Maisch's *Strong Hearts* (1937): 'it has the same mistakes as *White Slaves*. Too bourgeois and simple, without contour or contrasts.'[16] In opting to show Bolshevist revolutionary amorality, violence and class conflict, Third Reich directors were not going far enough. Hitler and Goebbels wanted historical portrayals of communism to correspond to contemporary Nazi ideas about a world-historical struggle of ideologies, especially in the context of the signing of the Anti-Comintern Pact, details of which were being worked out in the autumn of 1936. For this reason, Goebbels introduced a final scene into *White Slaves* where the global threat of communism, and the need to fight it, is spelt out.

Directors could produce propagandistic films, then, and still fail to meet expectations, or even commit a faux pas in Hitler's eyes. This was certainly true of Luis Trenker, of whose mountaineering films Hitler was a fan. In 1937, Trenker directed a feature film called *Condottieri*. Set in early sixteenth-century Italy, it focuses on Giovanni di Medici's struggle to regain his father's castle from Cesare Borgia with the help of mercenaries, and on his commitment to the idea of a united fatherland. Associations with the present were reinforced by modelling the condottieri on Mussolini's Blackshirts, and by employing sixty members of Hitler's own personal bodyguard formation, the SS Leibstandarte Adolf Hitler, to play the mercenaries.[17] Unfortunately for Trenker, the importance given to Catholicism in his film did not go down well with Hitler and Goebbels. Goebbels complained about Trenker's tendency to 'lose himself too much in mystical-Catholic magic'.[18] 'Not a heroic film,' wrote Goebbels, 'but a film by the Catholic Action.'[19] Trenker claimed later that Hitler angrily left the room after viewing a scene in which the condottieri genuflect before the Pope: 'he had probably expected his SS Leibstandarte to be put to a different use'.[20] Hitler was informed of protests in Munich against the film's Catholic focus, and Goebbels ordered cuts.[21] Hitler and Goebbels were in something of a dilemma. On the one hand, they did not want to support a film which appeared to celebrate Catholicism, especially not at precisely the moment of the Pope's encyclical criticizing Nazi ideas, 'With Burning Concern', had been read out in German Catholic churches.[22] On the other hand, the film, a German-Italian coproduction, celebrated the idea of nationhood and national strength, and served as a cultural affirmation of German–Italian friendship. Banning it, moreover, would have irritated the Italians.[23] The dilemma resulted in shifting policies. The film premiered on 25 March 1937. It was then withdrawn following a staged protest in the Rhineland when Hitler Youth members hurled rotten eggs at the screen during the controversial scene in the Vatican.[24] By this stage, Hitler had lost patience with the film and with Trenker,[25] but Goebbels ensured that cuts were made,[26] and *Condottieri* was rereleased.

Soliciting Hitler's Views

Another director who, like Trenker, had built up reliable ideological credentials only to blot his copybook was Karl Ritter. Ritter produced and directed a whole stream of nationalist feature films after the Nazis came to power, such as *Traitors* (1936), which warned of the threat posed by foreign spy networks to the Nazi armaments industry, and *Leave on Word of Honour* (1938), which follows the fates of four German soldiers at the end of the First World War; despite the fact that revolution is in the air, none of them opts to desert. In late 1937, Ritter himself took a period of leave from national duties when he decided to make a fantastical and baroque musical comedy called *Capriccio*. If Trenker in *Condottieri* had mixed nationalist propaganda with Catholicism, which was problematic enough, in *Capriccio* Ritter seemed to have abandoned propaganda in favour of farce. Goebbels tried to stop Ritter making the film, but as the project was already well advanced he restricted himself to issuing a severe warning: 'Ritter should only make large-scale political and national films.'[27] When Goebbels watched *Capriccio* in May 1938, he was horrified: 'terrible filth. Supposed to be a musical comedy. Trivial, boring, frivolous and tasteless. A disgrace for Ritter.'[28] Hitler, who viewed the film in June, was equally horrified, pronouncing it 'particularly bad [. . .] shit of the highest order'.[29] The film's spirit of utter disrespect is striking. It lurches between bad taste, frivolity and a refreshing satire of the Nazi entertainment industry. More by accident than design, Ritter had arguably produced the Third Reich's most interesting film, but, for Hitler and Goebbels, it was unacceptable. From depicting masculine heroism in his previous films, Ritter had switched focus to a sword-bearing woman dressed up as a man. Scenes in a bordello might also have caused offence, and the Reich Music Chamber did not like the music ('a mixture of swing and Beethoven').[30] Yet, on 16 June, Ritter received the 'miraculous news' that *Capriccio* was to be released 'without changes', and Hitler's devastating critique a few days later did not delay the premiere, which followed in August.[31]

Nevertheless, Goebbels did ensure that *Capriccio* did not run for long,[32] and Ritter's indiscretion also contributed to an important decision by Goebbels. On 16 June 1938, the very day that Ritter received the 'miraculous news', the Propaganda Ministry explicitly asked Hitler's Adjutants Office to inform it of every film Hitler viewed, and of his opinion.[33] This request was honoured from June 1938 through to at least July 1939. Goebbels interpreted *Capriccio* as a symptom of a deeper malaise in the German film industry, and stated his intention to 'take more drastic measures against film saboteurs within Ufa'.[34] On 12 May 1938, he issued a 'serious warning' to the chiefs of production.[35] Goebbels wanted Hitler's views of films in writing as a source of support in his struggle for total ideological control of the now more or less state-owned Ufa. He also wanted them because he was fed up of interference from other quarters. In 1935, Hitler had issued an edict forbidding individuals, professional groups or organizations from trying to bring about the censorship of films simply because they or members of these groups were portrayed negatively; only the Propaganda Ministry had the right to exercise censorship.[36] But this did not stop complaints. In 1938, the German press took exception to Victor Tourjansky's *Faded Melody* (1938) because one of the characters was a disreputable journalist, while doctors objected to the way they were depicted in the Austrian film drama *Mirror of Life* (1938), directed by Géza von Bolváry.[37] Having Hitler's views on films would make it easier to react to such criticisms, and enable Goebbels to be sure that opinions on film emanating from the Berghof really were Hitler's.[38] Knowing what films Hitler had watched, moreover, would help Goebbels find out if films were being sent to Hitler behind his back. German branches of American film companies sometimes sent films directly to Hitler, usually in the hope he would overturn a ban.[39] In October 1937, for instance, Paramount asked Hitler to consider lifting the ban on Alexander Hall's *Give Us This Night*, Wilhelm Thiele's *The Jungle Princess* and Cecil B. DeMille's *The Plainsman*, all released in the USA in 1936.[40] *The Jungle Princess* was passed by the Film Censorship Office in March 1938, despite its Jewish director William Thiele, and *The Plainsman* in March 1940.[41]

How useful Hitler's views really were to Goebbels in his control of the film industry, however, remains guesswork. A few days after the Propaganda Ministry's request to be kept informed of Hitler's viewing, Hitler was complaining to Goebbels about an overemphasis on professional problems in German films. Instead, Hitler wanted to see the portrayal of 'human problems'. Goebbels vowed to do his best,[42] but Hitler's complaint rather suggested he understood the objections of some professions to German films.[43] More often than not, Hitler's negative reactions to films had little impact on whether or not they were released.[44] Thus his poor opinion ('bad') of Harald Paulsen's *Woman Comes to the Tropics* – an admittedly preposterous melodrama set on a plantation in Cameroon – did not lead Goebbels, who also disliked the film ('boring and nonsensical'), to take any action.[45] It opened in cinemas on 28 July 1938. If Goebbels had hoped to use Hitler's comments as a lever to apply pressure of whatever kind on the German film industry, by late 1938, Hitler was applying pressure on Goebbels by using his film viewing to punish his propaganda minister. Goebbels' growing infatuation with the Czech actress Lída Baarová was threatening to ruin his marriage, career and relations with Hitler. Hitler's anger at the situation prompted him to slap bans on two films in order to embarrass Goebbels and bring him to his senses. Affected by the bans were two feature films, Carl Junghans' *Old Heart Goes on a Journey* (1938)[46] and Rolf Hansen's *Life Can Be So Wonderful* (1938).[47] *Old Heart Goes on a Journey* provided an at times unflattering portrayal of a farming community, while *Life Can Be So Wonderful* focused on problems created by housing shortages. Interestingly, the censorship problems faced by both films demonstrate only too well why filmmakers in the Third Reich often avoided depicting social issues: there was always a danger such portrayals would be understood as a critique of Nazi policies. Hence there was a preference for depicting problems in professional milieus seemingly removed from politics.

Documentary Film and Sterilization

Hitler usually only intervened in the fate of individual feature films at post-production and distribution stage, but his engagement in documentary film was more fundamental, and responded to longer-term goals as well as more immediate political concerns. This was the case with the twenty-five-minute documentary short *Victims of the Past* (1937), which set out to justify the forced sterilization of the mentally and physically disabled. The Law for the Prevention of Hereditarily Diseased Offspring had been passed on 14 July 1933, allowing for the sterilization of German citizens deemed to be suffering – in the opinion of pompously named Genetic Health Courts – from supposed genetic disorders. Soon after, the Racial Political Office of the Nazi Party began to make short films to support this legislation, such as *The Fathers' Sins* (1935), *The Inheritance* (1935) and *The Hereditary Defective* (1936). The most notorious in this series was *Victims of the Past*, directed by Gernot Bock-Stieber, and co-written by Bock-Stieber and Rudolf Frercks of the Racial Political Office. It was commissioned by Hitler following his viewing of *The Hereditary Defective*, which he found good, but clearly felt needed improving.[48] And it was Hitler who had the idea of taking a more 'professional' filmic approach to the subject;[49] the Propaganda Ministry collaborated with the Racial Political Office to ensure this would happen. Apart from *The Inheritance*, the precursors to *Victims of the Past* were silent 16mm movies, using captions to encourage the desired interpretation of the film. *Victims of the Past* was a sound film, with a voice-over and an at times dramatic score connecting the individual sections. This served to reinforce its drastic message.[50] It claimed the disabled were a financial drain on the community; that they lived in palatial care homes, while many Germans lived in poverty; and that if they continued to procreate at a greater rate than the healthy, the Germans would soon be a nation of imbeciles.

It is possible that Hitler first watched *Victims of the Past* in October 1936.[51] If so, then a repeat viewing was required in early 1937, when Goebbels had a copy sent to Hitler's Adjutants Office with a request that a decision be taken on whether it could be shown, a decision Hitler had reserved the right to make.[52] Goebbels duly noted that Hitler found *Victims of the Past* 'very good', and that the film 'has to be shown in all German cinemas'.[53] After a joint viewing, Goebbels and Hitler reiterated that the film should be deployed 'as quickly as possible [. . .] in all German cinemas within the framework of a normal and suitable film programme'.[54] This was to be the first public showing of such a film; earlier Racial Political Office films about the disabled had been designed for internal Nazi Party viewing and presented in an explicitly 'educational' framework, with accompanying lectures.[55] Objections to showing the film publicly were made, but overruled. Frercks, for instance, wrote to Goebbels' secretary Karl Hanke, impressing on him that even if he, Hanke, could not approve of all the 'repulsive' images, it was necessary to show the nation the 'hard and unsparing side of ethnic life'. Frercks also implied that the severity of these images represented a direct response to Hitler's instructions.[56] In April, the showing of *Victims of the Past* was made mandatory.[57] Following a viewing for party leaders and representatives of Nazi organizations in Berlin – Hitler was not present – the film made its way round Germany's 5,300 film theatres. The Reich Propaganda Leadership, writing to all Gau Film Offices, stressed that Hitler had insisted *every* 'people's comrade' must see *Victims of the Past*, and collaboration between the Racial Political Office and the Gau Film Offices was to be streamlined to ensure his order could be followed.[58] No cinema in the Reich was exempt from showing the film.[59]

Victims of the Past lent visual and textual support to one of Hitler's more axiomatic pronouncements in *My Struggle*: 'he who is not physically and mentally healthy and worthy cannot be allowed to perpetuate his suffering in the body of his child'.[60] Like its predecessor sterilization films, only more forcefully, it seeks to convince the viewer that it is both God's law and natural law not to allow the genetically enfeebled to procreate. In the words of Michael Burleigh: 'insidiously, the films appropriate the language of mercy, morality and religion in order to subvert them the more effectively'.[61] That Hitler triggered the production of a propaganda film about the disabled for general release was a reaction to the public unease the sterilization laws had caused, with the Catholic Church in some cases expressing open disapproval. Minister of the Interior Wilhelm Frick even issued a circular asking government institutions to take measures in response to such 'agitation' against the law.[62] The sequence in the film showing a bride-to-be seeking advice from a doctor on genetic health was clearly designed to promote acceptance of the October 1935 Marriage Health Law.

At the same time, the film's obsessive dwelling on images of infirmity aims to unsettle audiences so that any potential resistance to the planned radicalization of policy that resulted in euthanasia is nipped in the bud. Euthanasia, under cover of war,[63] was always what Hitler had ultimately envisaged, but it was clear to him it was not going to be a popular measure with most Germans.[64] At points, *Victims of the Past* associates mental illness with Jewishness, tapping into anti-Semitic sentiment to mobilize resentment and fear. Hitler was confident, clearly, that confronting German audiences with images designed to repel would have the desired effect. Here again was his faith in the visual. Yet he stopped short of directly confronting audiences with visual documentation of euthanasia. In August 1939, Philipp Bouhler, chief of Hitler's Chancellery, and Martin Bormann showed Hitler and others a film called *Unworthy Life*. To judge from the description of the viewing by Hitler's army adjutant, Gerhard Engel, this was a film about children's euthanasia, the first steps towards which were coordinated as of mid-1939 by Hitler's Chancellery on Hitler's express orders. Bormann suggested to Hitler showing the film in cinemas, but Hitler's doctor, Karl Brandt, rejected the idea: what would you say, he asked, if you discovered one of your own children in the film? Hitler rejected the idea of a public screening in this instance, presumably agreeing with Brandt's assessment that it would 'cause unrest'.[65]

There are moments in the gestation of *Victims of the Past* where the brutality of Goebbels and Hitler comes sharply into focus.[66] On 4 December 1936, Goebbels commented on having seen 'a film from the lunatic asylums to justify the sterilization laws': 'horrifying material [. . .] your blood freezes just watching it'.[67] A few days later, he writes in his diary of a 'nice little' dinner party attended among others by Eugen Klöpfer, Heinz Hilpert and Lída Baarová.[68] The evening's entertainment consisted of a film about the 'hereditarily ill' that was 'strongly applauded', followed by a 'bad' French film, and then *The Hound of the Baskervilles* ('suspenseful and entertaining'). Goebbels showed what was probably *Victims of the Past* to his guests as a titillating horror show, something to enjoy over a drink or two, without a thought for the debasement of the disabled in the film or their fate under Nazism. On 10 February 1937, Hitler, after seeing *Victims of the Past*, suggested to Goebbels adding a photograph of Helga, Goebbels' four-year-old daughter – to provide a 'nice final image'.[69] Goebbels took up and developed the idea. Ten days later, he sent Hitler a film roll showing his children, presumably seeking Hitler's approval for the images to be included.[70] '*Victims of the Past* with our children at the end,' Goebbels enthused; 'all three are so sweet!'[71] The final version of the film does include a clip of three children playing. These are almost certainly Helga, Hilde and Helmut Goebbels. They are used as an example of healthy German children, contrasting with the images of debility that have gone before, and anticipating the film's apotheosis – a visual celebration of athletic National Socialist youth groups, and, at the very end, of Hitler himself. The rush of sentimentality felt by Hitler and Goebbels at the thought of the Goebbels' children stands in sharp contrast to their absolute lack of empathy for the disabled. The world is imagined as a conflict between the unworthy and the worthy, darkness and light, illness and health, ugliness and beauty. *Victims of the Past* played a part in preparing the way for the killing of the 'unworthy'. Towards the end of the war, Goebbels and his wife Magda murdered their own children so that the 'worthy' would not fall into the hands of the 'unworthy' Allies. Given the putatively life-affirming contrast between Goebbels' children and the disabled in *Victims of the Past*, this was a bitterly ironic development.[72]

In Battle against the World Enemy

A second key example of Hitler prompting a documentary to promote hostility, this time towards the Soviet Union, is provided by a film about the Spanish Civil War (1936–39), a war interpreted by the Nazis as a campaign against Soviet communist imperialism. The Nazis made two longer films about this war. Work on the first of these went through several versions and titles. It began in 1936, with the film finally reaching cinema screens as *Heroes in Spain* in 1938. Hitler did not commission it, but he certainly interfered in its production. He did, however, commission the second film. In January 1939, he asked Karl Ritter to go to Spain and film what Hitler hoped would be the final stages of the war.[73] The result was *In Battle against the World Enemy: German Volunteers in Spain* (1939). Given

Hitler's disgust at Ritter's *Capriccio*, his choice of director might seem surprising, but Ritter had in the interim gone back up in Hitler's estimation following the premiere of his film *Pour le Mérite* portraying the build-up of the air force under National Socialism. Hitler, who was at the December 1938 premiere, described *Pour le Mérite* as 'the best contemporary film up to this point in time'.[74] There are several reasons why Hitler asked Ritter to make a film about the Spanish Civil War. First, he wanted a film focusing particularly on the role of the German Legion Condor, whose participation in the war remained officially secret until Franco's victory. Second, he wanted a film that presented German weaponry and German forces in action, to impress domestic and international audiences. Ritter, judging by *Pour le Mérite*, was surely an appropriate choice of director for this task. Finally, Hitler was not happy with *Heroes in Spain*; it did not make the global threat of Bolshevism as clear as he wanted. Just as he felt *Victims of the Past* would be an improvement on its predecessors, so Hitler sensed that Ritter would do a better job of filming the Spanish Civil War than the production team behind the making of *Heroes in Spain*.

The original idea for the film that became *Heroes in Spain* emerged from the Propaganda Ministry. Shortly after Hitler's decision to support the nationalist cause in Spain, Hans Weidemann, responsible for overseeing German newsreel production since 1935, took on the task of producing a documentary about the conflict. It was to be directed by Carl Junghans, with whom Weidemann also collaborated on a number of other film projects, such as *Youth of the World* (1936), a film about the 1936 Winter Olympics, and *The Great Time* (1938), which celebrated 'the reconstruction of the Reich' under Hitler. Junghans was a colourful character. In the 1920s and early 1930s, he had been a filmmaker for the communists before going over to the Nazis.[75] Today, he is only remembered for his affair with Vladimir Nabokov's sister Sonia, who was more than ten years his junior. Nabokov did not approve of the relationship, but it may have inspired him to write the novel *Camera Obscura* (1932), and even *Lolita* (1955).[76]

Perhaps Junghans was not entirely able to dissociate himself from the left-wing cause, because his film about the Spanish Civil War, *The Scourge of the World* (1936), met with the disapproval of Goebbels, who bemoaned what he saw as its lack of clarity and precision.[77] Weidemann made changes. While Goebbels found the new version 'usable',[78] Hitler decided against showing it, because it was *still* not clear and precise enough, and the text was too pathos-laden: 'so it's banned', Goebbels wrote.[79] Junghans, in short, had not managed to convey the forceful anti-Bolshevism that Hitler wanted.[80] The German-Spanish production company Hispano Film subsequently transformed *The Scourge of the World* into *Onward Spain* (*Arriba España*); Hispano had been set up by Goebbels to promulgate pronationalist and Nazi propaganda in Spain. *Onward Spain* was shown in Austria in early 1938,[81] before Bavaria Film in Munich acquired the rights to adapt it into what became *Heroes in Spain*.[82] *Heroes in Spain* premiered in Munich on 6 October 1938, with official approval: the Gauleiter of Munich and Upper Bavaria, Adolf Wagner, acted as patron, and representatives of the party, state and Wehrmacht attended.[83] But Goebbels had shown concern before the film was released that it was too violent: 'horrific portrayal of the civil war [. . .] unsuitable for us'.[84] Shortly before Christmas 1938, Hitler decided the film could not be screened in the rest of the Reich until changes had been made.[85]

Ernst Leichtenstern of the Propaganda Ministry, which issued the ban, approached Hans Schweikart, Bavaria's production chief, to ask for the script to see where cuts could be made.[86] Hitler, in other words, had wanted material excised, although it is possible the Wehrmacht also raised objections to particular passages.[87] Hitler also asked for additions.[88] Clearly, he wanted to see *Heroes in Spain* brought as up to date as possible, especially as the triumph of the nationalist troops became more and more likely.[89] To provide new footage, Bavaria and Hispano Film sent a film team to Spain in mid-January 1939. In the meantime, *Heroes in Spain* remained banned. In February, having been appraised of the financial damage this was inflicting on Bavaria, Hitler lifted the ban, only to impose it again shortly afterwards.[90] Bavaria kept on adapting the film 'in response to the events in Spain',[91] but, even when the Spanish Civil War was over, Hitler wanted additions. On 9 May 1939, just when Bavaria thought they would soon be able to release the film, Hitler's personal adjutant Julius Schaub rang up to say Hitler had asked for more changes – *Heroes in Spain* was to end with footage of Franco's triumphant entry into Madrid. Schaub indicated the film was now due to be released in Berlin on 10 May.[92] But, with all Hitler's meddling, it did not have its premiere until 8 June. All these delays cost Bavaria 300,000 Reichsmarks.[93] Hitler told Gerdy Troost, his architectural adviser and a member of Bavaria's board, that he had not wanted *Heroes in Spain* banned, just parts of it changed;[94] but it seems an academic distinction: as long as it was being altered, it was banned.

Hitler expected *Heroes in Spain* to be constantly adapted to events as they unfolded, and he also, like Goebbels, wanted some of the graphic footage of atrocities removed. One thing he did not do, however, was ask for *Heroes in Spain* to incorporate images of the Legion Condor. Neither *The Scourge of the World*, *Onward Spain* nor *Heroes in Spain* included reference to Germany's participation in the war. Hitler had persistently proclaimed that a strong German military was required only for peaceful purposes.[95] However, the deployment of German air force formations in Spain had not gone entirely unnoticed in the Reich. Germans able to tune in to foreign radio stations or read foreign newspapers had quickly learnt that German units had landed in Cadiz in 1936, while the families of those serving in Spain also began to have their suspicions.[96] Rumours circulated about what had really happened at Guernica, and those who had guessed that the German air force was involved in fighting were sceptical that the participants were really volunteers.[97] Hitler could have asked for *Heroes in Spain* to feature footage of the legion in an attempt to justify its involvement, but did not, probably because he did not anticipate it would only reach cinemas in its final form after Franco's victory, when Germans were to be informed of the Legion Condor. The function of *Heroes in Spain* was to persuade audiences of the righteousness of the Spanish nationalist cause, not to address German (or Italian) participation.

Hitler reserved this task for another film: Ritter's *In Battle against the World Enemy*, which was designed from the moment Hitler commissioned it in January 1939 as a celebration of the Legion Condor for showing in cinemas when the legion returned. In the end, both *Heroes in Spain* and *In Battle against the World Enemy* were released at more or less the same time (8 June and 16 June respectively). Hitler, albeit unintentionally, triggered a competition between film companies, and it was a competition Ufa was in a better position to win because, of the two films, only Ritter's appeared to offer a comprehensive version of events. The president of Bavaria's board, Döhlemann, complained bitterly about this. He also objected to the subtitle of the Ufa film (*German Volunteers in Spain*) which, he suspected, had been added to spell out to potential audiences that Ritter's film would reveal details about German participation.[98] That two films appeared on the Spanish Civil War within a week, one that omitted reference to the Legion Condor and one that placed it in central focus, must have led to discussions among cinemagoers about the vagaries of Nazi information and film policies.[99] Cinemagoers could, as it were, choose whether they wanted to experience the Spanish Civil War on screen with or without German participation, though most of them certainly wanted to see the German air force in action, especially now it was clear the war had been won. Döhlemann was right to feel aggrieved. *In Battle against the World Enemy* received more press coverage and official attention, with Göring, who had welcomed the German troops when they returned to Germany on 30 May,[100] coming to the premiere on 16 June. That evening, he awarded Ritter the Spanish Cross in silver.[101]

Heroes in Spain and *In Battle against the World Enemy* do have much in common. Both blame communism for the unrest in Spain that followed the election of the Popular Front in 1936. Both identify the Soviet Union and the Jews as the originators of this unrest, their interests allegedly personified in the figure of the Soviet ambassador to Spain, Moses

Rosenberg, portrayed in both films as the key rabble-rouser. And both present Franco's intervention as a humanitarian response to the intimidation by the radical left. That violence in Spain had many roots, that Franco staged a coup against an elected government, and that the Soviets initially pursued a non-interventionist policy towards the escalating situation in Spain are inconvenient facts both films ignore. But, of the two films, it is Ritter's that makes more of the anti-Bolshevik theme and casts communism in the role of the 'world enemy', in line with the film's title. It contains fewer images of supposed or actual Bolshevik atrocities than *Heroes in Spain*, because its focus, as Hitler wanted it, was not so much on the gruesome symptoms of Bolshevism as on its global ambitions and the need to resist them. *In Battle against the World Enemy* also stresses the collaboration of Spain, Germany and Italy, a collaboration presented as a united defence of civilization against Soviet imperialism. It is more dynamic than *Heroes in Spain*, with Ritter using his skills as feature film director to capture the energy of battle, and provide impressive images of German weaponry, manpower and aerial power. There are moments when *In Battle against the World Enemy* resembles the film of an air show, or depicts Spain as a training ground for German bomb-dropping. At such moments, it was closer to the truth than Ritter realized.

Hitler liked the film he had commissioned, and is not hard to see why.[102] It told the story he wanted of how the Legion Condor came to be formed, a story of a defensive moral mission against communism. Soaking in the images of German military power in the cinema, sceptical viewers were turned into admiring viewers – at least, that, was the intention. *In Battle against the World Enemy*, and *Heroes in Spain* to a less explicit extent, also helped to provide filmic support for the Pact of Steel, signed between Italy and Germany on 22 May 1939, two or three weeks before these films were screened. Both films had a longer-term function as well, preparing the Germans psychologically for the 'necessity' of war against the Soviet Union. That both films were released at the same time served to reinforce this message. Germans, after all, may not have chosen one film over the other, but gone to both.

Hitler's Building Projects

Hitler's film-related building projects also demonstrate the importance he attached to cinema, even if none of them came to fruition and details were not widely known outside the film companies involved. One of these companies was Bavaria, based in Munich. Without Hitler, Bavaria could have folded in 1937. Its studios were in a run-down condition, far inferior to those of other film companies in Berlin or Vienna.[103] A new company, Bavaria Filmkunst, was set up in February 1938, and Hitler provided assurances of economic support,[104] as well as personally advising on plans for new building developments.[105] He also explicitly asked for a huge new studio – Großatelier, or 'grand studio' – to be built as part of Bavaria's refurbishment. It was to measure 200 by 100 by 25 metres and cost some 4.8 million Reichsmarks.[106] According to Goebbels, 'the experts don't know what to make' of Hitler's proposal,[107] but this did not deter Hitler, who insisted the studio be built in the dimensions he had specified.[108] Hitler also refused to transfer the project to Berlin, while remaining open to the idea of a similar construction there at some point in the future.[109] Both Goebbels and Reich Commissioner for the German Film Industry Max Winkler eventually suggested taking the studio project out of Bavaria's budget and setting up a separate firm to administer it. If necessary, Goebbels said, Hitler would have to ask the Reich Finance Ministry for the means to support it.[110] But, with the advent of war, the 'grand studio' project gradually receded into the background; ultimately, it never got further than the drawing board.[111]

Hitler's Munich project did have a pragmatic rationale: according to Bavaria Filmkunst's production chief, Erich Walter Herbell, Hitler imagined that a vast indoor arena would save money by reducing the need to film outdoors, presumably because it could accommodate extensive sets. There would be less dependency on the weather. The 'grand studio', then, was planned as an experiment in self-sufficient indoor filmmaking – corresponding, perhaps, to Hitler's striving for economic autarky. But Max Winkler doubted that the production studio, if built, could be rented out frequently enough to cover the running costs.[112] The plans for it reflected Hitler's peculiarly inconsistent attitude to Bavaria. On the one hand, he helped to bail out the company and assign it a prestigious studio project; on the other, he saddled it with expenses it struggled to meet, as when he interfered with *Heroes in Spain*. Hitler's supportivenesss was matched by economic short-sightedness. He lost himself in visions of a vast modern production studio, outdoing Hollywood, without reflecting on the economic feasibility of the project for a small firm like Bavaria.

He also lost himself in a grand vision of a huge cinema. In July 1938, Max Winkler set up the Deutsche Lichtspielbau to oversee the construction of an enormous cinema in Berlin with capacity for 2,300 cinemagoers;[113] Ufa agreed to cover the costs of the interiors, and to rent the cinema on completion.[114] The idea for the cinema was Hitler's, and probably dates back at least to 1937.[115] It was envisaged as part the 'Germania' project, the architectural transformation of Berlin into what one historian called 'the gleaming new capital of a Greater German "World Empire" '.[116] Albert Speer was responsible for the Germania project, and he also became involved in the planning of the new cinema. Hitler was to have his own entrance leading up to his personal loge, and there was to be a 'Führer's lounge' and a 'Führer foyer'.[117] Construction never even began. The impact of the war, diverting resources elsewhere, was one reason. But matters were not helped by Hitler's interventions. In the course of 1941, he asked for a more elaborate design,[118] and for a larger air-raid shelter which alone would have cost 4 million Reichsmarks.[119] Contrary to what has been claimed,[120] the cinema project was not abandoned, despite Speer's letter of 26 February 1942 informing all Gauleiter that it was 'no longer appropriate to proceed with construction projects that are of no relevance to the outcome of the war'.[121] As late as 1944, the Propaganda Ministry set aside 300,000 Reichsmarks to help with planning for the cinema.[122] But defeat ended all of Hitler's dreams – and Speer's, who had planned an even more enormous cinema for Berlin, seating 6,000–8,000 people, a proposal which had Hitler's approval.[123]

In the end, Hitler's plans for a 'grand studio' and a vast cinema remained fantasies, as did his wartime plans for film studios in Linz,[124] and for a film company to be set up in the former seminary of Wilhering near Linz.[125] The latter idea foundered because Wilhering was plagued by mosquitos.[126] But for all three cities that mattered to Hitler – Berlin, Munich and Linz – there existed ambitious film-related plans. Hitler's interest in the 'grand studio' and especially the premiere cinema was as aesthetic, architectural expressions of the close relationship between political power and film, a relationship articulated above all through sheer size. The Berlin cinema, with its Hitler loge and its 2,300 seats, would have served as a centre for affirming the bond between leader and people. Yet, when war began, Hitler avoided the cinema. The conflict stopped the building plans, but so did Hitler's loss of interest.

Finally, Hitler was involved in plans to build studios for Leni Riefenstahl in Berlin. Riefenstahl, as the next two chapters will show, became Hitler's chief filmmaker. On 13 July 1939, Albert Speer, General Building Inspector for Berlin, wrote to State Secretary Paul Körner to inform him that a 'film building' was to be erected 'at Hitler's behest'. 'This building will provide Leni Riefenstahl with the studios she has so far lacked.'[127] In fact, Speer had been negotiating the construction of these studios with Riefenstahl since March 1939. At a meeting with Speer on 8 March, Riefenstahl's representative Walter Traut conveyed her wishes for a piece of land 5,000 square metres in extent.[128] As the land envisaged belonged to the Prussian state, discussions had to be conducted with the Prussian Building and Finance Direction – and Göring. Hitler decided that 'either the Party or Bormann' was to figure as building contractor.[129] Like the other film-related building projects, nothing came of Riefenstahl's studio scheme. In August 1942, the plans were still in place, but the fact that the Prussian Building and Finance Direction decided eventually to rent out the envisaged land for gardening purposes indicated that vegetables had more hope of establishing themselves there than Riefenstahl's studios.[130]

Hitler's interventions in film matters reflect his self-appointed political role as head diplomat, chief racial policymaker and master-builder. Where the possible effects of films had to be considered in relation to matters of foreign policy, Hitler – not von Neurath's or Ribbentrop's Foreign Ministry – decided on what course of action to take. Even during the war, when he had less time for film, Hitler preserved this prerogative. In 1941, he refused to allow Augusto Genina's Italian film about the Spanish Civil War, *The Siege of the Alcazar* (1940), to run in Germany until scenes showing the uplifting influence of the Catholic Church had been removed; as with *Condottieri*, he prioritized domestic anti-Catholic considerations, while hoping the Italians would accept cuts. Mussolini asked the actor Emil Jannings to tell Goebbels 'the film is set in Spain, not in Germany',[131] but Hitler insisted on scenes being excised.[132] His interventions in documentary film production can be divided into two categories. As we shall see, he used Leni Riefenstahl to create uplifting films about National Socialism. *In Battle against the World Enemy* was positive in its portrayal of the German military, but it was also designed as a warning against the Bolshevik threat, while *Victims of the Past* focused on the 'threat' of the disabled. Hitler was central to films that promoted the Nazi sense of community, and films that clearly stigmatized those who did not belong. His film-related building projects provide evidence of his belief in the representational power of architecture. He envisaged studios for his favourite director, a vast new modern studio for his favoured film company, Bavaria, and a huge cinema in Berlin designed mainly for premieres which he would attend, turning film into political statement.

3

Hitler's Director

LENI RIEFENSTAHL FILMS THE 1933 NUREMBERG RALLY

Of all Third Reich documentary film directors, Leni Riefenstahl was by far the most important. Her collaboration with Hitler began at the latest in 1933, and ended only with the death of Hitler in 1945. She produced several documentaries at his behest. Far from simply believing there should be 'political film' on the one hand, and 'entertainment film' on the other, with a clear separation between these two forms, Hitler wanted documentary films that blended political expression with the expressive visual aesthetics and story-telling techniques of feature film. The first of these was Riefenstahl's film of the 1933 Nazi Party rally, *Victory of Faith*. It was Hitler, not Goebbels, who grasped the significance of the rallies and understood that, in concentrated filmic form, they could reach and sway those tens of millions of Germans who had never experienced them directly.

Hitler's Director

Riefenstahl, if her account is to be believed, did not want to make any films for Hitler. In her memoirs, she recalls that, when she first met Hitler in May 1932, he said to her: '[W]hen we come to power, then you must make my films.' She declined, replying she could never make prescribed films, and that she was not interested in politics; she also voiced her objection to Hitler's 'racial prejudices'.[1] At the time, Riefenstahl was playing the lead role in Arnold Fanck's new film about an Arctic expeditionary force, *SOS Iceberg*. After meeting Hitler, she left for Greenland, where *SOS Iceberg* was being made on location at Umanak. While in Greenland, some of those involved in the film exploited the hospitality of their Eskimo hosts by sleeping with their wives. There is no evidence that Riefenstahl herself participated in the egregious boozing and wanton damage of Eskimo storerooms,[2] but, had word of the scandalous behaviour of Fanck's team got through to Hitler, Riefenstahl might have gone down in his estimation. As it was, in May 1933, having since come to power, he asked Riefenstahl to create a film about the Nazi martyr, Horst Wessel, who had been shot by communists in 1930. Again she declined.[3] When he renewed his efforts to win her support in August 1933, pleading with her this time to film the Nazi Party rally about to begin in Nuremberg, she gave in.[4] She became, whether she had wanted to or not, Hitler's director. It was a label she was to keep until her death – at the ripe old age of 101 – in 2003. After 1945, again and again she insisted that documentary films (which she admitted making) were not propaganda films (which she denied having made). Despite this, she remains, alongside Veit Harlan, the prime example of film directors' collaboration with Nazism.

There are several possible answers to the question as to why Hitler entrusted Leni Riefenstahl with the job of filming the rally. The answer provided by Riefenstahl's detractors was that Riefenstahl was Hitler's lover. Writing in American exile in 1942, the anti-Nazi writer Carl Zuckmayer remarked that Riefenstahl was known in Germany as the 'Reich's glacial crevasse'. Zuckmayer himself did not believe that she had slept with Hitler: 'we can assume they are both impotent'.[5] But rumours about her possible sexual relationship with Hitler were rife during the Third Reich. They found explicit expression abroad. In 1938, Riefenstahl's press secretary Ernst Jaeger accompanied her on a trip to the USA. He never returned to

Germany. Riefenstahl describes conflicts with Jaeger in her memoirs,[6] and Jaeger seems to have borne her a grudge, because in 1939 the *Hollywood Tribune* published his account of 'How Riefenstahl became Hitler's girl-friend'.[7] Jaeger knew Riefenstahl well enough to know she never had. After the war, Luis Trenker, a mountain-climbing actor who was something of a rival of Riefenstahl's, also determined on spreading stories about her.[8] Struggling to find his feet financially, Trenker came up with the idea of claiming that he owned a copy of Eva Braun's diary, which she had alleg-edly passed on to him in 1944. He sold its contents to the press.[9] Of course, there was no such diary: what Trenker was selling was a fake, for which he himself was probably responsible (although this has never been clearly ascertained). The French press began reporting on the diary under headlines such as 'Leni Danced Naked before Adolf'.[10] The fake diary was published in 1948 in French, then in Italian and English. In it, 'Eva' expressed fears she might be ousted by Riefenstahl. At one point, she is banished to her bedroom while Riefenstahl and other guests entertain themselves below: 'I wonder whether they are performing the nude dances [. . .] of which they always talk and which I must never attend.'[11]

The diary did contain a passage where 'Hitler' denies any sexual interest in 'Leni', but Riefenstahl was so incensed at the 'nude dancing' accusation that she took legal action (along with Eva Braun's family) to stop further dissemination of material from the diary.[12] Riefenstahl's denazification files contain statements by members of Hitler's entourage testifying that the relationship between Hitler and Riefenstahl was cordial, but strictly professional, and certainly never intimate. Fritz Wiedemann, Hitler's erst-while adjutant, declared bluntly that 'Frau Riefenstahl was never Hitler's lover', and that during his tenure (1935–39) she had very few personal meetings with Hitler.[13] Hitler's former chauffeur, Erich Kempka, dismissed the idea that Eva Braun could ever have been jealous of Riefenstahl. 'I never observed that Fräulein Riefenstahl's relationship to Hitler was an intimate one.'[14] Margarete Mittelstrasser, a maid and cook at the Berghof, declared that Riefenstahl had never stayed overnight; it was therefore 'pure invention' that she had danced naked for Hitler.[15] According to Goebbels, Riefenstahl did, at least once, *dance* for him and Hitler: 'Leni R. dances. Well and with effect. A supple gazelle.'[16] But this is not the same thing as dancing *naked*.[17] That Hitler had sexual relations with Riefenstahl, or that she displayed herself to him, can be dismissed as fantasy. While in this respect the victim of false allegations, Riefenstahl must, however, take some of the blame for their persistence into the present. In her memoirs, she claimed that Hitler made advances when they first met at Horumersiel in May 1932, before reining himself in with the dramatic remark: 'I cannot permit myself to love a woman till I have completed my task.'[18] Riefenstahl never stopped admiring Hitler till her dying day, and she relished the thought that he might have been attracted to her, while simultaneously wanting to put an end to the rumours that sexual intimacy had played any part in their relationship. Riefenstahl's account of this meeting with Hitler in 1932 does not ring true. What it does do is wilfully imply that Hitler sacrificed his interest in her to the greater good of the nation, a story designed to dignify the fact that nothing had happened between them.

While Hitler's choice of Riefenstahl cannot be traced to sexual interest, it may have had something to do with her being a woman – exactly what the male party faithfuls thought would disqualify her. In matters of the arts, Hitler often preferred liaising with women. Gerdy Troost, following the death of her architect husband Paul in 1934, became a kind of interior designer for Hitler. She played a major role in designing his home at the Berghof.[19] According to Hitler's former personal adjutant, Julius Schaub, Troost was the 'ideal conversation partner' for Hitler, with whom he could 'talk endlessly about his architectural plans'.[20] Hitler protected Gerdy Troost against the hostilities she faced in what she later called the 'Männerstaat' – a state ruled by men.[21] He was equally protective of Winifred Wagner, who ran the Bayreuth Wagner Festival from 1930 until 1944.[22] Not all Nazi leaders approved of Winifred, and few approved of the festival being run by a woman. It was precisely because Troost and Winifred Wagner were women that Hitler believed they were less likely to be drawn into one of the various cliques that formed within the Nazi Party, or to associate themselves with the interests of a particular state or party institution. They remained directly answerable to him. The same was true of Riefenstahl. Like Troost, she faced animosity from men. But unlike Troost, Riefenstahl was not a party member, and so the animosity was probably stronger. The effect of this animosity was to reinforce her dependence on Hitler, to whom she turned for help, or on those close to him. As we shall see, Riefenstahl did receive support, but so too did she face adversity from Goebbels and the Propaganda Ministry. While most of the funds for her films were sanctioned by Hitler personally, they were administered through various state and party offices. Nevertheless, her insistence after the war that she kept her distance from party networks was not untruthful.

The main reason Hitler asked Riefenstahl to film the Nazi Party rallies is the most obvious one: he was convinced she would do a good job. It was a conviction based largely on his admiration for *The Blue Light* (1932), a film starring Riefenstahl that she co-directed with another multi-talent, Béla Balázs. Balázs, a communist and a Jew, went into exile in the Soviet Union when Hitler came to power. Set in spectacular mountain scenery in the Dolomites, *The Blue Light* tells the tale of an outsider figure – Junta, played by Riefenstahl – who is able to climb dizzying heights to reach a grotto filled with crystals, while the young men of the nearby village plunge to their deaths in the attempt. With the help of a passing artist, Vigo, played by Mathias Wieman, the villagers finally find their way to the grotto and make off with the crystals; devastated, Junta herself now tumbles to her death. When Hitler first met Riefenstahl he said that, of all her films, *The Blue Light* had made the strongest impression on him: 'it is unusual that a young woman is able to assert herself against the resistance and the taste of the film industry'.[23] While this comment proves that Hitler had been struck by Riefenstahl's independent spirit, it tells us little about why he liked the film. It might have impressed him because of its multiple echoes of Wagner's *Ring* cycle, where it is the theft of gold, rather than crystals, which triggers disaster. He might have seen in it, too, an allegory of the rapacious effects of capitalism, or, by contrast, an anti-communist tale about what happens when wealth is redistributed among the common people. But what probably impressed him most was the film's mise en scène.

It has often been suggested that the German mountain films of the Weimar Republic were in a sense pre-fascist: here, then, was one Weimar Republic tradition to which Hitler could explicitly connect. Whether such claims are fair or not, many of those who directed or acted as cameramen for mountain films – key examples being Arnold Fanck, Luis Trenker, Sepp Allgeier and, of course, Riefenstahl – went on to have important careers under Nazism and, in the case of Riefenstahl, Fanck and Allgeier, to film Nazi documentaries. It seems it was a short step from filming mountains to filming fascism. That the Nazis saw mountain films as appropriate for the heroic occasion is demonstrated, for instance, by the inclusion of several of them in the list of recommended films for Heroes' Commemoration Day in 1934, where *The Blue Light* features alongside Fanck's *SOS Iceberg* and his *Storm over Mont Blanc* (1930).[24] All the qualities that made the mountain film genre so attractive to Hitler are present in *The Blue Light*. Junta is filmed again and again against a backdrop of mountains, craggy rocks, rushing waterfalls, rivers, swirling clouds and mists, sweeping skylines and thick forests. Until she falls from the mountainside following the theft of the crystals, she seems in control of the natural world around her. Riefenstahl as Junta places herself within vast panoramas of alpine scenery, yet makes it appear as if she stood at their centre. If Hitler thought she could transfer this skill to representing his role among the tens of thousands of followers at Nuremberg, then he showed a sure instinct.[25] Hitler, moreover, was well aware of Riefenstahl's skills as a dancer. He could hope she would be sensitive to the importance of investing film of the marching columns of men at Nuremberg with the required vitality.

Hitler's choice of Riefenstahl, who had no experience of documentary or political filmmaking and whose cinematographic aesthetic had developed through her work in feature films, must lead us to reconsider the typical view of Hitler as someone who did not believe that art and politics should be mixed. This, supposedly, was what he told the actress Toni van Eyck in an oft-quoted interview from 1933.[26] Yet, apart from this one source, we have no evidence that Hitler thought this. Most film historians tend to argue that Hitler believed in the production of explicit propaganda films, whereas Goebbels was more interested in insinuating propaganda discreetly into feature films. David Welch, for instance, distinguishes between the 'lie indirect' (Goebbels' way) and the 'lie direct' (Hitler's way).[27] There is much truth in this. Hitler did on occasion complain to Goebbels that a film was not directly National Socialist enough.[28] It is also true that Goebbels, in 1933, insisted he did not want to see the SA marching their way across the cinema screen. Nor did he want dramatizations of the party programme, stressing that film should seek to give artistic expression to the impulses it contained.[29] According to Fritz Hippler, as of 1939 head of the Propaganda Ministry's Film Department, Goebbels claimed that 'propaganda [. . .] is the art of simplifying and repeating without anyone noticing how you are doing it'.[30] But Goebbels was central to the Nazi newsreel and propaganda film production, which was characterized more by the 'lie direct'. He also oversaw the production of propagandistic feature films which – like *Jew Süss* (1940) – were saturated with Nazi ideology, even if they were set in the past. Equally, Hitler was not simply an advocate of politics-free feature films on the one hand and straightforward propaganda films on the other. For instance, he was a great admirer of Veit Harlan's feature film *The Ruler* (1937), about a leader figure clearly designed to parallel Hitler.[31] Hitler chose Riefenstahl to film the Nazi Party rallies because he believed she would produce something that far transcended the run-of-the-mill propaganda of the newsreel. Far from preferring 'his propaganda straight', as one film historian has put it, Hitler, at least for the rallies, wanted propaganda refined through aestheticization.[32]

Hitler's view of artistic commitment was not dissimilar to his view on political commitment. In his speech at the Nazi Party's Cultural Conference in 1933, which took place during the rally that Riefenstahl was sent to film, he stressed that 'art is a sublime mission, one which commands fanaticism'. In the same speech, he maintained that it is the political leadership which must create the 'material and actual conditions' for the arts. 'Every great political age in world history will demonstrate its right to existence through the most visible proof of its value: through its cultural achievements.'[33] Politics, then, must find expression in culture, and culture must be imbued with politics; the two were intertwined, for Hitler, in a reciprocal relationship.[34] So it was that Riefenstahl was drafted in to transform the political event of the rally into a cultural one, indeed to transform the transient rally into a permanent work of art. After the war, Riefenstahl defended herself against the charge of collaboration by insisting she had filmed the rallies from an artistic, not a political standpoint.[35] This argument was consistent with her understanding of her role during the Third Reich itself. In a 1935 publication on the making of *Triumph of the Will*, Riefenstahl asserted that Hitler had entrusted her with the 'artistic representation' of the rally 'for the second time'.[36] The Nazi press also presented her as responsible, at Hitler's express request, for the artistic design of both *Victory of Faith* and *Triumph of the Will*.[37] As Riefenstahl saw it, this absolved her of any responsibility for the political content of the rally films. For Hitler, by contrast, Riefenstahl's artistic skill was the guarantee that the political effect of the rallies would be heightened when converted to the screen. In the end, Riefenstahl's attempt to dissociate herself from the politics of the rally films does not convince.

There remains the question as to why Riefenstahl ultimately agreed to make films for Hitler. Her memoirs stress she did so reluctantly, but she is honest enough to admit she sought to contact Hitler in the first place, that Hitler fascinated her, and that she lacked the will to let him down. Careerism played a major part. Hitler's admiration of her was her ticket to fame. Later, when shunned on her visit to America in late 1938, she also found out that it was her ticket to notoriety. There is evidence that Riefenstahl sympathized with National Socialism even before Hitler came to power. 'She is full of enthusiasm for us,' writes Goebbels already in November 1932.[38] In mid-1933, he describes her as 'the only one of all the stars who understands us'.[39] After hearing Hitler, in late 1932, talk about the need to end unemployment and to place the common good before that of any individual, she was 'moved to the core'. She suggests it was the socialist aspect of National Socialism that attracted her,[40] while claiming she told Hitler she could never join the party, and disapproved of his racial prejudices.[41] One critic, Jürgen Trimborn, has contended that she was in fact anti-Semitic, and that this drew her to Hitler. But the evidence that Riefenstahl blamed Jewish critics for negative reviews of *The Blue Light* is anecdotal.[42] Nor does the fact that she asked the Nazi anti-Jewish rabble-rouser Julius Streicher (whom she befriended) to intervene in a financial dispute with – as Riefenstahl put it in her letter to him – the 'Jew Béla Balázs' necessarily prove her anti-Semitism.[43] One could just as easily argue that the examples of her having helped Jews, examples which emerged in the course of her denazification proceedings, proved her philo-Semitism. Riefenstahl helped the family of a former teacher, the German Jew Käte Reuber, in 1937 and 1939 after Reuber's husband was sacked.[44] She also supported the Jewish wife of Ernst Jaeger after he decided to remain in the USA in 1938.[45] Moreover, during the Third Reich she employed people of Jewish background, or who had Jewish spouses or other relatives.[46] She also helped communists.[47] But all this really proves is that Riefenstahl was ready to help others when it suited her. Equally, she was prepared to denounce to the Nazis those she perceived as obstructions when it furthered her interests, in the case of Balázs by exploiting Nazi anti-Semitism.[48] She was ambitious, with a ruthless streak, and was content to ply her trade in an anti-Semitic state. Yet she could also be kind-hearted and even prepared to court controversy, as when she shopped in a Jewish fashion shop in 1937, whereupon she was herself promptly denounced.[49] To describe her as anti-Semitic is to simplify things and construe a straight ideological affinity with Hitler. It was messier than that.

Making *Victory of Faith* (1933)

There has long been a degree of uncertainty surrounding exactly when Hitler commissioned Riefenstahl to film the 1933 Nazi Party rally. Riefenstahl herself claimed it was not until the last week of August 1933, a matter of days before the rally began, that she received this commission.[50] Entries in Goebbels' diary, however, might seem to suggest the commission came earlier. In mid-May 1933, after listening to Riefenstahl's film plans, Goebbels suggested to her that she make a 'Hitler film'.[51] In June, he mentions a 'new film' he has been discussing with her,[52] and, following a conversation between Riefenstahl and Hitler, Goebbels claims 'she is now starting with her film'.[53] In light of these diary entries, some critics have suggested that in her memoirs Riefenstahl simply lied about the date of the commission.[54] Whereas the impression conveyed by Goebbels is that her involvement was long planned, her version suggests she was thrown into the fray at the last minute. Her memoirs also depict Goebbels as her implacable enemy, following her rejection of his attempt to seduce her. By contrast, Goebbels' diaries suggest that, at this point, they had a good working relationship as film projects were discussed and planned. Riefenstahl did concede that Goebbels had suggested to her making a film about the press in mid-1933, and that Hitler around the same time tried to get her to make a Horst Wessel film.[55] But she claims she rejected these suggestions, and that no mention was made of a rally film until late August.

While Riefenstahl certainly played down the fact that, as of May 1933 at the very latest, she was a frequent guest at social events organized by Goebbels and Hitler,[56] her version of when she came to receive Hitler's commission for the 1933 party rally film nevertheless rings true. In suggesting to Riefenstahl in May 1933 that she make a 'Hitler film', Goebbels could hardly have been thinking of a film of the next party rally, because the decision to hold a rally in 1933, and hold it in Nuremberg, had not yet been taken.[57] Even if it had, surely he would have referred to such a film, as he did in an August diary entry, as a 'party rally film'.[58] After

Hitler came to power, it was hardly surprising that Goebbels – and others – wanted to make a film about the Führer's apparently meteoric rise; this, presumably, is what he meant by a 'Hitler film'.[59] As for the film referred to in Goebbels' diary on 14 and 20 June, there is no evidence that either a 'Hitler film' or a 'party rally film' was meant. Riefenstahl, after all, was trying to make headway with a spy film she planned, called *Madame Docteur*, to which the Foreign Office had objected. Moreover, it is hardly likely that Goebbels would have suggested she make a rally film after he had granted the Film Office of the Reich Propaganda Leadership the monopoly on filming all party events (on 11 May).[60] In one respect, perhaps, it matters little when Riefenstahl received the commission from Hitler. The late August date does not absolve her of complicity up to that point, for, as Goebbels' diaries show, she had reacted enthusiastically in May to the idea of making a film about Hitler, even if it never materialized. (She also, according to Goebbels, responded positively to the idea of making the rally film when it was discussed with Hitler on 27 August.) Riefenstahl may even have come up with the idea for a Hitler film herself, at least if Ernst Jaeger is to be believed.[61] But, in another respect, it does matter. Hitler, according to Riefenstahl, relayed his wish to the Propaganda Ministry that she make the film 'weeks' before their meeting in late August.[62] He was, so she writes, furious that his instructions had not been passed on to her. If this is true, then Goebbels' ministry had been quietly boycotting her. If it is not, and Hitler made a last-minute decision to commission Riefenstahl, then he did so because he did not trust the ministry to do a good job of filming. Either way, Hitler and the Propaganda Ministry did not see eye to eye on how best to film the rally.

Tensions between Riefenstahl and others hoping to make the rally film escalated towards the end of August 1933. On 25 August, the Nazi press announced that Riefenstahl, at Hitler's special request, was to take over the artistic direction. The announcement also stated that Arnold Raether – head of the Film Office of the Reich Propaganda Leadership – would be responsible for the 'overall supervision', while Eberhard Fangauf would be responsible for the technical organization.[63] Reading between the lines, Raether and Fangauf had been planning to make the rally film. Now they ran the risk of being upstaged by Riefenstahl. Both Raether and Fangauf were loyal Nazis who had already found influential positions within Goebbels' film bureaucracy, but neither of them had distinguished himself with his film directing.[64] They did not take kindly to the appointment of Riefenstahl, and Raether in particular started up a campaign to topple her by questioning her racial background.[65] Newspaper reports from late August and early September, sometimes omitting all mention of Riefenstahl's name, sometimes including it, suggest a behind-the-scenes tussle for control of the film.[66] Throughout the rally, Raether and Riefenstahl worked together – or, rather, against each other. How far Raether's 'overall supervision' extended, and where exactly Riefenstahl's 'artistic leadership' ended, was never clarified at the time. Raether and Fangauf certainly tried to curtail her influence by refusing to provide her with film equipment or cameramen. But Riefenstahl was already able to call on the support not only of Hitler, but also those close to him such as Albert Speer. Speer helped to recruit Walter Frentz to her camera team. Frentz, subsequently to become Hitler's photographer for the newsreels, later confirmed she had faced interference from the 'Nazi Party people, because they weren't the ones making the film'.[67] Hostility, according to Riefenstahl, also came from the SA, one of whose members denounced her to Rudolf Hess, Hitler's deputy, for supposedly claiming she had Hitler 'wrapped round her little finger'. Hess was placated the following day by Speer, who assured him she had said no such thing.[68]

In the early months after the Nazi accession to power, Hitler, it seems, could not always impose his will as easily as he might have liked. He also had to impose it firmly on Riefenstahl, if her version of events is to be believed. Hardly had filming finished than Riefenstahl, back in Berlin, was invited to lunch at the Reich Chancellery. Unable to restrain herself, she complained to Hitler – in Goebbels' presence – about the way she had been treated in Nuremberg. Hitler reacted by upbraiding Goebbels and insisting that Riefenstahl, not the party, create the film: 'That is an order!' When Riefenstahl despairingly objected that she could not go on with the commission, Hitler – icy-faced – made it clear she would have to.[69] That same day, 13 October 1933, Goebbels, by Riefenstahl's account, ordered her to come to the Propaganda Ministry and berated her: 'You are a dangerous person, you tell the Führer everything! Get out! I don't want to see you any more.'[70] In his diary, Goebbels also notes that Riefenstahl protested about the way she had been treated, but, in his version, this happened on 19 September, with Riefenstahl complaining specifically about Raether.[71] Goebbels claims that he 'made peace between Leni Rie. and Raether'.[72] Two days later, however, she was in tears because she 'thinks she has been treated wrongly by the party: I talked her out it'.[73] If Goebbels really had told Riefenstahl on 13 October he never wanted to see her again, he soon changed his mind. Two days later, he held a 'nice' reception at his home to which she, as well as actors Willy Fritsch and Renate Müller, were invited and where all 'manner of things were discussed'.[74] Riefenstahl exaggerated the degree to which Goebbels opposed her, but Goebbels' presentation of himself as peacemaker is not reliable. He had, after all, done nothing to stop Raether trying to boycott Riefenstahl, and quite possibly encouraged him. In the end, Hitler stepped in to make clear to Goebbels that Raether was to have nothing to do with the film, and to Riefenstahl that she was to complete it.

Even as Riefenstahl set about working through the footage of the rally to make her film, she remained, so she claims, a target of the wrath of the SA, who could not accept that a film of 'their' rally was to be made by a woman. Again, Riefenstahl had to depend on support from Hitler. She recounts that Rudolf Diels, head of the Gestapo at the time, told her he had orders to guard her.[75] While this story might seem like a product of Riefenstahl's imagination, it was quite likely true. Diels testified after the war that Riefenstahl had to suffer under the 'hatred of her opponents'. Hitler knew this, Diels said, and had to protect her.[76] There can be no doubt that Riefenstahl's filming for *Victory of Faith*, as the film of the 1933 party rally was to become known, was fraught with difficulties. It was one of the ironies of the rally that while it was supposed to affirm the unity of Nazi organizations, behind the scenes there was rivalry and gender bias, none of which of course found its way into Riefenstahl's film (although women rarely feature in it). In addition, she had too little time to prepare filming, and her camera team, put together at the last minute, was too small; to a degree, she had to rely on newsreel material of inferior quality. When she came to edit the footage, she found parts of it were almost unusable: sequences were unclear, images too dark or unstable, camera movements apparently unmotivated.[77] Motifs, and Hitler himself, were lost from view as people walked in front of the camera. Riefenstahl was unable to iron out all these problems. After the war, she dismissed *Victory of Faith* as an 'imperfect patchwork'.[78]

The End Result

Nevertheless, Riefenstahl did the best she could to shape the material into an effective film. It was her way of repaying Hitler for his faith in her, and the assistance he and others acting as his 'agents', Speer and Diels, had provided. Rather than begin the film with the rally itself, she includes a long prelude establishing a set of telling contrasts. To the accompaniment of Herbert Windt's dreamy score, *Victory of Faith* starts with smoky images of Nuremberg's medieval roofs, house facades and tourist attractions, before the cameras focus on the construction of a stand to hold rally visitors in the marketplace; gradually, the Wagnerian-style music gives way to the more assertive strains of the Horst Wessel song. While the initial shots of Nuremberg create an impression of a city emptied of its population, now the streets are shown filling up with bustle and festooned with Nazi flags. Trams and cars come into view, as if seeking to dispel the cosy medievalism of the opening. The film then concentrates on arrivals: first, groups of SA men sing vigorously as they march into Nuremberg; next, a train with a Nazi emblem pulls into the station, bringing Nazi dignitaries and guests; finally, Hitler himself arrives by plane, linking the most modern of travel technologies with the Nazi leader. Sepp Allgeier was allowed to accompany Hitler in his car as it made its way through a now crowded, cheering Nuremberg, filming him from behind.[79] The film's opening connects past to present, embedding Hitlerism in German history. It identifies Nazism with the revitalization of the old by the new, to render palpable the mobilization of the masses, the creation of the people's community, and to associate National Socialism with modernity.

To herald the beginning of the rally itself, Riefenstahl includes images and sounds of pealing bells that fade into the scenes of welcome extended to Hitler by Nuremberg's mayor in the town hall, scenes accompanied by solemn-sounding music. *Victory of Faith*'s narrative is strongly religious. In the town hall, we see and hear Hess opening the 'Congress of Victory' by emphasizing Hitler's supposed qualities: he was the 'guarantor of victory', remained 'steadfast where others wavered', was a source of renewed courage and 'took up the flag more resolutely' when others left the ranks. Hess, observed in close-up by the camera, delivers a panegyric on Hitler which accredits to him the kind of spiritual resilience one might associate more with a religious leader. Riefenstahl's film, at several junctures, shows Hitler as he walks towards the party faithful, approaching his congregation. She dwells at length on the honouring of the Nazi dead by Hitler. Towards the end, we hear Hitler deliver a speech to the SA in which he celebrates the overcoming of German guilt and shame – by which he means the Weimar Republic and the 'November criminals'. In priest-like fashion, he pronounces national absolution, and the film ends with an image of a Nazi flag blowing above the clouds, linking Hitler with Heaven. Riefenstahl does more than register the religiosity of the rally; she amplifies it through such symbolism. While the film also shows Hitler as he speaks of the new, supposedly classless society, the cinematography serves to reinforce the hierarchical division between leader and people that characterized the rally, and underpin its message that classlessness means, above all, uniform (and uniformed) adherence to the godlike Hitler and his idea of the nation. As Hess puts it in the film: 'the Führer is the future of the nation'.

To be fair to Riefenstahl, the film does have moments that appear to invite reflection. As the SA men march into Nuremberg, Riefenstahl shows children at the roadside thrusting out their arms in a Hitler salute. Four are lined up in order of height, in a posed and artificial manner. The next shot, just as brief, shows a cat behind a grille; it could be resting, but the image also suggests imprisonment. Shortly after, when a passing SA man waves to a girl, she does not wave back or raise her arm. Rather, she seems bemused, even frightened. Riefenstahl's inclusion of shots of the Neptune fountain will not have been to the liking of the local Nazis, because they regarded it as an eyesore and, during the rally, as an interference. Moreover, it had been donated by a Jew, Ludwig Gerngros: hence its Nazi nickname, 'the Jewish fountain'. Hitler ordered its removal in 1934. Riefenstahl's film, intentionally or not, pays filmic tribute to it. *Victory of Faith* also contains almost comic moments. In Nuremberg's town hall, we see Hitler, having just been presented with a bouquet of flowers by a young girl, dump it unceremoniously into Hess's lap. Later in the film, Hitler Youth leader Baldur von Schirach accidentally sweeps Hitler's SA cap from the rostrum with his bottom as Hitler waits to speak to the assembled Hitler Youth. In the same sequence, Hitler shoos a trumpeter away impatiently. And towards the end, overweight SA leader Ernst Röhm keeps fiddling with his belt behind Hitler as Hitler speaks to the SA ranks. Commentators assume Riefenstahl included this material through sheer lack of alternative footage.[80] But it is just as possible she saw no reason to edit out comic moments. She also found a way to cock a snook at Goebbels. The film shows Hitler, in his town hall speech, recalling 2 September 1923, the first time the Nazis entered Nuremberg in large numbers (for 'German Day'). When Hitler refers to the 'hostile environment' the Nazis had to face, the camera provides a close-up of Goebbels.

These moments of ambivalence do not amount to anything remotely subversive, however. For the most part, *Victory of Faith* is committed to visually affirming Hitler's role as redeemer and leader. The hour-long film takes the viewer through the various stages of the rally: the opening of the Party Congress in the Luitpold Hall; the roll-call of the masses of Nazi officials on the Zeppelin Field; Hitler's address to the throngs of Hitler Youth in Nuremberg's stadium; the parade of party formations on Nuremberg's Marktplatz; and the honouring of the dead, culminating in Hitler's address to the SA and SS. Riefenstahl and her team filmed this recalcitrant material from every conceivable angle to highlight Hitler's key role. Throughout, her approach was informed by the wish to suggest the bond between Hitler, Nazi leaders, and the rank and file members of the various Nazi organizations. During the party rally itself, Hitler was for most of those attending a remote figure. Thanks to Riefenstahl's use of the camera, cutting as it does between close-up images of Hitler and images of his followers, this remoteness is overcome for the cinema. We see the effect of Hitler's words mirrored in admiring, upturned faces. She is careful to alternate images of the masses with images of individual SA men and Hitler Youth, stressing both the extent of Hitler's support, and the personal way it is experienced. In the end, she instrumentalizes the serried ranks with her camera. The film includes several sentences from Hitler's speeches referring to the unity made possible by the Nazi assumption of power. As Hitler speaks, the cameras pan over the masses of well-organized and apparently united Germans, as if to prove the truth of what Hitler is saying.

Both Goebbels and Hitler viewed *Victory of Faith* in late November 1933. Goebbels described it as a 'fabulous SA symphony'. 'Riefenstahl did a good job,' he enthused, remarking how Hitler had been 'moved' by the film.[81] After the Berlin premiere on 1 December, Hitler threw a huge party. He was clearly very pleased, and any doubts Goebbels or Riefenstahl herself might have had were dispelled: 'Leni Riefenstahl is happy,' Goebbels noted enthusiastically; 'she has every right to be. She did her work well.'[82] The premiere, which Hitler attended, triggered a rhapsodic response in the German press: 'this is the freedom film of the nation, the first state film of the Third Reich!' declared one newspaper; 'a gigantic and triumphant symphony of images' proclaimed another.[83] Regional Film Offices like the Regional Film Office North-East had the task of 'taking this film out to the peoples' comrades of all classes and tribes so that they can share in this grandiose portrait'.[84] Some 20 million Germans saw the film, many of them without having to pay for their ticket.

Hitler's admiration for *The Blue Light* bore fruit. From the beginning, he imagined a documentary film that, rather than appearing spliced together from disparate newsreel sources, would be conceived and created as a whole, just as feature films are. At the time, Riefenstahl referred to her intention to make a film that, far from resembling a reportage-style news-reel, would be 'complete in itself'.[85] She was also able to breathe life into the often static material she had to film. In *The Blue Light*, she used light, scudding clouds and constantly shifting perspectives to create drama and rhythm around the mountainscapes. In *Victory of Faith*, she deploys perspective in a similarly shifting way: we see the massed audiences from every imaginable angle. She also uses deep and shifting perspectives to create an integrated portrayal of Hitler and his supporters. If natural light was not something she could use so effectively (the weather during the rally was bad), she made up for it in her focus on the wind blowing along lines of flags, a focus conveying movement even as the flag-bearers stand rigid. Only in the scenes depicting the march-past on the marketplace does Riefenstahl seem to run out of ideas as to how to vary the perspective. In addition to producing an energetic concentrate of the rally, she tells a story, one reflected in the film title's reference to 'faith'. It is the story of one man's spiritual triumph against adversity, the outcome of a struggle conducted in the name of the nation. Hitler may not have known exactly what she would do with the filmed material, but he knew he could rely on her cinematography, her sensitivity to the importance of movement and mise en scène, and her loyalty to him to bring out the rally to best visual and propagandistic effect.

Riefenstahl's insistence that she was only responsible for the artistic representation is in a literal sense borne out by the film's opening credits, which describe her role as one of 'artistic realization'. But while the *event* itself was not of her making,[86] the filming of it was, and she used her art, as we have seen, to turn the rally into a political-aesthetic experience, exactly as Hitler wanted. If it was indeed August when Hitler commissioned *Victory of Faith*, this was not long after the Nazi Party had been declared the only party in Germany, and not long before the Reichstag elections of November 1933. He needed a film that celebrated the triumph of National Socialism and his own personal triumph, as articulated at Nuremberg, as a form of redemption. Such a celebration, shared by millions in German cinemas, would help, so he surely hoped, to enhance the appeal of Nazism. Riefenstahl lent her artistic skills to the visual reinforcement of the myth of rebirth, helping to generate an utterly false view of National Socialism. Her choice of what material to film, and what not to film, reflected her wish to avoid any subject that might, depending on the viewer's perspective, have raised questions about Nazism's true character. Thus she totally ignores the racial aspect of the movement, although Goebbels, Rosenberg and Walter Gross all gave speeches at the 1933 rally on race, and Hitler certainly made reference to it too.[87] The triumph of Nazism had been secured by a level of genuine support among Germans, but also through the crushing of democracy and the violent, and at times murderous, removal of all opposition. Hitler's speeches at the 1933 rally suggested that the real criminals had been Weimar Republic politicians. Riefenstahl's film focuses several times on variations of this idea. A transformation achieved by coercion and repression she happily presents as a moral revolution. Her film provided Hitler with an ideal smokescreen.

4

Celebrating Hitler

TRIUMPH OF THE WILL AND *OLYMPIA*

In 1934, Riefenstahl filmed the sixth Reich Party rally in Nuremberg and, in 1936, the Berlin Olympics. Both films were commissioned by Hitler. If *Victory of Faith* declared that Hitler had arrived, the message of *Triumph of the Will* was that he was here to stay. It emphasized the consolidation of Nazi power within Germany, and of Hitler's power over the Nazi Party. *Olympia*, in turn, was designed to dupe international audiences into thinking that Hitler was all about peaceful sportsmanship and international collaboration. Riefenstahl delivered exactly what Hitler wanted and expected of these documentaries – and he arranged finance for her to ensure that she did.

Hitler Re-engages Riefenstahl: *Triumph of the Will*

When, in October 1933, Hitler insisted Riefenstahl complete *Victory of Faith*, he also promised her she would never again have to endure the kind of difficulties she had faced when filming it.[1] This sounded as if he expected her to film the next party rally, too; and indeed Riefenstahl later claimed she had already received this request in 1933.[2] In the spring of the following year, Hitler issued a letter commissioning Riefenstahl with the making of the 1934 rally film.[3] In contrast to the situation in 1933, then, Hitler was determined she should have more time to prepare, and she was from the start given both artistic and technical control. Riefenstahl, if her account is to be believed, tried to wriggle out of doing the film, first by engaging the documentary filmmaker Walter Ruttmann to do it instead and, second, by committing herself to another project – directing the film *Lowlands* – in the hope she could shake off her obligations to Hitler.[4] But he was not to be shaken off. Returning to Berlin in mid-August 1934, she found, among the 'basketfuls of unopened mail', a letter from Hitler's deputy, Rudolf Hess, saying that Hitler wanted *her* to make the film, not Ruttmann. Riefenstahl rushed to Nuremberg to meet Hitler, but he reiterated what Hess had written to her: she had to make the film. She claims Hitler assured her that the Nazi Party and Goebbels would have no influence over her. This also meant no financial influence.[5] Whether Riefenstahl actually had this discussion with Hitler must remain a matter for conjecture. When interrogated by the Americans after the war, Riefenstahl said that a discussion with Hitler at the time had not been possible; she got no further than Hess.[6] If the meeting did take place, Hitler cannot have told Riefenstahl that the party would play no part in the making of the new rally film, because by that stage it was already financing it.

In her memoirs, Riefenstahl claims her project was financed through her own efforts;[7] as evidence, she refers to a distribution agreement with Ufa.[8] But this agreement was finalized only a few days before she began filming in Nuremberg in September 1934, by which time she had already spent considerable sums of money.[9] This money was paid on Hitler's orders. Almost six months before the rally, in April 1934, he gave instructions that Riefenstahl, as 'special appointee of the Reich Leadership of the NSDAP [National Socialist German Workers' Party]', was to be supported to the tune of 300,000 Reichsmarks.[10] Riefenstahl knew this funding came through Hitler, because, in late 1935, she questioned having to pay tax on it, arguing she was not a businesswoman, but an employee of the NSDAP.[11]

After the war, in the course of an interrogation by the Americans, she also admitted that her firm had had a 'Reich Party Account' through which all expenditure on the film was 'booked'. The Brown House in Munich, the NSDAP headquarters, had then reimbursed her. She was unsure whether it was an office under the control of Rudolf Hess or the Nazi Party treasurer, Franz Schwarz, who administered the payments. Regarding the money she received from Ufa, she maintained in the same interrogation that this came directly to her firm, which then passed it on to the Brown House because 'the Party was the owner of copyright'.[12] Not only was Riefenstahl financed, then, through Hitler, but the agreement with Ufa was concluded in the name of the NSDAP – not on her private initiative or to her private advantage.

In August 1949, Riefenstahl changed her position virtually overnight after talking to her lawyer Eugen Krämer. Copyright, she now claimed, actually rested with her, because *Triumph of the Will* was her own 'intellectual creation', even if the NSDAP had financed it.[13] Krämer had presumably informed her that, if she admitted to the party having copyright, she might lose all control over the films she directed for Hitler, and not be able to benefit from any proceeds copyright ownership might bring in the future. As it became clear there was considerable post-war demand to show *Triumph of the Will*, or parts of it, Riefenstahl went a step further in her attempts to secure copyright by denying the party had financed her at all. This is the version, a self-exculpatory and commercially self-interested version, which she presents in her memoirs. Even if there is some uncertainty regarding exactly how Riefenstahl was paid, the US post-war investigators assembled enough testimony to indicate that Hitler was behind the payments. Hans Saupert, Schwarz's chief of staff, told the Americans that *Triumph of the Will* was financed directly or indirectly by the NSDAP's Treasury;[14] his estimate was that it had cost over 1 million Reichsmarks to make.[15] Schwarz's auditor, by contrast, claimed that the support came from the Adolf Hitler Fund of German Industry.[16] Hess's adjutant Alfred Leitgen, in yet another variant, assumed the money had come from the

Office of the Deputy of the Führer,[17] but also thought it could have gone through Schwarz. Finally, Hugo Fischer, who worked in the NSDAP's Reich Propaganda Leadership, recalled that the Film Department within that office was ordered by Schwarz to transfer a 'substantial sum' to Riefenstahl's company.[18] Nazi documents from 1935 suggest that the money could indeed have come from Schwarz.[19]

Having organized financial support for Riefenstahl, it was not surprising that Hitler would not countenance someone else taking charge of the film. Certainly, Riefenstahl overstated Hitler's objections to Ruttmann in a post hoc attempt to play down his contribution to the film; he helped produce the script, shoot material for the film and edit this material right up to February 1935.[20] But that Hitler wanted Riefenstahl to take overall charge is indisputable; she was the only one in whose skills he really trusted. The projected film of the 1934 rally took on greater significance for Hitler following the Night of the Long Knives in early July 1934, because, after this date, *Victory of Faith* could no longer be shown.[21] It placed a central emphasis on Hitler's party friendship with Ernst Röhm, the leader of the SA – a man he had subsequently had murdered for supposedly planning a 'second revolution'. *Victory of Faith* also included footage of Vice-Chancellor Franz von Papen. Von Papen had since fallen out of favour following a speech in Marburg on 17 June 1934, where he appeared to criticize both the SA and the Nazi government. Following the withdrawal of *Victory of Faith* because of now embarrassing, indeed hypocritical scenes of friendship between Hitler and Röhm, Hitler needed a new film that would serve to eradicate the memory of these scenes and emphasize the loyalty of the SA to him, as well as his control over it. And he had another expectation of the new film. Following Hindenburg's death on 2 August 1934, a referendum was held shortly before the rally to confirm the union of the offices of chancellor and Reich president in the person of Hitler. Of the 95.7 per cent of eligible Germans who voted, almost 90 per cent voted in favour. This seems an impressive acclamation of Hitler's decision to appoint himself 'Führer and Reich Chancellor'. Even artists such as the conductor

Wilhelm Furtwängler, the composer Richard Strauss and the sculptor Ernst Barlach rushed to offer their support for the merger.[22] But the referendum result was achieved in part by intimidation and terror. It would also be Riefenstahl's task, in her 1934 rally film, to provide powerful support for Hitler's self-promotion to the status of absolute ruler of state as well as of the party.

Riefenstahl embarked on the new film with great gusto. In contrast to the situation when making *Victory of Faith*, she was able to assemble a sizeable production staff to support her, including eighteen cameramen and eighteen camera assistants.[23] The German newsreel companies, as well as the European subsidiaries of Fox and Paramount, also put their teams at her disposal.[24] Talking at an event organized by the Reich Film Chamber in April 1935, Riefenstahl outlined three principles she followed when filming the 1934 rally. First, her team tried to create images that conveyed a sense of movement. Second, all effort was made to film people only when they did not know they were being observed; naturalness was important. Third, events, people and objects chosen for filming had to be interesting; artistic criteria stood in the foreground.[25] To ensure the first principle was met – avoiding 'immobility' – Riefenstahl had tracks laid to enable shots to be made from moving cameras, put cameramen on roller skates and even had a lift fixed to a flagpole. To fulfil all three principles, enormous quantities of film had to be used, as it was clearly not always going to be possible to convey the right degree of movement, or 'naturalness', at the first attempt, and not everything filmed was going to be 'interesting'. Riefenstahl set herself a mammoth task.

In her memoirs, she complains that, again, obstacles were put in her way: newsreel teams ignored her instructions, and officials at the security barriers proved uncooperative. When she tried to inform Hitler, she recalls, it was impossible to get through to him.[26] Hitler provided assistance indirectly, however. He instructed Rudolf Hess to watch over the situation. Hess in turn asked his adjutant, Alfred Leitgen, to ensure that any problems were resolved. Leitgen recalled after the war that Riefenstahl encountered 'a certain resistance from the Propaganda Ministry under its leader Dr. Josef Goebbels'. As Leitgen understatedly put it, 'it would have been thinkable that the film could have been made directly by the Propaganda Ministry'. Leitgen's job was to 'point out to those offices whose collaboration in the film' was required that Riefenstahl had the commission to make it, and that said offices were to support her.[27] It is difficult to know exactly how much Goebbels was involved in creating difficulties. Before the rally began, he had little faith in Riefenstahl doing the film well: 'not much is going to come of it. She is too jittery.'[28] By October, he had changed his mind: 'Leni Riefenstahl tells me about the party rally film. It's going to be good.'[29] On 22 November, after seeing some of the film material, he generously enthused: 'this afternoon, wonderful images of the party rally film. Leni is very capable. Just think if she were a man!'[30] Goebbels clearly found it hard to accept that a woman might be able to make such a film as well as a man could. Some SA men also regarded it as inappropriate that a member of the female sex should be asked to film such a masculine event.[31]

Hitler not only protected Riefenstahl against interference, he also consulted with her about the film, and quite probably gave her 'directives'.[32] He met Riefenstahl at Nuremberg on 21 August 1934, two weeks before the rally began. As the new SA leader Viktor Lutze was also present, one can assume she was being briefed about how to portray the SA.[33] When the rally was finished, Riefenstahl began viewing, editing and splicing 130,000 metres of film. Hitler took direct interest in her progress, intending to 'intervene decisively' if necessary.[34] On 6 December 1934, he visited her in her Berlin studio, accompanied among others by his personal adjutant, Julius Schaub. He spent two hours watching film of the rally. Riefenstahl explained how she intended to archive the material that was not going to find its way into the final product. Goebbels visited her at her studio on 5 December, Hess on 7 December.[35] By March 1935, Riefenstahl had whittled the material down to 3,000 metres,[36] and Hitler's advice had informed the editing process at least in part. After discussions with Riefenstahl, Hitler decided in late September 1934 on the title *Triumph of the Will*.[37] He also supported the publication of an accompanying book which appeared in mid-March 1935, just before the premiere, with Hitler's publishers, the Franz Eher Verlag. The book was apparently authored by Riefenstahl and included plenty of photographs of Hitler. After the war, Ernst Jaeger claimed he had ghostwritten it for her;[38] even if this is true, Riefenstahl found it quite acceptable to have the volume published in her name. Hitler himself provided a foreword describing Riefenstahl's film as a 'unique and incomparable glorification of the strength and beauty of our movement'.[39] The text presented as Riefenstahl's was equally effusive in its praise for Hitler: 'the Führer has recognized the significance of film. [. . .] The belief that a real, strong national experience could be re-experienced through film was born in Germany. The Führer gives contemporary film sense and mission.'[40]

When Riefenstahl was asked in April 1935 what part Hitler played in the making of the 1934 rally film, she answered that he was only responsible for the commission. Everything else was left to her: 'in this way, Adolf Hitler made clear that artists should create without directives'.[41] This remark severely downplayed Hitler's involvement in *Triumph of the Will*. His commission came with expectations, some of which he would have made clear in discussions with her about the film in advance of the cameras starting to roll, and subsequently. Riefenstahl did her best to fulfil these expectations. More so than *Victory of Faith*, *Triumph of the Will* was to be a film which foregrounded Hitler, helping to ascribe to him an omnipotent status, but also a status as supreme 'Künstler', artist. As one Nazi article put it, Hitler was the 'artist' who 'as master-builder, rebuilt his people and envisioned the sacred pilgrimage of his people to Nuremberg as a cultic festival'.[42] The rally, in other words, was a realization of Hitler's ideal of political experience as simultaneously religious and artistic experience. Carefully stage-managed, it aimed to give participants the feeling they were enacting a new national unity around their leader. Yet this was not mere theatre: what was being acted out followed a clear agenda. Hitler strove to overcome the old German dichotomy between 'spirit' and 'power', politics and art. This is why Riefenstahl's argument that she was responsible only for the artistic realization of *Triumph of the Will* misses the point that providing that realization meant subscribing completely to Hitler's vision of the party rally.

Triumph of the Will is almost twice as long as *Victory of Faith*. More effectively than in that shorter film, Riefenstahl employs all methods at her disposal to make the rally gripping viewing. There are even more dramatic shifts of perspective, from high above to close up and from below, utilizing all varieties of angles. In addition to using the movement, patterns and rhythms of the marching men to render them interesting, Riefenstahl includes shots of their flags, banners and spades in ways that are at times genuinely breathtaking: at one point, flags merge into one another in a manner suggestive of a field of wheat. Marching units are framed using watching crowds and nearby buildings, visually integrating them into the townscape in ways which imply the fusion of Nazism and Nuremberg. Riefenstahl is always mindful to keep Hitler at the centre of her film, more so than in *Victory of Faith*.[43] Ruttmann had originally intended to begin the film with the rags-to-riches story of how National Socialism brought an end to the shame of the Weimar Republic. All that has remained of this is a text at the start telling the viewer that Hitler's visit to the 1934 rally came twenty years after the outbreak of the Great War, and 'sixteen years after the beginning of German suffering'. *Triumph of the Will* did not focus on the overcoming of the Weimar Republic; *Victory of Faith* had done that. Rather, it set out to affirm the status quo. It asserted Hitler's incontestable position at the political centre of Germany. Images of Hitler's arrival at the start – we see his plane flying over Nuremberg – are intercut with shots of marching columns making their way into the city. Hitler and his followers are shown converging. *Victory of Faith* presented the 1933 rally as a union of people and leader. *Triumph of the Will* presents the 1934 rally as a well-coordinated and triumphant reunion.

In *Victory of Faith*, Hitler arrived in Nuremberg as redeemer. In *Triumph of the Will*, he is a returning hero. Riefenstahl makes sure she captures sharp, close-up images of ecstatically smiling faces in the crowd (particularly women and children) or among participants; at one point, we see women dressed in regional costumes gazing at Hitler as if they are about to swoon. In contrast to *Victory of Faith*, when Hitler is filmed being driven into the city, we are shown his facial expression, not just the back of his head. Riefenstahl portrays him as more relaxed and assured than in *Victory of Faith*, his expression a reflection, so the film implies, of the adulation around him. She takes care to show how he mingles with the crowd: we see him chatting informally to some young Reich Labour Service workers. Before Hitler speaks to the assembled Reich Labour Service, some of their members, while standing stock-still, chant out a partly choric dialogue in which they stress their regional diversity and unity, and their resolve to ensure – by means of spades, rather than guns – that the German soldiers killed in the World War have not died in vain. This static playlet, performed for Hitler's benefit, is designed to demonstrate the reciprocity of Hitler's relationship with Nazi organizations: he does not just talk, he listens. Riefenstahl's cameras capture him looking on with studied seriousness. We are shown youngsters at the Hitler Youth Rally climbing up flagpoles or standing on tiptoes as they desperately try to catch a glimpse of the approaching Hitler. The Hitler Youth burst out into a series of 'Heils' when they finally see him. Throughout, Riefenstahl has a predilection for filming scenes where Hitler is arriving, or where his speeches come to an end. At such moments, she shows the masses as they bellow out approval of their Reich chancellor. *Triumph of the Will*'s focus on the intense response to Hitler's presence has a clear purpose. It mobilizes the legitimizing power of feeling. The justification for Hitler's supremacy is to be found, according to the film, in the emotions he unleashes.

Riefenstahl has repeatedly argued that her film was a document of the rally, not propaganda.[44] But it was she and her team who chose what to film and how to film it, and at all times the result condenses powerfully the propaganda inherent within the rally itself. *Triumph of the Will* provides support for Hitler's recent politics, above all in its depiction of Hitler's relations with the SA. Riefenstahl may only provide a few sentences from Hitler's opening rally proclamation, but they are carefully selected, including the words 'revolution cannot be a permanent condition' – a clear criticism of the SA under Röhm. The apotheosis of the rally, Hitler's parting speech to Party Congress, also forms the final part of the film. We hear Hitler speak of the need to reject elements that have 'proven bad' and 'do not belong to us'. This is an attempted justification of the purge of the SA. Throughout, Riefenstahl provides viewers with plenty of supposed evidence of the re-established loyalty of the SA and Hitler's control over it. We are treated to a night-time sequence in which the SA declare their effusive loyalty to the new SA leader, squeaky-voiced Viktor Lutze. Lutze had aided Hitler in the purge of the SA. *Triumph of the Will* also features a long scene showing SA men filing into place as Hitler prepares to speak, underscoring the idea that the SA is 'falling into line'. Hitler then talks of 'a shadow' cast over the SA, of 'sins' committed against it, a scene in which blame is implicitly projected away from Hitler himself and onto Röhm.

Riefenstahl showed a sure sense for including key statements from Hitler's rally speeches which assert the right of the party leader to wield total control, and the duty of all other National Socialists and non-party members to follow this authority. Her film makes clear that any kind of opposition – not least from within, but also more generally – would be ruthlessly dealt with. It shows, above all, the triumph of Hitler's will and his power; it was not for nothing that the 1934 rally was subsequently called the 'Party Conference of Power'. When *Triumph of the Will* premiered in Berlin on 28 March 1935, it was not Riefenstahl who was the star, but Hitler. The police busily controlled crowds eager to get a sight of Hitler as he arrived; sightseers climbed onto every available elevation – the chairs and tables of nearby cafes, lamp posts, canopies and fences. Riefenstahl took her seat in her box at 8.30 p.m., but it was Hitler who was the last to enter. The audience of 2,500 stood silently, arms outstretched in the Hitler salute. The SS Leibstandarte Adolf Hitler played the Führer's favourite march, the Badenweiler, before the film began. When Hitler was shown standing on the balcony of his Nuremberg hotel in *Triumph of the Will*, cheers broke out in the auditorium, echoing those to be heard in the film.[45] After the showing, the audience stood and continued singing the Horst Wessel song with which it had ended. As the lights came on, Hitler stood at the railing of his box to receive a resounding ovation of 'Sieg Heil'.[46] Leni Riefenstahl got a bouquet of flowers from Hitler, and a 200,000 Reichsmarks cheque for her efforts. But the film was Hitler's success.

The premiere marked the beginning of the propaganda process whereby *Triumph of the Will* circulated through Germany, helping to promote the notion that Hitler had protected the Nazi movement and the nation, united the regions and overcome class barriers, all of which entitled him to his position as both Reich chancellor and president.[47] Early Nazi feature films such as Hans Steinhoff's *Hitler Youth Quex* (1933) had celebrated the Nazi battle against communists during the Weimar Republic and anticipated the Nazi revolution. *Triumph of the Will* also recalls the old struggle against political enemies, but more than anything it marks the end of the revolutionary phase in the Nazi movement's history and the inner consolidation of the party under Hitler. Now, Goebbels was enthusiastic, finding the film 'grandiose': 'Leni's masterpiece'.[48] On 1 May 1935, Riefenstahl, with Hitler present, received the state prize from Goebbels. Both Hitler and Goebbels sent her congratulatory telegrams. At the prize-giving, Goebbels described her film as 'the great filmic vision of the Führer, who is represented here with an intensity the likes of which we have never seen before'.[49] After the premiere, the main Nazi newspaper, the *Völkischer Beobachter*, declared that, in *Triumph of the Will*, 'the soul of National Socialism is given life', adding that, at one point, the camera had revealed the 'innermost depths of the Führer'.[50] The Nazi press reacted as if the film were an epiphany. Comparisons of it to other art forms such as a 'song', an 'oratorium' or a 'ballade' implied the poeticization of politics.[51] This would not have been possible without Riefenstahl's art.

Day of Freedom

In August 1934, shortly before the rally began, Hitler had become Supreme Commander of the Armed Forces or Reichswehr. Yet in *Triumph of the Will* Riefenstahl virtually overlooked the Reichswehr, which became the Wehrmacht on 16 March 1935. In December 1934, as she was editing the film material, Riefenstahl was visited by General von Reichenau, chief liaison officer between the Armed Forces and the Nazi Party. According to her account, he asked to see footage of the military her team had filmed at Nuremberg, and was disappointed to hear she did not intend to use it in *Triumph of the Will*. The quality was too poor, she claimed; bad weather during the army exercises was to blame. Reichenau found the quality acceptable, but Riefenstahl refused to change her mind, so he complained to Hitler. Hitler suggested to Riefenstahl she preface *Triumph of the Will* with images of Nazi Party and military leaders. She rejected this idea, fearing that a parade of heads would spoil the atmospheric opening. Hitler lost his temper, calling her an 'obstinate donkey'. Then she made an alternative suggestion: she would make a film of the Armed Forces at the next party rally. Hitler said he would 'leave that to her'.[52] Ufa, according to Riefenstahl, did insist she include 'a few metres' of film of the military in *Triumph of the Will*.[53] This was hardly likely to satisfy the generals, however, especially as conscription had been introduced two weeks before the premiere.[54] So it was that Riefenstahl made her way to Nuremberg in September 1935 to film Hitler's speech to the Armed Forces, and their military display and exercises.

The September 1935 party rally was called 'Rally of Freedom', a reference to the supposed 'liberation' from restrictions placed on German remilitarization and the size of the Armed Forces by the Versailles Treaty. By this stage, Hitler had stopped being cagey about proclaiming his intention to rearm. Riefenstahl produced a twenty-eight-minute documentary with the title *Day of Freedom: Our Wehrmacht*. It begins with scenes of army camp life, as men get themselves shaved, brush their teeth and consume their soup-kitchen breakfast. Pressed into uniforms, soldiers then stand before the Führer as he delivers a speech insisting on the importance of sacrificing personal freedom for virtues such as obedience, decency, duty and honour. Freedom from the Versailles Treaty, then, translated directly into loss of freedom for the conscripts and those who soon would be conscripts, as Hitler in his speech anticipated generations of young Germans swelling the ranks. Next, soldiers and artillery parade past Hitler, and the final scenes show the army and air force carrying out all kinds of military manoeuvres. Riefenstahl's reorganization of the actual series of events makes it appear as if the manoeuvres are a response to Hitler's speech, whereas in reality they preceded it. The film visualizes Hitler as military commander, ordering troops and tanks into battle.

Day of Freedom does have some interesting moments. The acoustic and visual focus of the final section of the film on artillery and guns, even if men do appear in control, could be taken to suggest an impersonal mechanization at odds with the cheerful singing of the soldiers and their individuation at the start. Peter Kreuder, a film music composer, provides accompanying music that sometimes sounds like a cross between a military march, Offenbach and fairground music. At least to today's ears, it seems slightly sarcastic. None of this, however, seems to have undermined the propagandistic function of the film. *Day of Freedom* was first shown at the Reich Chancellery in Berlin in late December 1935. The invited audience included generals wearing military uniforms studded with medals, and their wives in evening dress.[55] Hitler no doubt organized the showing to patch up the relationship between Riefenstahl and the Wehrmacht.[56] Riefenstahl had arrived late, and had feared her tardiness would spoil the occasion. But after the film was over, the response was enthusiastic. 'Hitler showed a sense of humour,' Riefenstahl recalled; 'for Christmas he sent me a porcelain Meißner clock with an alarm feature.'[57] Ufa had already viewed the film on 28 November, and decided to show it in combination with the feature film *The Higher Order*, directed by Gerhard Lamprecht and starring Lil Dagover.[58] The premiere of both films duly took place on 30 December. *The Higher Order*, set in 1806, focused on the need for British–Prussian collaboration against Napoleonic France, exactly mirroring Hitler's attempted leanings towards Britain in the present. Together with *The Higher Order* – a very successful Third Reich feature film – *Day of Freedom* was shown all round Germany. Right up until 1938, it served as the 'central public relations film of the new Wehrmacht', and 'found regular use in German schools'.[59]

Riefenstahl's triptych of rally films promoted deceptively benign images of Hitler's politics, helping to foster cosy myths about Nazism and Hitler, and giving to the rallies an aesthetic gloss which concealed brutal realities. *Victory of Faith* emphasizes the idea that 1933 meant the overcoming of adversity and the creation of unity, as if Nazism had emerged triumphant from persecution, rather than from the ruthless crushing of opposition. *Triumph of the Will* suggests a protective purification of the party, an act of necessary defence in the people's interest, thus helping to obliterate the savage murders of SA leaders and others ordered by Hitler. *Day of Freedom*, for its part, implies that Hitler's remilitarization of Germany was all about restoring pride in military tradition, about honour, duty and toughness, and about ensuring the nation was able to defend itself. Yet, even as it seeks to mask aggressive intent, its focus on military exercises actually confirms precisely such an intention. It was a very flexible piece of propaganda.

Riefenstahl's Film of the 1936 Berlin Olympics

Riefenstahl did not produce any more Nazi Party rally films for Hitler, but he did commission one more major film from her, of the 1936 Berlin Summer Olympics. In the summer of 1935, she recalled, she was summoned to the Reich Chancellery: 'there Hitler told me that it was his wish I make the *Olympia* film, because he knows of no one else who possesses the experience required for the successful completion of such a film'.[60] But she has also claimed it was the secretary general of the Organizing Committee of the Berlin Olympics, Carl Diem, who asked her to make the film.[61]

Nowhere does she admit that Goebbels also played a significant role in the assignment of *Olympia*. On 28 June 1935, just after Riefenstahl had received the Film Prize for *Triumph of the Will*, Goebbels 'discussed the plan of the *Olympia* film with her'; they had further conversations about the proposed film in August and October 1935.[62] There was, then, a consensus between Hitler, Goebbels and Diem that Riefenstahl was the right choice of director. That it was Hitler who first asked her, though, seems likely. If *Day of Freedom* helped justify a militarized society, Riefenstahl's film of the Olympics was to serve the purpose of assuring the world that National Socialist Germany was more interested in peaceful competition on the sports field than in war, and was tolerant towards all ethnicities and nationalities – though of course it was precisely the exclusion of Jews from the German Olympic team that nearly caused the USA to withdraw from the games.[63]

As one commentator has remarked, Riefenstahl 'told lies about this film, as she did about so much else'.[64] After the end of the war, she claimed she had secured independent financial support for *Olympia* from the film company Tobis.[65] The reality was different. In October 1935, the Propaganda Ministry considered trying to secure funding for *Olympia* through the Film Credit Bank. This fell through, however, because the Credit Bank only financed feature films produced by private companies, not culture films commissioned by the Reich.[66] The ministry then considered turning to the Reich Credit Company, but baulked at the prospect of interest payments.[67] So it was that the Propaganda Ministry itself decided to finance the film through its own budget to the tune of 1.5 million Reichsmarks. The money was to be paid in tranches over the period 1935–37.[68] A contract was signed with Riefenstahl to this effect, as Goebbels confirmed on 7 November 1935: 'Riefenstahl gets her contract for the Olympics film. 1.5 million. She's delighted.'[69] As with *Triumph of the Will*, Hitler ensured that Riefenstahl was amply funded, but in the case of *Olympia* the finances came from the Reich rather than the party. An 'Olympia Film Company' was set up to disguise the Reich's involvement:

'the company has had to be established because the government does not wish to appear publicly as the producer of this film'.[70] It was also created so that Riefenstahl could avoid having to pay any kind of commercial tax to which she would be liable if acting as an entrepreneur.

Riefenstahl knew very well that Hitler was behind the monies and contracts that came her way in 1935 and 1936, however this money was paid. And she knew exactly what was expected of her. In May 1936, Tobis wrote to Riefenstahl's Olympia Film Company offering her technical staff and equipment for filming the Olympics – at a good rate. They did so because her company had indicated that the Olympics film was to be made 'exclusively with state funds' and used 'exclusively as propaganda for Germany'.[71] It was precisely because Riefenstahl knew money was coming from the wealth of the Reich that she was profligate in spending it. A Propaganda Ministry report had doubts that all the expenditure was needed, questioning the amounts spent on meals, for instance. Olympia Film did not even deem it necessary to keep a safe: the clerk responsible kept the firm's ready cash in his pockets.[72] When the Propaganda Ministry wanted to let the Film Credit Bank scrutinize Riefenstahl's books to find out whether the spending was appropriate, Riefenstahl resisted, saying she must be free to dispose of the money as she saw fit: 'she said she was acting on the authority of the Führer'.[73] Riefenstahl's technical manager, Wilhelm Lipke, highlighted numerous examples of what he clearly regarded as unnecessary expenditure. Thus, when Riefenstahl's film team moved into Castle Ruhwald, between eight and ten chaises longues were purchased, as well as several new clothes cupboards, and garden tables with chairs and sunshades. After filming was over, much of what had been acquired was sold off or given away.[74] To be fair, investigations in early 1937 into Riefenstahl's expenditure – undertaken by the Reich Film Chamber – revealed no irregularities, despite Lipke's allegations.[75]

Still, Riefenstahl and her team made sure they were comfortable when filming *Olympia*. And her firm continued to spend eagerly at the Reich's expense. Riefenstahl's decision to create two films out of the Olympic material, rather than just one, drove up the costs.[76] By November 1938 – several months after the premiere of *Olympia* – the Reich had paid out 1.8 million Reichsmarks to Olympia Film, 300,000 more than originally envisaged. Moreover, the Film Credit Bank had now chipped in after all, providing 550,000 Reichsmarks. Money taken at the box office was immediately used to pay off the Film Credit Bank loan and the money that had come directly from the Reich; most of the debt had been repaid by November 1938.[77] Still Olympia Film went on spending, as Riefenstahl's team set about producing short films from leftovers taken from the material filmed in Berlin during the 1936 games.[78] Olympia Film also purchased a brand new BMW sports car, despite the fact that the company was soon to be wound up.[79] It was struck from the trade register on 9 January 1942. By this time, certainly, remaining debts had been paid, and even a small profit made of about 114,000 Reichsmarks.[80] As part of the agreement she signed on 9 December 1935, Riefenstahl received 250,000 Reichsmarks followed by another 100,000 at the first performance.[81] This was subsequently raised to 400,000 Reichsmarks.[82]

The making of *Olympia* thus represented a significant state investment initiated by Hitler, one that Riefenstahl happily exploited. Yet she did face difficulties. During the games, Riefenstahl and Goebbels clashed a number of times. Tensions came to a climax when Riefenstahl lost her temper with an Olympic referee who refused to allow one of her cameramen, Gustav Lantschner, to film the hammer throw competition – which, because two Germans were among those competing for the medals, promised to be of particular interest. The referee, whom Riefenstahl called a 'swine', complained to Goebbels, who gave Riefenstahl a dressing down: 'her behaviour is impossible. A hysterical woman.'[83] According to Riefenstahl, he also told her not to set foot in the stadium again until she agreed to apologize to the referee.[84] Friedrich Mainz bears out her story of the threatened stadium ban, adding: 'the Propaganda Ministry as well as the leadership of the SA and SS started up an extreme campaign against her'. Riefenstahl's old enemy Arnold Raether informed Mainz that

Riefenstahl had become 'intolerable'; leading representatives of the party and government 'rejected' her.[85] Riefenstahl also fell out with Hans Weidemann of the Propaganda Ministry over whether her cameraman, Hans Ertl, should be filming for her or for Weidemann, who was making a feature on the 1936 party rally; Weidemann sent in the SS to ensure Ertl did his bidding.[86] Goebbels also refers to Riefenstahl's spat with Weidemann: 'she is extremely hysterical, yet more proof that women simply cannot master such tasks'.[87] Faced with these problems, Riefenstahl did what she had done in the past when she did not get her way. She went to Hitler.

In fact, according to Mainz, she would never have finished *Olympia* had it not been for Hitler's intervention.[88] Wearied by disagreements with Goebbels and following, so she claimed, a press ban he imposed on all mention of her name, she decided to abandon the film. Hitler forbade her from doing so. To protect her, he ensured that, in future, she would not work directly with the Propaganda Ministry, but through the offices of Hess and then Bormann.[89] There is evidence that Goebbels and his ministry continued to be involved in liaising with Riefenstahl's firm right up until 1942.[90] Yet Hitler's former adjutant, Julius Schaub, more or less confirmed Riefenstahl's version of events. During her denazification proceedings, he testified that she had come to him in the winter of 1936 in a state of nervous exhaustion as a result of her 'differences with Goebbels', who was trying to prevent her completing *Olympia* and threatening to withdraw funding. She asked Schaub to engineer a meeting with Hitler, who then ordered that the payments for Riefenstahl's film would be managed not through the Propaganda Ministry, but through the Party Chancellery. Bormann was given the task of mediating between Riefenstahl and Goebbels.[91] Fritz Wiedemann, Hitler's former adjutant, testified that she had also approached him and asked for a meeting with Hitler, and, like Schaub, he recalls that Hitler transferred responsibility to Bormann for overseeing payments to Riefenstahl's company.[92] The hostility she faced drove her back to Hitler, to seek his support. In return, Riefenstahl did her best to produce a film that would, above all, please the man who had commissioned it.

If Goebbels did prohibit any mention in the press of Riefenstahl's name, he was forced into undermining his own ban in June 1937 following a report in *Paris Soir* that he had slapped Riefenstahl and called her a Jewess. *Paris Soir* also claimed Riefenstahl had fled to Switzerland. None of this was true, but, faced with a smear campaign, Goebbels was stung into action: 'the foreign press has published a series of malicious insults against Leni Riefenstahl and me; I issue a strong denial'.[93] When news of these press claims leaked through on Radio Strasbourg, Hitler organized a seemingly convivial get-together at Riefenstahl's house. Hitler's photographer Heinrich Hoffmann took a number of photographs meant to demonstrate entirely amicable relations between Goebbels, Riefenstahl and Hitler, and give the lie to the rumour that Riefenstahl had left the country.[94] These photographs appeared in the German and international press. From this point on, Goebbels in his diary has only the highest praise for Riefenstahl and her developing film: 'watched parts of the *Olympia* film. Indescribably good. Magnificently filmed and presented. A massive achievement. Some parts deeply moving. Leni really is extremely capable. I am enthusiastic.'[95] Finally convinced, it seems, that a woman could create a film worthy of his praise, Goebbels told Hitler in November 1937 how impressed he was with *Olympia*; Hitler, he notes, 'was very pleased that it is a success'. Yet Goebbels could not resist withering sarcasm: 'we must honour Leni a little in some way, she has deserved it, she has had to do without fame and recognition for so long'.[96] With her films for Hitler, she demonstrated that it was she, not Goebbels' ministry, who could produce the best film propaganda. Hans Weidemann's film of the 1936 and 1937 party rallies, *Festive Nuremberg*, was poor.

Riefenstahl did not really need Goebbels to organize accolades; she was quite able to do this herself, not least by ensuring that the two-part *Olympia* film – consisting of *Festival of Peoples* and *Festival of Beauty* – would be premiered on the evening of Hitler's birthday on 20 April 1938. The original intention had been to first show the film in early February 1938.[97] In January 1938, Propaganda Ministry press conferences kept postponing any pre-release reporting on the film, initially until 31 January, then until 15 February, and then until mid-March.[98] Riefenstahl had spent over a year and a half making *Olympia*, but these last-minute postponements had nothing to do with her. They were the result of the Austrian crisis, and, when Hitler finally marched into Austria on 12 March 1938, the premiere had to be postponed yet again. And indeed it would have been problematic to premiere a film about international sportsmanship and friendship just as Hitler was effectively invading another country. Riefenstahl, however, was not happy about an indefinite delay. She followed Hitler to Innsbruck when, in early April 1938,[99] he set off on an election tour of Austria. There, she suggested to him the premiere be held on 20 April.[100] In fact, the newspapers had already announced in late March that it would take place on 19 April.[101] But she wanted it on Hitler's birthday itself. In her memoirs, Riefenstahl implies the idea came to her spontaneously. Her request, surely, was more calculated than that. By having the premiere on 20 April, she could be certain of receiving the widest possible publicity. It was a shrewd piece of marketing.

There might have been another reason for Riefenstahl's suggestion, one to which she did not admit after the war: namely that she wanted to align herself and her film as closely as possible with Hitler's political interests. This would be quite consistent with her behaviour at the time. On 10 April 1938, Hitler had the annexation of Austria confirmed by referendum. Like a number of actors and directors, Riefenstahl lent her voice to the intimidating 'Yes' campaign, declaring in the Nazi press that the 'liberation' of Austria was like a 'miracle', and that the vote on 10 April will be a 'unanimous proclamation of loyalty to our Führer Adolf Hitler'.[102] *Triumph of the Will* found new use as election propaganda in the run-up to the referendum, showing to packed houses in Vienna.[103] Newspapers reported on the positive response among Viennese audiences, particularly among the 'many thousands of unemployed' who were able to watch the film for a mere twenty pfennigs. According to one report, the unemployed Viennese experienced the film as an indication that a better future was coming their way.[104] So that the rally film was seen by as many Austrians as possible, mobile cinema units toured rural areas. *Triumph of the Will* played a part in persuading Austrians that the Third Reich was all about peaceful formations and a charismatic leader, helping to displace the much more aggressive image conveyed by the occupation of Austria. Riefenstahl presumably condoned this use of her film; she certainly did not try to stop it. And in setting Hitler's birthday as the date for the premiere of *Olympia*, she allowed that film to be drawn into attempts by Nazi propaganda to mend the diplomatic damage done by the occupation. *Olympia* set out to portray Hitler as thoroughly urbane and benign.

When Riefenstahl's *Olympia* opened in the presence of Hitler, the Nazi press celebrated it as evidence of his 'love of peace'.[105] Gathered to receive this message at the premiere were many ambassadors to Germany, and representatives of the International Olympic Committee.[106] How many of them believed it was a different matter, especially as Hitler had spent the morning watching a massive military parade. At the premiere, the Greek ambassador handed Riefenstahl an olive branch from the holy grove near ancient Olympia, and Hitler presented her with a bouquet which, among the red roses, included white lilac. The Ufa Palace, its facade pompously fitted out for the occasion in neoclassical style by Albert Speer, sported swastika banners alongside the white colours of the Olympic flag. Nazism and the Olympic ideals appeared united, and indeed Riefenstahl's film did much to promote this supposed unity. *Olympia* is fairly comprehensive in its coverage of the 1936 Summer Olympics disciplines, and judicious in focusing not just on the achievements of German participants, but also on the successes of athletes from other nations, such as the USA, Finland, Italy, Japan and Great Britain. Famously, it devotes several minutes to showing the athleticism of the black track and field sportsman Jesse Owens. Some have interpreted this as Riefenstahl's way of protesting at Nazi racism, but in effect it creates an illusion of ethnic tolerance. Riefenstahl went to great lengths to get shots of the athletes from all angles.[107] *Olympia* is a technically perfect film. It sets out to suggest harmony. Athletes are

seen competing in the best possible spirit, and the crowds applaud enthusiastically. There are few if any images of frustration, disappointment,
anger. We see no injuries, and only an occasional mishap. Competitions,
medal-winning boards and award ceremonies follow one another in
compressed elegance. *Olympia*'s most striking feature is its smooth surface.

A smooth surface was what Hitler had tried to create during the
Olympics themselves: all visible signs of anti-Semitism were removed from
Berlin. But, of course, German Jews remained excluded from athletics in
the Reich, and from the German Olympic team, apart from the 'half-Jew'
Helene Mayer. During the games, Berlin's branch of the Gestapo reported
regularly on communist underground activities, which included distrib-
uting illegal leaflets and sending letters to athletes in the Olympic Village
protesting against Hitler's suppression of fundamental freedoms. The
Gestapo intercepted a letter sent from Southampton to Jesse Owens asking
him to refuse acceptance of his Olympic medals and openly complain
about Nazi racial hatred.[108] Riefenstahl will probably not have known
about any of these letters and protests. However, she spent much time with
foreign athletes (particularly the Americans, with one of whom, decathlete
Glenn Morris, she had an affair). Some of them would surely have expressed
their concerns to her about Nazism. And she will have known about the
exclusion of German-Jewish athletes and Nazi anti-Jewish discrimination
in general. She would not have been able to address this in *Olympia*. But
its aesthetic perfection, its unperturbed projection of harmonious sportsmanship, seems like an exercise in denial – a pernicious denial given that,
by the late spring of 1938, the Nazis had not only stepped up their anti-
Semitic campaign, but extended it into Austria with immediate, drastic
effect. The foreign press reported in detail on, as the *Guardian* put it,
'Nazi terrorism' against Austrian Jews.[109] On the day *Olympia* was
premiered, the same newspaper was reporting on what it anticipated would
be the destruction of Jewish life in Austria.[110]

Audiences were treated in *Olympia* to a smiling, laughing, cheering
Hitler, reacting with childlike enthusiasm to the games. This was Hitler at

leisure. He is depicted as enjoying the achievements of others, rather than as standing in the centre of his own supposed achievements. He appears tolerant of the weaknesses of others, too, as when he dismisses the disappointment of the German women dropping the baton during the 4 × 100 metres relay with a mild hand gesture. Riefenstahl's portrayal of him in the film was designed to disarm those who saw in him what he really was: a ruthless dictator. His part in *Olympia* is not a mere cameo role, as some of the post-war versions of the film, from which he has been partly culled,[111] might lead one to think. Riefenstahl's images of Hitler are invested with significance. After the film's dreamy prelude, we hear and see the tolling Olympic bell, superimposed upon the Olympic stadium; this sequence then fades into a close-up of Hitler's head. In this way, Riefenstahl imprints Hitler on the events that are about to unfold. For all the film's suave internationalism, Riefenstahl includes enough sequences showing sections of the crowd and Hitler doing the Nazi salute to suggest that the games are really being held in honour of the Führer and the Nazi movement. In one scene, she seems to impute special powers to Hitler. As Hans Woellke prepares to launch into the throw that won him the shot put competition, Riefenstahl shows Hitler's intense focus on him, as if telepathically conveying the will to victory. Afterwards, Hitler claps elatedly, and shakes Woellke's hand.

Olympia's images of a congenial Hitler were soon to be seen in Switzerland, Italy, Norway and Denmark as the film was shown around Europe. Hitler saw in it a useful way of solidifying German–Italian friendship, because he gave Mussolini a present of *Olympia* when visiting Rome in May 1938.[112] Riefenstahl, obligingly, had included a lengthy take of the women's 80 metres hurdle winner, Ondina Valla, as she does the Hitler salute on the victory rostrum and Hitler appears to salute back – the medal ceremony is transformed into a celebration of the deep understanding between Italian fascism and National Socialism. Goebbels was delighted by the success of *Olympia*; 'it's a smash hit everywhere'.[113] When Riefenstahl told him about the impact *Olympia* had made in Scandinavia, Goebbels commented: 'she really has done a lot for the German cause. And now she is going to America. I give her a few instructions on how to behave.'[114] But Riefenstahl's America trip did not turn out as planned. A few days after she left for the USA, the Nazis launched Reichskristallnacht. In the States, Riefenstahl was boycotted, and there were protests. She was unable to secure a contract for the showing of *Olympia* there. In the context of the Nazi assault on Jews, *Olympia* now appeared as the sham it really was.

Performing National Socialism

When Hitler speaks to the assembled Reich Labour Service in *Triumph of the Will*, he tells them that, at this moment, they are not only being seen by the hundreds of thousands at Nuremberg, but also by all of Germany. Hitler was given to such grand rhetorical statements, but, when he made this particular assertion, he was well aware the Reich Labour Service at the rally would indeed soon be seen by all of Germany – in the cinema. This raises the question as to what degree Hitler's rally speeches, and indeed the whole rally ritual, in 1934 were fashioned for Riefenstahl's cameras. It is not a question that can be answered, at least not from the archives. But one thing can reasonably be assumed. Hitler knew he was being filmed close-up by Riefenstahl in Nuremberg in 1934, and that knowledge surely prompted him to try particularly hard to muster the full range of theatrical posturing and facial expression of which he was capable, and use it to best effect. So, when Riefenstahl claimed she was just filming the event, she overlooked the possibility that the event was in part being staged for her camera. That was certainly much less the case in 1933, or in 1936 when she filmed the Olympics, though in the latter there are moments when Hitler sweeps into the arena as if he knows he is being filmed. In other words, Riefenstahl filmed events that were to a degree imagined from the beginning by Hitler as films, because he was convinced that, as visual spectacles in the relatively small space of the cinema, they would captivate and overwhelm.

Riefenstahl's films were shown around the Reich, to public audiences, party organizations and young people. They became part of school education. In May 1935, for instance, *Triumph of the Will* was shown to 60,000 schoolchildren and students in the Cologne area.[115] Hitler's message was amplified and disseminated, thanks to Riefenstahl, to every corner of Germany. It is hard, certainly, to gauge the effect of her films on German audiences at the time, but it should not be underestimated. In 1935 and in the following years, *Triumph of the Will*, in what Riefenstahl framed as its rousing conclusion, blared out Hitler's message about the intention of the Nazi Party, once it had taken power, never to share it and never to let it go. It asserted over and again, far and wide, the absolutist stance of Nazism, while making clear what happened to those, like the 'traitors' in the SA, who challenged its authority. Riefenstahl made virulently *political* films for Hitler, exactly as he intended, supporting the triumph and consolidation of his regime, and supporting his diplomacy.

5

The Führer at the Movies

HITLER IN GERMAN CINEMAS

Hitler was present in German cinemas in a number of ways. He was, for a start, present in person. Unlike his private film viewing, his viewing of film in public was politically motivated. He chose films with which he wished to associate himself or the Nazi movement. He exhibited a remarkable sense of timing, seeking to make immediate political capital out of going to particular film premieres. Hitler was also present in cinemas through the sound of his speeches, and, on a regular basis, in the weekly newsreel or Wochenschau. Finally, Hitler reached cinema screens indirectly in the various Third Reich feature films which celebrated great historical leader figures. Given these multiple interfaces between Hitler and cinema, German cinemas between 1933 and 1945 became vehicles not just for transmitting Nazi ideas, but also for reinforcing in various ways the personification of these ideas in Hitler.

Hitler at Film Premieres

No sooner did Hitler become Reich chancellor than he attended the first Berlin performance of Gustav Ucicky's feature film *Dawn* (1933), along with other leading representatives of the new Reich cabinet, on 2 February 1933. The day before, Reich President Hindenburg, at Hitler's bidding, had dissolved the Reichstag and announced there would be new elections. *Dawn* celebrated the fighting spirit of a German submarine crew during the First World War. Hitler's viewing of *Dawn*, reported in all national newspapers, was designed to encourage the association of his politics as chancellor from the very beginning with the spirit of the First World War and its military traditions. Given the restrictions on the German army and navy at the time, Ucicky had to borrow a Finnish submarine to make the film. Advertising for *Dawn*, though, showed a 'new U-boat ploughing through the shimmering waves towards new deeds', and the Nazi daily the *Völkischer Beobachter* emphasized that the 'timeless value' of *Dawn* lay in its 'uncompromising depiction of what was, what is, and what always will be: war!'[1] Hitler's appearance at the premiere implicitly underscored his commitment to re-armament, and to reversing the terms of the Versailles Treaty. *Dawn* also portrayed the supposed deceitfulness of the British, who lure the Germans into a trap. The British Conservative politician Charles Cayzer protested at this, but Foreign Affairs' Secretary Sir John Simon, not prepared to risk a diplomatic spat just after Hitler had come to power, defended the film against the charge that it had represented the British navy as 'treacherous'. It is unlikely Simon would have held this view had he actually seen the film.[2]

Hitler's attendance of the Berlin premiere of *Dawn* was not his only appearance at the showing of a First World War film. On 20 February 1934, he was at the premiere of *Shock Troop 1917*, directed by the author Hans Zöberlein, upon whose novel *Faith in Germany* (1931) it is based; film and novel celebrate the bravery of German soldiers. The day before, on 19 February, Hindenburg had issued a proclamation stipulating that the Nazi insignia would henceforth be used in the army. If this indicated the beginning of a Nazi takeover of the military, Hitler's viewing of *Shock Troop 1917* artfully suggested rather his respect for the army's history and achievements, and his personal bond with the ordinary infantryman. A few hours before watching the film, Hitler had been in conference with

Eric Phipps, British ambassador to Germany, and Lord Privy Seal Anthony Eden. The main topic of conversation was a proposed arms convention, with Hitler veering between insisting on the German right to rearm and showing willingness to curb the military power of the SA. Neither the German nor the British public learned the details of Hitler's discussion with the British representatives.[3] But that Hitler spent the evening watching *Shock Troop 1917* will have assured the Germans of his firm commitment to the need for a strong military. At the same time, because *Shock Troop 1917* ends with German soldiers sharing their Christmas with a dying British soldier, his viewing of the film could have been construed as affirming his belief (at that time) in German–British friendship. The next day, the film no doubt still fresh in his mind, he exchanged personal memories of the First World War with Eden; according to the latter, Hitler 'thawed materially' in the course of the discussion.[4]

Hitler's appearance at First World War film premieres was intended to underscore the point that the deaths of German soldiers had not gone unanswered: the victory of National Socialism, supposedly restoring German pride, was, as it were, the compensation for those losses. Newspaper reports on Hitler's attendance of war films stressed that Hitler was 'the unknown soldier of the Great War', as if to demonstrate that any ordinary soldier could rise to fame, or that the success of one unknown soldier somehow made sense of the sacrifices of the others.[5] Hitler identified himself with films about sacrifice – in *Dawn*, two members of the submarine crew sacrifice their lives to save the others. In 1933, Hitler also attended the first showings of *Storm Trooper Brand* (1933) on 14 June, and *Hitler Youth Quex* (1933) on 12 September. These films celebrated the spirit of sacrifice in the case of the SA and the Hitler Youth in their fight against communism during the Weimar Republic. Goebbels had reservations about *Storm Trooper Brand*. After the first showing, he complained it was 'too full of talking' and would need 'drastic cuts'.[6] And, in early October 1933, Goebbels, after conferring with Hitler, decided to ban a film about Nazi martyrdom at the hands of communism, Franz Wenzler's *Horst Wessel*, which he dismissed as 'the worse kind of dilettantism'.[7] A revised version under the name of *Hans Westmar* reached cinema screens on 13 December 1933. Despite the relative failure of Nazism to produce persuasive feature films about its political struggles during the Weimar Republic,[8] Hitler's attendance of the premieres of *Storm Trooper Brand* and *Hitler Youth Quex* surely achieved its aim. Self-sacrifice for the cause was a quality Hitler wished to encourage through his presence; he wanted a nation, after all, that would go to the utmost for his goals, and not question their value in the process.

Just to make sure members of the premiere audience got the point of *Hitler Youth Quex*, leader of the Hitler Youth Baldur von Schirach spelt it out in a pre-performance speech in which he said that the death of Hitler Youth member Herbert Norkus – upon whose fate the film was based – had not been in vain. Peddling Nazi rhetoric about productive sacrifice, Schirach claimed that today, a million and a half young 'warriors' had sprung up from the site of Norkus' murder.[9] A glance at the way Hitler distributed his public film viewings shows he used them to demonstrate his solidarity with a range of important groups whose loyalty mattered to him: the German navy (*Dawn*), army (*Shock Troop 1917*) and then, in December 1938, air force (the subject of Karl Ritter's *Pour le Mérite*), as well as the SA (*Storm Trooper Brand*) and the Hitler Youth (*Hitler Youth Quex*). Sometimes, his supposed bonds with these groups were acted out at the cinema. Approaching the cinema to watch *Storm Trooper Brand*, Hitler made his way through an honorary cordon of SA men, mainly Nazis who had served in SA units active in Berlin's communist districts.[10] After the screening of *Hitler Youth Quex*, representatives of the Hitler Youth appeared on stage and raised their arms towards Hitler. Hitler got up from his seat and thanked them, smiling benevolently.[11] When Hitler came to the premieres of Riefenstahl's *Victory of Faith* in late 1933, and especially of *Triumph of the Will* in 1935, there were similar rituals. First, all the Nazi dignitaries representing the mass organizations portrayed in *Triumph of the Will* arrived at the Berlin's Ufa Palace, to be followed, finally, by Hitler himself. Crowds watched the spectacle, participating in a symbolic coming together of the people's community outside the cinema before Riefenstahl's film reproduced this collective bonding on the cinema screen inside.

Most of the film showings at which Hitler was present were attended by select audiences of high-ranking Nazi politicians, representatives of Nazi organizations, generals, cultural officials and other dignitaries, but there were exceptions. On 3 April 1939, he watched Wolfgang Liebeneiner's comedy *The Florentine Hat* (1939), starring Heinz Rühmann, along with 1,000 German workers. This was a film without an obvious political message. But, even if *The Florentine Hat* appears to be a harmless comedy, the showing Hitler was at – a 'pre-performance' anticipating the premiere the next day – was framed in a politically significant way. Here was Hitler mixing with the ordinary people, showing himself to be close to them, apparently sharing in their leisure activities and their collective amusement. The setting for the showing was not an ordinary cinema, but a ship, the *Robert Ley*, and the occasion was special, because this was the *Robert Ley*'s maiden voyage. The *Robert Ley* had been specially built by the Nazi leisure organization Strength Through Joy (KdF), after whose leader it was named. Its purpose was to provide cruises for the German people as a reward for their industry. But Hitler's sojourn on the *Robert Ley* was not just about bonding with the *Volk*, it was also about providing a counterpoise to the more militaristic part of his visit to Wilhelmshaven. Here, two days earlier, he attended the launch of the battleship *Tirpitz* and delivered a speech in which, among other things, he condemned supposed British aggression – a response to Chamberlain's announcement on 31 March 1939 of a British–Polish alliance. The days he spent on board the *Robert Ley*, relaxing not least by watching a film comedy, were designed to convey the impression of a peace-loving Hitler – and yet it was probably in early April, too, that Hitler secretly gave orders for the planning of the German attack on Poland.[12] In the end, Hitler was more interested in strength than joy, whatever his pleasure in viewing *The Florentine Hat* – and he must have liked it, because it was ordered for his private viewing later in April. Hitler classified it as 'very good'.[13]

It was not always German films that Hitler watched in the cinema. On 8 March 1937, Goebbels noted in his diary that *Mario*, an Italian youth film about the early years of Italian fascism, was to be shown 'in grand style' on Hitler's birthday at Berlin's Ufa Palace. Elaborate plans were drawn up for the occasion. A thousand Hitler Youth members lined the nearby streets to welcome Hitler. To stress the unity of Italian and German youth, a choir from the Italian colony in Berlin opened the evening with a rendering of the Italian fascist youth organization song, echoed by a Hitler Youth choir's performance of the Hitler Youth song.[14] Italian and German youths assembled in impressively tiered groups on the stage.[15] 'With the Führer to the Ufa Palace,' writes Goebbels on 20 April.[16] *Mario* he describes as having a 'powerful effect', even if it was not 'a great film'. He comments positively on the 'atmospheric framing' of the film showing, and indeed this was the most important aspect of the evening. That Hitler should spend part of his birthday watching an Italian film sent a clear message to Mussolini of Hitler's admiration for Italian fascism and its cultural expressions. It was a gesture designed to lend support to the negotiations for an Italian–German Film Agreement which had been proceeding earlier in the month.[17] This cultural collaboration, in turn, helped pave the way for Mussolini's state visit to Germany in September, after which Italy, in November, joined the Anti-Comintern Pact. Viewing a film, for Hitler, could constitute a form of diplomacy, as was the case when Hitler was present along with numerous ambassadors to Germany at the first performance in 1938 of Riefenstahl's film of the 1936 Berlin Summer Olympics.[18] What was important about all Hitler's appearances at cinema showings was the message he thereby hoped to convey. The films themselves, and the occasions, were used as a means to that end.

The Sound and Sight of Hitler

When the Nazis came to power, they did not take long to transform radio and film theatres into vehicles for party propaganda. New radio technology, from the moment it was introduced, was connected with the regime even in name. Thus the Nazi People's Receiver of August 1933 bore the name VE301 in honour of 30 January, the day the Nazis seized power. The German Labour Front People's Receiver – designed for radio broadcast in factories and public places – was called DAF1011, in honour of Hitler's speech to Siemens' workers on 10 November 1933. Most German cinemas continued to bear the names they had always had, such as Metropol, Ufa or Apollo, although some were renamed in compliance with the new regime, while others found themselves, following the Nazi renaming of streets and squares, situated on the Adolf-Hitler-Straße or the Adolf-Hitler-Platz. And cinemas were soon put in the service of showing Nazi propaganda films. When such films were shown, cinemas were expected to adorn their facade, foyer and/or auditorium with Nazi symbols. It was above all the use of radio and cinema to convey the sound and sight of Hitler which made them a potent instrument for transmitting National Socialist values. From 1933 onwards, as one would expect, Hitler's important speeches were broadcast on the radio. But they were also relayed to cinema audiences. In May 1933, the Reich League of German Cinema Owners declared its expectation that all cinema owners in a position to do so broadcast Hitler's May Day speech live to cinema audiences through loudspeakers, interrupting the film programme if necessary.[19] This soon became a habit. When Hitler was due to speak in the German Reichstag in May 1935, German film theatres were instructed to organize their evening opening hours so that cinemagoers could listen to Hitler's speech at 8 p.m. either after the main feature film or before it.[20] In some cinemas, Hitler's voice boomed out into the foyer so that people gathered there could also listen. Audiences sat for two hours as Hitler's seemingly interminable speech continued. At first unsure how to react when they heard Reichstag members applauding, they began to applaud themselves. There was no visual accompaniment, apart from the swastikas embellishing the cinema safety curtain.[21]

Goebbels' Propaganda Ministry used the cinemas to immerse audiences in the sound of Hitler not just to strengthen the hold of Nazi ideas generally, but also quite specifically in the interests of election propaganda. It was with Reichstag elections approaching that Hitler, on 10 November 1933, gave his speech to German workers at Berlin's Siemens factory. A day later, thanks to the organizational efforts of Berlin's Regional Film Office, Berliners were able to *see* as well as listen to the speech at fourteen public places in the city. Similar showings were organized throughout the Reich, with newspaper reports claiming that they were viewed all in all by hundreds of thousands of people. Responsible for projecting the film were mobile cinema trucks, elongated vans designed for showing films in public areas. One of the trucks was provided by the Margarine-Union AG, a German branch of Unilever, which thereby played its part in mobilizing Berliners for the election.[22] Soon, however, the Nazi Gau Film Offices all had their own mobile cinema trucks, used in cities, towns and even small villages to disseminate propaganda.

Just over two weeks after Reich President Hindenburg died, the Germans were asked to vote on 19 August 1934 on whether the positions of Reich president and chancellor should be united in the person of Hitler. Ufa, at Goebbels' behest, swiftly released two short films, composed largely of newsreel material, the first showing the 'high points' of Hindenburg's career (*Hindenburg*), the second those of Hitler's (*Our Führer*). *Hindenburg* stressed the supposed bond between the geriatric general and Hitler. *Our Führer* did this as well. It also treated the viewer to excerpts from Hitler's speeches and footage from events such as Hitler's opening of the Autobahn construction programme. The *Hindenburg* film replaced the weekly newsreel and began running on 3 August – a mere day after Hindenburg's death – in about 2,500 German film theatres.[23] Goebbels, and Ufa, were clearly well prepared. *Our Führer* started showing in Berlin, Kurmark in eastern Germany, and sixty-six other German cities as of 13 August.[24] What were now called the Gau Film Offices showed *Our Führer* in public places, such as the Parade Square in Stettin on the evening of 14 August. To keep the gathering crowd entertained as darkness fell, march music and Nazi Party songs blared out from the loudspeakers before the film itself was projected onto an enormous screen. Showings of *Our Führer* were planned every evening in Stettin right up to election Sunday.[25]

By the time of the April 1938 Reichstag elections, simultaneously designed to gain popular approbation for Hitler's seizure of Austria, the Nazi propaganda machine was working with high efficiency. Whenever Hitler gave a talk in a German city prior to these elections, the cinemas in that city were expected to relay his speech.[26] *All* German and Austrian cinemas were called upon by Goebbels to broadcast Hitler's last electoral speech, given in Vienna.[27] Film programmes were affected in another way. The culture film – a short which usually accompanied the main film – was replaced with one of several brief election films browbeating cinemagoers into casting their vote for Hitler. The election films then went on tour throughout the Reich, including the newly annexed Austria. Nazi newspapers proudly reported on the mass turnouts. In Vienna, 120,000 people came along to an open-air viewing of election films including *Word and Deed* (1938), which celebrated all that Hitler and the Nazi Party had achieved up to that point.[28]

The degree to which Hitler engaged personally in promoting this election propaganda is not clear. Certainly its implementation lay for the most part in the hands of the Film Department of the Propaganda Ministry, with input from Hans Weidemann (responsible for the newsreel coordination within the ministry) and with the collaboration of German film companies. The Film Office of Goebbels' Reich Propaganda Leadership, responsible for overseeing the work of the Gau Film Offices, was also involved. German film directors, such as Hans Steinhoff and the Austrian Gustav Ucicky, offered their services: Ucicky co-directed *Word and Deed*, Steinhoff the short 1938 election film *Yesterday and Today*.

Many of the documentary shorts produced between 1933 and 1939 with the aim of inculcating or reinforcing belief in Nazism followed the same pattern. Aspects of the political, cultural, economic and social achievements of National Socialism since Hitler's coming to power are set in a contrastive relation to the Weimar Republic, with its financial problems, unemployment, political conflicts and supposed enslavement to the will of the Allies and the terms of the Versailles Treaty. This is the message in one of the earliest Nazi documentaries to appear after Hitler became Reich chancellor, *Germany Awakens!* (1933), and it is still the message in the 1939 Tobis film *Victory over Versailles*, directed by Wilhelm Stöppler, in which Hitler's occupation of the Sudetenland (1938) and of Memel (1939) are celebrated. Again and again, Germany's resurgence after 1933 is presented in messianic terms, an interpretation Hitler was only too willing to support. Hans Weidemann's short film chronicle of the 1936 and 1937 Nazi Party rallies, *Festive Nuremberg* (1937), ends with an excerpt from a speech in which Hitler describes developments in Germany as 'the miracle of the rebirth of a so deeply humiliated people [. . .] the miracle of re-emergence'.[29]

In 1933, the Nazi emphasis on rebirth both reflected a real sense of the need for change, as the Nazis perceived it, and served to conceal all the murder, repression and skulduggery to which they resorted as they set about silencing anyone who might challenge that 'rebirth'. The continued evocation of this 'rebirth' three, four or five years later might seem anachronistic. In *Word and Deed*, we see a clip from March 1932 in which Social Democrat Otto Braun, minister president of Prussia at the time, warns against the dishonesty of National Socialist agricultural politics. This is followed by a scene showing Hitler paying homage to the importance of farmers: Braun, we are to infer, got it completely wrong. Yet Braun had long since vanished into Swiss exile. By the time Weidemann's *Years of Decision* (1939) was produced, a Nazi documentary contrasting images of the inflation-wracked, 'decadent' Weimar Republic with images of a resolute Hitler set on bringing it to an end, the Republic was history. Nazi propaganda films, however, depended for their effectiveness on conveying an impression of Hitler's constant political activism and dynamism in the face of difficult odds. As there were no longer any opposing political parties, it was the Weimar Republic that continued to form the contrastive foil to Nazism. Moreover, the danger supposedly posed by Jews and

Bolsheviks in the present, at least until the Second World War, was most frequently spelt out in Nazi propaganda by summoning the memory of the Weimar Republic. And, as long as aspects of the Versailles Treaty remained in force, the Republic, associated with that treaty, was not absolutely over-come in the Nazi imagination. Hitler's politics between 1933 and 1939 were aimed at overturning the Versailles Treaty step by step, and Nazi documentaries over that period were always able to find new political triumphs to celebrate as a result. The process of national regeneration, as films such as *Years of Decision* suggest, began with Hitler's rekindling of economic and social life, before encompassing territorial expansion. *Years of Decision* ends with footage of Hitler entering Memel – ceded to Germany by Lithuania in March 1939. Versailles, the film tells us against a back-ground of marching soldiers, is finally 'dead'.

Hitler's autobiography *My Struggle* (1925) could only become a kind of National Socialist 'bible' by keeping the memory of the Weimar Republic alive. In 1936, the German civil service made Hitler a birthday present of a medieval-style handmade copy of *My Struggle* produced on parchment, weighing 70 lbs. A short film – called *The Book of the Germans* – recorded the making of the volume. Directed by Richard Skowronneck, it was shown at the Great Exhibition of German Art in 1937, featuring as a demonstration of 'German genius'.[30] *The Book of the Germans* begins with images of the First World War, post-war chaos, industrial standstill, marching communists, unemployment and hunger. Then the clouds break, and Hitler's *My Struggle* comes into view, followed by shots of Germans of all classes reading it. The voiceover tells us: 'Thanks to Hitler, the German people found itself again; he freed it from destitution, class-war, dishonour and despair.' The film suggests the regenerative power of the very act of reading Hitler's text, which, so we are told, is 'the iron foundation of German reconstruction'. The memory of that reconstruc-tion is evoked in an attempt to invest *My Struggle* with a continuing iconic national status.

Hitler in the Wochenschau, 1933–39

Nazi documentaries were largely retrospective and summative in character, seeking to overwhelm audiences with accumulated evidence of Hitler's success. Hitler was presented in a much more regular fashion to audiences in the Wochenschau, the weekly newsreel, which naturally focused on very recent events. Here, he was one piece of news alongside others, and not framed within narratives in the same way as in the documentaries. Newsreels tended to concatenate reports, sometimes in a manner that seems random – although major political issues, which tended to involve Hitler, usually featured first. The weekly newsreels stood at the heart of the systematic visual exposure to Hitler not least because, until the outbreak of war in 1939, there were *four* of them circulating in Germany, two produced by Ufa (under the name of Ufa and Deulig), one by Fox and one by Tobis (which took over the Bavaria Wochenschau in 1938).[31] From 1935, these newsreels were coordinated from within the Propaganda Ministry by Hans Weidemann, until he was replaced by Fritz Hippler – later to direct *The Eternal Jew* – in January 1939. Goebbels was thus quick to supervise the weekly news broadcasts, long before they were merged into the single 'German Wochenschau' in November 1940.[32] From 1933 onwards, cinema audiences could relive on a regular basis the high points of Hitler's activities, as filtered through the lens of the Wochenschau cameramen. For the most part, Hitler was represented in the pre-war years in ways that reinforced the propaganda image of a politician close to his people. He was shown and heard giving speeches, often at mass events where he was the main attraction, be this the yearly Nuremberg Party Rally, or the Reich Harvest Festival on the Bückeberg, or the November commemorations of the Nazi 1923 putsch in Munich. He was the centrepiece of the Nazi calendar, his stage-managed reappearance at key annual events caught by the cameras year after year. Over time, the newsreels helped to instil a Nazi sense of time, so often were the Nazi anniversaries, to a degree superimposed upon the existing Christian calendar and on war commemoration events, reported on.

At the same time, newsreels reflected the careful choreography of Nazi events, in that they presented Hitler not only as standing at the centre of the people's community, but also as apart from it – and above it. One Nazi newsreel reporting on the Reich Harvest Festival in 1936 shows us Hitler, first, walking through a sea of spectators, shaking hands with one or two of them. He is then filmed ascending a set of steps before beginning his speech, looking down upon the masses from his raised podium. But the newsreels also enabled viewers to *share* in Hitler's perspective.[33] They alternate between affirming visually the subservience of the German people to their leader, and allowing viewers to imagine they are party to Hitler's own superior vantage-point, and even permitting them the privileged perspective of looking down from above on Hitler. A good example is a 1939 newsreel of the May Day national holiday celebrations in Berlin. We see Hitler approaching the Lustgarten, where he is due to speak to the masses, in his motor cavalcade. Hitler's arrival – whether by plane, ship or, usually, car – is always a key point in the newsreels, which capture the moment of supposed union of the Führer and his Volk. The cameras show the approaching cars from the front, above and behind; they show us Hitler standing in his usual pose in the passenger seat, arm outstretched; and they also show the crowds as if from the perspective of Hitler's passing car: Hitler's implied gaze becomes that of the newsreel viewer. Through such deft shifts of focus the newsreels sought to implicate the viewers in the exercise of power, while always making clear the elevated status of Hitler. Whether Hitler is filmed from above, behind or below, and regardless of the position of the crowds in relation to him in any given take, he remains the object of the cinemagoer's gaze, the axis around which everything turns.[34]

In the Nazi pre-war newsreels, cinemagoers also had plenty of opportunity to *hear* Hitler. Despite some exceptions,[35] however, the Wochenschau only provided snippets of Hitler's speeches: his often long and poorly structured public speeches were reduced to a few aphoristic statements which acquired significance through the very act of their selection. A newsreel report on Hitler's 30 July 1933 speech to the masses gathered in Stuttgart to celebrate the 15th German Gymnastics Festival highlights his evocation of a future dominated by a new kind of human being: one combining 'radiating intellect' with a 'wonderful body'. The explicitly racial and racist theory the speech also contained is not included in the newsreel.[36] Newsreel coverage of his 1933 speech to the party faithful commemorating the 'fallen' of the Munich putsch gives prominence to his claim that the goals for which the Nazis had marched in 1923 had now been achieved. 'If they [the dead] were to get up from their graves they would cry for happiness now that the German army and the awakening German people have formed a unity.' In this one statement, history and the present are fused, death is given meaning, and National Socialism appears as the creator of national harmony.[37]

Germans going to the cinema in the Third Reich watched the newsreel and a feature film, and indeed both had their place in the theatre of illusion. The newsreels after 1933 portrayed Hitler as he liked to be seen: a positive, forceful figure, radiating optimism and certainty. Little of the aggression and few of the threats in his public speeches found their way into the Wochenschau. Hitler, right up to and even after September 1939, insisted in public statements that he was a man of peace, and that it was other nations, not Germany, who were agitating for war. The newsreels echoed this message. In 1935, Hitler introduced general conscription. Lest the German people read into this an aggressive intention, Nazi propaganda did its best to present the measure solely as a protective one. The advantage of the newsreel was that it was able to disseminate propaganda messages throughout the Reich with a visual power not possible in other media. Following a 1935 ceremony for the war dead in Berlin, Defence Minister Blomberg gave a speech in which he interpreted conscription as an assurance of peace and Hitler's politics as harvesting the crops sown by the war dead. This harvest took the form of a 'Reich of unity, strength and honour, a Germany of peace in a Europe made peaceful'. Blomberg's speech is lent weight by newsreel reports, not least when the camera focuses suddenly on a solemn Hitler as Blomberg speaks of the Reich's security.[38]

Hitler himself had been watching newsreels at the Berghof at least since 1936 – and intervening in their production. According to Goebbels, Hitler stepped in in April 1937 to ban a newsreel report on the SA's 'Offering of Thanks', a campaign to collect monies for Hitler's birthday,[39] and in August of that year, Hitler had telephoned to ask for some sections to be removed from the Wochenschau.[40] In the course of 1938, not least as the political crisis over the Sudetenland was brewing, Hitler complained to Goebbels and his Propaganda Ministry about the quality of the Wochenschau. He wanted it to be cleverer in its political treatment of its subjects. He also wanted images of Czechoslovakia's 'nervous preparations' and, at the end, a 'close-up of the German soldier': 'no week should pass in which we do not see images of the navy, army and air force'.[41] Hitler no doubt hoped to impress the Czechs into easy submission through this powerful show of arms, or to prepare the Germans for the anticipated invasion of Czech lands and assure them of the Reich's military supremacy. As the Sudetenland crisis reached boiling point in the autumn of 1938, the German newsreels – perhaps as a result of Hitler's intervention – were particularly skilled in deploying text and image to present his politics as a reaction to Czech 'aggression'.

To convince viewers that the real aggressors were the Czechs, one news-reel provided harrowing images of Germans fleeing from the Sudetenland, and reported on the refugee camps set up on the German–Czech border to accommodate them. The reality, however, was concealed from cinemagoers: most Germans who fled were either Nazi sympathizers fearing Czech coun-termeasures, German civilians worried about a war breaking out, or German males trying to avoid an anticipated call-up to the Czech army.[42] After Hitler occupied the Sudetenland in early October 1938, the newsreels, learning from documentary films, constructed overarching narratives in which Hitler starred as a national saviour. One newsreel begins with reports on the oppression of Germans and Poles by the Czechs, and ends with images of Hitler all but hidden from view by bouquets of flowers proffered to him by jubilant Germans in Eger (Sudetenland). In between, the newsreel comments on the peaceful outcome of the Munich Agreement – as if this had been Hitler's achievement.[43] Another follows a similar structure. It begins with images of bridges and schools allegedly destroyed by Czechs, before celebrating Hitler's 'liberation' of the Sudetenland. We then see an excerpt from Hitler's 1938 speech in support of the Winter Aid campaign. Hitler speaks of all the 'run-down' Sudeten German towns and 'undernourished' Sudeten Germans he had personally seen, before calling on fellow Germans to help them. As he talks, images of needy Sudeten Germans are woven into the report. Hitler had planned aggression, but was frustrated. German cinemagoers were treated instead to a version of events that interpreted his motives as grounded in social solidarity, charity and concern for human rights.[44]

Yet, even as the Wochenschau sought to convince audiences of Hitler's peaceful intentions, from 1933 onwards it portrayed him again and again in the presence of military formations. This was, to a considerable extent, a reflection of reality. Many of the mass events attended by Hitler had a military character or dimension. If Germans did believe Hitler embodied peace, then it will have been clear to them this was going to be a peace defended and, if necessary, imposed by military means. The newsreels not only reflected reality, however, they also subtly used visual juxtapositions to encourage viewers to accept the predominance of the military and its special relationship with Hitler. In this way, they prepared German audiences for the acceptance of war. In one 1934 newsreel, we see Hitler greeting police units marching by his balcony window, before the perspective shifts to the waving crowds standing behind, and then back to Hitler, who appears to greet the crowd. The newsreel reinforces the sense of hierarchy: the military formation has priority over the civilian.[45] When Hitler turned fifty in April 1939, the newsreels reported extensively on his birthday. The highlight for the Berliners was probably the opening of part of the new road known as the East–West Axis (part of Albert Speer's plan for reinventing Berlin). But

Hitler's triumphant drive down it does not form the centrepiece of the Ufa newsreel. Rather, the focus is on the celebratory military parade – the longest and largest military parade in the Third Reich's history. It lasted four hours. In the newsreel, the viewer is treated to a long report on the parade, in which we see artillery and soldiers pass in front of Hitler. There is then a sudden cut to a scene showing Hitler on a balcony, arm outstretched in acknowledgement of the cheering crowds below. Images of military strength are suggestively juxtaposed with images of Hitler's popularity.

Hitler Figures in Nazi Feature Films

Hitler was not represented in Third Reich feature films – although brief documentary footage of him at the 1936 Olympic Games was included in Eduard von Borsody's *Request Concert* (1940), and he can be heard on radio in Gustav Ucicky's *Homecoming* (1941). Yet he was indirectly present in feature films which promoted the so-called 'leadership principle'. The strong leaders depicted in a number of Nazi film epics created historical parallels to Hitler; these in turn were designed to provide justification for Hitler's style of rule.

The greatest resemblance can probably be found in *The Ruler* (1937), a film very loosely based – to the point of travesty – on the drama *Before Sunset* (1932) by Gerhart Hauptmann. The storyline of *The Ruler* is straightforward.[46] Following the death of his wife, steelworks owner Matthias Clausen (Emil Jannings) falls in love with his secretary, Inken Peters (Marianne Hoppe). Fearing that the firm and family fortune might fall into the hands of Peters, Clausen's family try to have him declared incapable of managing his own affairs. Their attempt to disinherit him fails and, at the end of the film, Clausen bequeaths his firm to the 'people's community' in the expectation that 'from the ranks of my workers and employees [. . .] the man will emerge who is destined to continue my work'. According to the film's director, Veit Harlan, this final speech was not in the original script, but added at the insistence of Walther Funk, state secretary in the Propaganda Ministry at the time.[47] But it is not out of keeping with the rest of the film, where Clausen is portrayed as a strong leader admired by his workers. When celebrating the fortieth anniversary of the steelworks, they greet him with outstretched arms in the manner of a Hitler salute. At a board meeting, Clausen declares his will to be 'the supreme law' to which everything else is subject. It is this declaration, as well as Clausen's outbursts of temper, that his family think will convince the legal authorities he is not in control of his faculties. But the film makes clear Clausen's rage stems from a justified moral indignation, and that he does not dictate to his workers. His autocratic tendencies are exercised in their interest and directed against the greedy self-interest of board and family. They are also exercised in the national interest. For financial reasons, the steelworks board had decided in Clausen's absence to discontinue a research project which, if successful, would have contributed to Germany's striving for autarky. Clausen's iron rule ensures the project continues, a project which constituted, as one critic put it, 'a variation on an idea of the Führer's'.[48]

German industry protested against the film because of its negative portrayal of a managerial board. Their complaints were taken up by others.[49] But Hitler very much liked *The Ruler*, and chose, according to Goebbels, to see the 'funny side' of the protests.[50] *The Ruler* remained a favourite of the Nazi propaganda machine long after its opening run had come to an end. It was screened eighty-eight times during the Youth Film Hours in 1938/39, for instance.[51] It served to remind audiences of the ostensible bond between the people's community and Hitler. It helped to sustain the myth that Hitler, like Clausen, had reined in capitalism and tied it to the national and collective interest. Clausen was by origin 'a simple locksmith', and it was not beneath his dignity despite his ascent to wealth to court a secretary of equally humble origins. He has no sense of class hierarchy. In this, he is also supposed to resemble Hitler: Nazi propaganda liked to present him, too, as of humble origins. *The Ruler* provided confirmation of the socialism which, according to the theory at least, underlay the nationalism of Nazism. Above all, *The Ruler* implicitly confirmed the absolute authority Hitler possessed. It was this that made the film a very useful propaganda tool.

Observant cinemagoers might have noticed that the idea of a ruler's will and law being one and the same had already found expression in an earlier film, Hans Steinhoff's *The Old and the Young King* (1935), starring Werner Hinz as the young Frederick the Great, with Emil Jannings playing his tempestuous father, Frederick William I of Prussia. *The Old and the Young King* was one of six films about Frederick the Great produced during the Third Reich, the most famous being *The Great King* from 1942. Films about Frederick the Great had been a regular feature of German cinematic production since the early twentieth century, and in fact most of them were made during the Weimar Republic, when the actor Otto Gebühr – a great favourite of Hitler's – carved out a niche for himself as 'the' screen Frederick. All pre-1933 Frederick the Great films took episodes from Frederick's life and adapted them without much respect for historical accuracy.[52] *The Old and the Young King* was a new departure in that it focused not on the mature Frederick, but – as the film sees it – the immature Frederick who, in the course of the action, gives up his youthfully indulgent life of idleness, pleasure-seeking and gambling to commit to his future role as head of state. This is a film, then, about how Frederick came to be Frederick. It is a film about imposing paternal authority. In a gesture in which some critics have seen an echo of the 1933 book-burnings, Frederick's father hurls his son's books into the fire, as well as snapping his flute in two, in an angry effort to persuade him to focus instead on matters military and political. Fed up with the constrictions of life under his father, Frederick plans to decamp to his mother's family in England with the help of his friend Katte, but the plan fails. Frederick William, not afraid of drastic educational methods, has Katte executed and makes his son watch. This is the turning point. Frederick pledges loyalty to his father and now does his bidding. The shadow of Katte's death, as Frederick puts it, still falls between him and his father, but he develops into a dutiful son. At Frederick William's deathbed, the two are reconciled in an emotional scene.

The scenes around Katte's execution are a turning point, not least because of the confrontation between Commandant von Reichmann and Frederick. Frederick, indignant at Katte's execution, accuses his father of murder. 'The king does not murder,' replies von Reichmann, adding, 'his will is law, and whatever does not bow to his will he has to destroy.' Von Reichmann reminds Frederick that he, too, will one day have to demand obedience and embody duty, an argument which proves persuasive. *The Old and the Young King* was first shown in February 1935, not that long after the Night of the Long Knives (30 June/1 July 1934), when Hitler had decapitated the SA, ostensibly because its leader Ernst Röhm was planning a 'second revolution'. A law passed on 3 July 1934 on 'measures regarding state self-defence' declared the crushing of the Röhm 'putsch' to be legal. The killings were subsequently justified by Hitler in his speech to the Reichstag on 13 July 1934: 'in this hour, I was responsible for the fate of the German nation and therefore the German people's supreme judge'. Hitler, then, as leader, embodied the national interest; acting on its behalf automatically conferred legal status on his decisions. This was essentially the interpretation provided by the philosopher Carl Schmitt when he argued that 'the true Führer is always also a judge; being a judge flows from leadership'.[53] Similarly, in *The Old and the Young King*, the execution of Katte is given the force of law because King Frederick William, with Prussia's future in mind, willed it. Possibly more than any other Third Reich historical film, *The Old and the Young King* serves to justify a ruler's right to set himself above the law, to *be* the law, even and especially when acting in an apparently brutal manner. Brutality is but the harsh face of justice. Not only that: on his deathbed, Frederick William admits to having treated his son too strictly, but claims to have done so only out of love. Frederick accepts that his father was right to have been severe. 'Make Prussia great', Frederick William says to him before he expires. Frederick looks up into the camera in a long take, as if lost in a vision. Accepting firm leadership, then, is the key to a better future.

Reviews of *The Old and the Young King* elevated the film to the status of a national treasure. According to one newspaper, the film encapsulates the 'mentality of the whole land in which it was made' and 'fulfils the highest mission a work of art can ever fulfil'.[54] On 21 March 1933, with President Hindenburg in attendance, the new Reichstag had been ceremonially constituted at Potsdam's Garrison Church, the burial place of Prussian kings Frederick William I and Frederick the Great. Hitler thereby implied that he stood in an august Friderician lineage. Feature films such as *The Old and the Young King* and the 1937 film *Fridericus* reinforced this genealogy. Directed by Johannes Meyer and starring Otto Gebühr as the now mature Frederick the Great, *Fridericus* focuses on Frederick's struggles against France and Austria in the Seven Years' War (1756–63). Its theme is the need not so much to impose supreme authority as it is to defend the country against outside aggression. An on-screen text at the start tells audiences: 'surrounded by the dynastic European superpowers, upward-striving Prussia has been struggling for decades for its right to exist'. At one point, Frederick tells Graf Wallis that he does not want Prussia to be 'the plaything of East and West', and that he wants to put an end to Prussia's 'shameful slavery'. He declares more than once that his interest is peace, but war – which he ultimately wins in the film – has been forced upon him. The links to the present are unmistakable. In 1935 Hitler introduced conscription, and by 1937 rear-mament was well under way. This, of course, was supposedly all in the interest of the re-establishment of the necessary balance of military power, and the preservation of peace. *Fridericus* makes of Frederick an inspired leader with the interests of his people at heart, and invites audiences to understand Hitler's politics as similarly motivated. Goebbels was not impressed with *Fridericus*, describing it as 'messed up'.[55] He oversaw the addition of a speech at the end in which Frederick appears to anticipate new conflicts if Prussia is not to starve – pointing forward to Hitler's quest for 'Lebensraum' for the Germans. But, even if it had not had this ending, and despite Goebbels' misgivings, *Fridericus* does an effective job of generating parallels between Frederick and Hitler.

Feature films, then, could be used to lend support to the Nazi tenet that Hitler's politics were a visionary response to present and future threats. During the war, the German film industry, in addition to making more films about political giants such as Bismarck and Frederick, brought to the screen a number of films focusing on pioneering creativity. One of the earliest examples is *Robert Koch*, made in 1938 and 1939, and first shown in September 1939. It follows microbiologist Robert Koch's search for the pathogen behind tuberculosis, a search which seems to earn him only enmity. He is dismissed as a charlatan and as satanic. Rudolf Virchow, a German physician known at the time as the 'pope of medicine', is also portrayed as rejecting Koch's research, until he is forced to acknowledge its successful outcome. Towards the end of the film, with fame now assured, Koch is praised for his 'unimaginable diligence' and 'intuitive genius'. *Robert Koch*'s depiction of its eponymous hero as an embattled visionary draws implicit parallels with Hitler. Hagiographic accounts of Hitler's rise to power liked to stress his struggle against adversity as he sought to realize his designs for a better Germany. Like all subsequent genius films, *Robert Koch* asks us to accept that the genius is above society, and beyond its rational and moral comprehension – a view which encouraged unquestioning acceptance of the politics of the allegedly inspired Führer. *Robert Koch*, starring Emil Jannings as Koch and Werner Krauß as Virchow, was one of the best-acted Nazi propaganda films. 'The *Robert Koch* film has become a positive experience for almost virtually everyone,' enthused one Security Service report.[56] It won the first prize at the 1939 Venice Biennale. Hitler sent a telegram to the director, Hans Steinhoff, to congratulate him. In his reply, Steinhoff, who had also directed *Hitler Youth Quex* and *The Old and the Young King*, promised Hitler to continue in the spirit of his previous films. 'To give you one-and-a-half hours of pleasure is a stimulus for me and a deeply felt wish,' Steinhoff wrote.[57] He continued to produce propaganda films, notably the anti-British *Uncle Krüger* (1941).

Images of Hitler

National Socialism, in its official pronouncements, was about the need for community, bonding, sacrifice, will, leadership and national self-defence.

117

The propaganda messages conveyed through Hitler's appearances in documentary film and newsreels, as well as through Hitler-like figures in feature films, were not different from messages conveyed in other media in the Third Reich. But cinema screens enabled audiences to get closer to Hitler than most of them otherwise managed in their lives. The sound of Hitler could be heard on the radio, but only the cinema provided moving image and sound. The attempt to immerse Germans in the sight and sound of Hitler even reached out to the countryside, as the Gau Film Offices brought film showings and newsreels to rural communities. When converted to the screen in excerpted form in newsreels and documentaries, Nazi meetings were concentrated into highlights which cameramen and cutters felt most effectively symbolized Hitler's supposed relationship with the people. Thus it was that newsreels and documentaries, supported by feature films, constantly reaffirmed the embodiment of community, bonding, sacrifice, will, leadership and national self-defence in the figure of the Führer himself. Hitler helped this process of identification by attending film premieres which focused on such values. Cinemas, physically and symbolically as well in terms of what was shown on screen, became a Nazi space, even as audiences went to the cinema to 'forget' their daily lives for an hour or two.

Cinema audiences were to be made to feel they had special access to Hitler through newsreels in particular, especially when they showed Hitler's more private moments, for instance relaxing at the Berghof. In 1938, the IG Farben chemical firm proposed producing copies of narrow-gauge films made by Hitler's pilot, Hans Baur, presumably for use in home cinemas.[58] The films included *The Führer Taking a Break* (in Wiesbaden), *The Führer's Birthday* and *Our Führer*, a combination of these two films.[59] Baur filmed Hitler on board his plane, as well as on a birthday boat trip on the *Scharnhorst*. He made sure he captured touching, kitschy images of young girls enthusiastically or shyly greeting the Führer.[60] If these films were indeed sold to some of those few wealthy families who had home cinemas, they will have given them the feeling they had particularly privileged access to the more private side of Hitler's life. The destructive side to Nazi politics, where it featured in newsreels or Nazi documentaries, was rarely connected to Hitler. As far as I can tell, the first direct connection drawn in newsreels between Hitler and Nazi politics towards Jews was the report on Hitler's 30 January 1939 speech to the Reichstag, where he threatened the 'annihilation of the Jewish race in Europe'.[61] The exclusionary aspects of the people's community were played down in newsreels in favour of inclusive, uplifting images of Hitler among the Germans. Documentaries related over and over his overcoming of the Weimar Republic, but were silent about his crushing of the rights and freedoms of minorities after 1933. Nazi feature films presented genius figures faced by all manner of difficulties; by implication, then, those who objected to Hitler were backward and opposed to progress. German cinemas became a place for fostering an image of Hitler as a caring, if at times strict and demanding patriot, a 'clean' image designed to encourage the broadest possible support for the Nazi leader.

6

Holding Court

HITLER AND ACTORS

Most German and Austrian actors who remained in Hitler's Germany proved willing to ply their trade under National Socialism. Hitler gave actors the feeling they mattered: he granted them tax concessions, attended their film premieres, sent them presents, gave them awards and titles, and sometimes offered his help and protection when they ran into difficulties. In return, actors starred in films that Hitler enjoyed, and which kept the masses entertained. And they participated in propaganda films when called upon, helping Hitler's political cause. But Hitler did not have affairs with actresses; he left that to Goebbels. Goebbels would have sacrificed his career for the sake of one actress, Lída Baarová. Hitler prevented this. In his own case, such a sacrifice would have been unthinkable.

Memoirs and Fact

Until the Second World War, Hitler spent much leisure time with artists of all kinds, particularly actors, as did Goebbels. A surviving guest list for an evening meal with Hitler and Goebbels at the Propaganda Ministry in October 1937 features the names of actresses such as Hilde Körber, Carola

Höhn, Erika Dannhoff, Fita Benkhoff, Lída Baarová and Lil Dagover, as well as the actor and director Veit Harlan.[1] Goebbels refers in his diary to social events, private or official, at which Hitler and actors were present. Hitler regularly invited film stars such as Brigitte Horney,[2] Renate Müller[3] and Jenny Jugo[4] to his home at Obersalzberg, and to events at the Reich Chancellery. To make issuing invitations easier, the Propaganda Ministry sent a list of the telephone numbers and addresses of 'all those involved in filmmaking' to Hitler's Adjutants Office in 1937.[5] Hitler's telephone book (as of 1939) contained, as one might expect, the names of Goebbels', Rosenberg's and Hitler's dentists, for instance, but it also included actors, particularly actresses, the latter including Leni Riefenstahl, Trude Marlen, Camilla Horn, Jenny Jugo, Jutta Freybe and Magda Schneider.[6]

During denazification, actors were cautious of admitting that they had attended social events at Hitler's behest, or spent time in his company on other occasions – unless they had no option. Even then they did their best to play the evidence down. When confronted with a photo showing her sitting beside Hitler at a concert, Russian-born actress Olga Chekhova awkwardly tried to explain this away as a coincidence.[7] But when they came to write their memoirs in the 1960s, actors were only too keen to relate the details of the afternoons or evenings they spent with Hitler. Now, their careers were no longer threatened by denazification, and their colourful accounts helped satisfy a never-ending public hunger for details about the Führer and his private life. Camilla Horn, for instance, recalled dining with Hitler and Goebbels. In contrast to other invitees such as Jugo and Chekhova, she was wearing make-up; no-one had informed her that Hitler preferred it if women did not.[8] The boxer Max Schmeling remembered that Hitler liked to 'pay court' to stars from the world of sport and the arts, including his actress-wife Anny Ondra, by sending them congratulations, flowers and invitations.[9] Veit Harlan, whose film *The Ruler* (1937) had pleased Hitler, recollected being invited together with the film's male lead, Emil Jannings, to the Reich Chancellery in 1937.[10] In 1939, the Dutch actor and singer Johannes Heesters received an invitation

to attend a reception for artists of all kinds in Munich organized in celebration of the Day of German Art. Heesters had no wish to go, as he had
engagements in Berlin. But then he received a telegram telling him Hitler
wanted him to appear as Danilo in a special performance of Hitler's
favourite operetta, Franz Lehár's *The Merry Widow*. The train to Munich,
Heesters relates, was full of artists: painters, musicians, singers, dancers,
writers and actors, all on their way to the reception. The journey cost
nothing, and neither did the wine and food enjoyed en route. Heesters did
his bidding as Danilo before attending the lavish reception at the House of
German Art. He was starving when he arrived; he remembers how Hitler
took a personal interest in ensuring he was given something to eat.[11]

In the reminiscences of actors, Hitler is often portrayed as a rather
ridiculous figure. Anecdotes are carefully chosen and theatrically shaped so
that, in one way or another, Hitler is cut down to size – by the actors themselves, who suggest to their post-war German readers that social occasions
involving the Nazi leader had offered them an opportunity to cock a snook
at him. In her memoirs, Hungarian actress, singer and dancer Marika
Rökk describes how celebrities at Hitler's receptions had to queue up to
meet the Führer. But, in contrast to others, she resolved not to do the
Hitler salute.[12] The Austrian actor Paul Hörbiger recounts that, at one of
Hitler's non-alcoholic receptions, he and fellow actors Theo Lingen and
Georg Alexander surreptitiously downed two bottles of champagne.[13]
Actress Zarah Leander recalls that, when she found herself standing next to
Hitler, she asked him whether he had never thought of doing something
with his hair, to which Hitler – after a moment of irritation – replied that
he had tried everything from oil and pomade through to various tinctures.
Nothing helped: 'my hair keeps falling down over my forehead'.[14]
According to her mother Olga, at a reception held in honour of a Mussolini
visit, the actress Ada Chekhova simply ignored Hitler's adjutant when he
told her no-one was allowed to leave before Hitler himself, a moment of
defiance which supposedly led to Olga Chekhova being 'struck from the
Reich Chancellery guest list'.[15] Chekhova also regales her post-war readers

with one of the most well-known theatre anecdotes from the Third Reich. At a reception in the Propaganda Ministry, the grande dame of German theatre, German-Dutch actress Adele Sandrock, was holding forth on her days as a star at Vienna's Burgtheater when Hitler interrupted with his own memories of the Burgtheater. When he pronounced it a pity that Jewish actors had achieved fame and honour there, Sandrock riposted: 'Herr Reich Chancellor, let's drop the subject. I don't want to hear about it. But – in case it's of interest to you, and between you and me – my best lovers were always Jews.' Hitler, allegedly, turned to stone.[16]

There are countless other examples in such autobiographies of Hitler – and Goebbels – being mocked, undermined and upstaged by actors. These stories may contain a grain of truth amongst the embellishments. That Theo Lingen and Georg Alexander might want to stage a small show of defiance by secretly consuming alcohol behind Hitler's back certainly rings true. Alexander's wife was Jewish, Lingen's 'half-Jewish', and both had problems in the Third Reich as a result.[17] But Hörbiger was one of several actors and directors to publicly declare their support for Hitler's annexation of Austria in 1938.[18] While in his autobiography he claimed he voted against the 'reunion' of Austria with the Reich, in a Viennese newspaper of 7 April 1938 he offered unequivocal support.[19] What most retrospective accounts by actors who had pursued their careers between 1933 and 1945 are missing is any exploration of the degree to which they might have admired Hitler or aspects of his politics. Rarely do actors ask if they were implicated in supporting the Nazi regime, directly or indirectly, preferring to present themselves as opposed to Nazism. The ridiculing of Hitler in their autobiographies is problematic however we view it: if they did not take Hitler seriously at the time, they displayed a crass political ignorance. If they decided not to take him seriously in retrospect, they were trivializing him and their own role during the Third Reich.

Other sources suggest that actors might have had a more positive attitude. In April 1933, Goebbels and Hitler enjoyed a 'film tea' with a host of actors such as Brigitte Helm, Renate Müller, Käthe Dorsch and Friedrich

Kayssler. 'They all feel very happy among us,' Goebbels notes.[20] He may have mistaken politeness for contentment, but perhaps the invited actors were happy to attend the 'film tea'. Actors often responded to Hitler's gifts,[21] or words of congratulations, with sycophantic telegrams or letters. When Hitler praised Emil Jannings for his performance in the title role of *Robert Koch*,[22] Jannings replied with a telegram assuring Hitler that 'your recognition gives me strength and motivates me to go on committing myself with all my ability to the global reputation of German film'.[23] Such telegrams and letters were not only penned in response to a gesture from Hitler. Marika Rökk may or may not have refused to do a Hitler salute, but she certainly wrote to Hitler in 1937 asking him to send her two signed photographs. He kindly obliged. One of these she passed on to her parents in Budapest, while the other found pride of place – as she claims in an effusive letter of thanks to Hitler – on her writing desk, providing her with inspiration for her future work.[24] At a reception after the 1937 Berlin premiere of a new production of Schiller's *The Maid of Orleans*, Hitler's personal adjutant Julius Schaub told Luise Ullrich, who was playing the lead role, that Hitler had long admired the play: 'there are certain parallels, he and Joan are from simple backgrounds, close to the people, chosen to rescue their nation. She heard voices, he hears the voice of destiny.' Ullrich, to judge from this sarcastically delivered anecdote in her autobiography, had little respect for Hitler.[25] Yet in January 1938 she wrote to him fondly recalling the time she had spent with him after the premiere of the *Maid of Orleans*. She remembered he had given her the 'great pleasure' of asking her to let him know when she was performing again – which she now duly did, adding it would bring her 'the greatest joy' to act for him once more.[26] Actors were not averse, either, to providing endorsements of Hitler's political mission. Erika von Thellmann, later to star in the first German colour feature film *Women Are the Better Diplomats* (1941), sent a birthday greeting to Hitler in 1937: 'We live as if on an oasis, surrounded by confusion, horror and destruction in the outside world, and with deep gratefulness we then think always of you, my Führer, and wish that God may continue to protect and to bless you.'[27]

Actors, of course, knew it was professional common sense to accept Hitler's invitations (which later they claimed to have repeatedly turned down). The actor Axel von Ambesser was more self-critical than most when, in the 1980s, he admitted to having been 'enthusiastic' about the chance to meet Hitler at an artists' reception in 1939, and to seeing in this meeting opportunities for his career. He even asks himself why no-one tried to kill Hitler, openly admitting his own cowardice. He justifies his failure to do so by arguing that actors are unsuitable for political or revolutionary acts; deeds were not their metier, rather they were 'players'.[28] This was a view shared to a degree by Goebbels: 'with the Führer among artists,' he wrote in his diary on 6 September 1938, 'at last something unpolitical again'. Artists, for Hitler and Goebbels, were a form of relaxation from politics – or, more generally, from the world of politicians, diplomats and the military. But it cannot be inferred from this that actors can be absolved of responsibility for participating in a film industry operating under a dictatorship – especially when, paradoxically, it was their very appearance of being unpolitical that made them politically useful. They were paraded by the Nazis as evidence that the Third Reich was also about glamour, not just ideology.

Securing Loyalty

Hitler paid court to actors, other artists and sports personalities, on one level at least, because he admired them. Given that he had once lived as a bohemian, tried to make a living as an artist and taken acting lessons from an opera singer, spending time with artists of all kinds was a way of reconnecting to a past lifestyle, of imagining an alternative biography. Given that he spent so much time watching films, moreover, it is not surprising he would want to surround himself with those who starred in them – that is, simply, a privilege of power. He seems to have been genuinely keen to impress actors through his presence, although whether he chose the right subjects to discuss is debatable. The actor and director Luis Trenker recalls

Hitler holding forth to assembled actors on the subject of tanks, cannons and machine-guns as early as 1934, 'hardly a year after he had come to power'.[29] In the same year, Hitler delivered a lengthy monologue on the subject of synthetic rubber to actresses Berta Drews and Maria Bard.[30] Perhaps Hitler regarded actors as an appropriate audience for testing out his rhetorical abilities, as if their admiring presence would confirm the quality of his own acting skills. On occasion, Hitler's guests were subjected to a lengthy showing of newsreel material, as Paul Hörbiger recalled of his invitation to the Reich Chancellery in 1935. He and fellow actors Theo Lingen and Georg Alexander, no doubt with ironic intent, decided to applaud the next time Hitler appeared in close-up in the newsreel, where-upon Hitler stood up to take a bow.[31] In his memoirs, Hörbiger arrogantly compares Hitler's bow to that of a 'ham actor'.[32] He overlooked the fact that Hitler was himself quite capable of irony. Hörbiger did recognize that the whole occasion was Hitler's way of staging a self-celebration.[33] Indeed, there was something significant about these private showings of newsreels, particularly to audiences of captive actors. It was Hitler's way of demon-strating that, in the Third Reich, he was the leading actor. 'The Führer must sway the masses like an actor,' Hitler had said in 1933.[34] What better way to prove his skills than by swaying actors themselves?

Max Schmeling believed that Hitler genuinely felt at home in the company of actors and other artists. He also recognized that Hitler's wish to share their company combined 'sincere feelings with an element of calculation'.[35] Whether actors were 'unpolitical' or not, by inviting them to sit at his table, Hitler sought to flatter them by allowing them to get close to the centre of power. Like Goebbels, Hitler wanted to ensure actors played their parts in Nazi public life as well as on stage and on screen, and the best way to do this was to give them the feeling they were special. This was done not just through invitations and presents, but by indulging actors' appetite for large fees. Despite constant complaints from the Nazi press up to the mid-1930s at least that actors were overpaid,[36] neither Hitler nor Goebbels seriously tried to put a stop to the problem.[37] And it was Hitler who pushed for tax concessions to be granted to 'all those prominent in the world of the arts', as Goebbels put it.[38] He decided that up to about 33 per cent of their income could be declared non-taxable as work-related expenditure. He soon increased this to 40 per cent for 'prominent artists'. The Finance Ministry complained that the list of 253 names suggested by Goebbels as eligible was too long. In the case of most of these names, largely actors,[39] the actual work-related expenditure was much less than 40 per cent.[40] However, a ruling was drawn up on 28 November respecting Hitler's wishes. It defined a 'film artist' as 'prominent' if he or she earned more than 100,000 Reichsmarks a year.[41] Hitler's tax concessions represented a substantial entitlement: in 1937, Hans Albers earned 562,000 Reichsmarks, for instance, Käthe Dorsch a more modest 152,700 Reichsmarks.[42] To the probable disappointment of actors, however, the ruling on tax concessions did not apply for long, because Goebbels withdrew the privilege when the war began.[43] Goebbels and Hitler also set about overseeing the introduction of general pension plans for those working in the arts.[44] A pension scheme for members of the Reich Theatre Chamber came into effect in 1938, benefiting many who had acted in films as well as theatre.

Hitler's much-publicized visits, as Reich chancellor, to the cinema, his commissioning of films by Leni Riefenstahl, and his regular presence at film-related events between 1933 and 1939 helped to create the impression that, under Hitler, actors and directors were to enjoy the highest state profile. Even if Goebbels was the driving force in film matters, Hitler played his part too. In 1937, Goebbels set about a state takeover of Ufa and made renewed efforts to restructure the film company to improve production. Hitler, who approved of Goebbels' measures, was kept informed.[45] One of these measures was to include actors and directors in Ufa's supervisory board: Mathias Wieman, Eugen Klöpfer, Paul Hartmann and Karl Ritter, for instance, were allowed to imagine they had a serious role to play by becoming members of it. More generally, Goebbels, with Hitler's agreement, oversaw the inclusion of directors and actors in administrative positions within the Reich Theatre and Reich Film Chambers, for instance. Entrusting them with such quasi-official positions ensured their collusion. It may have been Goebbels who was behind the establishment of the Reich Film Archive or the creation of the National Film and Book Prize, but Hitler attended the opening of the former on 4 February 1935[46] as well as the award ceremonies for the latter. Together with Goebbels, he chose the directors who won the National Film and Book Prize,[47] and they were appreciative; after winning it in 1936, director Carl Froelich sent a telegram to Hitler to express his 'joyful and heartfelt thanks'.[48] Hitler also had a hand in choosing which actors should be awarded the Nazi accolade of 'state film actor', and in awarding professorial titles – to Karl Ritter, for instance, in 1939.

This conferral of privileges upon directors and actors inevitably impli-cated them in Nazi politics, and with it came the expectation that they would, when called upon, place themselves at the disposal of the regime – during the annual Winter Aid programme, for instance, when they did their bit to collect money. Winter Aid had been set up under Chancellor Heinrich Brüning in 1931, but the Nazis soon turned it into propaganda for their supposed social conscience. Actors helped to popularize the charity drive. Photographs were published of Hitler inserting coins into the cans they carried, adding to the overall effect. To be fair, actors were put under pressure to take part, and to contribute a donation themselves. If the donation was not forthcoming, they were reminded by letter 'not to exclude' themselves 'from the Führer's great social undertaking'.[49] The Nazis also organized widely publicized Film Balls. These were not simply actor get-togethers. In 1935, the Film Ball took place in Berlin during the International Film Congress, attended by delegates from various European countries. The congress was designed to place Nazi Germany at the head of a project to create a more integrated European film market.[50] The Film Ball was the social part of this political enterprise. Goebbels, 'to give this event an appropriately representative character', insisted that those involved in the film industry make themselves available.[51] In 1938, Hitler financed the Film Ball in Munich because it was attended by the Yugoslavian minister president and his wife: actors and directors provided a pleasant ambience for his visit.[52] In such situations, actors were placed in the roles of cultural representatives of Nazism, whether they liked it or not.

Often, they were used as ambassadors for Nazism's efforts to be perceived as international and open to the outside world, for all its nationalist ethos and dismissal of cosmopolitanism as 'Jewish'. A significant number of leading Third Reich actors were not German or Austrian at all, particularly actresses: Lída Baarová was Czech, Pola Negri Polish, Marika Rökk of Hungarian descent, Olga Chekhova was born in the Russian Empire (in what is today Armenia) and Zarah Leander was Swedish. Lilian Harvey was half-English, Ilse Werner half-Dutch. Several Third Reich actors were international stars, such as Emil Jannings. A number starred in films not just in Germany, but elsewhere, such as Brigitte Horney, who acted in British and German films in the 1930s. In 1938, Goebbels began to express concern that there were too many foreigners in German films.[53] But he hardly discouraged this; his relationship with Lída Baarová appeared more like an encouragement.[54] Besides, the international flavour to the German film industry could be used to demonstrate Nazi Germany's supposed urbanity. Film historian Gerd Albrecht, in a seminal study from 1969, came to the conclusion that, of the feature films made under Nazism, only 153 could be classified as propaganda films, while 941 were 'non-propaganda films'.[55] This assumed discrepancy is often pointed to, not least by former Third Reich actors, as evidence that most German films produced between 1933 and 1945 were unpolitical. But, if we accept this debatable claim for a moment, it misses a very important point. When Nazi-period films that appeared charming and harmless were shown in democratic countries such as Britain and the USA, this helped to create an impression abroad that Germany was perhaps not quite as bad under Hitler as it might seem from the newspapers. And, when German cinemagoers streamed into cinemas to watch German film comedies, they escaped both mentally and emotionally from the National Socialist world. 'Unpolitical' films momentarily released and neutralized any dissatisfaction audiences might feel with the political order.

That Third Reich film directors produced and actors acted in comedies and musicals, then, is hardly a sign of quiet protest. That Hitler wanted more propaganda films than Goebbels was able to deliver may be true, but it does not follow from this that he did not want comedies and musicals – his private film viewing proves the opposite. Actors who remained in Germany after the exclusion of Jews and others from cultural life, and who went on to participate in light-hearted films, were aiding in the production of a pernicious illusion. Besides, when asked to take part in propaganda films, not many of them refused. The few examples of actors who did demonstrates that some flexibility was possible. Albrecht argues that only a seventh of all German films premiered during the Nazi period were propagandistic.[56] But he classes some films as non-propagandistic which were, in fact, propagandistic.[57] Moreover, according to his own statistics, eighty-four actors had leading roles in one or more of the propaganda films. Many more had smaller roles.[58]

One only needs to look at key propaganda films from the pre-war period to identify the level of involvement of leading actors in films promoting Nazi beliefs. Paul Wegener, for instance, famous for his role in the classic horror film *The Golem: How He Came into the World* (1920), featured in Franz Wenzler's SA film *Hans Westmar* (1933). Hans Albers and Eugen Klöpfer took lead roles in Gustav Ucicky's anti-Soviet feature film *Refugees* (1933), while Maria Koppenhöfer and Friedrich Kayssler starred in Peter Hagen's *Frisians in Distress* (1935), the distress in question being experienced by Volga Germans at the hands of the communists. Karl Ritter's anti-British espionage film *Traitors* (1936) starred Willy Birgel and Lída Baarová, while Ritter's First World War film *Operation Michael* (1937) praising self-sacrifice featured Mathias Wieman, Heinrich George and Willy Birgel. Hitler's beliefs and politics were relayed and reinforced through propagandistic feature films to which important actors lent gravitas and credibility by taking part. This was the loyalty Hitler had reckoned with in exchange for the special status he accorded actors.

Hitler and Actresses

Film stars may have enjoyed special status, but it is unlikely Hitler slept with actresses. Max Schmeling's comment about Hitler's attitude to artists being 'calculating' is the key here.[59] He may have been attracted to actresses, and he certainly admired them and enjoyed their company, but his approach to them was also based on expediency, and that left little room for intimacy. Yet rumours of his affairs with actresses abound, sometimes sensationalized by adding sordid details. According to film director and producer Alfred Zeisler, Hitler not only slept with Renate Müller, but insisted she satisfy his masochistic impulses, rolling around on the floor and asking her to kick him.[60] Müller died in hospital after falling, inebriated and under the influence of morphine, from the first floor of her villa in Berlin in 1937. Her death can be connected to the pressure she was under from Goebbels because of her relationship with a Jew, Georg Deutsch, but there is no evidence she was murdered by the Gestapo, as is sometimes claimed. Nor is there evidence of a relationship with Hitler.[61] But the Zeisler story about Müller continues to circulate.[62] As do the stories about Müller, as well as the actress Jenny Jugo and Hitler, which were served up in the fictitious and utterly salacious memoir *I Was Hitler's Maid*. Probably written by one John Beevor, this was first published in 1940 under the name of Pauline Kohler as anti-Hitler propaganda, and subsequently republished in 1993 without so much as a word of critical commentary. It describes how Jugo was filmed doing a striptease at the Berghof. Hitler, so the fiction continues, then watched the film in his private cinema.[63] Admittedly, such stories are complemented – or contradicted – by tales of monk-like sexual abstinence on Hitler's part. In her book on actors Gustaf Gründgens and Marianne Hoppe, Carola Stern relates the following anecdote. When invited by Hitler to dinner in 1934 – at that time, he was residing opposite the Hotel Kaiserhof in Berlin – Hoppe asked him to tell her something about his private life. By way of answer, he showed her his bedroom: all it contained was an iron bedframe, a chair and a light bulb. 'How uncomfortable,' she said, and left the room.[64] Views of

Hitler as ascetic or as freely indulging in sado-masochistic bedroom games seek to explain his criminality either in terms of pathological sexual self-denial or perversion. Hoppe also relates that Hitler rubbed his knees and 'had a kind of orgasm' when watching a violent scene in Trenker's film *The Rebel* (1932), an anecdote which prompted German author Volker Pilgrim to suggest that a sadistic form of sexual deviance drove Hitler to become a mass-murderer. What propelled those Germans who led normal married lives to commit genocide, Pilgrim does not tell us. In any case, as psychologist Erich Fromm puts it, Hitler's sexual life does not 'explain anything more about him than what we know already'.[65]

Other actresses were rumoured to have been Hitler's lovers – Pola Negri, for instance, the star of *Mazurka* (1935). In her memoirs, Negri writes of the 'extraordinary rumour' she heard when she returned to Germany in 1936 to make her next film, *Moscow–Shanghai* (1936). People thought she was 'under the special protection of the Führer' and began to pay her 'very special attentions'. Her simplest wish 'was granted with the speed of a royal command'. Yet, as she says, 'I had never even met Hitler.'[66] Dancer and actress Lea Kruse, or Lea Niako as she called herself, is another name mentioned in connection with Hitler's supposed amorous escapades. According to director Géza von Cziffra, Hitler's chief adjutant Wilhelm Brückner organized secret trysts between Hitler and Niako – at exactly the same time she was having a relationship with the Polish spy Jurik von Sosnowski (1933–34). Hitler, Cziffra writes, was 'infatuated' with Niako.[67] Hitler, we read elsewhere, 'worshipped' Niako.[68] In 1934, Niako helped German counterintelligence to uncover the spy network; Sossnowski was arrested, and two women working in the Reichswehr Ministry who had furnished him with military secrets were executed.[69] According to Cziffra, it was Hitler's Reich Chancellery that was responsible for amnestying Niako. Goebbels claims it was he and Julius Schaub, Hitler's personal adjutant, who 'got the little dancer Kruse off the hook, as she is clearly innocent'. He adds with a note of self-satisfaction: 'it is nice to give unhappy people their lives back'.[70] Niako clearly wanted to return to her dancing career, but Goebbels was unsure: 'a difficult topic considering the treason trial'.[71] In the end, he helped her out by arranging for the German Opera House to give her a contract,[72] but she was rarely if ever allowed to perform. In 1939, unhappy at this situation, Niako turned to Hitler, but found herself negotiating instead with one of Hitler's adjutants, Alwin-Broder Albrecht.[73] She wanted a permanent contract at Ufa, but Albrecht and Goebbels were only able to get an agreement from Ufa that she would be 'given the possibility to act in films with dance sequences'.[74] When Niako protested vehemently at this, Albrecht effectively washed his hands of the matter: 'I won't answer any more of your letters.'[75]

Niako is a mysterious figure whom Hitler may have assisted, but there is no more to it than that. Géza von Cziffra's memoirs are based on unsubstantiated speculation. In any case, Hitler soon tired of being bothered with her problems and passed her on, as so often with those who wrote begging letters, to his adjutants. Niako suggested she enjoyed 'the protection of the Führer', but, had that been the case, Albrecht would hardly have broken off contact.[76] What the Niako–Albrecht correspondence demonstrates is that actresses were prepared to use whatever contact they had once had with Hitler to try to reignite their careers. Hanna Ralph, for instance, who had played Brunhilde in Fritz Lang's *The Nibelungs* (1924), a film much admired by Hitler, wrote to him on 12 May 1939 asking for the 'brief audience' he had promised her when they met at a reception. In a severe professional and personal crisis, Ralph told Hitler in her letter he was the only one 'into whose hands I can put my fate'.[77] Hitler left his adjutant Schaub to deal with the matter, and she sent Schaub letter after letter beseeching him to arrange a meeting with Hitler.[78] Schaub, a past master in handling requests of Hitler, politely shilly-shallied. The meeting with Hitler did materialize, however; he met her in his flat in Munich on 15 July 1939.[79] Hitler himself suggested finding her a permanent position at the Burgtheater in Vienna. Heinz Hilpert at the Deutsches Theater in Berlin eventually took her on for a year, but was reluctant to do it for a second year. Writing to Reichsdramaturg Rainer Schlösser, Hilpert stated that 'an actress who needs high connections to find any kind of work can't be very highly qualified'.[80]

Those who addressed pleas for help to Hitler, such as Niako and Ralph, were well aware they were living in a dictatorship. The same applies to those who turned directly to Hitler's adjutants, such as the young dancer Lilo Schneider. In 1939, she appealed to Wilhelm Brückner, with whom she was personally acquainted, for help in securing positions both for herself and her fiancé.[81] The assumption was that a word from Hitler or one of his influential personal aides would get the help needed. It was important, in other words, to be able to play the Hitler card.[82] In all three cited cases, the help provided by Hitler and Brückner did bear fruit, but Hitler soon tired of playing the kind uncle. And he was not prepared to impose actors or actresses on unwilling film or theatre companies.[83] Niako was no doubt expecting her connections to him to open any doors she wanted. Another actress to discover that appealing to the Führer was a source of help, but not indefinitely, was Lída Baarová, a Czech actress first hired by Ufa in the mid-1930s. She fell in love with her co-star Gustav Fröhlich and remained in Germany, becoming a favourite with moviegoers. Baarová's connections with Hitler and, most famously, Goebbels, with whom she had a turbulent affair, deserve further exploration. Baarová found herself at the centre of a political and emotional tussle which reveals clearly that Hitler's admiration for actresses had its limits.

Hitler probably first met Baarová in January 1935 during a visit with Goebbels to the film set for Gerhard Lamprecht's *Barcarole*, a love story set in Vienna.[84] According to Baarová, Hitler was interested in her, and invited her to tea.[85] There, Hitler said she reminded him of somebody both beautiful and tragic in his life: 'to her horror, she later realised this was Hitler's former lover and half-niece, Angela Raubal, who was found dead in her Munich flat in 1931, aged 23, after shooting herself in the heart with a pistol'.[86] Baarová herself could only speculate on why she reminded Hitler of Raubal: 'perhaps [Raubal] had Sudeten German ancestors, from whom she had got slightly Slavic features'.[87] Hitler invited Baarová once or twice more for afternoon tea, but after that they only met at social gatherings. Baarová's lover at the time, Gustav Fröhlich, claimed it was she who initiated the meetings with

Hitler. When Nazi officials tried to get her thrown out of the film business because she was Czech and not German, Baarová, recalling how positively Hitler had reacted to her when they first met, contacted his adjutant Schaub. Schaub then arranged a rendezvous with Hitler, who immediately put an end to attempts to oust her. Not only that: 'from then on, Lída could choose whatever roles she wanted, and set her own fees'.[88] Baarová's meetings with Hitler prompted Fröhlich's jealousy. After the third encounter, he quipped sarcastically, 'if you intend to become the mother of the nation, please let me know in time, so I can emigrate'.[89] But there is no reason not to believe Baarová's claim that her relationship with Hitler remained platonic. Fröhlich had nothing to fear from Hitler. Goebbels, however, was a different proposition.

Baarová got to know Goebbels well during the 1936 Berlin Olympics. Their affair inevitably put strain on Baarová's already faltering relationship with Fröhlich. One evening, Fröhlich saw Baarová standing next to Goebbels' car. 'Now, at last, I know exactly what I have to contend with,' he shouted at Goebbels. This confrontation was embellished in the recounting until it took on the form in which it circulated throughout and beyond Berlin's film business: Fröhlich, so the story now ran, had slapped Goebbels.[90] Cabarettist Werner Finck, certainly not one to kowtow to the Nazis (in 1935, he was imprisoned in Esterwegen concentration camp), came up with a comic line which also did the rounds in Berlin. Literally translated, the humour is lost in English: 'Who wouldn't like to be cheerful?' The key to the joke is the German word for cheerful: 'fröhlich'. The relationship between Goebbels and Baarová was an open secret. According to Baarová, journalists in film magazines and popular newspapers began to hint at it in their reporting, so that knowledge soon spread.[91] Extraordinarily, it took much longer to reach the ears of Magda Goebbels. Initially, she seemed prepared to tolerate her husband's affair, but eventually told Hitler. This was in the late summer of 1938, at the politically sensitive time of the German–Czech crisis. Hitler was furious. The last thing he wanted was a propaganda minister consorting with a Czech actress while his ministry oversaw the production of anti-Czech propaganda.

On 16 August 1938, Goebbels confided to his diary that he had had a long and serious conversation with Hitler about the situation, and recognized he would have to give Baarová up: 'a hard, terrible life, dedicated only to duty. My youth is at an end.' Furtively, he tried to go on seeing her, but a further meeting with Hitler in October proved decisive. Hitler flew into a rage at the suggestion that Goebbels divorce Magda – their marriage, after all, which so far had produced five children, was promoted in the Third Reich as exemplary.[92] Hitler imposed a three-month cooling-off period during which he expected matters to be resolved.[93] According to Graf von Helldorff, police president of Berlin, who was present at the meeting of Goebbels and his wife with Hitler, Hitler had told Goebbels, 'He who makes history has no right to a private life.'[94] Helldorff informed Baarová that she was prohibited from taking on any new roles in films or plays. She was also forbidden from leaving the country.[95] A few days later, a film in which she was starring, Gerhard Lamprecht's *The Gambler* (1938), had its Berlin premiere. When General Kirileff, played by Eugen Klöpfer, suggested to his daughter, played by Baarová, that she try to get money from 'her doctor' (meaning Dr Tronka, played by Albrecht Schoenhals), people in the auditorium began to laugh. There were catcalls. It was likely to have been Himmler or Hanke – state secretary in the Propaganda Ministry as well as confidant (and lover) of Magda Goebbels – who organized this 'protest'.[96] It culminated in calls for the 'minister's whore' to be 'thrown out'. Baarová took the decision to leave Germany. Sensing she might do this, Hitler, reluctant to see her depart lest she provide the foreign press with unsavoury details of her affair with Goebbels, sent his chief adjutant, Julius Schaub, to instruct her not to cross the border: 'otherwise something unpleasant might happen to you'.[97] Whether Schaub was warning her or threatening her, or both, was unclear. Baarová nevertheless fled to what was left of Czechoslovakia in November 1938, and returned to her home city of Prague.

Goebbels never lost interest in Baarová despite ending the affair. In November 1940 he visited Prague's Barrandov studios. To ensure he would not be able to meet Baarová, the Gestapo, or at least so it was claimed, whisked her away, and kept a close eye on Goebbels, reporting that he reacted furiously when he realized she was not among the actresses present at a reception held in his honour.[98] Hitler did not forget her either. Trying to rebuild her film career in Prague, she faced obstruction from Nazi officials who wanted to make her pay for her relationship with Goebbels, or believed she was subject to a ban in the Protectorate as well as the Reich.[99] In late 1941, Martin Bormann wrote to Goebbels telling him that Hitler wanted Baarová to be permitted to act in German and Czech films.[100] Goebbels confirmed this in conversation with Karl Hermann Frank, state secretary for the Protectorate, in June 1942.[101] Frank then informed Baarová, adding that Goebbels wanted permission extended to other Czech actors provided they were prepared to make their names more German-sounding; Baarová promptly declared herself ready to take the name of 'Frau Baar'.[102] Still she could not find work. In July and again in November 1944, Karl Hermann Frank wrote to Ernst Kaltenbrunner, head of the Reich Security Main Office, asking him to 'clarify the matter' so that Baarová could take part in German films.[103] Reich Film Superintendent Hans Hinkel called on Baarová in June 1944 to assure her of Goebbels' support. Hinkel also suggested she talk to Hitler, who was 'very well-disposed' towards her.[104] The end of the war ended Baarová's hope of a re-engagement in German film. She fled Prague in April 1945.

Baarová later suspected that Magda Goebbels had been behind her difficulties in finding work.[105] When Hinkel indicated to Baarová in June 1944 that he might have a word with Hitler, he said he would 'first have to negotiate with a certain person in private', although this person was 'always ill'. He probably meant Magda Goebbels, whose health had been stuttering for some time.[106] That Magda remained suspicious of Baarová is quite possible. One can only speculate as to why the Nazi Security Service took such an interest in Baarová and Goebbels in 1940, or why Frank needed the Reich Security Main Office to 'clarify' Baarová's status as a film actress as late as 1944. Magda may have been behind all this, or Himmler. It may also have had to do with Baarová's relations with Paul Thümmel, a double agent working for the Nazis and the Czech resistance.[107] What is certain is that there was distrust of Baarová. Allowing her to act in German films would, perhaps, have brought her back into contact with Goebbels at some level.[108] Surprisingly, this concern does not seem to have been shared by Hitler. Then again, he did not unduly persevere in his attempts to help her find work. As with other actresses who asked for help, he eventually just lost interest.

Goebbels' affair with Baarová nearly ended his career as Propaganda Minister, and there were those who would have liked to see him fall: not least Alfred Rosenberg, chief Nazi ideologue, who, in December 1938 – in connection with Goebbels' affair with Baarová – told Himmler that Goebbels represented 'morally the biggest burden for National Socialism'. Himmler, for his part, told Rosenberg about the 'dozens of cases' of women whom Goebbels had 'sexually coerced' and who had reported this to Magda Goebbels and the Gestapo. Some of these reports Himmler had passed on to Hitler.[109] In this instance, however, Rosenberg and Himmler missed the point. Goebbels had not coerced Baarová: they had fallen in love. Hitler was prepared to tolerate Goebbels' sexual excesses. What he was not prepared to accept was a love affair which threatened to end Goebbels' exemplary National Socialist marriage and lead to his resignation. The case of Baarová makes clear that, while Hitler and Goebbels both enjoyed the company of actresses, this is as far as any similarity between their interest in them extends. Hitler's relationships with actresses did not go beyond occasional private audiences and conversations at receptions. Goebbels' relationships with them began, by all accounts, on the casting couch.[110] Hitler kept a certain distance; Goebbels lost it completely. In 1935, the close connections between politicians and actors in the Third Reich found harmonious expression in the extravagant wedding between Göring and Emmy Sonnemann. For a brief period in 1938, in the case of Goebbels and Baarová, it seemed as if these connections might lead to a political disaster, at least from Hitler's point of view.[111]

Baarová became a political liability because her affair transgressed the boundaries that ultimately divided cultural and political life in the Third Reich. At certain times, without knowing it, she became a pawn in the power game between Rosenberg, Himmler and Goebbels, and, to a degree at least, a victim of the intersecting loyalties between Hitler and Magda Goebbels, Magda Goebbels and Hanke, and Goebbels and Hitler. Baarová, to judge from her memoir, never really grasped the political implications of her affair. She was not the only one. On 14 March 1939, the Viennese-born actress Hilde Körber, who was married to Veit Harlan at the time, wrote a desperate letter to Hitler. Körber, a close friend of Baarová's, had acted as a go-between for Goebbels and Baarová in 1937 and 1938. She possibly prevented Baarová from attempting suicide when Goebbels broke with her. Subsequently, she found herself ostracized. 'What have I done, my Führer,' she asked, 'to make you exclude me from every community of artists, so that I am not invited to receptions any more and have to bear all the resulting rumours, shame and injury?'

The sycophantic tone of Körber's letter is typical of quite a few of the telegrams and letters that actors – and particularly actresses – wrote to Hitler. It ends with an intense plea on her own behalf for forgiveness, but also on behalf of her children:[112] 'if I were only able to stand before you, my Führer, you and you above all would see into my soul, see who I am, what I am, how I am. If I have done anything wrong, then I will atone for it ten times over, but I beg you, my Führer, to recognise the goodness in me.'[113] Körber almost relates to Hitler as one might to a divinity. As we have seen, actors and actresses retrospectively cast Hitler as a somewhat ridiculous figure, and there will have been those who saw him that way from the beginning. But the truth is that a number of actors idealized him, or at least imagined him as standing above the rough world of politics, despite the fact that he stood at its very summit. There were actors who chose to view Hitler as he saw himself, as Germany's redeemer, as a moral authority, rather than by what they surely must have known about his racism and persecution of opponents. At best, this was naïve.

Useful Idols

In a 2007 German TV series, the popular historian Guido Knopp argued that media stars such as actors Hans Albers, Heinrich George, Heinz

Rühmann and Marika Rökk had placed themselves at the disposal of the Nazi regime. They had, as Knopp put it in the title of the series and accompanying book, been 'Hitler's useful idols'.[114] Hitler knew that, in the Third Reich, the only public figures who could seriously compete with him in terms of popularity were actors. It was better, then, to bring them onside, so that they would not rival his popularity, but place theirs in the service of his. In early January 1939, Hitler held a New Year reception in the New Reich Chancellery for Wehrmacht and police leaders, and foreign ambassadors to Germany. 'Here, I am the representative of the German people,' he portentously declared.[115] In early March, it was the turn of those involved in German cultural life to view the New Reich Chancellery.[116] According to actress Anneliese Uhlig, Hitler took the greatest pleasure in showing off the impressive interiors, and providing detailed information on the material used, the origins of the furniture and the dimensions of the rooms. Uhlig stresses that *all* the invited guests from the world of the arts accepted the invitation, so curious were they to see the new building: 'there, for instance, sailing through the guests like a frigate with convoy, was Zarah Leander with dark glasses and her mane of red hair'.[117] The reception for artists at the Reich Chancellery was intended to impress on them that Hitler, through his architecture, was the grandest artist of them all. In attending, they not only satisfied their curiosity, they also paid homage to the power manifest in that architecture. Hitler liked to be acknowledged by famous actors because their fame then reflected his even greater fame. Actors do not seem to have realized this at the time, or if they did, subsequently they were not prepared to admit it. Nor were they ready to admit that the process was a reciprocal one: they felt elevated to the highest status by Hitler's attentions, and responded by cooperating with the Third Reich. They were indeed Hitler's 'useful idols'.

7

Watching over War
HITLER AND WARTIME CINEMA

During the war, Hitler used individual films to assert his authority. Dissatisfaction at the film *Victory in the West* (1941), which documented the defeat of France, prompted him to step up ideological training within the army, and he used a feature film about Frederick the Great, *The Great King* (1942), as a vehicle for admonishing his generals. His interest in film and the newsreels became bound up almost entirely with the Nazi war effort. Overall, he remained the supreme arbiter in film matters; Goebbels still deferred to him in disputes over individual films, and issues of general film policy.

Documentary Film

In 1944, Hitler told his generals: 'everyone can imagine this war is not comfortable for me. I've been cut off from the outside world for five years now. I haven't visited a theatre, listened to a concert, seen a film. I live only for the single task of [leading] this battle.'[1] Hitler's wartime abstinence from film viewing was later confirmed by some in his immediate entourage. 'Hitler did not view any more films, just the newsreels,' writes Karl

Wilhelm Krause, Hitler's valet.[2] Hitler's pilot Hans Baur even recalls Hitler making a solemn declaration: 'as long as the war is on, I will not go to the cinema or the theatre, or to a concert'.[3] Julius Schaub, Hitler's personal adjutant, claims Hitler did not watch any more films,[4] while Traudl Junge, Hitler's secretary, tells us Hitler 'denied himself this form of entertainment' after the outbreak of war.[5] Even Goebbels asserts that Hitler 'is not watching any films during the war'.[6] This seems plausible: Hitler had more pressing things to do. Whereas before the war he would have been watching films at 10 p.m., during the war 10 p.m. was a time reserved for briefings.[7] He was directing a very real global drama of far greater moment than anything that might be represented in film. Nevertheless, that Hitler desisted completely from film viewing is overstated. Such claims help to foster a Nazi-period myth: namely that Hitler, dedicated as he was to the defence of his people (as he interpreted the war), simply had no time for culture. Above all, in the case of documentary films, he kept a close eye on developments.

The first Nazi documentary to chart the effects of the Wehrmacht's onslaught was Fritz Hippler's *Campaign in Poland* (1940). From Hitler's adjutant Max Wünsche's record of Hitler's activities in late 1939,[8] we know Hitler watched this film at least twice. Produced by the Reich Propaganda Leadership, *Campaign in Poland* was first shown on 8 October 1939 to a select audience.[9] The Army High Command expressed reservations, objecting that the film did not adequately reflect the army's role.[10] Hitler first watched *Campaign in Poland* on 10 October.[11] The fact that reporting on it effectively stopped, and that a second version had to be produced, may suggest his support of the army's concerns. According to Goebbels, a new draft script was drawn up, and Goebbels himself made changes.[12] The resulting new version Goebbels found 'really excellent'.[13] But Hitler, who watched the revised version on 11 December, was still not satisfied, and asked for further alterations.[14] On 14 December, Hitler's adjutant Alwin-Broder Albrecht wrote to Hippler, informing him that Hitler had taken exception to the fact that, on a map, the Protectorate of Bohemia and

Moravia was distinguished by a different colour from the rest of the Reich.[15] Clearly, any unintended implication that the Protectorate was under other than Nazi control was to be avoided.

Film historian Jürgen Trimborn has suggested that *Campaign in Poland* was originally planned as a Leni Riefenstahl film.[16] At the outset of war, Hitler ordered that a 'Special Film Troop Riefenstahl' be set up by the Propaganda Ministry; among the team were Walter Traut, Sepp Allgeier and Gustav and Otto Lantschner, all experienced cameramen who had worked with Riefenstahl before.[17] After the war, Riefenstahl was vague about the function of this group. At one point, she claimed that, with Germany and Poland at war, she was expected to make propaganda films 'vital to the war effort'.[18] At another, she maintained that she organized a group of cameramen so she could provide reports directly from the front.[19] The activities of her group attracted much less attention after the war than the fact that, while filming in Poland, Riefenstahl had witnessed Wehrmacht atrocities against Jews on 12 September 1939 in the town of Konskie. This is proven by a famous photograph of her looking on in horror.[20] Yet she consistently claimed she had witnessed the mishandling – not the killing – of Poles, and that she looked horrified because soldiers had pointed their guns at her when she protested.[21] If Riefenstahl had been making her own documentary about the Polish campaign, one wonders why she had to send material back to the Propaganda Ministry. Yet Hippler denied that Riefenstahl had played any part in the gestation of *Campaign in Poland*. That Riefenstahl met with representatives of the Wehrmacht to discuss her film unit's activities also raises as yet unanswered questions.[22] It is possible Hitler entrusted her with a special film focusing on his role in the war against Poland.[23] What is certain is that part of the material her 'Special Film Troop' filmed did find its way into *Campaign in Poland*, as both Sepp Allgeier and Gustav Lantscher are among those credited in the documentary.

Hitler's wishes (beyond minor changes to maps) for *Campaign in Poland* are as unclear as Riefenstahl's role in it. But we know from Hitler's involvement in *Heroes in Spain* that he liked documentaries to be up to date. The initial version of *Campaign in Poland* only covered the period up to 20 September 1939, ending with Hitler's entry into Danzig.[24] The second version concluded with Hitler's triumphant entry into Warsaw on 5 October 1939. Hitler's intervention ensured that *Campaign in Poland* became a Nazi film monument to the total crushing of Poland. When the film went on general release in February 1940, some viewers still complained it was in essence a concatenation of old newsreel clips.[25] But Goebbels hailed it as 'a huge success'.[26] Security Service reports tell of spontaneous applause in some cinemas, and the film was frequently sold out.[27] Even if it was no longer current news, *Campaign in Poland* served to disseminate the view of reality Hitler liked to project: that Germany, surrounded by enemies bent on annihilating the Reich, had had no option but to respond to aggression by taking up weapons. According to the film, Hitler wanted peace, not war, and the Wehrmacht only marched into Poland to rescue persecuted Germans and liberate Danzig from Polish 'terror'. The film ended with a map of 'Greater Germany', now including western Poland, as if the war had solely been about restoring German borders. In effect, *Campaign in Poland* was a filmed version of Hitler's 19 September 1939 speech in Danzig; it reproduced every one of his defensive arguments for invading Poland.[28]

That the film did not reach German cinemas till February 1940 had the advantage that its portrayal of the West, and above all Britain, as hypo-critical and bellicose helped prepare the Germans for the attack on Western Europe. In April 1940, another film premiered in Germany which, like *Campaign in Poland*, stressed the supremacy of the German military: *Baptism of Fire*, directed by Hans Bertram. *Baptism of Fire* had been commissioned by the German air force to highlight the role of air power in the defeat of Poland.[29] The effect of these two films on another branch of the German Armed Forces, the army, was not entirely positive. If *Campaign in Poland* had set out to glorify Hitler, *Baptism of Fire* glorified Göring's pilots. The army felt overlooked. To ensure that its achievements got the appropriate film coverage in future, Commander-in-Chief of the

German Army Walther von Brauchitsch commissioned the Army Branch of Armed Forces' Propaganda under Kurt Hesse to produce a feature on the army's role in the campaign against Western Europe.[30] Goebbels, wary of Brauchitsch, immediately set about planning his own film. Brauchitsch offered to cooperate, while reminding Goebbels that the army would continue to produce its own film, and pointing out that Hitler had agreed to be filmed for it.[31] The army's film, *Victory in the West* (1941), was put together from material filmed by the Army Film Centre's film teams and propaganda companies, as well as from captured British, French and Belgian footage. It was directed, among others, by Svend Noldan, and focused largely on the conquest of the Low Countries and France. The first version was viewed in the Propaganda Ministry on 21 November 1940. Armed Forces weapons inspectors objected to the showing of particular types of artillery on the grounds that Hitler did not want foreign weaponry on display.[32] This criticism was echoed by the Armed Forces censorship department.[33] Meanwhile, Kurt Hesse was incensed to discover that the Propaganda Ministry had pressed on and was producing its own documentary film, *On the Roads of Victory*.[34]

So, even before Hitler saw *Victory in the West*, Goebbels was in dispute with the army over who got to produce film propaganda. On 22 December 1940, Goebbels notes in his diary that he and Hitler had 'watched the Army High Command's film about the campaign in the West. It is not quite satisfactory.'[35] There was no overall line of argument, Goebbels complained, and the collaboration between different parts of the Armed Forces had not been brought out clearly. Goebbels was for banning it: Hitler, he wrote, agreed.[36] Kurt Hesse, recalling Hitler's viewing of the film many years later, writes not of a ban, but of Hitler's requests for the message behind certain passages to be strengthened or toned down.[37] Certainly, changes were required, and a revised version was seen by Hitler on 21 January 1941 in the Reich Chancellery. According to cameraman Hans Ertl, who also attended the screening, Hitler was 'visibly impressed'.[38] Goebbels now also found the film 'quite usable'.[39] It premiered on

31 January 1941 – and was an unexpected success with the public. While Goebbels was happy to accept a 'usable' *Victory in the West*, a successful one was less to his liking. Irked, he ordered the Propaganda Ministry to 'reduce somewhat' the propaganda campaign for the film, arguing that it could not disguise its 'significant defects'.[40] Goebbels did not rest until he had ousted Hesse from his position as head of the Army Propaganda Branch,[41] thereby dealing a blow to Brauchitsch, to whose vanity – and that of his wife – Goebbels took exception.[42] Hesse had not endeared himself to Hitler, either, by publishing an article in the leading Nazi newspaper which implied that the army itself mattered more than Hitler did.[43]

In the end, Hitler must have had persisting doubts about *Victory in the West*. After viewing it for the first time, he set about implementing measures to curtail the influence of the army's Propaganda Branch. On 23 December 1940, an agreement was drawn up between the head of the Armed Forces' High Command, Wilhelm Keitel, and Alfred Rosenberg, the chief Nazi ideologue responsible for the 'intellectual and philosophical education of the NSDAP [National Socialist German Workers' Party]'.[44] Effectively, it stipulated that Rosenberg's office was to be given greater control over the ideological training of the Armed Forces.[45] And, on 10 February 1941, some two weeks after Hitler had seen the revised version, he decreed that propaganda and military censorship were to be 'exclusively the task of the High Command of the Armed Forces'.[46] If ever a film prompted Hitler to take political-ideological measures, then it was *Victory in the West*. It is not hard to see why. The film's preamble provides a potted history of Hitler's rise to power; it refers to his military skill and genius; and it concludes with images of a victorious Hitler. But most of the film focuses on soldiers. We see them marching, on horseback, manning the artillery, laying bridges, eating, drinking, washing clothes, cleaning their boots and washing down horses. We hear them singing cheerful military songs. Herbert Windt's heroic score accompanies the images of energetic infantrymen and artillerymen. Artillery also dominates the film. A matter-of-fact commentary, unlike that of the Nazi newsreels, means that the action, rather than voiceover rhetoric, takes centre stage. There are some nods along the way towards the generals and military strategy, but for the most part the film is preoccupied with the soldiers themselves, and the sounds and rhythms of battle.

It was *Victory in the West*'s unideological approach to war which annoyed Goebbels and Hitler. Not that Brauchitsch or Hesse did not intend the film as propaganda, but in their eyes it was in propaganda for the army. As Hesse put it, the 'film should inspire enthusiasm in the viewer and above all in young people for the soldier's life'.[47] The war is not primarily about Nazi ideals, the film could be understood to imply, but about the courage, thrill and adventure of life at the front. Hitler's response was to boost ideological education within the Armed Forces, and to place responsibility for propaganda firmly in the hands of Wilhelm Keitel, a general utterly loyal to Hitler – in contrast to the vacillating Brauchitsch. And it was probably in reaction to *Victory in the West* that Hitler set up a military history department within the Armed Forces.[48] Its job was to produce documentation emphasizing the ideological character of the war and the Nazi rationale for waging it. Its function was also to stress the brilliance of Hitler: *Victory in the West* had not adequately represented Hitler's view of himself as an inspired military genius. In March 1942, Walter Scherff, head of the department, instructed his staff to collect sayings by poets, thinkers and 'men of action' about the nature of genius. These were gathered together in a parchment-bound volume called *Lived Genius* and presented to Hitler for his birthday on 20 April 1942.[49] In the end, not much came of Scherff's department. Nor were any other significant Nazi documentaries produced after *Victory in the West* – unsurprising, perhaps, given that the war began to turn against Germany following the attack on the Soviet Union.[50]

However, Hitler did follow the making of a film about the Atlantic Wall, the coastal defence system the construction of which he had initiated in 1942. It was designed to prevent an invasion of Nazi-occupied Europe from Britain. Hitler watched versions of *The Atlantic Wall* on 26 May 1943 and then again on 18, 19 and 20 July 1943.[51] The film's director was

Arnold Fanck, one of the mountain-film pioneers who placed his skills at Hitler's disposal. After the war, he told the denazification authorities that the Nazis had 'frozen him out' in 1939 – neglecting to mention that he made a number of films for Albert Speer in his capacity as head of Operation Todt as of 1942.[52] Speer only did Hitler's bidding, and the film about the Atlantic Wall – like Fritz Hippler's 1939 film about the Siegfried Line, *The West Wall* – probably came about because Hitler asked for it.[53] As so often, Hitler's interest was in films premised on the need for defence. By 1943, the option of attack as a form of 'defence', the message of *Campaign in Poland*, seemed less realistic. Hitler now pinned his hopes on a supposedly insuperable bulwark along the coast. *The Atlantic Wall* was to inspire audiences with confidence in Germany's defences – and to discourage the Allies. The twenty-minute film was never shown in public. But the Atlantic Wall was a recurring theme in Nazi newsreels in 1944,[54] and some of Fanck's footage may have been used. In the end, the Atlantic Wall quickly gave way under the impact of Operation Overlord.

Fanck made *The Atlantic Wall* as a member of Riefenstahl's production team. Riefenstahl conveys the impression in her autobiography that she spent most of the war making *Lowlands*, a feature film based on an opera by Eugen d'Albert. She does not mention that Hitler supported the making of *Lowlands*. In early 1941, Ufa's board felt obliged to offer her studio space because *Lowlands* was being promoted from 'the very top'.[55] She also fails to mention that Hitler commissioned her to make a film about the New Reich Chancellery in Berlin in May 1940.[56] The cost, originally estimated at 700,000 Reichsmarks, was covered by Hitler's personal Culture Fund.[57] The money was paid through an account held by Speer as General Building Inspector for the Reich Capital. His inspectorate oversaw regular payments to Riefenstahl's company from at least mid-1941 until late 1944. The 700,000 Reichsmarks were all spent by December 1944.[58] In addition to the film about the Reich Chancellery, Riefenstahl's company worked on other films for Speer and Hitler: *The Führer Builds his Reich Capital*, *Building the Air-Raid Shelter* and *Bombing Damage* – and *The*

1 Fritz Lang's *Die Nibelungen* (1924) was possibly Hitler's favourite film. The story of Siegfried, speared in the back by Hagen, resonated with Hitler because it seemed to anticipate the supposed 'betrayal' of the German army by democratic politicians in November 1918.

2 Hitler greatly admired Greta Garbo, and he personally intervened in September 1937 to ensure that *Camille*, an American film starring Garbo, would be shown in German cinemas despite the fact that its director, George Cukor, was Jewish.

3 Goebbels gave Hitler a present of twelve *Mickey Mouse* films for Christmas in 1937. Hitler was delighted by the gift. He also ordered up *Mickey Mouse* films through his personal adjutant, Wilhelm Brückner.

4 A still from John G. Blystone's *Swiss Miss* (1938), starring Laurel and Hardy, whose films Hitler greatly enjoyed. The humour of Laurel and Hardy owes much to the pre-talkies era, and Hitler, who was sceptical of film dialogue, appreciated the visuality of their films.

5 Hitler welcoming the return of the Legion Condor in Berlin, 1939. Hitler provided military support to Franco in the Spanish Civil War, but kept this secret. He commissioned a film on the Legion Condor which was shown to German audiences when the Legion returned, in 1939, in an attempt to justify its involvement.

6 Hitler consulting with Leni Riefenstahl at Nuremberg prior to the 1934 Nuremberg Rally. He met with Riefenstahl several times to discuss her film of this rally, *Triumph of the Will*, which he commissioned from her. Following the purge of the SA, Hitler needed a new rally film which would emphasise the SA's loyalty to him.

7 Scene from Leni Riefenstahl's *Triumph of the Will* (1935). Riefenstahl's second rally film, even more than her first (*Victory of Faith*), provided spectacular views of Hitler standing at the centre of massed Nazi organisations, suggesting a deep bond between Führer and followers.

8 The premiere of Leni Riefenstahl's *Olympia*, her film of the 1936 Olympic Games, at the Ufa Palace in Berlin, 20 April 1938. Nazi flags and Olympic flags hang side by side. *Olympia* created the illusion that Nazi Germany was a movement tolerant of the outside world.

9 Hitler congratulates Riefenstahl at the premiere of *Olympia* in Berlin, 20 April 1938. Riefenstahl ensured that *Olympia* was first shown on Hitler's birthday. This was a good marketing ploy on her part, but it also meant that the film was immediately associated with Hitler and his political interests.

10 Hitler and Goebbels on the set of Gerhard Lamprecht's film *Barcarole* in early 1935. It was probably during this visit to Ufa's film studios that Hitler met Lída Baarová, a Czech actress. She may have reminded him of his half-niece Angela Raubal, who committed suicide in 1931.

11 When Goebbels' relationship with Lída Baarová threatened to ruin his exemplary Nazi marriage, Hitler insisted he break off the affair, which Goebbels reluctantly did. After Baarová left Germany for Prague, she struggled to find work in German films, and Hitler intervened in an attempt to help her out.

12 A still from *Victory in the West* (1941), a Nazi propaganda film about the conquest of France. It was made by the army, not the Propaganda Ministry. Goebbels and Hitler took exception to its unideological celebration of the soldier's life, and Hitler reacted by increasing Nazi propaganda within the Armed Forces.

13 Otto Gebühr as Frederick the Great in Veit Harlan's *The Great King* (1942). This was one of a number of Nazi 'genius' films, which suggested parallels between great historical figures and Hitler. Hitler used *The Great King*, which depicts vacillating generals, to give his own generals a dressing down.

14 Ferdinand Marian as the title character in the notorious anti-Semitic feature film *Jew Süss* (1940), directed by Veit Harlan. *Jew Süss* brings to the screen many of the anti-Semitic cliches in Hitler's *My Struggle*. Harlan's film was used to support the Nazi ghettoisation, deportation and genocide of Jews.

15 Advertising for the Nazi 'documentary' *The Eternal Jew* (1940). Images from it and *Jew Süss* 'were endlessly replicated in Nazi anti-Semitic posters or publications, all over the Reich and occupied Europe' (Saul Friedländer). *The Eternal Jew* includes an excerpt from Hitler's 30 January 1939 speech threatening the annihilation of the Jews.

16 Hitler in the last Nazi newsreel, March 1945. Over the course of the war, Hitler became more and more reluctant to show himself in Nazi newsreels: he was afraid audiences would notice signs of ill health. Here, he is seen receiving members of the Hitler Youth. The newsreel implies that the Reich's defence now depends on youngsters.

17 Henny Porten, one of Hitler's favourite actresses. She had made a deep impression on Hitler when he saw her for the first time on screen while on leave in Lille during the First World War. During the Third Reich, she refused to divorce her 'half-Jewish' husband Wilhelm von Kaufmann-Asser, and appealed to Hitler for help.

Atlantic Wall. Fanck was probably chiefly responsible for them, but he remained 'under Riefenstahl's supervision'.[59] By 7 August 1943, her company had racked up costs of 1,023,298.93 Reichsmarks.[60] All that came of Riefenstahl's Berlin projects were two short films, directed by Fanck, about Hitler's favourite sculptors Josef Thorak and Arno Breker, both of whom had created sculptures for the New Reich Chancellery.[61] In view of the generous financial support for Riefenstahl, these were meagre results indeed.[62]

Hitler's and Speer's plans to rebuild Berlin never materialized, which might explain why *The Führer Builds his Reich Capital* never saw the light of day, but what became of Riefenstahl's film about the New Reich Chancellery is harder to fathom. However, that Hitler wanted it made remains significant. Hitler's Riefenstahl commissions have one thing in common: her role was to film representations of power, be these Nazi rallies, the Nazi staging of the 1936 Olympics, or Hitler's political architecture. Given that these representations of power were, from Hitler's point of view, also expressions of Nazi artistry, whether in the form of the orchestration of mass consensus (Nazi rallies) or of Speer's neoclassical designs for Berlin, Riefenstahl's role was to translate one form of art into another. And, because these representations were effectively representations of Hitler's ostensible genius and limitless authority, her films were also a form of visual hagiography – one which could be disseminated, as was *Triumph of the Will*, around the Reich to impress audiences. By the end of the war, Berlin was reduced to rubble. The Soviets demolished the New Reich Chancellery. Hitler's megalomaniac dreams had ended in destruction; most of Riefenstahl's and Fanck's footage disappeared into obscurity.

Feature Film

Evidence that Hitler watched feature films during the war is less conclusive than in the case of documentary film. However, even if it was mostly Eva Braun and her family and friends who populated the Great Hall at the

Berghof to watch films,[63] or repaired to the skittle alley after dinner to watch them there,[64] it is difficult to believe Hitler avoided viewing feature films entirely. Adjutant Max Wünsche's record of Hitler's activities in late 1939 includes references to the word 'film', usually followed by 'Wochenschau', newsreel.[65] A record of Hitler's activities for the 1943 period indicates he watched at least one film, on 4 December 1943, together with Traudl Junge, among others.[66] A further possible indication of film viewing is provided by Heinrich Himmler's service calendar. On 12 July 1942, Himmler took supper with Hitler at Führer HQ before watching Wolfgang Liebeneiner's *The Dismissal*;[67] and, on 1 March 1942, he lunched with Hitler before watching Veit Harlan's *The Great King*.[68] Himmler's diary, however, does not make clear whether Hitler accompanied him to these screenings – and Goebbels writes that Hitler was not present at the showing of *The Great King* at his HQ in March 1942.[69] Goebbels' comment that *Germanin: The Story of a Colonial Deed* (1943) 'earned little applause in Führer HQ' is also inconclusive: we do not know if Hitler was among those who watched it.[70] Directed by Goebbels' brother-in-law Max Kimmich, *Germanin* was an anti-British advertisement for Germany's civilizing effects in Africa and its right to colonies. Goebbels had high hopes of the film[71] but was disappointed by the final result, objecting that it was awkwardly perched between a culture and a feature film.[72] Whether Hitler watched it or not, *Germanin* triggered a discussion about the awarding of inappropriate official film ratings in which Hitler was involved.[73]

Goebbels' diaries alternate between stating that Hitler did not watch any films during the war[74] and suggesting he might have. In March 1941, according to Goebbels, Hitler said he intended to watch *Uncle Krüger*, Hans Steinhoff's anti-British film about the Boer War,[75] and a little later, Goebbels recounts that Hitler 'liked our U-boat film very much', which certainly sounds as if he had watched Günther Rittau's *U Boats Westwards* (1941), a propaganda film about the Battle of the Atlantic.[76] Former members of Hitler's personnel also appear to contradict themselves. Herbert Döhring, Berghof manager, states that Hitler did not watch any films for entertainment after September 1939 – a sentence after informing his readers that one of Hitler's favourite films was Herbert Selpin's *Carl Peters*, an anti-British propaganda film celebrating Peters' achievements in German East Africa.[77] *Carl Peters*, starring the popular actor Hans Albers, was released in March 1941, so Hitler must have seen it in late 1940 or early 1941. Not all of those who had access to Hitler during the war present him as abstemious. Hitler's photographer Heinrich Hoffmann recalls that a film Hitler watched repeatedly was Helmut Weiss' *The Punch Bowl*, a comedy starring Heinz Rühmann first shown in January 1944 (though perhaps Hoffmann confused this film with *Such a Rascal*, an earlier film version of the same novel by Heinrich Spoerl released in 1934).[78] Hitler's bodyguard Rochus Misch recollects that Hitler watched Victor Fleming's *Gone with the Wind* (1939) at least three times, a film which did not reach Goebbels until July 1940. Goebbels was massively impressed by the epic film of the American South, admiring its use of colour and its overall effect, particularly the crowd scenes.[79] So, according to Misch, was Hitler, who, after watching the film, summoned Goebbels and viewed it a second time, telling Goebbels afterwards: 'Now that, that is something our own people should also be able to do.'[80] Allegedly, Clark Gable, who played Rhett Butler in *Gone with the Wind*, was one of Hitler's favourite actors. Gable joined the US Air Force, and, in 1943, was stationed in England, from where he flew at least five combat missions. Rumours persist that Hitler offered a reward to anyone who could capture Gable. Gable told fellow actor David Niven that he feared Hitler would 'put him in a cage and charge 10 marks a look all over Germany'.[81]

Regardless of whether Hitler continued to watch feature films, he remained the supreme arbiter when disagreements over films could not be resolved.[82] Despite Goebbels' attempts to stop complaints from various quarters about films, they continued with vigour. The National Socialist Teachers' League objected to the 1941 youth film *Jakko* by Fritz Peter Buch, which, they found, made teachers look laughable.[83] Doctors bemoaned the ridiculing of the medical profession in the 1942 film *Doctor*

Crippen, directed by Erich Engels.[84] Most famously, the Armed Forces' High Command protested against the Zarah Leander blockbuster *The Great Love* (1942), directed by Rolf Hansen, because a Luftwaffe pilot is shown spending the night with a singer. 'The Armed Forces' High Command,' wrote Goebbels, 'feels this to be a moral slight and declares, no flight lieutenant would do such a thing. But Göring is right when he says, if a flight lieutenant let such an opportunity pass unused then he wouldn't be a flight lieutenant.'[85] When Hitler's generals spoke out against Veit Harlan's *The Great King*, which drew parallels between Frederick the Great's determination to fight on after defeat at the Battle of Kunersdorf (1759) and Hitler's commitment to winning the war, Goebbels went to Hitler. Hitler had taken an interest in the making of this film, deciding that Otto Gebühr should play Frederick (not Werner Krauβ, who was Harlan's choice),[86] and that the premiere should take place at Christmas time (1941) in Berlin's Ufa Palace.[87] Various delays meant the premiere was postponed until 30 January 1942, and then 3 March 1942. The film was shown to Wehrmacht generals at Hitler's HQ at the very beginning of March. Hitler, one presumes, listened to their objections, but dismissed them, deciding that the premiere should go ahead as planned.[88] Goebbels heard later from Hitler's adjutant Julius Schaub that there had been a 'hard struggle' over the film, which Hitler, unsurprisingly, had won.[89]

Hitler's generals were disgruntled because they saw in *The Great King* a critique of their own conduct during Operation Barbarossa. In the film, Prussia's generals, as Goebbels puts it, 'let Frederick the Great down in the decisive hour'.[90] They are portrayed as having effectively fled from the Russians, and they urge Frederick to sue for peace; this he refuses to do, leading the way for a dramatic turn of military fortune in Prussia's favour. Without doubt, amendments made to the film, not least at Goebbels' instigation, in the months before its release helped to imply that there were analogies between Prussia's generals at Kunersdorf and Hitler's generals outside Moscow. In January 1942, Goebbels noted how dissatisfied Hitler was with the 'defeatism' of former Army Commander-in-Chief von Brauchitsch, whom he had dismissed in December 1941. German generals, wrote Goebbels, were 'at the end of their physical powers of resistance'; if the 'critical situation' had been overcome, 'then this is entirely down to the Führer'.[91] *The Great King,* from Hitler's point of view, was timely. When the generals sat down to watch it, they were to receive a dressing-down in the form of a history lesson: they had failed as Frederick's generals had done. Their job was to rally round Hitler, and prevent a repeat of Frederick's isolation.[92] No doubt they were to see in Frederick's punishment of the disobedient Sergeant Treskow in *The Great King* a corroboration of Hitler's treatment of General Erich Hoepner, thrown out of the Wehrmacht by Hitler for defying orders in December 1941. *The Great King* functioned as education at the highest level. Hitler asked for a copy to be sent to Mussolini.[93] Perhaps this was a hint that , following Italian defeats in Africa, Mussolini needed to be firmer with army leaders.

The Great King was used to promote the image of Hitler as a genius by means of historical analogy, only now both Goebbels and Hitler set about redefining genius in response to recent military setbacks. On the eve of Hitler's birthday, 19 April 1942, Goebbels spoke on the radio to praise the representation of Frederick the Great in Harlan's film as a 'struggling Titan', before going on to extol Hitler's leadership qualities. Hitler, in other words, was to be admired not just for his military successes, but also for his strength of character in dealing with those of his enemies. *The Great King* was to help Germans get used to the idea that war was not all about easy victories.[94] In his 26 April 1942 speech to the Reichstag, Hitler spoke 'as a man who feels he has the worst struggle of his life behind him' and 'as a leader of armies who mastered a fate imposed on them as the severest test designed only for those destined for the highest things'.[95] Hitler was asking his listeners to imagine that withstanding the Soviet counteroffensive was a sign of victories to come. In his Reichstag speech, Hitler (surely with Hoepner in mind, who had protested against his exclusion from the Wehrmacht) arrogated to himself the right to act as supreme judge in the interests of winning the war, a right also exercised by Frederick in Harlan's film. Hitler did not mention *The Great King,* but it echoes throughout his speech.

Hitler also intervened to settle a dispute over another 'genius' film, namely Wolfgang Liebeneiner's *The Dismissal* (1942), about former Reich Chancellor Otto von Bismarck, starring Emil Jannings. *The Dismissal* was a celebration of Bismarck's political wisdom. Lest there be any doubts that the cinematic Bismarck was to be understood as an anticipation of Hitler, Jannings wrote an article explicitly connecting Frederick the Great, Bismarck and Hitler.[96] But Liebeneiner's film displeased the Political Archive of the Foreign Office, which objected to the portrayal of Foreign Office official Friedrich von Holstein as a villain who brought down Bismarck. Another concern related to the film's emphasis on Bismarck's support for an extension of the Reinsurance Treaty with Russia. The Political Archive thought this might upset the Turks because a secret clause in that treaty had offered Germany's support to the tsar in the event of a dispute over access to the Black Sea. Finally, the Political Archive criticized the film for suggesting Germany was to blame for the First World War, fearing this might sour relations with some of Germany's current allies.[97] Ernst Woermann, head of the Political Department of the Foreign Office, also worried that *The Dismissal* was too critical of the Foreign Office, and suggested changes be made.[98] Goebbels himself had doubts about the depiction of the Reinsurance Treaty in the film; this did not 'fit the political landscape'.[99] Hitler, after all, was at war with the Soviet Union: the Hitler–Stalin Pact had not lasted. Liebeneiner had to make changes.

Goebbels was also cautious lest the film's negative portrayal of Kaiser William II upset those with sympathies for Germany's monarchic traditions.[100] Rather than risk 'putting noses out of joint', Goebbels decided to show *The Dismissal* in private to 'a number of categories of human beings' to test the response.[101] One of these 'categories' consisted of Nazi Gauleiter. Goebbels was pleased by their reaction; they argued for the film's immediate release. One can rely, he enthused, on 'the old guards of Nazi revolutionaries'.[102] But he was still hesitant, and approached Hitler. Hitler, reluctant to make a decision immediately, came up with the idea of doing a test run in 'some town or other' to gauge public reaction.[103] Goebbels opted for Stettin in Pomerania, which was far enough away from Berlin for a possibly negative reaction not to do any real harm, but, as Germany's third-largest city, represented a substantial sounding-board. The film was shown there to great acclaim on 15 September 1942. Goebbels informed Hitler,[104] but remained concerned about the continuing broadsides against *The Dismissal*. Hitler told him not to worry, and to release it 'in grand style'.[105] This duly happened on 6 October in Berlin's Ufa Palace. According to Goebbels, the film was a 'sensational success'[106] – albeit one that, because it showed no 'female conflicts', was restricted to male audiences, with women tending to reject the film.[107]

The 'continuing broadsides' comment was above all a reference to Alfred Rosenberg, head of the Foreign Policy Office of the NSDAP. Rosenberg saw the film and immediately protested to Walter Tießler, the Party Chancellery's liaison to the Propaganda Ministry. Rosenberg, picking up earlier criticism, objected to the portrayal of the Foreign Office and Kaiser William. Tießler was not worried about any of this;[108] nor was Hitler. The test runs and the premiere had not led to any substantial complaints. *The Dismissal*, as well as Liebeneiner's earlier film *Bismarck* (1940), fitted neatly into the sequence of Nazi feature films aligning Hitler with great historical personages. It ended with Bismarck asking dreamily who will come to finish the imperial construction work he has begun, a question, of course, to which there could only be one implied answer in a Nazi-period film. Hitler would also have approved of its criticism of Kaiser William, whom he despised.[109] Films criticizing the military, or the monarchy and the Foreign Office, could only serve to lend support to Hitler's belief that traditional elites needed to be brought to heel. That it was Hitler who decided over films with potentially significant diplomatic and domestic repercussions shows that when cinema became high politics, Goebbels recognized the limits of his own authority – or of the risks he was prepared to take. Hitler seems to have been less concerned about 'putting noses out of joint'. Nor was he concerned the film might set a bad example. In July 1942, the Reich Ring for Propaganda reviewed *The Dismissal* and expressed concern that it showed how one man could topple a great leader.[110] Arnold Bacmeister, head of the Film Review Office, responded to this by arguing that no-one watching the film could ever think that Hitler might also be brought down by 'one individual scumbag'. He was too powerful and popular for that.[111] Hitler would surely have concurred.

A final example of Hitler's wartime intervention is provided by *The Punch Bowl* (1944), starring Heinz Rühmann. In his 1982 autobiography, Rühmann relates how the film had only just been finished when Minister of Education Bernhard Rust insisted it be banned. Rust did not approve of its unflattering portrayal of the teaching profession, especially at a time when it was proving difficult to find new teachers. Rühmann contacted someone he knew in the Air Ministry, who promised to see if he could get Reich Minister of Aviation Hermann Göring interested in the film. Göring asked Rühmann to bring a copy to him directly at Hitler's HQ in East Prussia. Rühmann duly obliged. The film was shown in the evening – Hitler was not present, according to Rühmann's account – and the following day, Göring told Hitler he had no idea why *The Punch Bowl* had been banned, but 'we were all roaring with laughter'. 'Then the film must be shown immediately,' was Hitler's reply.[112] Hitler subsequently told Goebbels he was not to let himself be intimidated by objections from teachers or the Education Ministry: the film was to be shown.[113] It premiered on 28 January 1944 and proved to be very popular.[114] By the time Rühmann came to write his autobiography, taking a copy of a film to Göring in the Wolf's Lair was nothing more than a colourful anecdote. Yet, in the immediate aftermath of the war, Rühmann was at pains to deny he had ever been to Hitler's HQ.[115] Admitting that to the Allies in 1946 might have got him into trouble. Rühmann, in early 1944, had happily appealed to Göring and, through him, to Hitler to secure the release of a film, evidence of how well he, like other actors, knew how to play the system. Right up to the end of the war, Hitler remained the ultimate authority on the showing of controversial films, and was sometimes lenient towards films that caused offence to particular professional groups. Rühmann is likely to have known this.

General Matters of Film Policy

During the war, Hitler certainly still liked to talk about film. He would ask his personal adjutant Julius Schaub over breakfast if he had been to the cinema.[116] Lunchtime conversation at the Berghof often revolved round theatre and cinema – including American colour films.[117] Goebbels kept Hitler regularly apprised of issues pertaining to the German film industry.[118] Moreover, Goebbels liked to talk film politics with Hitler, especially when he wanted Hitler's support. In 1934, Goebbels set up the Reich Film Archive, a vast store of domestic and foreign film productions from which interested parties could borrow films.[119] After war began, Goebbels used the archive to collect Hollywood films and other foreign films confiscated from occupied countries.[120] But, following a conversation with Hitler, Goebbels declared that neither he nor Hitler approved of showing 'enemy films to party or state groups for so-called educational purposes'. Goebbels had learnt from experience, so he wrote, that this 'always has a depressing effect'. Hitler authorized Goebbels to 'absolutely reject' such showings for the duration of the war. 'That goes particularly for *Gone with the Wind*.'[121] Clearly, neither Goebbels nor Hitler had been depressed by *Gone with the Wind*, yet so concerned were they about its possible effects that it was actually excluded from the Reich Film Archive itself and kept in a special safe – along with Charlie Chaplin's *The Great Dictator* (1940).[122] The Nazis claimed Chaplin was Jewish, and banned his films.[123] Hitler may have seen *The Great Dictator*, but Goebbels kept it securely under wraps. According to Hans Barkhausen, archivist at the Reich Film Archive, Chaplin's portrayal of Hitler caused 'paroxysms' of rage – whether on Goebbels' part or Hitler's, or both, he does not say.[124]

In the end, Hitler did not impose a total ban on the showing of foreign films held at the Reich Film Archive, but ordered that borrowing them needed the permission of Goebbels. Goebbels furnished himself with a letter to this effect from Hitler's secretary Bormann on 27 December 1942, which he brandished whenever necessary. The letter also entitled Goebbels to ensure that all foreign films were handed over to the film archive for safekeeping.[125] Goebbels, of course, watched foreign films of all kinds at home in Berlin.[126] And he did cede to pressure from actors, journalists and even members of the military, allowing special viewings of the forbidden fruits.[127] But in his ongoing turf war with Alfred Rosenberg, who had become Reich Minister for the Occupied Territories following the attack on the Soviet Union, Goebbels gave no quarter. Expressing concern lest Soviet propaganda should 'corrupt' some of Rosenberg's personnel,[128] Goebbels insisted Rosenberg hand over Soviet films to the archive. Rosenberg complained bitterly about this to Hans Lammers, head of the Reich Chancellery, arguing that he needed the films for educational reasons.[129] In the end, this dispute was about Goebbels' narcissistic obsession with control of all film matters. It was decided in Goebbels' favour by Hitler in May 1943.[130] But Goebbels did not always get his way on the issue of foreign films, especially when he tried to relax his own rules. He found the 1939 British propaganda film *The Lion Has Wings* so 'unbelievably daft'[131] he wanted it shown publicly in Berlin, convinced that its over-the-top anti-German propaganda would invite ridicule. *The Lion Has Wings*, directed among others by Michael Powell, proved popular with Nazi and military authorities. Heydrich ordered one of the two copies for viewing in Prague,[132] and the Wehrmacht showed great interest.[133] Eventually the film was sent to Hitler's flat in the Reich Chancellery.[134] According to Fritz Hippler, Hitler then rejected Goebbels' idea of a public viewing. Hippler did not know why.[135]

In fact, during the war, Goebbels, following Hitler's interventions, had to give way on one or two issues regarding film policy, as his attempts to impose total control were resisted – for instance by the German Labour Front (DAF), which had been in a long tussle with the Reich Chamber of Culture over the production of films. On 2 July 1941, Bormann informed Goebbels that party organizations such as the DAF did not have to be members of the Reich Film Chamber: the party cannot be answerable to 'a state organization'.[136] Goebbels immediately protested.[137] The DAF nevertheless withdrew its membership, whereupon the Reich Film Chamber began to complain about the Labour Front's filmmaking activities.[138] The DAF in turn claimed that it was only answerable to the Film Office of the Reich Propaganda Leadership, a party organization.[139] Goebbels was head of both the Reich Chamber of Culture and the Reich Propaganda Leadership, which appeared to be pulling in different directions, because the Propaganda Leadership's Film Office supported the Labour Front's wish to be free of Reich Film Chamber control.[140] A ruling issued by Bormann on 20 February 1942 stipulated that NSDAP organizations had the right to make and disseminate films 'for enlightenment purposes'.[141] A Hitler order on the party's legal status of 12 December 1942 provided further clarity,[142] and on 23 March 1943, Hitler's Party Chancellery unequivocally stated that the party and affiliated organizations did not need to be members of the Reich Film Chamber.[143] This was largely a dispute between Goebbels' subordinates and rivals in competing state and party organizations. In the end, Goebbels still retained influence over the DAF through the Reich Propaganda Leadership. But he did not sacrifice supervisory control through the Reich Film Chamber willingly. Hitler favoured party over state. While Goebbels usually had Hitler's ear, Hitler's preference for a polycratic style of rule meant that Goebbels was never able to exercise absolute authority in film matters.

Goebbels also had to concede ground in a dispute over the right of local communes ('Gemeinden') to own cinemas. While Goebbels was prepared to countenance a degree of such ownership, he was not willing to see this happen at the expense of other cinema owners. In September 1943, with Hitler's agreement, he wrote to the Reich Film Chamber decreeing that the status of Reich-owned, private and local commune-owned cinemas should not change. If Gemeinden wanted to take over a privately owned cinema, then they needed both 'good reasons' for doing so and his permission.[144] When Goebbels wrote to all Gauleiter to reinforce his position, Bormann informed him that, in fact, he was acting *against* Hitler's wishes. Hitler, claimed Bormann, had repeatedly emphasized that local communes must have their own sources of income – one of which was running cinemas.

Bormann recommended enabling Gemeinden to acquire privately owned cinemas 'to the fullest extent'. Bormann could also not resist taking a swipe at Goebbels' attempts to absorb as many cinemas as possible into the Reich Film Theatre Company, a process he described as a 'damaging centralization of cultural life in an important area': 'generally, the Führer has considerable reservations about over-large central companies'. Bormann effectively reprimanded Goebbels for not following the 'political will' of the Führer, but suggested that Lammers approach Hitler and ask him to settle the dispute.[145] Ultimately, Goebbels was forced to issue a ruling giving local communes the right to acquire privately owned cinemas as these became available.[146] Hitler's wish to respond to the economic needs of the Gemeinden overrode his support for Goebbels' drive for control of cinemas. And he was ably assisted by Bormann and Lammers in their wish to clip Goebbels' wings.

That Hitler occasionally disagreed with Goebbels on film matters is borne out by a conversation he had with Alfred Rosenberg and Goebbels himself (among others) in December 1939. According to Rosenberg, who probably played the incident up because he hated Goebbels, Hitler claimed the Nazi revolution appeared to have had no impact at all on German film production.[147] Goebbels, after noting that Hitler had been critical of both feature film and weekly newsreels, described the criticism as 'not quite justified'.[148] In July 1942, Hitler complained that German films had taken no interest in the Autobahn – a statement which was untrue, he himself had banned one of them[149] – and followed this up with the objection that 'in contrast to England and France, it is unfortunately the case in Germany that all great things that are created do not find expression in film'. The only exception, he noted, was Vienna, adding the caveat that 'Vienna is represented so much in film it makes you sick.'[150] It is difficult to know how seriously to take Hitler's complaints. Goebbels himself often noted his own discontent with individual films and his problems with the film industry. Indeed, his diaries comment on various attempts to encourage better films, though he never wonders to what extent any loss of quality might be put down to censorship and state interference. Hitler's complaints, in turn, spurred Goebbels to bring about improvements.[151] That said, Goebbels was largely happy with film production, and his diaries provide evidence that Hitler was also full of praise for specific German films and German film production; criticism and praise alternate in no particular order.[152] Hitler's outburst on 11 December 1939 was one of his sporadic rants, not so much the expression of any cumulative frustration, although he may have been annoyed that Goebbels had not provided enough propagandistic films to accompany the start of the war.[153]

What makes it a surprising outburst, too, is that it was preceded by Hitler's pathos-filled assurance to his assembled guests on 11 December that he had no time for culture: 'I will defeat Britain, whatever the cost. All my thoughts and actions are focused on this. Film, theatre and music no longer interest me.'[154] Yet, that very evening, he watched *Campaign in Poland*.[155] When Goebbels reports, then, that Hitler during the war intentionally denied himself 'all forms of distraction', including film, we need to take this with a liberal pinch of salt.[156] The transition from aesthete to ascetic was in part mythical. In the end, if Hitler watched fewer and fewer films, then this was not as a matter of principle, but because he did not have the time. Goebbels surely relished being able to oversee the film industry without Hitler watching every film it produced, but, as we have seen, he did not hesitate to approach Hitler when he needed him. Hitler mostly, if not always, backed Goebbels in his various disputes over the showing of films with the National Socialist Teachers' League, the Foreign Office, Rosenberg and even Bormann,[157] and he also supported him when it came to disappointing Mussolini. In May 1943, Hitler agreed with Goebbels that the 1942 Italian film about the North African campaign, *Bengasi*, was unsuitable viewing for German audiences. As Goebbels put it trenchantly: 'One can't really beat a retreat from African territory and at the same time show a film claiming we'll soon be in Bengasi.'[158] Hitler asked Goebbels to suggest to Mussolini a 'postponement', but the film never ran in Germany. Throughout the war, Hitler was content to see films annoy sections of the party, military or state, and use them to keep them on their toes and 'educate' them into accepting their subservience to his will. He took a particular interest in historical films that provided supposed corroboration of his own self and actions; where the present did not yield enough by way of justification for his policies, then screen Bismarcks and Fredericks were mobilized in support. He never lost his sense of the importance of film for the purposes of representing power or promoting propaganda.

8

Preparing Genocide

THE NAZI FILMS *JEW SÜSS* AND *THE ETERNAL JEW*

Three Nazi anti-Semitic films reached cinema screens in the summer and autumn of 1940: the feature films *The Rothschilds* and *Jew Süss*, and the 'documentary' *The Eternal Jew*. Of these three, the latter two are the most notorious. Goebbels may have initiated the films, but singling him out is to overlook the role of Hitler. The development of *Jew Süss* in particular needs to be seen in relation to the evolution of Hitler's anti-Semitic policies and ideas. The genocidal message in *The Eternal Jew* is even more explicit. It connects this message directly with Hitler and his threat in January 1939 to annihilate the Jews.

The Making of Anti-Semitic Films

In mid-July 1935, Goebbels' newspaper *The Attack* (*Der Angriff*) claimed that German-Jewish cinemagoers had protested against a Swedish anti-Semitic film, Per-Axel Branner's *Pettersson & Bendel* (1933), which was showing in a Berlin cinema on the Kurfürstendamm. *The Attack* called upon National Socialists to react to what it regarded as Jewish effrontery with a 'firm hand'.[1] Goebbels also threatened a response during a speech in

Essen.[2] A Danish journalist who witnessed the resulting wave of anti-Jewish violence clearly identified the 'party badges' of those who attacked his car when the rioters mistook him for a Jew.[3] There can be little doubt that the Kurfürstendamm riots in 1935 were in significant part unleashed by the Nazis and in particular the Storm Troopers (SA), despite Goebbels' attempts to make it look as if they were entirely the expression of spontaneous popular rage. Goebbels turned on Jewish cinema-owners by falsely accusing them of having made alterations to their copies of *Pettersson & Bendel*. Jewish-owned cinemas were then Aryanized.[4] Hitler was concerned about the international protests against the 15 July violence, and that Germans, disturbed by this and other examples of unrest in 1935, might lose faith in his ability to keep order. Two months later, the Nuremberg Laws, which stripped Jews of German citizenship and forbade sexual relations between Jews and Germans, were rapidly promulgated. By radicalizing the state's legal position on Jews, Hitler hoped to keep violence off the streets.

There can be no doubt, then, that an anti-Semitic film was used by the Nazis in 1935 to promote anti-Semitism. What is surprising is that it was not made by Germans. On the one hand, the Nazis could point out that this served to prove that the Jew was perceived as a threat in other European countries.[5] On the other, it raised the question as to why the Nazis had not yet produced such a film. Arzén von Cserépy's *Don't Lose Heart, Suzanne*, first shown in January 1935 and starring Veit Harlan, did provide a scathing condemnation of Jewish film producers, but was poorly made. Goebbels objected to its 'dreadful dilettantism'.[6] In the early years of National Socialist rule, Goebbels' main concern had been 'de-Jewifying' the film industry, rather than pushing for anti-Semitic films. *Pettersson & Bendel*, in which the blond Pettersson is trapped in a web of corruption by the devious Jew Bendel, caused Nazi critics to ask if the time had not now come for German film to show the supposedly pernicious influence of Jews. In a discussion of *Pettersson & Bendel*'s success in Germany, one critic even suggested that the film branch was resisting representing National Socialist ideas – as if still under the 'spell' of the Jews.[7] Yet Goebbels still did little to stimulate anti-Semitic films. He was also quick to find fault with films that did contain anti-Semitic scenes or characters, such as Jürgen von Alten's *Togger* (1937), which condemned the 'international Jewish press'. Goebbels found Alten's directing 'too rigid', and the film flopped at the box office.[8] Goebbels was no less dissatisfied with Hans Zerlett's comedy *Robert and Bertram* (1939). It portrayed Jewish corruption in the figure of Nathan Ipelmeyer. Goebbels complained that it handled the Jewish problem too 'superficially'.[9]

Filming for *Robert and Bertram* began in early 1939; it was first shown on 7 July 1939. Heinz Helbig's film about a monopolistic Jewish textile firm, *Linen from Ireland*, was also produced in the first half of 1939 and reached cinemas on 16 October. Goebbels was seemingly happy with it.[10] It is likely that these two films represented the first responses to the radicalization of anti-Semitic film policy which set in after Reichskristallnacht (8/9 November 1938), though work on the script for *Robert and Bertram* may have begun earlier. Certainly the three notorious anti-Semitic films which appeared in 1940 originated in the aftermath of Reichskristallnacht: Erich Waschneck's *The Rothschilds*, which is set during the Napoleonic period and seeks to demonstrate the supposed manipulation of markets by a corrupt international Jewry; *Jew Süss*, which depicts the disastrous influence of a wealthy Jewish financial adviser, Joseph Süss Oppenheimer, on Duke Karl Alexander of Württemberg in the early eighteenth century; and *The Eternal Jew*, which takes us to the twentieth century, seeking to prove how ghetto Jewry has fanned out into the wider world to wield a destructive influence on all aspects of non-Jewish political, cultural and social life. After the war, the director of *Jew Süss*, Veit Harlan, was put on trial in Hamburg charged with collaborating in racial persecution.[11] Alf Teichs, the former chief dramaturge of Terra, which produced *Jew Süss*, claimed at the trial that the Propaganda Ministry commissioned all state-owned firms to produce an anti-Semitic film.[12] This commission was probably given in November 1938.[13]

By the autumn of that year, Goebbels had fallen from grace as a result of his affair with Lída Baarová. His central involvement in Reichskristallnacht was his way of demonstrating his anti-Semitic loyalties and rallying Germans behind the Nazi programme.[14] After the pogrom, he oversaw a massive propaganda campaign designed to blame the Jews for Nazi violence. He set out the need for 'a huge anti-Semitic campaign for the press, radio and party gatherings'.[15] Films played their part in this campaign. A thirty-five-minute compilation film, *Jews Unmasked*, was shown at local Nazi Party gatherings.[16] Its aim was to expose Jewish dominance of the film industry prior to 1933. Like the later film *The Eternal Jew*, it included a clip from Fritz Lang's 1931 film about a serial killer, *M*, starring German-Jewish actor Peter Lorre. In the context of *Jews Unmasked*, the clip invited viewers to associate Jews with brutality and murder. Goebbels also took steps to ban Jews from cinemas,[17] and remove the remaining Jews from the German film industry. More significantly, the Swedish film *Pettersson & Bendel* was reshown in cinemas in November 1938, this time dubbed rather than subtitled.[18] That Goebbels had to resort to reshowing a Swedish film about Jews will surely have made him aware of the need for indigenous, German anti-Semitic films.

Yet a more important impulse for his decision to commission these films may have come from Hitler himself. The intensification of anti-Semitism following Reichskristallnacht aimed to speed up the pace of Jewish emigration. Whatever the role of Goebbels and Göring, it was Hitler who was behind this 'systematic policy of expulsion' and the measures implemented to achieve it.[19] But there is more to it than this. Reichskristallnacht led to weeks of international protest at Nazi violence. On 30 January 1939, Hitler gave his notorious speech before the Reichstag. He uttered what appeared to be a genocidal prophecy: 'should international finance Jewry in Europe and beyond succeed in plunging the nations into another world war, the result will not be the bolshevization of the earth and thereby the victory of Jewry, but the destruction of the Jewish race in Europe'. He also threatened a series of anti-Semitic films should American film companies produce 'anti-Nazi, i.e. anti-German' films, as they had declared they would. The 'times of propagandistic defencelessness among the non-Jewish peoples are at an end,' he added.[20] His speech was interpreted as an explicit call for the production of German anti-Semitic films in the Nazi press; Goebbels will have got the message.[21] Later, too, Hitler weighed in to keep Goebbels on his toes, for instance by complaining about the (in his view) inferior quality of *Robert and Bertram*, which he found more critical of Germans than Jews. Given that the two title characters are escaped prisoners, Hitler's reaction is understandable.[22] Particularly in the case of *Jew Süss*, there is evidence, moreover, that Hitler's ever-radicalizing policies towards Jews impacted on the development of the script.

Jew Süss

After the war, the director of *Jew Süss*, Veit Harlan, did his best to dissociate himself from the film.[23] Goebbels had originally entrusted Peter Paul Brauer with directing it, but changed his mind in late 1939, passing the chalice to Harlan.[24] It is also true that the original script was not Harlan's work, but that of Ludwig Metzger and Eberhard Wolfgang Möller. And Harlan may have been put under pressure. He later claimed Hitler had issued a military-style order that he was to make *Jew Süss*,[25] and that Goebbels threatened him with Dachau if he did not consent.[26] There is, however, no evidence for this. In his diary, Goebbels presents Harlan as cooperative. Although not unhappy with the original script,[27] for instance, Goebbels notes that Harlan had 'lots of new ideas' and is going to 'work over the script again'.[28] Goebbels described Harlan's ensuing changes as 'grandiose'.[29] Contrary to Harlan's post-war claims that he toned down the anti-Semitism of the pre-existing script,[30] he exacerbated it. This is clear from a comparison of the original script by Metzger and Möller with the version by Harlan.[31] In the stage directions of Harlan's script, Süss is referred to simply as 'the Jew', a clear indication of Harlan's intention to strip him of individuality and represent him as a 'type'. Harlan bolsters the original script's identification of Jewry with sadism,[32] promiscuity and indeed sadistic promiscuity; thus Harlan's version develops considerably the scene in which Süss rapes the 'Aryan' Dorothea, and connects it with the torture of her fiancé. In its final form, *Jew Süss* contains a scene added by Harlan in which the Jewish girl Rebecca leans lewdly over a balcony. Harlan's script and the final film also develop Süss's attempt to use Jewish money to plunge Württemberg into a civil war, thus lending historical support to Nazi wartime propaganda about the Jews being behind the Allied war effort. The original Metzger–Moeller script presented western Germany's Jews as 'Asiatic' and 'oriental', seeking thereby to justify the need for their emigration. Harlan intensified this characterization. In depicting Europe's Jews as essentially eastern, alien and amoral, Harlan's script now justifies not so much their emigration as the Nazi policy of deportation and ghettoization being practised in occupied Poland. For now the war had begun, the Nazis had to 'deal' not just with German, Austrian and Czech Jews, but also Polish Jews.

On 29 September 1939, Alfred Rosenberg recorded a conversation in which Hitler told him about his impression of Poles – 'a thin Germanic layer, terrible beneath' – and Polish Jews: 'you cannot imagine anything more horrible'.[33] In December, Hitler was complaining to Goebbels and Rosenberg about the failure of Nazi film to tackle the theme of 'Jewish Bolshevists'.[34] Harlan was not party to these conversations, but Goebbels kept him informed of Hitler's views on anti-Semitism, as Harlan's autobiography makes clear.[35] It is certainly striking that the Jews in *Jew Süss* share the supposed communist traits of infiltration, sedition and greed. Harlan did everything he could to make the Jews of Frankfurt and Stuttgart resemble Eastern European Orthodox Jews. He also introduced a ghetto scene.[36] To ensure that a reluctant Ferdinand Marian took the part of Jew Süss, Harlan persuaded him to dress up like a ghetto Jew, with kaftan and forelocks, for a screen test.[37] According to Otto Lehmann, head producer of the film, Harlan watched footage of Łódź ghetto designed for inclusion in *The Eternal Jew* to inform himself about Jewish customs.[38] While Marian took on the central role, Werner Krauß insisted on offering to take over the other Jewish roles. Krauß may have assumed that Goebbels, who was known to dislike actors playing more than one role in a film, would refuse.[39] During his denazification trial, Krauß claimed, by contrast, that he played the secondary Jewish characters because he wanted to ensure there would be no competition between different actors to appear more 'Jewish' than the others.[40] Whatever his intention, by taking on these parts, Krauß helped to reinforce the Nazi idea that all Jews were expressions of the same racial type – and that the embodiment of their destructive uniformity was the supposedly devious European Jew on whom Krauß's roles are modelled.[41]

To 'study' eastern Jews, and amplify the eastern Jewish aspect to the film, Harlan travelled to Lublin in Nazi-occupied Poland in January 1940, together with his set manager Conny Carstennsen and his assistant Alfred Braun. According to Carstennsen, they also wanted to organize a train to bring 150 Jews to Berlin to participate in the crowd scenes, but fear of spreading typhus led to the idea being dropped.[42] In his autobiography, Harlan makes the trip sound like a pleasant outing to meet accommodating Jews only too keen to get away from Lublin's Jewish quarter and be in his film – though he does not reflect on why they might be so desperate to leave, beyond making the comment that 'they believed they would be safer in Berlin'.[43] In late 1939 and early 1940, Lublin was a hub of the so-called Nisko Plan for concentrating and deporting Jews.[44] Surely, Harlan must have sensed something of the large-scale Nazi deportations of Jews to the Lublin area, who were dispatched there not just from the annexed Polish territories, but also from Vienna, Mährisch Ostrau and Kattowitz. He must have witnessed the conditions under which Jews were living. He visited several ghettos, including Łódź, not just Lublin. After watching Jewish dances marking the festival of Purim, Harlan opined: 'the negroes have more in common with us than this race'.[45] Harlan knew he was making *Jew Süss* at a time of heightened persecution of Jews, when his film was likely to contribute to the anti-Semitism which drove that process. Yet he continued to make the film, and remained set on creating as 'alien' an impression of the Jews as he could. After the fruitless trip to Lublin, Harlan filmed the synagogue scenes in Prague. Although he claimed that Prague Jews volunteered to act out their religious rites for the film, the synagogue scenes show the religious observances of *Eastern* European Jews. It is quite possible the synagogue Jews were brought to Prague by the SS Central Office for Jewish Emigration, who subsequently complained about not being given free tickets for the premiere of *Jew Süss*.[46] At any rate, the synagogue sequence, which shows ululating, chanting Jews moving in apparently chaotic restlessness across the set, was filmed by Harlan to reinforce the impression that Jews had 'nothing in common' with Germans.

The production of *Jew Süss* stands in close relation to three major events in the history of the Nazi persecution of Jews to which Hitler was central: Reichskristallnacht, Hitler's 30 January 1939 Reichstag speech, and the implementation of anti-Semitic measures in occupied Poland. The film's depiction of the alleged threat of Eastern European-style Orthodox Jews ensured that it acquired an incisive topicality when first shown in 1940. Like *The Eternal Jew* and *The Rothschilds*, and in contrast to earlier Nazi anti-Semitic films, the danger posed by the Jews in *Jew Süss* is depicted as total: after inveigling himself into the duke's home, Süss nearly brings down the state. The ejection of the Jews from Stuttgart at the end is presented as an act of German self-preservation. *Jew Süss* thus provides pseudo-historical support for the processes of Jewish deportation in the present. Süss is executed in the film because he had sex with a Christian, creating a radical precedent for the 1935 Nuremberg Laws, which forbade such sexual relations under threat of imprisonment. In a way, the film points forwards to the Holocaust, insofar as it recommends killing as the ultimate answer to the perils of racial intermingling. According to Fritz Hippler, head of the Film Department in the Propaganda Ministry, Harlan had rejected the initial script for *Jew Süss* by Metzger and Moeller as 'dramatized *Stürmer*', a reference to the crudely anti-Semitic newspaper edited by Julius Streicher, Gauleiter of Franconia.[47] During the war, the *Stürmer* constantly reminded its readers that the Jews were the source of all Germany's problems. Yet, in the end, this is what Harlan's film does. For the most part, it is little more than well-acted *Stürmer*.

In laying all responsibility at Goebbels' door for *Jew Süss*, Harlan tried to conceal his own anti-Semitic track record: thus in 1933 he had provided the leading Nazi newspaper with an anti-Semitic account of his father's death,[48] and he acted in one of the first Nazi anti-Semitic films, *Don't Lose Heart, Suzanne* (1935). Harlan also endeavoured to hide the fact that his film, to adapt Hippler's phrase, is a 'dramatized *Mein Kampf*'. In *My Struggle*, Hitler wrote, 'so every court had its "court Jew" – as these beasts were called, who tortured honest folk to the point of despair and provided the princes with eternal pleasure'.[49] He went on to make the claim that Jews, not satisfied with being Jews, insolently endeavour to transform themselves into Germans – one of the most infamous pieces of deception, according to Hitler, it is possible to imagine. But, while they may acquire the language of the Germans, they remain Jews, according to Hitler, because being German is a matter of race, not language.[50] Elsewhere, he describes how the 'black-haired Jew boy' waits for hours for the helpless girl whom he 'defiles with his blood'.[51] Hitler was hardly giving voice here to original ideas; rather he was peddling the stock-in-trade clichés about Jews that had been circulating in Germany and elsewhere for years. But it was *My Struggle* which popularized these ideas. Even if only some of those Germans who acquired one of the almost 12.5 million copies produced during the Third Reich actually read it,[52] many cinemagoers will surely have recognized its ideas in the film *Jew Süss*. Here too we have a court Jew who provides an aristocrat with the money to indulge in 'eternal pleasure'. Here too we have a Jew who, in imposing arbitrary taxes, brings hardship to ordinary people. Here too we have a Jew who assumes the identity of a gentile, but whose Jewishness is recognized by a non-Jewish German who can 'sense' Jewishness behind the mask. And here, too, we have a dark-haired Jew leering over a defenceless Aryan woman. The links between Hitler and *Jew Süss* are many.

The Reception of *Jew Süss*

The premiere of *Jew Süss* took place at the Venice Biennale on 5 September 1940. Goebbels was satisfied with its impact.[53] He sent a report for Hitler's perusal.[54] Goebbels was ecstatic about the success of the German premiere in Berlin on 24 September 1940, which was attended by almost the entire Reich cabinet. 'There is only enthusiasm,' he wrote: 'the auditorium went wild. That's how I had wanted it.'[55] Hitler was not present: since the start of the war he no longer attended film showings in cinemas. Goebbels informed him of the film's success and Hitler was impressed.[56] From Berlin, where 60,000 people had seen it in the Ufa Palace by 7 October,[57] *Jew Süss* made its way around the Reich, pulling in large audiences. In Frankfurt, where *Jew Süss* was first shown in November 1940, the premiere cinema was bedecked with flowers in honour of the occasion. Newspapers reported record audiences in German towns. By mid-December 1940, for instance, 75 per cent of those living in the Saarland town of St Wenzel had seen *Jew Süss*, and 66 per cent of the population of Mährisch-Ostrau in Moravia. Seventy thousand crammed into Munich's Atlantik Palace in the first twenty days of the film's showing.[58] The 100,000th cinemagoer to have seen *Jew Süss* in Königsberg was rewarded with a spray of white chrysanthemums and a present of marzipan bearing the Ufa logo. She appeared delighted.[59] The Nazi propaganda machine soon ensured that *Jew Süss* was shown in Nazi-occupied territories such as Denmark, Belgium, Holland, Luxemburg and northern France.[60] Only in the unoccupied zone of France were there significant protests, and the French resistance planted bombs at screenings.[61] *Jew Süss* was also dispatched to Axis countries such as Bulgaria and Hungary. In Budapest, the film showed to packed houses for four weeks. Overall, *Jew Süss* was a huge success. According to Otto Froböse, Terra's financial auditor, about 450 copies of *Jew Süss* were made, with another 150 copies going out to the Wehrmacht, Nazi Party organizations, SS and propaganda offices; a film would be considered to have done well if 250 copies had been produced. Fröböse reckoned that some 21 million people had seen the film; omitted from this figure are those who saw it outside of commercial cinemas. It brought in about 20 million Reichsmarks at the box office.[62] The Nazi press declared it the most viewed film of 1940, and it still reached 6 million viewers in 1941.[63]

Critics have sometimes been reluctant to make judgements about the power of *Jew Süss*. Such caution underestimates the potential impact of a plot designed to appeal to all the stereotypical neuroses about 'the Jewish enemy' on German audiences already steeped in anti-Semitic propaganda.[64] 'Surely no other film has succeeded in having such an effect on so many parts of the audience as this,' claimed a Security Police report for the Bielefeld area.[65] 'Half-Jew' Ralph Giordano, later to become a famous writer, remembered seeing the film as a teenager. He describes the 'heavy atmosphere' in the cinema as the lights came back on at the end: 'the murderous effect of the film was oppressively palpable'.[66] Helene Rothenberg, whose Jewish husband was forced out of the banking business in 1936, later recalled that, on leaving a Berlin-Neukölln cinema after watching *Jew Süss*, she overheard fellow cinemagoers calling for the Jews to be strung up: 'the Führer said the Jews are to blame for our problems'.[67] Young Germans were particularly susceptible to the film. Franz Mahler was thirteen when, in 1942, he had to watch it during a Youth Film Hour. He and his comrades took *Jew Süss* for historical truth; the 'badness of the Jews' made a deep impression, generating a 'strong mood of hatred towards Jews'.[68] In Buchau in Württemberg, when the film was shown in November 1940, Jewish citizens had their windows smashed. Members of the Hitler Youth built a makeshift gallows on the square where Buchau's synagogue had stood before being burnt to the ground during Reichskristallnacht. From the gallows dangled a life-size dummy, representing a Jew.[69] There will have been other similar incidents throughout the Reich, and the Security Police in their report on the impact of the film refer to protests against Jews. In Berlin, there were calls for Jews to be expelled, an indication that *Jew Süss* was proving efficient preparation for widespread acceptance of the deportation of German Jews envisaged by Hitler and Goebbels.[70] In mid-1941, shortly before the introduction of the 'Jewish badge' and the large-scale deportation of German Jews as of October, both *Jew Süss* and *The Rothschilds* were again promoted in German cinemas.[71]

The film's impact on audiences in the occupied territories and in Axis countries was also considerable. In Antwerp, after *Jew Süss* was screened in the autumn of 1942 to invited members of the nationalist Flemish organization Vlaams Nationaal Verbond and Léon Degrelle's Rexist Party, the audience streamed out of the cinema cursing Jews. They smashed Jewish property and committed acts of violence against Jews.[72] According to a report that Goebbels showed to Hitler, tumult broke out in Budapest's Ufa cinema at the premiere there in 1941, with members of the audience calling out during the scene showing Süss's execution that 'we should do the same with the Jews in Budapest'.[73] In Italy, the showing of *Jew Süss* led directly to anti-Jewish violence in Casale and Trieste.[74] While it is clear that the protest and violence in Antwerp, Budapest and in some cases elsewhere emanated from fascist groups, it would be a mistake to assume, as one historian has done, that it was therefore merely 'staged'.[75] It would also be a mistake to imagine that, because Hitler Youth groups in Germany were made to watch the film and encouraged to 'react', this reaction was merely 'a performance'. In any case, planned anti-Semitic violence is hardly any less reprehensible than spontaneous violence, if indeed the two forms can be truly separated. Nor can we simply assume such violence, physical or verbal, was restricted to fascist groupings. Béla Angyal, a Hungarian teacher living near the Urania Cinema in Budapest at the time, remembered seeing cinemagoers streaming out of the cinema issuing threats against Jews or shouting 'Down with the Jews!'[76] Belgian Jew Rudy Rosenberg recalls that, when he saw *Jew Süss* in Brussels, the audience stood up cheering.[77]

So convinced was Heinrich Himmler of the film's power that he quickly ordered its deployment as part of the preparatory 'training' of the SS. On 30 September 1940, Himmler sent out an order that all SS and police members watch *Jew Süss* in the course of the winter.[78] On 15 November, he issued another ruling insisting that all members of the Order Police and Security Police who had not yet seen the film be made to do so.[79] Himmler's orders were followed. Thus, a mere week after the second edict, the SS and police leader for the district of Lublin informed local SS commanders that special showings for SS and police members had been organized; units serving outside Lublin were to be transported to the cinema by bus.[80] This was the very town from which Harlan had wanted to take his Jewish extras. Now, ten months later, *Jew Süss* was being used to help reinforce the anti-Semitism driving the already murderous forced labour programme to which Jews were being subjected in the Lublin area.[81] Harlan's film was routinely shown at Nazi concentration camps to camp personnel. The commandant at Buchenwald ordered that *Jew Süss* be viewed by guards 'as a collective' in October 1940,[82] and it was mandatory viewing for female guards at Ravensbrück camp north of Berlin.[83] According to a former inmate of Dachau concentration camp, Max Kronfelder, it was used 'more or less as a training film' for the SS guards there.[84] Former prisoners testified during the post-war Harlan trials that such viewings at concentration camps led to violence. One witness stated there was systematic brutality against Jews at Sachsenhausen after the film was viewed.[85] This is confirmed by another former prisoner, who claimed Jews were tortured after the showing of *Jew Süss* at Sachsenhausen more than on any other occasion.[86] Similar testimonies exist which indicate that *Jew Süss* triggered anti-Semitic violence in Neuengamme and Auschwitz.[87] While not all of this testimony could be adequately verified,[88] enough has accrued over the decades to suggest that camp guards reacted to viewing *Jew Süss* by taking out on prisoners the anti-Semitic anger it generated. There is also evidence that the Nazi Einsatzgruppen (task forces) were shown the film prior to deportations or the shooting of Jews.[89] *Jew Süss* was also widely shown to the German army. In November 1940, the Supreme Command of the Wehrmacht even ordered extra copies of the film in response to high levels of demand.[90] *Jew Süss* was still being shown to troops in the late stages of the war. One officer in a troop camp near Lüneburg recalled that it was shown twice a week, and that the effect of its anti-Semitic agitation on the soldiers was 'catastrophic'.[91]

Jew Süss, and to a lesser extent *The Eternal Jew* and *The Rothschilds*, was regarded by the Nazis as a flexible tool which could be usefully deployed in a number of situations, as one example will illustrate. In October 1940, Arthur Greiser, the Gauleiter of the Warthegau (formed from Nazi-occupied territory in Poland) organized a showing of *Jew Süss* in Posen for Nazi officials. He wanted to celebrate the anniversary of the incorporation of the Warthegau into the German Reich and the programme of German resettlement in the area. Greiser informed Hitler's chief adjutant Wilhelm Brückner, presumably hoping Hitler could be tempted to come. Frustrated by obstacles placed in his path as he tried to clear the Warthegau of Jews and Poles, Greiser no doubt hoped the film showing would strengthen the anti-Semitic resolve of local Nazi leaders.[92] We certainly need to know more about the range of specific contexts between 1940 and 1945 in which *Jew Süss* was shown, and to trace more connections between showings and anti-Semitic acts; we also need to know more about effects on different audiences, and changes in effects over time. Nevertheless, we know enough to understand that the film was used to support the anti-Semitic programme of deportation, ghettoization and, ultimately, genocide. Had Hamburg's Regional Court had more archival evidence at its disposal in 1950, it surely would not have acquitted Harlan of being implicated in crimes against humanity. In 1942, Goebbels told Harlan that Hitler regarded Moses as the father of anti-Semitism, and anti-Semitism itself as having originally been designed to strengthen solidarity among Jews. Now, according to Goebbels, Hitler had redirected anti-Semitism to protect Germans from Jews.[93] The message of *Jew Süss* is precisely of the need for solidarity and resolve on the part of Germans in the face of the 'Jewish threat'. The film presents the murder of Süss and the expulsion of Jews as acts of self-defence, exactly in line with Hitler's insistence in public rhetoric that anti-Jewish measures were purely protective. Harlan brought Hitler's anti-Semitism to the screen.

The Eternal Jew

In November 1937, the Nazi travelling exhibition *The Eternal Jew* opened in Munich.[94] It set out to present the physical attributes of Jews in the worst possible light, to highlight their dominance in pre-National Socialist culture and politics, to link Jews with Bolshevism, and to encourage the belief that they were 'alien'. To be seen in the exhibition was a short film, *Jews Unmasked*, which aimed to demonstrate the negative influence of Jews on the German film industry. Immediately after Reichskristallnacht, on 12 November 1938, *The Eternal Jew* exhibition opened in Berlin. A series of associated film showings under the heading 'The Eternal Jew Disturbs Peace in the World' was organized for party gatherings, with *Jews Unmasked* as the main attraction.[95] Goebbels, however, had a poor opinion of the propagandistic power of *Jews Unmasked*.[96] The idea for the 1940 film *The Eternal Jew* probably emerged in the wake of Reichskristallnacht and against the background of Goebbels' wish to 'improve' on *Jews Unmasked*. But concrete plans for an extended anti-Semitic documentary film were only set in motion with the Nazi invasion of Poland and under the impact of Nazi anti-Semitic measures there.

In early October 1939, Goebbels discussed the making of a 'ghetto film' with Fritz Hippler, head of the Film Department within the Propaganda Ministry. Goebbels wanted it to contain 'the most vicious anti-Semitic propaganda that one can think of'.[97] In a further conversation with Hippler and Eberhard Taubert (responsible for the screenplay), Goebbels emphasized that the film was to be based on material filmed in Poland, and 'should be finished in 3 to 4 weeks'.[98] 'These Jews are not people any more,' Goebbels wrote, 'they are predators possessed of a cold intellect, who must be dealt with.'[99] Hippler left for Łódź in Poland. After the war he claimed that, at the time, he had no idea the material Goebbels wanted him to film was intended for use in a 'documentary'; he had assumed that it was destined for the archive. Goebbels had said to him he wanted his camera team to record Jewish life 'at its point of origin' because soon there would be no Jews living there any more. 'The Führer,' Goebbels had told Hippler, 'wants to deport them all, to Madagascar or to other areas.'[100] Film scholar Felix Moeller accuses Hippler of being a 'brazen liar'. Rather, Hippler was being selective with the truth.[101] In early October 1939, Goebbels voiced his dissatisfaction with the material filmed by the propaganda companies.[102] Among other things, he wanted more images of 'Jewish types of all kinds',[103] and complained that film reports had so far failed to register the 'completely devastated' Jewish quarters. To remedy the situation, Goebbels dispatched Propaganda Ministry officials Eberhard Fangauf and Josef Henke to Poland to act as advisers to the 8th Army's propaganda units.[104] Camera teams – including Hippler and Taubert – were sent to Warsaw, Łódź and Cracow to 'fulfil special tasks'.[105] While Goebbels was indeed thinking of using some of the resulting material for 'archive purposes',[106] it was also intended for the newsreels, and, in the case of the ghetto sequences, for what became *The Eternal Jew*.[107] In 1940, Hippler talked quite openly about his involvement in the project in Nazi media.[108] In any case, had his footage only been intended for the 'archive', this would hardly have made it innocent. It would have acted as a celebratory record of the Nazi destruction of European Jewry.

Hippler returned to Berlin with, as Goebbels put it, 'lots of material for the ghetto film'. Goebbels immediately informed Hitler, who showed great interest, of preparations for the film. After viewing the material, particularly the scenes of ritual slaughter, Goebbels wrote: 'this Jewry must be annihilated'.[109] On 18 November 1939, Goebbels noted that a rough cut of the film was ready.[110] He talked again to Hitler about it, and Hitler made 'a few suggestions'.[111] Towards the end of November, Goebbels declared the film, which he hoped would be a 'propagandistic masterpiece',[112] to be ready.[113] Yet work continued on it through December and January 1940.[114] Following a meeting with Hitler, Goebbels wrote: 'I will have to make more alterations to the Jew film.'[115] The film was presented on 1 March 1940 to a group of Nazi representatives including, from the Chancellery of the Führer, Victor Brack, notorious for his involvement in the Nazi euthanasia programme. At this point, *The Eternal Jew* was to begin with scenes of swarming rats and end with images of Jewish ritual slaughter.[116] Already planned, too, was the inclusion of a sequence from Hitler's 30 January 1939 speech threatening the annihilation of the Jews. All participants responded to viewing it by bursting into spontaneous applause.[117] Otto von Kursell of the Staatliche Hochschule suggested ending the film with this sequence, and indeed, in the final version, it comes almost at the end. By early April, Goebbels was confident that the revised version of *The Eternal Jew* could now be shown to Hitler,[118] but still further amendments were required,[119] including alterations to the voiceover text.[120] In September, Goebbels declared his belief that 'now the documentary film is quite excellent'.[121] Even now, following a presentation of the film to representatives of the party, Wehrmacht, SA and SS, a further cut was required so that two versions of the film would be available: one with ritual slaughter scenes, one without – for the squeamish.[122]

Clearly, changes resulted from Hitler's interventions, particularly in early January and again in early May 1940. At these times, Hitler was either planning to launch or in the process of launching an attack on Western Europe. On 10 January, he felt compelled to call off the planned attack on Belgium following the so-called Mechelen incident, when papers detailing outlines of the plan fell into enemy hands; on 10 May 1940, the postponed attack on the West went ahead. In his diary on 8 May 1940, Rosenberg castigates Goebbels for lacking political instinct in his management of the film industry; according to Rosenberg, Goebbels had overseen the production of pro-English films when it was clear a conflict with Britain was on the cards. And now, in *The Fox of Glenarvon* (1940), pro-Irish sentiment was 'laid on with a trowel'.[123] One day later, Goebbels wrote of the need for revisions to *The Eternal Jew*.[124] Did revisions have to be made because the film drew connections between Britain and Jewry at a time Hitler regarded as politically inopportune, or, quite the opposite, because connections were not drawn strongly enough?[125] Or did changes have to be made simply to keep pace with material facts? On 5 January

1940, Leslie Hore-Belisha, the British secretary of state for war, resigned, to be replaced by Oliver Stanley.[126] It is quite likely the condemnation of the 'Jew' Hore-Belisha in *The Eternal Jew* had to be adapted, at least at a textual level, to take account of his resignation. But a key motive for changes surely lay in the wish to radicalize the anti-Semitic message. On 9 May 1940, Goebbels noted in his diary that Himmler had spoken of the need to impose 'iron discipline' on Poland's Jews, and of Hitler's fury that Jews had been put to work among German workers, rather than segregated from them. It was also in May that Hitler responded positively to Himmler's memorandum proposing the 'emigration of all Jews to Africa'.[127]

The Eternal Jew finally premiered in Berlin on 28 November 1940. Lest *The Rothschilds* and *Jew Süss* be understood as propaganda, Goebbels ruled that the word 'anti-Semitic' not be applied to them in the advertising campaign and in the media; they were to speak for themselves.[128] His absence from the premiere of *The Eternal Jew* was similarly motivated: audiences were not to think that the documentary film was Nazi propaganda. The first showing was preceded by a documentary short, *The German East*, and a performance of Beethoven's *Egmont* Overture. The combination of *The German East* with *The Eternal Jew* reinforced the message that Jews had no place in an expanded Germany and German-controlled East. Film scholar Stig Hornshøj-Møller argues that *The Eternal Jew* was intended to provide propagandistic legitimation for the deportation of German Jews.[129] This may indeed have been part of the original motivation. In September 1939, Hitler had given his approval for establishing a 'reservation' for Reich Jews in eastern Poland. But the mass deportation of German Jews did not begin, by and large, until October 1941. That Hippler was sent by Goebbels to Łódź in late 1939 to film Eastern European Jews indicates that *The Eternal Jew*'s main function lay elsewhere. It was to justify to German audiences the measures taken by the Nazis in Poland against Polish Jews. 'International Jewry' had always been a target of Nazi propaganda, but, before the Second World War began, dealing with Eastern European Jews had been less of a concern to Hitler than forcing the emigration of Germany's own Jews. After September 1939, the threat, according to the Nazis, now emanated from eastern Jews. *The Eternal Jew* shows Polish Jews living in terrible poverty. That they lived in abject conditions seemed to belie the Nazi claim about their incredible power, but, as the film goes on, it 'shows' how such destitute Jews transform themselves into what the Nazis understood to be *Western* Jews: Jews, in other words, who disguised their Jewish origins so as to infiltrate the Western world and acquire power and money. *The Eternal Jew* presents this poverty as a mask, a choice and a temporary state. Germans had to be convinced of the Polish-Jewish threat.

The Eternal Jew is in some respects a documentary version of *Jew Süss*, providing pseudofactual evidence of a supposed trend of which *Jew Süss* was a case study.[130] *The Eternal Jew* argues that, from their base in Eastern Europe, greedy and scheming ghetto Jews fan out into the world – in a manner the film graphically compares to the spread of rats – to take control of other nations. Parasitically trading in goods produced by others, they grow rich, rising to positions of dominance in politics and the arts, bringing corruption and threatening to eliminate the Aryan race. Disturbing scenes of the Jewish ritual slaughter of a cow are followed by the information that Nazism has forbidden this practice and has gone on to ban sexual relations between Jews and Germans, as if one prohibition leads naturally to the other. The 1937 exhibition *The Eternal Jew* had ended with a room detailing the Nuremberg race laws, as if these were the answer to the 'Jewish problem'. In the 1940 film *The Eternal Jew*, such laws are no longer enough. Towards the end, the film shows footage of Hitler issuing his 30 January 1939 threat about the annihilation of Jews in the event of war. Given that this war had now begun, the viewer was surely to assume that annihilation might at some point follow. The Hitler footage is immediately followed by images of jubilant Germans, marching into the future. Through such juxtaposition, *The Eternal Jew* suggests that Hitler's vision of the annihilation of Jews finds the enthusiastic support of the German people, and that the war is being fought in the interests of upholding purity of blood. Like *Jew Süss*, *The Eternal Jew* makes clear to Germans, if they had not already understood, that the war was a racial one, a life-and-death struggle against Jews. It makes of Hitler's words of 30 January 1939 a statement of intent and a call to arms, spoken – in the context of the film – against the background of images of supposed Jewish savagery.

According to Security Service reports, audiences in Munich applauded 'as if liberated' during the scene of Hitler's speech. Nevertheless, even Hitler's cameo appearance – for all its significance in shaping the film's message – could not rescue *The Eternal Jew* from a rather lukewarm reception at the box office. In Berlin, it was initially envisaged that *The Eternal Jew* would be shown in sixty-six cinemas as of 29 November 1940, but only a day later, this number had sunk to thirty-six; by 13 December 1940, it was only showing in one cinema in the city.[131] The same Security Service report that told of positive reactions in Munich also commented on the fact that, while attendance was initially high, audience numbers soon dropped off, perhaps because *The Eternal Jew* came too soon after *Jew Süss*, or because the scenes of Jewish ritual slaughter were too much to take; women and younger men, according to the report, had fainted.[132] Some commentators have suggested that Hitler and Goebbels had kept tinkering with *The Eternal Jew* because they feared it would not prove effective as propaganda, or would flop, or both.[133] It has also been suggested that they delayed its premiere until after that of *Jew Süss* in the hope that it would benefit at the box office from the latter's anticipated success. The opposite was the case: by the time *The Eternal Jew* reached the cinema, German audiences, it seemed, had already got the point about the Jewish threat. Unlike *Jew Süss*, which offered positive German figures (such as the innocent Dorothea) with whom audiences could identify, *The Eternal Jew* mostly presented only a parade of supposedly evil Jews. For all its attempts to do so, *The Eternal Jew* never really resolved the apparent contradiction between the images of Jewish poverty it showed and its claims that Jews wielded enormous power. Its mixture of supposed statistics, collage, horrific images and recycling of older film material was simultaneously imaginative and crude, manipulative and sordid.

Yet as Saul Friedländer points out, the varying commercial fates of *Jew Süss* and *The Eternal Jew* should not be viewed 'as contrary results in terms of Goebbels' intentions. Images from both films were endlessly replicated in Nazi anti-Semitic posters or publications, all over the Reich and occupied Europe.'[134] Moreover, like *Jew Süss* and to a degree *The Rothschilds* following its reintroduction in 1942, *The Eternal Jew* was repeatedly deployed – not least in the occupied countries – in support of anti-Semitic measures. Thus it was shown in mid-June 1942 in Paris to help prepare the way for the introduction of the yellow star for Jews, albeit without attracting large numbers of cinemagoers.[135] There is no doubt that Hitler was kept well informed by Goebbels about the making of *Jew Süss*, and no doubt either that he closely monitored and influenced the making of *The Eternal Jew*. These films accompanied the radicalization of anti-Jewish policy which emanated from Hitler, their gestation reflected that radicalization, and their screening aimed to promote it. In a review stressing the importance of *The Eternal Jew*, the main Nazi newspaper the *Völkischer Beobachter* argued that, contrary to what some might think, the 'Jewish question' was not yet over and would not be 'until the very last phase of the war is complete'.[136] Anti-Semitic film was to be a source of constant racial mobilization. *Jew Süss* and *The Eternal Jew* were useful in this respect because they reinterpreted the story of the wandering Jew not as a tale of Jewish punishment (for taunting Christ), but as one of Jewish conspiracy. They sought to intensify neurotic fears of the Jews. Film production and the politics of destruction in the Third Reich 'collaborated closely'.[137] At the centre of this politics of destruction stood Hitler himself.

9

From Hero to Camera-shy

HITLER IN THE NAZI WARTIME NEWSREELS

Throughout the war, Hitler maintained a consistent interest in the Wochenschau, the weekly newsreel. His interventions ranged from trivial corrections to demands for newsreels that showed more action. At times, Goebbels could not wait for the next military campaign to start, so desperate was he to present Hitler, as well as the German population, with newsreels that packed the required punch.[1] Military events were to be portrayed in a way that fulfilled Hitler's wish to see ongoing success, something that became harder to do as the war continued. What also became harder was securing Hitler's agreement to appear in the newsreels. His gradual disappearance created a dilemma for Goebbels, who knew how important it was for German audiences to be able to see Hitler.

Wochenschau, War, Hitler

When the Second World War began, the Wochenschau had already been significantly streamlined by Goebbels, not least in response to Hitler. On 17 December 1938, Goebbels noted in his diary that the 'Führer had complained about the Wochenschau'. This was not the first time. During the summer of 1938, as tensions with Czechoslovakia grew, Hitler had called for the weekly newsreels to be 'politically cleverer' in their propagandistic handling of the crisis. Goebbels resolved to set things straight by 'putting new people at the helm' of the newsreel production.[2] By early 1939, the 'reorganization of the Wochenschau' was in hand, and Goebbels anticipated that Hitler would be more satisfied than he had been.[3] An essential part of that reorganization was replacing the then head of coordinating the Wochenschau, Hans Weidemann, with the fanatical Nazi Fritz Hippler.[4] Centralization of the Wochenschau was well under way by the start of the war. A renewed intervention on Hitler's part in December 1939, however, caused Goebbels to accelerate the process. Hitler, according to Goebbels, had expressed 'severe criticism' of film, 'particularly the Wochenschau, and that in front of all the officers and adjutants'.[5] Alfred Rosenberg also records Hitler's criticisms of the Wochenschau, albeit more drastically: Hitler, wrote Rosenberg, found the newsreels 'unimaginative and disinterested'.[6] Goebbels responded by complaining to army liaison officer Bruno Wentscher about the inferior quality of the footage being provided for the Wochenschau. Among other things, it was too dark; the army had been insisting that reporters do extensive military drill during daylight hours, which meant they were filming in twilight conditions. Goebbels subsequently became embroiled in a dispute with Army High Command about the prioritization of military discipline over good propaganda material.[7] And he made further organizational changes to the newsreel production, as he did after renewed complaints from Hitler in early 1941.[8] The Wochenschau, as Goebbels once put it, was Hitler's 'favourite child' in the area of film production.[9] No doubt that was the reason why Goebbels arguably overreacted to Hitler's concerns, and why he was so keen to note Hitler's generally positive responses to the newsreels in his diary.

No amount of reorganization could change the fact that Hitler would always exercise his right of veto. Hitler was both indirectly and directly involved in the production of weekly newsreels – at the beginning and at the end of the process respectively. Like all Nazi propaganda, the news-reels were shaped in general terms by the directives and statements of Hitler himself, and to an extent also by the pronouncements of Göring and Reich Press Chief Otto Dietrich.[10] More specifically, of course, they were steered by Goebbels' Propaganda Ministry. The ministry issued 'propaganda instructions' on a regular basis to the propaganda companies. The material filmed by the companies was subject to military censorship when sent back to the Wehrmacht's Propaganda Department in Berlin – clearly, it was important not to release images that might provide the enemy with unwanted insights into the workings of the Wehrmacht's mili-tary operations and weaponry.[11] Then it was the task of the Propaganda Ministry to choose and collate material garnered from the propaganda companies and other sources (such as the Army, Navy and Air Force Film Offices). Overseeing this process – needless to say, under the close control of Goebbels – was Fritz Hippler. Representatives of the ministry, the army, the Foreign Office and the Reich Labour Service would then view the draft newsreel, as would Goebbels. The Wochenschau could not be released, however, until it had passed the final hurdle: Hitler himself. Hippler sent on a copy of the weekly newsreel, with a typescript of the text that was to serve as voiceover, to Hitler's Adjutants Office.[12] Goebbels' diaries refer to frequent wartime discussions with Hitler about the Wochenschau.[13] Other archival sources confirm Hitler's newsreel viewings. Hitler's adjutant Max Wünsche noted 'Wochenschau' showings in October 1939.[14] Hitler's valet Heinz Linge also documented regular newsreel viewings by Hitler.[15]

That no Wochenschau could be released until Hitler's alterations were made was confirmed by his former personal adjutant Otto Günsche and valet Heinz Linge. Hitler would ask for images to be changed or for the accompanying text to be revised.[16] Hitler's personal orderly, Karl Wilhelm Krause, recalled in his memoir that the newsreels were shown to Hitler without sound while one of his adjutants read out the text. When Hitler thought that the text did not fit the image, he changed it.[17] A few of these changes survive for three newsreels from mid-1940, although the alterations are barely legible, and some may have been made by Goebbels rather than Hitler. In the case of the changes that can be attributed to Hitler, it can be said that he occasionally sought to sharpen the tone, or made corrections to military terminology. Thus the original text for a July 1940 newsreel, following a report on British bombing raids, claims that 'everywhere our aircraft are getting their weapons ready for deployment against England'. Hitler has changed this to 'getting their weapons ready for the hour of retribution', making clear that German raids are an act of retaliation.[18] In the text for a newsreel of late June 1940, in a passage about crossing the Rhine, Hitler crosses out 'dinghy' and replaces it with 'raft'; elsewhere, the phrase 'reporting to the battery' has been replaced with 'report to the artillery', and 'armoured car' substituted with 'armoured combat vehicle'.[19] These minute changes suggest a particularly sharp eye. Possibly, though, Hitler was here being advised by the military personnel with whom he also watched the newsreels. Hans Baur, Hitler's pilot, recalled Hitler's scrutiny of the Wochenschau at the Reich Chancellery, with Chief of Army Staff Alfred Jodl and Wehrmacht Chief Wilhelm Keitel also in attendance.[20] In his various headquarters, too, Hitler also watched the Wochenschau with Armed Forces representatives. It was Goebbels who made sure that Hitler also had access to the newsreels at his HQ. He had a projector sent there so that Hitler could watch the Wochenschau. 'That's also very important for my work,' Goebbels wrote.[21]

As Supreme Commander of the Armed Forces, Hitler naturally had an interest in ensuring that the image propagated by newsreels – which were also shown in modified form in the occupied countries and watched by Allied intelligence – corresponded to the military and political interests of the Reich. He had, of course, already acted as news censor before the war. The ban he placed on the showing of film material of the battle of Narwik in 1940 until the British withdrew from Norway had a pre-war equivalent:[22] his embargo on any reporting of the Legion Condor's involvement in the Spanish Civil War. He had also followed newsreel reporting of military matters before the war, sometimes not so much acting as censor as counteracting the censorship imposed by the army's weapons inspectorate. Thus, in April 1939, he insisted on including footage of heavy-duty long-barrelled cannons which the inspectorate had cut out of the report on a military parade.[23] But during the war Hitler strove to make the propagandistic message even more forceful. In March 1942, for instance, while pleased at seeing film of U-boats, he asked for the accompanying commentary – 'several are launched weekly' – to be changed to 'they are being launched continually'.[24] When the Wochenschau did not provide the impressive images he wanted to see, he asked for them to be produced. In the spring of 1940, he had a film team sent to the Krupp factory in Essen to film as a matter of urgency the manufacture of cannons, shells and tanks for Wochenschau purposes.[25] Goebbels could usually count on Hitler being prepared to allow the showing of armaments in the newsreels when the Wehrmacht preferred to exercise caution.[26] Even in 1944, when Hitler's Wochenschau viewing became irregular, he reserved the right to decide in important cases whether armaments should be shown. Thus, after some hesitation, he permitted the release of images of the V1 rockets in July 1944.[27]

Hitler saw in the Wochenschau a means of impressing and reassuring the Germans, as well as intimidating the occupied countries and the Allies. As long as the German forces were advancing, Hitler was satisfied with the Wochenschau because it reflected the dynamism he wanted to see. When there was a lull or a setback, or there was nothing exciting to report, he became impatient. Goebbels invested considerable energies in overseeing the production in the Wochenschau of a constant impression, week after week, of German triumph or at least military strength. Sometimes this impression corresponded to the facts; sometimes it did not, especially during and following the disastrous battle of Stalingrad in 1942–43, when it became harder and harder to sustain. On the other hand, Hitler was also quite prepared to countenance the showing of Soviet atrocities to warn the German people as to the possible effects of Bolshevism. Some negative impressions were acceptable. For instance, he rang Goebbels in early July

1941 to tell him that a newsreel showing 'Bolshevik atrocities' in Lemberg (Lviv) was the best he had ever seen.[28] He also appeared to support Goebbels' wish to include footage of Soviet crimes at Katyn in the newsreels; the Germans had found the graves of murdered Polish officers there in early 1943. But Hitler's generals succeeded in having the footage cut out, on the grounds that relatives of German soldiers missing in action would be upset by the gruesome images.[29] As with feature film, Goebbels had to contend with interference from various quarters when it came to the Wochenschau. Shortly after the discussions about the footage of Katyn, he complained that there were far too many military personnel present at newsreel censorship meetings, and far too few Propaganda Ministry representatives.[30] As Hitler withdrew more and more in 1944, Goebbels had to sift Hitler's opinions about the Wochenschau from those of others at his HQ purporting to represent his views. In December 1944, a supposed Führer edict forbidding the showing of footage of defusing unexploded bombs turned out to be an invention of others at Führer HQ; Hitler had not even been present at the newsreel showing.[31]

There was only so much Goebbels could do to respond to Hitler's constant need for newsreels in which he could see a confirmation of progress. When Goebbels wanted to include 'homeland subjects' in the newsreels, to compensate for the lack of good material from the front, Hitler rejected the idea.[32] And there was little he could do to stop Hitler, as the war wore on, from insisting that any images which suggested defeat be removed and replaced with footage from earlier in the war when things were going better for the Nazis.[33] As Goebbels planned from Wochenschau to Wochenschau, Hitler was thinking in terms of copying Wochenschau material onto metal to preserve newsreels for later generations as a 'report of experience'.[34] The newsreels were to be his legacy, as well as propaganda for the present. With palpable frustration, Goebbels complained in mid-1942 that 'the Führer wants somewhat more from the Wochenschau than it can do'. 'The Wochenschau,' he went on, 'is not in a position to deliver, every time, an instant documentary film. It can only use the material that is momentarily available.'[35] Hitler wanted the Wochenschau to provide a well-rounded overview of a military event, a documentary record for posterity, rather than simply a snapshot of the front. In mid-1941, Hitler asked Goebbels to include more polemic in the newsreels; Goebbels wanted the images to speak for themselves.[36] We could read this as proof that Hitler wanted more explicit propaganda, while Goebbels was interested in the more implicit form (what David Welch calls the 'lie indirect').[37] But it can be read differently. Images would not speak so easily for themselves in the future; polemic would ensure their 'correct' interpretation.

Hitler in the Wartime Wochenschau

As the Germans notched up victory after victory, Goebbels and Hitler not only desired dynamic newsreels of events at the front, they also wanted to connect Hitler to them visually. The Hitler iconography of the pre-war period, in the press and newsreel, was to be intensified as Hitler sent his Armed Forces into battle. Hitler wanted to ensure he would be filmed in a manner that best reflected his importance. The man responsible for shooting much of the footage of Hitler during the Second World War was Walter Frentz, who had worked with Leni Riefenstahl on both *Triumph of the Will* (1935) and *Olympia* (1938). He accompanied Hitler as cameraman on his election tour of Austria in 1938. Riefenstahl's company Olympia-Film 'leased out' Frentz to the Reich Chancellery in July 1939.[38] After 1 September, he became Hitler's personal film-cameraman for the newsreels. Thus it was that the triumphal and celebratory aesthetics of Riefenstahl's style, conveyed through the camera of Walter Frentz, found their way into the Nazi Wochenschau particularly in the earlier part of the war. Not that Frentz was the only person to film Hitler:[39] when Hitler's cavalcade entered Danzig in September 1939, for instance, camera teams occupied different positions to provide different perspectives. But Frentz often enjoyed exclusive access.[40]

Without doubt, the highpoint of Hitler's representation in Nazi newsreels began in September 1939 and culminated in the imagery surrounding the defeat of France in 1940. Goebbels' propaganda machine generally set out to present Hitler's war as a necessary act of self-defence. The attack on Poland, like the occupation of the Sudetenland, was, according to the newsreels, but another example of Hitler acting in the interests of threatened Germans. A newsreel of February 1940 treats the viewer to an excerpt from a 30 January 1940 speech by Hitler in which he insists on the 'right to life' of 80 million Germans. The excerpt is preceded by a history lesson. The speaker tells us that Germany has smashed the Treaty of Versailles and created a 'people's empire' in the heart of Europe – one which, according to the map we are shown, includes the area of occupied Poland known as the General Government (which was never a part of Germany in the past). But Western powers, the speaker continues, want to carve up Germany and leave nothing of it for the Germans, with Saxony to be given to the Czechs, for instance, and Schleswig-Holstein to Denmark.[41]

This narrative, with Hitler as the dynamizing force of German self-preservation, underlies many Nazi newsreels. Germans who went to the cinema in September 1939 could watch Hitler visiting his troops near the Vistula, driving them on, so the voiceover puts it, to 'unimaginable achievements'. They could see him flying off to the front, chatting to soldiers and nurses, eating soup at the field kitchen, and watching as soldiers crossed the San river. And they could share in his triumph as he was chauffeured in regal style into Łódź, Gdynia and Danzig, crowds cheering as they had when Hitler entered Austria and the Sudetenland following their annexation.[42] To remind audiences of the supposed source of the international conspiracy against Germans, the Wochenschau also showed images of Polish Jews 'whose brothers in England and France', according to the speaker, 'are agitating for a war of annihilation against the German people'.[43] 'I am nothing, German people, but your spokesman,' Hitler said in his 30 January 1940 speech; 'I am he, then, who represents your rights.'[44] In the early stages of the war, Hitler was depicted to audiences as the modest but determined embodiment of their interests, while the Jew was portrayed as the embodiment of the threat to that interest. Hitler's triumph, it was made clear, was to be built on the containment, ghettoization and forced labour of the Jews – all themes of 1939 newsreels.[45]

According to a September 1939 newsreel, Hitler and his soldiers had formed a community committed to live or die for the cause.[46] And it was a good cause even for the dead. A March 1940 Wochenschau shows Hitler honouring the fallen at Berlin's famous Zeughaus (Arsenal) on Heroes Commemoration Day. In his accompanying speech, he asks fate to grant the Germans victory: then the 'spirits of our fallen comrades will rise from their graves' in thanks. He concludes with a solemn assertion that a German victory will be the consequence of the war 'forced upon the Greater German Reich' by capitalist France and Britain.[47] In early June 1940, with German victory over France already on the horizon, Hitler 'came to his soldiers', as the reporting newsreel tells us, on the Western Front. 'He visited the battlefields where he himself had fought as a soldier,' the voiceover continues, before paying his respects at the Heroes Cemetery at Langemarck, the site of a 1917 battle where the 'volunteers of 1914 stormed against the enemy as they sang the German national anthem'.[48] The footage of Hitler at the location of First World War battles, following a particularly mendacious report on the 'total destruction' of the British Expeditionary Force at Dunkirk, implies that the losses of the Great War were not in vain; Germans' deaths had been made good. The wartime newsreels continued to promote the message of pre-war newsreels: Hitler's politics was a politics of redress. Reversing the outcome of the First World War through victory in France, in other words, was presented as an extension of the process that had driven Hitler's reversal of the effects of the Versailles Treaty. Hitler was shown to be setting right the wrongs of history and fulfilling the legacies of past generations.

The Nazi Security Service, or SD, recorded the population's reactions to the newsreels from 1939 through to 1944. The response to the footage of the successful campaign in the West, if we are to believe the SD, was almost ecstatic. In June 1940, many Germans were walking out of the cinema after the newsreels because they found the sequence of Wochenschau and 'shallow feature film' unbearable.[49] There were requests for even longer weekly newsreels (their length had already been extended in September 1939, and the number of copies in circulation increased from 800 to 1,600).[50] So popular was the Wochenschau at this point – and so important its influence – that Goebbels ordered 'newsreel cinemas' to be established throughout the Reich.[51] The SD reported that a Wochenschau of mid-June 1940 was, in the view of the people, 'the best ever'. While the sequences showing Stuka attacks and victory in Dunkirk were one reason for this, it was the images of Hitler that impressed viewers most. Calls of 'Heil!' from within the auditoriums greeted his appearance on screen, followed by a hushed silence when the newsreel showed Hitler walking through the park with his generals, and studying the map. Viewers, so the SD report continued, scrutinized Hitler's every movement, and particularly every movement of his face, 'from which they hoped, as it were, to find out the feelings of Germans as a whole'. But while cinemagoers admired Hitler's presence at the front, they worried for his safety, and his strained, serious expression also gave cause for concern.[52] Here, as in other SD reports – even allowing for a degree of exaggeration – it is clear that the impression of a symbiosis between Hitler and his people that the newsreels sought to convey found a receptive audience. Many Germans had come to believe that Hitler was the personification of the nation, of its collective hopes, aims and concerns. They were prepared to allow their own moods and thoughts to be determined by a newsreel projection of Hitler. Seeing him in the Wochenschau became, for some, a regular 'fix' – a visual need.

The Wochenschau endeavoured to create and disseminate images which suggested Hitler's popularity, but this did not always require effort; sometimes, all that was needed was to have the cameras at the ready when Hitler was mobbed by his fans. The Wochenschau was propaganda, but it also mirrored the adulation it helped to instil. The best example of this is a July 1940 newsreel in which Hitler features for longer than in any other wartime newsreel – at least twenty minutes. As does many a Nazi newsreel, it presents Hitler as Germany's saviour. France has fallen, and the armistice has been signed. But the destruction of France is positively presented as the liberation of Alsace-Lorraine by the Wehrmacht. When we first see Hitler, he is greeting his soldiers in Alsace, before stepping out of his car to feed a horse – the first of many sentimental moments with which this newsreel is replete. Having stressed the 'inseparable bond' between the 'Führer and his soldiers', the newsreel follows Hitler as he enters Strasbourg cathedral. Its bells can be heard celebrating the occasion, and the newsreel adds in a recording of a choir singing an eighteenth-century German folk song about the city and its soldiers. Such images and sounds, welding the Christian with the popular and military, were designed to reinforce the idea that Hitler was a man for *all* the people.[53]

The central section of this long Hitler sequence shows him traversing the country from Strasbourg to Berlin by train, with Germans lining the route as he passes. A farmer waves from his tractor, a brief but powerful moment suggesting Hitler's bond with the rural communities. We see his train passing through Marbach, linking Hitler with a poet-dramatist much lionized by the Nazis – Friedrich Schiller, born in Marbach in 1759. The train stops occasionally for Hitler to allow a young boy to jump into the train beside him or accept a gift from a girl – the bond with youth is not overlooked. At one point, we see Hitler signing photographs of himself and handing them out to a crowd at a station. The newsreel consciously stylizes him (and he stylizes himself) as a figure comparable to a film star, overlooking the difference that Hitler's starring role was not in a film, but in a war he had started. When he arrives in Berlin – again to the sound of church bells – the streets have been strewn with flowers to welcome him as his cavalcade drives from the station to the Reich Chancellery building. He is welcomed as a bringer of peace. Up to this point, one might argue, the newsreel is a skilful piece of stagecraft, manufacturing an impression. But, when Hitler stands on the balcony of the Reich Chancellery and looks out over an immense sea of Germans cheering, waving and swaying with an enthusiasm the security cordon can hardly contain, no more stagecraft is needed. This is a moment, to quote Goebbels, when the images can speak for themselves. For several uncommentated minutes, cinema audiences are invited to share the collective passion. Of course many Germans hoped that, with the fall of France and Britain's retreat, the war would soon be over. In this sense, Hitler *did* appear to be promising peace, and the enthusiasm may reflect a degree of relief. Yet these images are still disturbing. Propaganda and reality overlap, for Hitler's popularity is at its height, despite the brutal subjugation of Poland, Denmark, Norway, Luxemburg, Belgium, Holland and France. Or, perhaps, because of it.

The weekly Nazi newsreels were never able to film such scenes of mass adulation again, because the success of 1940 did not repeat itself. Hitler did still show himself to the people, but with decreasing frequency, and manifestations of popularity captured by the newsreel reporters were usually smaller in scale and unspectacular.[54] In August 1941, just after the campaign against the Soviet Union had begun, and again as the Case Blue plan was launched in mid-1942, Hitler was filmed visiting cheering troops on the Eastern Front. But as it became clear the war against the Soviet Union was not going to be won, Hitler showed little inclination to be filmed among his regular troops. Right into 1944, there were newsreel reports on Hitler's meetings with his generals, and the Wochenschau featured scenes of Hitler handing out medals to members of the Wehrmacht and the SS at his headquarters. Hitler was shown acknowledging military courage, but it was no longer possible to portray him as the First World War veteran keen to share the experience of being with his soldiers at the front. Occasionally, the Wochenschau did show him taking the time to greet and console soldiers maimed in war, as after his traditional Heroes Commemoration Day speech in March 1941 and 1942.[55] Moving as these scenes were, they were not complemented by scenes of Hitler showing a concern for the fate of German soldiers getting ready to face action.

In late 1940, there were newsreels showing Hitler among armaments workers.[56] After this, it was only the armaments that appeared to interest him.[57] He was filmed delivering speeches at the Zeughaus on Heroes

Commemoration Day in March 1940, 1941, 1942 and 1943 (in 1944, Dönitz laid a wreath in his place).[58] In May 1941, newsreel cameras filmed Hitler giving a speech to officer cadets in the Berlin Sportpalast. The same newsreel reported on his speech to the Reichstag in May 1941, and the cameras were also there when he gave what was to be his last Reichstag speech on 26 April 1942.[59] In November 1941, 1942 and 1943, the Wochenschau was there to record him lecturing the party faithful in Munich on the occasion of the commemoration of the 1923 Munich putsch.[60] Cinema audiences could thus, to a diminishing degree, experience Hitler as public speaker in the 1941 to 1943 period, but the public was usually carefully selected, consisting of (often high-ranking) military and political personnel. The newsreels, after mid-1940, were no longer able to provide many images of Hitler which showed him enjoying the attention of crowds of ordinary German citizens.

Hitler's Disappearance from the Newsreels

It is often claimed that Hitler gradually disappeared from the weekly newsreels as the war ground on. This is true, but with qualifications. If we take the number of newsreels in which he appeared, this was higher in 1941 and 1942 than 1940; a significant decrease came in 1943 and particularly 1944 (he only appeared twice in 1945). What was subject to an almost continuous decrease as of mid-1940 was the length of his appearances in any given newsreel. The footage of Hitler became briefer. Just as significant is the manner in which Hitler came to be filmed, with cameras often keeping their distance and largely avoiding close-ups. In sequences showing him awarding medals at his headquarters, Frentz was careful to film him from behind as he approached the awardees, or from the side. Rarely is he seen from the front. Hitler became camera-shy. Scenes in which cinema audiences did get to see him came to resemble one another. The stereotypical predominated, not the (impression of) spontaneity the newsreels had captured in the pre-war and early war period. In addition to showing repetitious scenes of Hitler handing out medals, newsreels included sequence after sequence of various foreign diplomats and politicians – from Japan, Slovakia, Hungary and Italy, for instance – visiting Hitler. Sometimes Hitler did not even appear in these sequences. In October 1940, when Hitler travelled to Hendaye to meet Franco, and then to Florence to meet Mussolini, the newsreel accompanied his train and allowed the cinema audience the privileged sense of travelling with the Führer, and of sharing in Hitler's private (and clearly amusing) conversations with Göring. The same newsreel included images of enthusiastic Italians cheering Mussolini and Hitler in Florence. Later newsreels also showed Hitler meeting Mussolini at the Brenner Pass (1941) and in Salzburg (1942). But for the most part, as of 1941, the newsreels had to content themselves with showing cursory, rather dull images of foreign dignitaries appearing at the Berghof, the Reich Chancellery and Hitler's HQ. They could be seen shaking hands on arrival and departure, but doing little else. Of course the intention was to demonstrate to German audiences the centrality of Hitler and Germany in matters of international diplomacy. Whether German audiences were excited by images of Tiso or King Boris or other Eastern European satraps visiting Hitler is another matter.

Viewers of the Wochenschau did have many opportunities to see Hitler attending funeral ceremonies, mostly in Berlin. He was filmed at official ceremonies in memory of Reich Minister of Justice Franz Gürtner in February 1941, and of the German flying aces Ernst Udet and Werner Mölders in November and December 1941.[61] The fact that Udet had committed suicide following a series of rows with Göring was kept quiet; the official story was that Udet had died trying out new weapons. The newsreels also showed Hitler attending the funeral of Armaments Minister Fritz Todt in February 1942, with whom he had fallen out because Todt insisted it would not be possible to win the war against both the Soviets and the Americans.[62] Rumours that Hitler 'arranged' for the plane accident that killed Todt have never entirely subsided. And the newsreel cameras were present when Hitler attended the funeral ceremony for Reinhard

Heydrich, chief of the Reich Security Main Office, in June 1942 following his assassination in Prague. Heydrich was subsequently turned into a Nazi martyr.[63] At these and other solemn occasions,[64] where he was seen laying wreaths and sometimes offering condolences or conferring special medals, Hitler could stage an intense and impressive show of seriousness. The fact nevertheless remains that, between 1941 and 1944, the Wochenschau screened him attending at least eleven funerals, but could no longer show him celebrating victories. The focus was now on a cult of death.[65] While the pre-1939 newsreels had also reported on the elaborate commemorative rituals surrounding the dead – such as the 'martyrs' of the 1923 Munich putsch – at that time it was always made clear that their deaths had paved the way for the Third Reich. But in 1943 and 1944, the question of the purpose of death remained unanswered. When snippets of Hitler's speeches were conveyed through the Wochenschau in the later years of the war, they often emphasized the importance of sacrifice, whether at the front or in the homeland. Now, fighting was all about the burdens and losses that would have to be borne, not victory.[66]

That Hitler did not appear enough in the newsreels, or only briefly, was a constant gripe. This becomes clear from Security Service reports. Already in June 1940, the SD noted that the population wanted to see more images of Hitler.[67] According to a report of November 1940, footage of Hitler met with 'the greatest interest': 'it is as if a newsreel not showing the Führer is not regarded as a proper Wochenschau'. The same report also claims that there had been complaints that Hitler's own voice had not been heard in the newsreels 'for a long time'.[68] This was an objection repeated more and more over the next three years. Thus, although cinemagoers were grateful to see newsreel images of Hitler in February 1941 – 'every single move-ment of the Führer and every movement of his face is followed with utmost attention' – they expressed regret that they could not hear him speaking.[69] After Operation Barbarossa was launched in June 1941, the SD registered complaints that Hitler was absent from the newsreels reporting on events at the Eastern Front.[70] Hitler's reappearance among his soldiers at the front in August 1941 triggered a powerful response. SD reports related that there had been a 'deep silence' in the auditorium; many viewers had registered every one of Hitler's movements. The sight of his hands moving in circles across the General Staff maps made a great impression, 'because people saw in these movements the sealing of the fate of further Soviet armies'.[71] But, as Hitler's newsreel appearances became fewer and shorter, so the public dissatisfaction grew, to judge from SD observation.[72] The visual exposure of the German population to Hitler since 1933 had created a dependency. What the SD reports describe are withdrawal symptoms – not on Hitler's part, but on the part of a public for whom seeing Hitler had become a source of spiritual and ideological sustenance. Because many Germans had abandoned themselves to Hitler, when he abandoned them by not showing himself, some of them, at least, lost orientation.

There can be little doubt it was Hitler himself who was responsible for withholding images of his own person from the Wochenschau. On 6 October 1942, Goebbels confided to his diary that he was in a 'proper dilemma: on the one hand, the Führer does not want to be shown, while on the other we receive countless letters from the public demanding not only that we show the Führer, but also that we show him for as long as possible'. In an entry two days later, he expresses his displeasure that, while it was Hitler's decision not to be shown, the general public assumed the blame lay with the Propaganda Ministry. Complaints and requests for 'more Hitler' in the newsreels inevitably landed on his desk, as when Nazi Gauleiter suggested that Hitler be shown more regularly so as to give the lie to rumours about Hitler's state of health.[73] Goebbels was well aware of the propaganda value of Hitler's presence in the newsreels. He feared that Hitler's reluctance would become 'general practice', such that *no* leading figures in the Nazi establishment would be willing to appear, leading to the newsreels losing personal charm and becoming too matter-of-fact.[74] Goebbels' efforts to persuade Hitler to allow himself to be filmed met with at best limited success. After the attempt on his life in July 1944, Hitler's radio and Wochenschau appearances became even rarer. On

3 December 1944, Goebbels complained in his diary that he was being 'bombarded' from all over the Reich with requests that he get Hitler to 'show himself in public', whether this be at a reception or in a newsreel, or to speak on the radio. Hitler eventually insisted that all film material showing him as in any way 'stooped or broken' be destroyed.[75] Newsreels came to include older footage of Hitler. In late September 1943, following the death of the Bulgarian King Boris, archive material of a Hitler meeting with Boris were shown.[76] Hitler did not attend the funeral of fighter-ace Walter Nowotny in November 1944; instead, archive images of him receiving a medal from Hitler were shown.[77]

The main reason Hitler appeared 'stooped and broken', of course, was because of his failing health. According to former personal adjutant Otto Günsche and valet Heinz Linge, Hitler thought 'the German people would be horrified if they saw him like that'.[78] In April 1943, Goebbels expressed concern at the 'shock' felt by the German people on seeing Hitler in a newsreel where he appeared 'grief-stricken and plagued by worries'.[79] This was just after the defeat at Stalingrad, on the occasion of Heroes Commemoration Day in Berlin. In fact, in the newsreel in question Hitler seems to fall asleep at one point.[80] Goebbels much preferred it if Hitler appeared in the newsreel as a relaxed private person, playing with his dog Blondi,[81] as in a Wochenschau of May 1942, and again in August and September 1943.[82] But while it was possible to counterbalance images of Hitler looking anxiety-ridden – as well he might after Stalingrad – with images of him at play, it was much harder to mitigate the effects of signs of his physical deterioration. The extent of this deterioration became particularly clear to Goebbels when, in March 1944, he watched some of Eva Braun's private pre-war films of Hitler and compared these with others she had taken in 1942. 'In 1939,' he wrote in his diary, 'he was a young man still; in the course of the war he has become older and older, and now he is quite stooped when he walks.'[83]

It is assumed today that Hitler in all probability had Parkinson's.[84] One German professor, Ellen Gibbels, studied eighty-three editions of the

German Wochenschau from 1940 to 1945 and found evidence, as she saw it, that Hitler was suffering from the disease. She detected 'a left-sided hypokinesia [loss of muscle movement] from about mid-1941', 'postural abnormalities' as of 1943, abnormalities in gait as of mid-1944 and 'clear signs of hypomimia' – a reduced degree of facial expression – in 1945.[85] Whether Hitler's physical decline was down to Parkinson's alone, however, or indeed to Parkinson's at all remains unclear; his doctor, Theo Morell, may have been treating him with the wrong drugs, and the attempt on Hitler's life on 20 July 1944 shook him to the core. Besides, Gibbels' ability to detect that something was wrong with Hitler does not mean that ordinary German cinemagoers in the 1940s would have been able to do so. After all, they were not scrutinizing the newsreels for pathological indicators, and, unlike Gibbels, probably only watched them once. But what is clear from Gibbels' research is that, despite the best efforts of cameraman Walter Frentz and of German censors, Hitler's illness can be detected with a careful eye in those sequences he did allow to be included in the Wochenschau.[86]

Arguably, too, as of mid-1944 even a less expert eye might have noticed peculiarities in Hitler's movements in newsreel footage. Walter Frentz was normally careful to avoid filming Hitler in ways that would draw attention to symptoms of illness, particularly the tremor in his left hand. Thus, in the later war newsreels we usually see Hitler from the right side rather than the left. Hitler in any case sought to conceal the tremor by clutching gloves in his left hand, putting his hand in his pocket or clasping both hands behind his back. After 20 July 1944, Hitler's physical problems became less easy to conceal, and Hitler, it seems, no longer always watched the Wochenschau before it was released. Carelessness creeps into the editing. When Hitler visited those wounded by the 20 July bomb attack, a scene of rare pastoral concern, the camera focuses on him as he seizes his right arm with his left, as if to steady it.[87] In September 1944, Hitler, having just awarded a medal to Erich Hartmann – probably the most successful German fighter pilot there ever was – is seen needing help to sit down, and then failing to grasp an object on the table before he slumps back into the chair.[88] And in the last two newsreels in which Hitler appeared, Gibbels writes, 'the censors obviously failed to notice the tremor which eyewitnesses were able to see as of 1942'.[89] Already in 1943, according to an SD report, German cinemagoers had remarked how exhausted and aged Hitler looked.[90] They put it down, so the report goes on, to the 'great worries' he had to bear. Unfortunately, the reports tell us little about audience reactions to the newsreels in late 1944.

In the aftermath of defeat at Stalingrad (February 1943), German cinemagoers' interest in the newsreels waned. Viewers streamed out of the cinema after the feature film, not waiting for the Wochenschau.[91] The main reason for this was that they had lost faith in the by now rather forced-sounding optimism. But if the Wochenschau never recovered the status it had enjoyed with filmgoers in the early years of the war, this also had to do with the decrease in footage of Hitler. While the main motive for Hitler's reluctance to appear in the newsreels was his deteriorating health, another reason may have been his sense that, unable as he now was to present himself as a successful leader riding the crest of a wave of victories, it might be better not to show himself very much at all. His absence is explicable, but it came at a cost. Hitler had been projected in the newsreels since 1933 as a dynamic leader; his facial expressions, voice and striding figure, not to mention his vigorous arm movements when speaking, had conveyed an image of unrelenting determination. The war was presented as the acting out of Hitler's powerful bond with his people: Hitler was leading them out to fight off the destruction threatened by the 'capitalist plutocrats' in the West and the 'Jewish bolsheviks' in the East. Repeatedly, Hitler had emphasized his will to defend Germany; now, as he absented himself from the screen, he appeared to be abandoning it to its fate.

The close identification of the war effort with the person of Hitler had been encouraged in the newsreel to the point that German audiences – to judge at least from SD reports – invested images of the Nazi leader with a higher meaning. His features became a barometer of the current state of events.[92] If Hitler looked sure of victory, then viewers felt sure of victory.[93] Hitler's withdrawal from visual representation accompanied and surely strengthened the German population's mounting loss of belief in the prospects of German triumph. Whether the cost of including more footage of the Führer – and thereby providing repeated evidence of his physical decay – might have been even higher, we do not know. In the end, Nazi newsreel propaganda lost its credibility because Hitler's frequent absence implied he no longer believed in it.

The Divinely Gifted

MOVIE STARS IN HITLER'S WAR

During the war, despite his diminished interest in feature film, Hitler still made sure actors were treated well. In return for exemption from military service, Hitler expected actors to do service on the screen. Now, their participation in propaganda films not only supported the ideals of the Nazi regime within Germany but also its military campaigns and the implementation of its policies in occupied countries. Cinema remained connected to Hitler to the end. Continuing to show films in an ever-shrinking Reich and devastated cities came to symbolize the supposed invincibility of the German spirit.

Lists

On 20 November 1940, Hitler dined with the actress Maria Holst at Vienna's Imperial Hotel. On the menu were chicken paprika, dumplings and rice, followed by pancakes.[1] Hitler continued to meet Riefenstahl.[2] Bormann's diary of Hitler's activities tells us that he met the actors Hertha Feiler and Willy Fritsch at the Platterhof Hotel on the Obersalzberg in 1942.[3] Magda Schneider, the mother of Romy Schneider, was a guest at the

Berghof in 1941.[4] And Hitler kept up his habit of sending presents: in February 1940, actress Jenny Jugo wrote to thank him profusely for the 'wonderful coffee'. She was overjoyed he should have thought of her. 'Heil, mein Führer!' she concluded energetically.[5] Overall, though, Hitler's interest in actors declined after September 1939. Before the war, he liked to consort with artists of all kinds because this implied the openness of the Nazi movement to the world. Once war began, in this respect at least, the international status of Germany's actors was no longer as useful. In fact, some months before the war started, Oswald Lehnich, president of the Reich Film Chamber at the time, sent letters to German film stars asking them to swap their foreign cars for German-made models – actors were to cast off any international allures.[6] But just because Hitler spent less time with actors after 1 September 1939 does not mean he ceased to influence their lives.

Deportation lists will forever be associated with Hitler's regime. But there were other, less well-known lists. In October 1939, Hitler ordered that the 'most capable' of those working in the arts should be kept back from military service because their services could not be dispensed with in times of war. Leopold Gutterer, ministerial director in the Propaganda Ministry, was instructed to draw up a list of eligible candidates.[7] On 5 January 1940, the High Command of the Armed Forces issued a decree proclaiming the so-called Führer List, a list of artists, writers, musicians and actors whom Hitler wished to exempt from military service. Individual film companies were confidentially informed of the actors included in this list in 1941.[8] At this time, it probably did not feature the names of actresses. When Hitler heard in late 1941 that actresses and female dancers were being drafted for work service, he insisted they should stay in their professions.[9] During the war, the Propaganda Ministry also issued special lists of actors (among other artists) it wished to see released from military service. The various lists and the alterations to them caused confusion among film companies. Confusion exists to this day. Scholars generally assume that Hitler – or Goebbels, after discussion with Hitler – first drew up the List of the Divinely Gifted ('Gottbegnadetenliste') in August or

September 1944. At this stage in the war, when the German war effort needed everyone it could get, to escape a call-up was a privilege indeed. Numbering among the divinely gifted were film actors whom Goebbels and Hitler felt German cinema production simply could not do without. But there is evidence that the earlier Führer List was already known as the List of the Divinely Gifted, and that the autumn 1944 Divinely Gifted List was actually the second (reduced) list.[10] To add to the confusion, a list of film actors frequently cited by historians as a part of the List of the Divinely Gifted may actually be part of a list called 'other individual artists exempt from military service'.[11] The archives do not tell an unambiguous story.[12]

The original Führer List sparkles with the names of leading Third Reich actors: Hans Albers, Willy Birgel, Paul Dahlke, Karl Ludwig Diehl, Willy Fritsch, Heinrich George, Paul Hartmann, Werner Hinz, Eugen Klöpfer, Viktor de Kowa, Theo Lingen, Ferdinand Marian, Viktor Staal, Paul Wegener and Mathias Wieman.[13] The 1944 Divinely Gifted List of theatre actors includes Rosa Albach-Retty, Anna Dammann, Käthe Dorsch, Maria Eis, Hermine Körner and Paula Wessely.[14] Another 1944 Film List of actors exempted from military service includes most of the above as well as actresses Käthe Haack, Maria Koppenhöfer, Hilde Krahl, Henny Porten, Leni Riefenstahl, Marika Rökk, Kristina Söderbaum, Gisela Uhlen and Ilse Werner.[15] These actors could hardly be more different. Albers liked to throw his supersized ego around, annoying the Nazis in May 1943, for instance, by refusing to vacate his hotel suite to make way for King Boris of Bulgaria, arguing: 'I am a king, too.'[16] Heinrich George, a former communist, collaborated with Nazism, but never concealed his loathing of it in private, any more than Paul Wegener did.[17] After the war, it was rumoured that Ilse Werner had sung songs by Hans Pfitzner for Hitler – a dubious anecdote not least because Werner's lively temperament and the sluggish late romanticism of Pfitzner's music go together like chalk and cheese. Werner, of Dutch-German extraction, tried repeatedly to leave Germany during the Third Reich.[18] Rosa Albach-Retty, by contrast, greatly admired Hitler, as Riefenstahl did.[19] Ferdinand Marian drank himself into the ground after playing the lead in *Jew Süss*. Käthe Dorsch repeatedly tried to help actors in need, and went regularly to Goebbels on their behalf.[20] Eugen Klöpfer, director of Berlin's Volksbühne, proved particularly accommodating, joining the Nazi Party in 1937, and taking on several functions within Nazi cultural organizations.[21]

Yet for all their differences, virtually all the exempted actors had one thing in common: they had roles in wartime propaganda films. Heinrich George starred in *Jew Süss*. Ilse Werner not only whistled her way through the light-hearted Helmut Käutner film *We Make Music* (1942), she also starred in Günther Rittau's *U Boats Westwards* (1941), an admittedly flatly directed film celebrating the achievements of German submarines in the war against the British. Werner Hinz acted in a number of anti-British Nazi propaganda films, including Max Kimmich's *The Fox of Glenarvon* (1940), in which he played a brutal English officer. After the war, Hinz provided a range of typical excuses for his involvement in propaganda films: he had not read the script, Goebbels kept changing it,[22] he sought to 'humanize' the negative characters he portrayed.[23] Not surprisingly, the British were not convinced by his claim that he attempted to inject humanity into his portrayal of the English officer in *The Fox of Glenarvon*; he is shown striking out at Irishmen with a whip and ordering hangings. One Major Lovell described Hinz's role as 'propaganda of a particularly obnoxious kind'.[24] Führer List actors Albert Florath, Karl Ludwig Diehl and Ferdinand Marian also had parts in *The Fox of Glenarvon*. Hinz had a slightly more sympathetic part in a later Kimmich film, *My Life for Ireland* (1941), where he plays an Irishman, Michael O'Brien. But this does not alter the fact that the whole film is designed to demonstrate the inhumanity of the British and intensify anti-British feeling. Anna Dammann and Paul Wegener also featured in *My Life for Ireland*. The 'Divinely Gifted' Käthe Dorsch played the lead role in Gustav Ucicky's *Mother Love* (1939), in which a woman, following the sudden death of her husband, dedicates her life to her children, and sacrifices the cornea of one of her eyes to enable her blind son to see. Goebbels was ecstatic, describing the film as a 'true masterpiece'.[25] Premieres of *Mother Love* became celebrations of German motherhood. In Salzburg, 100 women who had been awarded the Nazi Mother's Cross of Honour attended the first performance.[26] Productivity – sons and weapons – was the order of the day.

It is true that some of the directors and actors in Hitler's Germany did resist making or taking part in propaganda films. After the war, Führer List actor Aribert Wäscher related that Goebbels wanted him to act in an anti-British film, but he had refused, and Gründgens protected him by offering him a lead role at the Prussian Staatstheater.[27] But such stories are often hard to verify. Goebbels found most actors accommodating, if his own pronouncements are to be trusted. Speaking at the opening of the yearly Film Hours for German Youth in Berlin in 1941, Goebbels praised the films that had resulted from state commissions, such as Eduard von Borsody's *Request Concert*, Wolfgang Liebeneiner's *Bismarck*, Veit Harlan's *Jew Süss* and Hans Steinhoff's *Uncle Krüger*. Far from trying to avoid 'fulfilling this national task', he added, German filmmakers had set about it with 'great enthusiasm and artistic fanaticism'.[28] It is also true that most actors on the special lists took part in the far more numerous 'entertainment films' ('Unterhaltungsfilme'), but, as comedies, musicals and action films helped to lift spirits for a few hours, they also served the war effort. Moreover, Goebbels exploited the power of the propaganda films as far as possible. Their premieres were surrounded by Nazi media hype and attended by Nazi dignitaries. They were shown to youths – for instance during the Youth Film Hours – to steer their sentiments and thoughts in the direction desirable to Nazism. They were shown in occupied, Axis and neutral countries to the same ends.[29] They were also shown to the Wehrmacht. So, of course, were entertainment films. But against the dominance of Nazi entertainment films, it can be argued that propaganda films were recycled more intensively. Anti-Soviet films that had been mothballed after the Hitler–Stalin Pact were recirculated after Hitler's attack on the Soviet Union. In late 1944, as Goebbels stepped up his 'total war' campaign, a number of propaganda films were rerun in Berlin and elsewhere 'within the framework of the special deployment of reshowings of films of soldierly and national character'. These included *The Fox of Glenarvon*, *The Dismissal*, *My Life for Ireland*, Harlan's *The Great King* and Josef von Báky's *Annelie* (1941), the latter, like *Mother Love*, celebrating a mother's spirit of endurance.[30]

Protection, Intimidation, Setting Examples

The various lists of actors exempted from military service included names that seem surprising. Hans Brausewetter had problems with the Nazi regime because of his homosexuality. Yet he featured on the Führer List. Winnie Markus became involved in a lesbian relationship with photographer Charlotte Serda in 1943 and was placed under Security Service observation, but was on the Film List.[31] Also on the Führer List was Theo Lingen, despite his Jewish wife. Paul Henckels, classified by the Nazis as a 'half-Jew' and married to a Jew, was on a list of 'indispensable actors'. Austrian actor Hans Moser had a Jewish wife, but was on the Führer List and the List of the Divinely Gifted.

Film actors married to Jews came under pressure to divorce them, under threat of being barred from acting. Yet divorce risked exposing their Jewish partners to greater discrimination and, ultimately, deportation. Affected actors tried to find a way round this dilemma. Karl Etlinger, for instance, lied to the Nazi authorities in 1935 that he had filed for a divorce from his Jewish wife. Three years later, the Reich Film Chamber found out he had done nothing of the sort, and was still living with her.[32] When he did finally divorce her, she was murdered in 1942 in Ravensbrück concentration camp. Etlinger, incorrigible from a Nazi point of view, then married the daughter of a converted Jew, but still featured on a list of 'indispensable actors'.[33] Actor Heinz Rühmann, on the Führer List, did divorce his Jewish wife Maria Bernheim in 1938. But he only did so after taking up Göring's suggestion that he arrange for Bernheim to marry 'a neutral foreigner'.[34] This she duly did – a Swede. She fled to safety in Sweden in 1943.[35] Hans

Albers broke up officially with his Jewish partner, Hansi Burg, in response to pressure from the Nazi authorities,[36] but helped her to emigrate to England in 1939. The couple were later reunited. Things, however, did not always end well. When Goebbels found out in 1941 that actor Joachim Gottschalk had still not separated from his Jewish wife, Meta Wolff, he ordered her deportation, whereupon Gottschalk and his wife took their own lives. Actors who were married to Jews or who were themselves 'half-Jews' were subjected to inconsistent policies by the Nazis. Some were excluded from acting altogether.[37] Others were employed from film to film on the basis of 'special permission' for which film companies had to apply. Some were on exemption lists. Some were made scapegoats.

On occasion, actors turned directly to Hitler for help. Knowing, no doubt, that Hitler was a great fan of his,[38] Hans Moser wrote to him in 1938 asking for his Jewish wife, Blanca, to be exempt from having her passport marked with the letter J, and changing her forename to Sarah.[39] His petition met with success. In late 1939, Blanca was able to use her passport to flee to Zurich and then Budapest, where she sat out the war, simultaneously pampered by Moser and terrified of what might happen to her.[40] Hitler also helped actress Henny Porten, who was married to her 'half-Jewish' producer, Wilhelm von Kaufmann-Asser. During the Third Reich, she struggled to find employment. On 3 August 1939, she wrote to Hitler's personal adjutant, Julius Schaub, asking for an audience with Hitler,[41] and, as of 1941 at least, she appeared on screen in more significant roles. According to Goebbels, Hitler 'worshipped' Henny Porten, deeply regretting that because of her marriage she was 'not one of us'.[42] She had made a deep impression on Hitler when he saw her for the first time on screen while on leave in Lille during the First World War. The 'Permanent Stock' of films at the Berghof included the Carl Froelich film *Mother and Child* (1924), starring Henny Porten.[43] To help her out, Hitler granted her a pension in 1944.[44]

Hitler would even declare Jews non-Jews when he cared to, a process whereby Jews became 'honorary Aryans'. In 1938, Hitler had allowed

Tobis production chief Herbert Engelsing to marry a Jew because of her 'racial appearance' – that is, she did not look as Hitler imagined a Jew to look – and because Engelsing had supposedly taken part in the Munich putsch in 1923.[45] When in 1941 the actor Heinrich George intervened on behalf of the 'half-Jewish' actor Robert Müller (who also had a Jewish wife), Hitler decided that Müller 'should no longer be considered a Jew'.[46] Wolfgang Liebeneiner, director of *Bismarck*, was reluctant to divorce his wife, Ruth Hellberg, because she feared the consequences for her half-Jewish son from a previous relationship. In November 1942, via Bormann, Hitler assured Liebeneiner that there would be no threat to Hellberg's son in the event of a divorce.[47] His Jewishness was simply to be overlooked.[48] In the end, actors married to Jews and 'half-Jewish' actors depended on the forbearance of Goebbels and Hitler to continue their careers. Sometimes they lived in a strange twilight world between screen stardom, ostracism and fear. Paul Henckels spent the last years of the war living a cloistered life with his Jewish wife in Berlin's noble Hotel Bristol, eating meals in his hotel room and never venturing into the restaurant in case it drew attention.[49] It is likely Hitler held his hand over Henckels, whose acting he admired. Henckels acted in several films included in the Berghof's 'Permanent Stock'.

There was a reason why Hitler and Goebbels were prepared on occasion to exercise a degree of leniency on issues of racial policy when it came to actors: they needed them on screen. Like others of their profession, actors in mixed marriages and 'half-Jewish' actors usually had to take on some kind of role in Nazi propaganda films. In their cases, the obligation must have weighed heavily. One wonders how actor Otto Wernicke, whose wife was Jewish, felt about his role as camp commandant in the 1941 anti-British film *Uncle Krüger*, in which responsibility for concentration camps is foisted onto the British at a time when Jews were being incarcerated, ghettoized and murdered. This was no secret, especially not to actors performing for the troops in Eastern Europe. Actress and singer Lale Andersen, for instance, recalled being taken with other actors on a 'tour' of the Warsaw ghetto.[50]

Wernicke also had roles in other Nazi propaganda films such as *The Great King* and *Kolberg* (1945). Another actor with a Jewish wife, Paul Bildt, also had a part in *Uncle Krüger*. Both Bildt and Wernicke were on the Führer List. 'Half-Jew' Ernst Stahl-Nachbaur, listed as an actor needed for film production during the war, found himself playing John Knox in the anti-British Carl Froelich film *The Heart of the Queen* (1940), which features a particularly negative portrayal of Elizabeth I, with Zarah Leander playing the much more sympathetically portrayed Mary, Queen of Scots.[51]

Generally speaking, the principle of indulgence with caveats was one Hitler and Goebbels followed in the case of actors and directors. They kept them under control on the one hand by pampering them and allowing them a degree of freedom to flaunt their egos, and on the other, by subjecting them to a carefully modulated degree of moral and ideological pressure. While Hitler and Goebbels spent time in the company of actors, it is doubtful they took them seriously as people; what interested them was their stage and screen personas. Goebbels regarded most artists as unpolitical: 'they are neither for nor against the state, they just want to be left in peace and earn their money'.[52] So, according to Goebbels, did Hitler, who was inclined 'not to be too strict in political matters' where film actors were concerned: 'artists should not be taken seriously when it comes to politics'.[53] Hitler and Goebbels responded to misbehaviour on the part of artists with a mixture of condescending tolerance, irritation and threats, as is evidenced by the case of the actor Emil Jannings. In early 1942, Jannings denounced a colleague for having organized an anti-National Socialist demonstration in his studio.[54] It turned out Jannings had invented this story, Goebbels writes, 'out of envy towards a better actor'. At first, Goebbels wanted to teach Jannings a lesson, but he relented. He notes in his diary that 'the Führer also understands that most artists, above all actors, have their quirks'.[55] While condemning Jannings' behaviour, Goebbels writes, 'one can't take all this as seriously as one might in the case of normal people'. Actors, then, were a special case. Goebbels' tolerance, however, did have limits. In August 1943, he decided he wanted to 'make an example of someone' to issue a warning to 'unreliable elements' in the film and theatre branch.[56] Two months later, he identified a person he could abuse in this way: the actor Robert Dorsay, who was executed for critical remarks about Hitler; 'in wartime, artists do not have carte blanche to rant and go around being defeatist,' Goebbels wrote.[57]

Despite their privileges and despite threats from Goebbels, as the war wore on, actors began to show signs of recalcitrance. They found ways of refusing to take part in films being made in bomb-battered Berlin, hiding out in country residences or getting involved in film projects in Prague, which was safe from air attacks. If summoned to Berlin, actors hired 'prominent doctors' to fabricate letters testifying to various medical conditions.[58] Sometimes they simply vanished without leaving an address where they could be contacted.[59] 'Such a pity,' remarked Goebbels sarcastically, 'that a number of our leading artists have been struck down by an almost pathological fear of bombs';[60] these included the conductor Clemens Krauss and Emil Jannings. Jannings was particularly reticent about coming back to Berlin, which earned him Hitler's contempt. By contrast, Hitler expressed to Goebbels his admiration for the actor Heinrich George, who, in March 1944, had set up a makeshift stage in the refreshment room of the Schiller Theatre in Berlin so that performances could continue.[61] Goebbels eventually secured Hitler's agreement for measures to punish actors 'deserting' the cities affected by the bombing war.[62] But the actors still found ways to steer clear.

Where morale broke down, tongues loosened and denunciation was rife. On 9 August 1944, Magda Goebbels was sent an anonymous letter telling her – in the expectation she would pass this on to her husband – that Wien Film was 'saturated with communist and monarchist elements', all of whom openly expressed regrets about the failure of the July 1944 attempt on Hitler's life. Wien Film's legal adviser liked to make 'vile jokes' about Hitler and Goebbels, to the delight of other board members.[63] What particularly angered Goebbels was the fact that a number of actors had leapt to the defence of Major Friedrich Goes when he was denounced by the actress Marianne Simson for saying he found it a 'pity' that Hitler had survived Stauffenberg's bomb.[64] Goes was hauled before a Wehrmacht Special Court. Actors Anneliese Uhlig, Gertrude von Steuben, Viktor de Kowa, Kurt Weitkamp and Just Scheu, as well as Tobis production chief Engelsing, testified against Simson, and Goes was acquitted. Goebbels instructed Reich Film Superintendent Hinkel to haul them over hot coals, which he did, accusing them of having 'directly or indirectly stabbed the state in the back' in its struggle against 'treachery and defeatism'.[65] Hitler and Goebbels insisted Goes be subjected to retrial, this time by the notorious People's Court, which had been instructed to find him guilty. But the war ended before he could be sentenced. In one or two cases, actors became associated with the anti-Nazi resistance, notably Viktor de Kowa. De Kowa helped Wolfgang Harich, later to become a leading philosopher in the German Democratic Republic, to rebuild the resistance group that had formed around social democrat Theodor Haubach (who was arrested in July 1944).[66] The Nazi Security Service does not seem to have known about de Kowa, but they certainly knew about actor Paul Hörbiger's involvement with the 'Austrian Freedom Front', a resistance group spearheaded by Alois Parsch. Hörbiger was arrested and interrogated by the Gestapo in 1945.[67] One or two actors may also have become involved with spying networks.[68]

Concerns about 'attitudes' after 20 July 1944 among artists generally led Goebbels to instruct Hinkel to solicit from prominent art-world figures a 'profession of loyalty to the Führer' ('Führerbekenntnis').[69] Hinkel sent out 365 letters in early November 1944, informing most of the addressees that he hoped the collected responses would provide Goebbels with a 'little Christmas joy'.[70] By 1 December 1944, Hinkel was able to inform Goebbels that, so far, 100 people had answered. He also told Goebbels that his letters had caused much 'racking of brains', with 'friends' putting their heads together to work out the best way to answer. Actors at Vienna's Burgtheater even sent in a 'collective confession', while the actress Ethel Reschke decided to provide her response in rhyming verse.[71] Two weeks later, Hinkel provided further feedback. Friedl Czepa, director of Vienna's

Stadttheater, had responded to the call with a letter titled 'Another Confession', in which she and other Austrian actors including several on the Divinely Gifted List (e.g. Hedwig Bleibtreu and Maria Eis)[72] declared their support for actress Alma Seidler, who was married to a Jew and had been omitted from a list of 'theatre personnel of above-average talent'. Actress Käthe Dorsch also tried to help Seidler.[73] To respond to Hinkel's letter with a plea on behalf of a disadvantaged actress seems courageous. Hinkel reacted by requesting of Goebbels that 'nothing happen' to Seidler and her husband, i.e. the husband be protected against deportation.[74] On the other hand, Czepa and the other signatories will have known that Goebbels and Hitler made concessions to actors in mixed marriages. Czepa, in any case, was hardly a rebel; she offered a public vote of thanks to Hitler following Austria's annexation in 1938.[75] To have expressed support for Seidler's Jewish husband would have constituted a more significant — but very risky — act of courage. Not all actors reacted to Hinkel's letters. Gustaf Gründgens, director of the Prussian State Theatre, declined to respond. One might find Gründgens courageous; Goebbels found him cowardly.[76] Lizzi Waldmüller, a hot-blooded Austrian actress who fell out with the Nazis on several occasions before being killed in an Allied bombing raid in 1945, also proved uncooperative.[77]

Sending Goebbels the responses split between three folders, Hinkel wrote: 'a 4th folder, for rejections, was superfluous'.[78] Goebbels found the responses to be 'more than 100 per cent positive'.[79] No-one working in the arts who valued their life would have answered rejecting loyalty to Hitler. But the real point of soliciting 'professions of loyalty' was to make artists sweat. Never before had actors, for instance, had to provide on demand an explicit written endorsement of Hitler and his politics (although some of them had provided endorsements voluntarily).[80] Hinkel did not find it a bad thing that artists had got together to provide collective replies, as 'a significant number of these artists write the most miserable German and chew on their pens with an understandable lack of self-confidence'.[81] The psychological stress caused by Goebbels' extraction of statements, as well as the ever-present threat of being called up despite appearing to be in a privileged position, helped to counter signs of ill-discipline and keep most key actors in their place until the collapse in May 1945.

Film in Hitler's Service

German and Austrian actors, to judge from their post-war autobiographies, never grasped, or wanted to grasp, that the cost of their privileges was helping to promote Hitler's war. There can be little doubt that his policies impacted on film production. Certainly, unexpected changes of political direction meant this influence was not always beneficial from the German film industry's point of view. The Hitler–Stalin Pact led to anti-Bolshevist and anti-Russian films being broken off in mid-production; either that or their first performances were shelved, an example being Karl Ritter's *Cadets*, in which the Russians take young German cadets hostage during the Seven Years' War (1754–63). When Hitler launched Operation Barbarossa in mid-1941, anti-Russian propaganda films such as *Cadets* came back into fashion, but films produced during the period of the pact which portrayed the Russians positively, such as Veit Harlan's *The Great King*, had to be changed. Hitler's vacillations on what to do about Great Britain, at least in 1940 and 1941, meant that the production or showing of anti-British films was interrupted or delayed. But, overall, German wartime propaganda films were built on the consistent basis of anti-British and anti-Russian stereotyping, with anti-Semitic and anti-Polish elements also strongly represented (sometimes in combination); in projecting their damning view of the British, Russians and Jews into the past, as well as presenting it in a contemporary context, they reflected precisely Hitler's understanding of history.

As we have already seen in this book, Nazi propaganda cinema nourished the illusion that Germany was fighting a reactive and defensive war, and that Hitler – embodied in the various cinematic leader-figures and geniuses – stood in a tradition of the great misunderstood, ahead and outside of their time. This view of the world was Hitler's, even if it was more often Goebbels who promoted it. By 1943 and certainly 1944, reality had caught up with the vision: Germany really was surrounded by a world of enemies. Hitler, moreover, was becoming the increasingly isolated figure so typical of the Nazi genius films such as *The Great King* – with the difference that Hitler proved unable to turn defeat into triumph. Nazi propaganda films and newsreels, in short, were implicated in encouraging the Germans to believe what many of them wanted to believe anyway: that others were to blame, that the war was not the fault of Germany, that right and innocence were on their side, and that Hitler's actions were beyond question because he stood in a line of historical giants. Actors were complicit in this game of dishonesty. Thus Führer List actors Paul Hartmann, Emil Jannings, Otto Gebühr and Werner Krauß played lead roles in films about the Führer's supposed forebears: Hartmann was Bismarck in Wolfgang Liebeneiner's 1940 film of the same name, Jannings was Bismarck in Liebeneiner's 1942 *The Dismissal*, Gebühr was Frederick the Great in Harlan's *The Great King*, Werner Krauß Paracelsus in Georg Wilhelm Pabst's 1943 film *Paracelsus*, about the famous sixteenth-century Swiss doctor and alchemist.

The discussion of *Jew Süss* (Chapter 8) demonstrated that a Nazi propaganda feature film could be directly used to support Hitler's wartime policies, but *Jew Süss* was no exception. While some Nazi propagandistic feature films were outstripped by events and policies to the extent that they could no longer be deployed, or effectively deployed, others proved to be much more flexible tools, such as Wolfgang Liebeneiner's 1941 film *I Accuse*. In October 1939, Viktor Brack, head of Department II of Hitler's Chancellery, began overseeing the production of films that would help foster acceptance of 'mercy killing' among the German public. Blueprints for one of these openly addressed the issue of gassing: gas was used to kill patients in a number of Nazi psychiatric institutions. But, in late 1940, plans for a euthanasia documentary were temporarily shelved.[82] In December, Heinrich Himmler wrote to Brack expressing his concern that the local population of one killing centre, Grafeneck, had guessed what was going on. In view of mounting public disquiet, Himmler asked Brack for films on the subject of the disabled which would provide enlightenment in a 'clever and responsible way'.[83] In response to this, and perhaps also to a February 1941 call from Goebbels for more 'invisible' forms of propaganda,[84] the Chancellery of the Führer decided that a feature film might be more suitable than a documentary. The result was the Tobis film *I Accuse*, in which a woman suffering from multiple sclerosis is given a fatal overdose by her doctor husband – but only after she has asked to be killed. The husband, Thomas Heyt, is put on trial, so that the film appears to allow for a fair and legal consideration of the pros and cons of his actions. A key role is played by Heyt's friend, Dr Lang. Initially horrified by Heyt's decision to kill his wife, Lang changes his mind about euthanasia when he learns that a child whose life he fought to save is permanently disabled. *I Accuse*, therefore, justifies voluntary and involuntary euthanasia. And, in showing a doctor converting to the pro-euthanasia camp, it seeks to overcome the doubters in the audience.

The film was approaching its premiere on 29 August 1941 when, on 24 August, Hitler called a halt to the euthanasia action (although the killing did in fact continue). This was probably a consequence of Bishop Clemens August von Galen's protest against euthanasia in a sermon of 3 August 1941;[85] the disquiet Himmler had referred to in 1940, fomented further by the churches, had not gone away. So when *I Accuse* reached cinema screens, it could hardly serve the purpose, now, of providing a 'clever and responsible' rationale for a killing process which Hitler had apparently terminated. But it could serve another purpose: conveying the impression the Nazis were moving away from mass slaughter of the disabled to a case-by-case approach to euthanasia, individualized and grounded in law.[86] Gauleiter reports to the Party Chancellery indicate that *I Accuse* was, for the most part, well received by the population, and that the film's emphasis on due legal process was sympathetically interpreted.[87] Goebbels' more 'indirect propaganda', with the tendentiousness of the film disguised beneath an apparent open-endedness – it concludes before a verdict has been reached – proved effective because audiences felt they had freedom to discuss possible outcomes. There is a contrast here to *Jew Süss*, where the court case ends with Süss's sentence for 'miscegenation' and the film with his execution. Audiences could be expected to accept a judicial fiat of the harshest kind when it came to Jews, but needed the illusion that euthanasia was still under discussion.[88]

The relevance of Gustav Ucicky's 1941 film *Homecoming* was also seemingly overtaken by events, yet in certain respects it came to prove timely. It depicts the brutal treatment of Volhynian Germans living in Poland prior to the outbreak of the Second World War. Work on the film began in late 1940. Its function was to present Poles as savages and Germans as victims, and justify the resettlement of Volhynian and other ethnic Germans as of 1939 as a reaction to this savagery. In reality, of course, Germans were resettled because Hitler and Stalin, as they carved up Eastern Europe, agreed they should be moved. Following Hitler's attack on the Soviet Union in June 1941, the Wehrmacht occupied the areas from which the Volhynian Germans had been resettled. Some Volhynian Germans must have wondered why they had been resettled in the first place. But when *Homecoming* was first shown in Austria and Germany in October 1941, audiences might well have associated scenes imagining the 'liberation' of the ethnic Germans in Luzk in 1939 with the Nazi advance into eastern Poland in June 1941. Implicitly, *Homecoming* became a film about the need to defend Germans not just against the Poles, but also the Soviets, and in so doing seemed to provide a justification for Hitler's invasion of the Soviet Union. It also served to justify the Nazi forced labour programme to which Polish and Soviet citizens were subjected.

Goebbels stressed *Homecoming*'s function as an 'educational memory for all the Germans', and he awarded it the highest accolade: 'Film of the Nation'.[89] On his orders, the audience at the German premiere of *Homecoming* in Berlin on 23 October 1941 consisted largely of wounded soldiers and armaments' workers.[90] The film was also shown to soldiers on the Eastern Front – for instance, in Lemberg (Lwów) in Galicia,[91] not far from Luzk. At one point in *Homecoming*, the blind Dr Thomas senses the arrival of German tanks in Lemberg's suburbs in 1939; now, in 1941, Germans really had taken control of Lemberg. Lemberg, like Luzk, had been the site of a Soviet massacre of Ukrainians, killed before the Germans conquered the town. The Nazi authorities blamed Lemberg's Jews, 3,000 of whom were slaughtered by Einsatzgruppe C. German soldiers in Lemberg who watched *Homecoming* would most likely have known of these events. *Homecoming* served to remind them that the real savages were the 'others', the Poles, the Slavs and the Jews, represented in the film by the anti-Semitic caricature Salomonsson.[92] As the German offensive against the Soviets began to slow down, it reminded them, too, of the need to be merciless against the 'Jewish-Bolshevik' enemy if they were not to fall prey to bestiality. *Homecoming* infuriated the Polish resistance. They murdered Igo Sym, an Austrian-born Polish actor, for helping to cast Polish actors for the film. Some of these were imprisoned after the war by the Polish authorities for collaboration.[93] By contrast, Austrian and German actors in *Homecoming*, such as the female lead and 'Divinely Gifted' Paula Wessely, continued their careers after 1945.[94]

The End

In 1944, as Goebbels cranked up his efforts at total war, and as Germany began to buckle under the Allied advance and air war, staffing and material shortages hit every area of the economy. Cinema was no exception. Already by July 1944 petrol shortages nearly led to the collapse of the newsreels, and film production had in some cases almost come to a standstill because it was becoming difficult to arrange for the transport of props.[95] Film production was also hit by the loss of saltpetre (potassium nitrate) factories in the west. By late 1944, there was a chronic shortage of film stock.[96] In August 1944, Goebbels ordered a reduction of the Propaganda Ministry; the individual departments for theatre, music and the visual arts were dissolved and subsumed under a single Culture Department under Rainer Schlösser.[97] In the same month, the Nazi press announced that there would be no further production of culture films or advertising films. The production of educational films was also to be severely restricted. Staff were needed for the armaments industry and the army.[98] Goebbels also issued guidelines stipulating that anyone involved in the film industry had to do some kind of work service in between making films.[99]

Yet even as the situation in the Reich deteriorated in the course of 1944, cinema remained important. Ufa worked hard to reinstate bombed-out film theatres and created emergency cinemas in huts to ensure that viewing continued.[100] Tellingly, while Goebbels ordered the closure of theatres in September 1944, cinemas were to remain open, and in fact many theatres were turned into cinemas. Film was required not just to keep up the spirits of German audiences. In June 1944, Himmler expressed concern that allowing foreign workers into cinemas was reducing the seats available for Germans. But Goebbels' Propaganda Ministry insisted that foreign workers be offered a minimum of distraction, especially given the 'unsatisfactory situation' regarding their accommodation and food.[101] Slave labourers from Eastern Europe were still being provided with film and newsreel viewings in the summer and autumn of 1944.[102] In December 1944, Goebbels ordered that 150,000 metres of raw stock for copying films be reserved by the Reich Propaganda Leadership for use in providing film viewings to foreign workers and POWs. The majority of available stock, of course, was still destined for German viewers: 500,000 metres for use by the units providing viewings in rural areas, and 500,000 for film showings to the troops.[103] Conditions in the Reich may have been chaotic, but Hitler's favourite director, Leni Riefenstahl, feverishly continued work on her epic film *Lowlands*, financed by Hitler seemingly with no limits. In 1942 and 1943, despite protests from Minister for Economic Affairs Walther Funk, who was concerned at the drain on foreign currency reserves required for the war effort, Riefenstahl had procured large amounts of pesetas and lira to film in Spain and Italy. Hitler's factotum Martin

Bormann ensured she got what she wanted.[104] Now, in late 1944 and early 1945, she was restricted to filming in Kitzbühl, but mobilized all her resources to 'recruit a whole series of former crew members and friends' to come and help her finish the film.[105] It was not premiered until 1954.

While film production generally stalled, the making of new propaganda films had not ceased. In August and September 1944, the Central Office for the Regulation of the Jewish Question oversaw the production of a documentary film designed to deceive the Red Cross into thinking that Terezin ghetto and concentration camp was a pleasant place to live. Jewish inmates forced to participate in the film, such as the director Kurt Gerron, were murdered by the Nazis after the film was complete (it was never shown in public), while excerpts were shown in the weekly newsreels to contrast the supposedly comfortable life of Jews in Terezin with the hardships endured by soldiers at the front.[106] After the war, ghetto survivors sarcastically named the film *The Führer Gifts the Jews a Town*.[107] In the autumn of 1944, the ever obliging Veit Harlan came up with the idea of filming Shakespeare's *Merchant of Venice*. Reich Film Adviser Kurt Frowein wrote to Goebbels that the 'propagandistic suitability of the material is obvious'.[108] Even at this late stage in the war, indeed particularly so, Jews were to be scapegoats. Germans, by contrast, were to be presented as victims. In 1943, the German Foreign Office had suggested creating a documentary film about the 'Anglo-American bombing terror'. Titled *Woe to the Guilty* and produced at the behest of the Reich Propaganda Leadership, it was completed after repeated changes by December 1944 and mainly designed, like the Terezin film, for showing abroad. The aim was to demonstrate that the real 'air gangsters' were the Allies, not the Germans, who, in deploying V2 rockets, had merely been reacting to the violence visited on the German population.[109] The films about Terezin and Allied bombing were also intended as a moral self-defence in the now increasingly likely case of defeat and the passing of post-war judgment on Germany. In the final months of the war, Wolfgang Liebeneiner was entrusted with directing *Life Goes On*, a feature film starring Führer

List and 'Divinely Gifted' actors such as Heinrich George and Viktor de Kowa. It depicted the tenacity of Berliners under the impact of the Allied bombing raids in 1943, but was never completed.[110]

In late 1944 and early 1945, Nazi newspapers were replete with reports of Allied bombing raids, referred to as 'Air Terror'. Dresden's bombing was labelled a 'desecration', while Soviet treatment of Germans in the east was summed up in one *Völkischer Beobachter* headline as 'Murder, Plunder, Desecrate, Burn'.[111] That National Socialism might have provoked this treatment was, of course, not an interpretation to be found in the Nazi press. Goebbels and Hitler tried to persuade the public that the destruction of the German Reich by its enemies was, as Hitler put it in his 1945 New Year address, an act of 'cultural desecration': for Hitler, German culture was all that stood between the West and the profanity of Jewish–Bolshevist world domination.[112] Given that cinema was the only cultural site still operating by this stage, albeit with difficulty, its continuity became the symbol, for the Nazis, of the resistance of German culture to the threat of Allied 'annihilation'. Veit Harlan's historical epic *Kolberg* (1945), the last Nazi blockbuster to reach cinema screens, epitomized culture as resistance because it was actually about resistance. In the film, the Pomeranian town of Kolberg fights off Napoleon thanks to the resilience of the citizens' defence led by the military commandant Gneisenau. Resistance was to be its message already when it was first planned in 1943. In a June 1943 letter to Harlan, Goebbels said he wanted the film to show that a 'people united in the homeland and at the front can overcome every enemy'.[113] But, by 1945, when it was premiered, *Kolberg* had become a film about last-ditch resistance, defiance against seemingly impossible odds. With the German army facing defeat, culture led by example. *Kolberg* was premiered not just in Berlin, but simultaneously in the German-occupied French town of La Rochelle, which had become, like Kolberg in Harlan's film, an isolated fortress.[114] A copy of the film was flown into La Rochelle like a secret order. Germans in Berlin and in La Rochelle were to see in the film what was possible when home front and battle fronts worked together.[115]

After the war, Veit Harlan claimed that an 'order' had come from Hitler personally to make *Kolberg*.[116] But former Reich Film Superintendent Fritz Hippler testified that the 'Hitler order' was in fact an invention designed to put Harlan under pressure.[117] Certainly Goebbels did what he could to associate the film with Hitler. It was first shown on 30 January 1945, on the anniversary of the Nazi takeover in 1933. That same evening, Hitler appealed in his radio speech to the 'whole German people' to arm themselves with 'an even greater and tougher spirit of resistance'. He made it clear he expected everyone – including town-dwellers and farmers, even the sick and the weak – to play their part in the struggle. Even as he celebrated his survival of the 20 July 1944 bomb attack as a sign of divine protection, he railed against the cowardly and characterless who 'stab the nation in the back'.[118] These messages, about the need for a total mobilization of the Germans and to be wary of the shirkers and dalliers, were echoed, loudly, in *Kolberg*.

Several of the actors we have already mentioned in this chapter had roles in *Kolberg*: Heinrich George, Paul Wegener, Kristina Söderbaum, Otto Wernicke and Paul Bildt, for instance. Actors provided their services to Hitler through to the very end. They helped, through propagandistic feature films, to sustain belief in German military strength, the threat of 'Jewish Bolshevism' and the insuperable might of the genius. The trouble with *Kolberg*, for all that it was trumpeted by Goebbels as a 'document of the unwavering steadfastness' of the German people,[119] was that its message was so starkly contradicted by the fact of the total German collapse. Harlan claimed after the war that Hitler had insisted Napoleon be portrayed positively in the film.[120] In 1943, when work on the film began, Hitler may still have been imagining he could achieve what Napoleon had achieved, or indeed even more. The scene in *Kolberg* of Napoleon standing at Frederick the Great's grave is meant to recall Hitler bowing before Frederick's grave in March 1933. But, by late January 1945, it was clear he would fail: the Soviets had already crossed the border into the German Reich. They would soon be in Berlin. With *Kolberg*, Nazi film reached a kind of culmination point. A delusional Goebbels entrusted to it the power to change the outcome of the war. But at the same time, because defeat now appeared to most Germans inevitable, *Kolberg* exposed the hollow duplicity of Nazi propaganda more sharply than any other propaganda film before it.

Epilogue

On 21 June 1938, Hitler spent the evening, as usual in the pre-war period, watching a film: in this case, the Laurel and Hardy classic *Swiss Miss*. As we saw in the opening chapter of this book, Hitler enjoyed *Swiss Miss* despite the fact it starred a Jew (Grete Natzler).[1] Later that evening, at 10 p.m., he was present at a private celebration of the summer solstice.[2] During the Third Reich, the Nazis encouraged the welcoming of the winter and summer solstice in their attempts to revive Germanic customs. Hitler moved easily from enjoying a product of 'Jewish' Hollywood to celebrating a Nazi ritual. On 30 June, he began watching the mystery film *The Great Gambini* (1937) and the romantic comedy *Bluebeard's Eighth Wife* (1938). He broke off the showings, but that he started them at all seems surprising given that both films were directed by Jews, Vidor and Lubitsch respectively. That night, he sat down to write a long tract on the building of fortresses.[3] As a private viewer of films, Hitler was able to simply suspend not so much his disbelief as his ideology, only to pick this up again a few hours later. Some films did not require such a suspension, of course, and Hitler was equally able to enjoy Nazi propaganda films. Yet this makes the incongruities all the more striking. Personal pleasure, for Hitler, did not always operate according to the principles that governed his personal and public politics. In private, he did not hesitate to indulge his liking for cheap entertainment, comedies and the like.

But he made sure the public image of his film viewing was shaped by his attendance of solemn Nazi films. In the public realm, Hitler took film very seriously as a supreme propaganda tool. Whether it was celebrating Nazism or promoting anti-Bolshevism, eugenics, anti-Semitism or the Nazi military campaigns, he entrusted film and newsreels with the power to convince: 'Films could change the world,' he told Riefenstahl in 1940.[4] He imagined the power of film operating far beyond the present. Hitler rarely philosophized on the subject of film, but, when he did, he developed grand visions. It would be 'fantastic', he said in the same conversation with Riefenstahl, if 'today we could see films from the past, about Frederick the Great, Napoleon and the historical events of the ancient world'.[5] Hitler here meant films made *at the time* of Frederick the Great, for instance. He asked Riefenstahl to contact the Kaiser Wilhelm Institute in Berlin and discuss the possibility of the production of a film material 'made from the finest metal' that would resist the ravages of time and last for centuries: 'just imagine if, in a thousand years, people could see what we are experiencing today'.[6] Hitler, here, was envisaging the present as history, with film as a surviving record of its existence. In 1943, the NSDAP set about preparing a film documenting Hitler's career as a politician, beginning with the First World War and ending with the Second. Provisionally entitled *But I Decided to Become a Politician*, the film was never made, and Hitler's part in its planning is not clear.[7] In 1942, the Propaganda Ministry came up with the idea of filming Nazi leaders to create an 'Archive of Personalities'. Nothing materialized in this case either. Both of these film projects nevertheless reflect something of Hitler's view of film as a resource for the future, not just the present.[8]

In Hitler's eyes, the longevity of film was to be matched by its monumentality. Hitler complained about Trenker's films being 'worm-eaten' with Catholicism in his 'Table Talk' on 20 August 1942;[9] and, on 20 May 1942, while welcoming Goebbels' idea of a film on Lola Montez (the mistress of

Bavarian King Ludwig I), Hitler insisted she be portrayed as someone who 'resisted the Catholic Church'.[10] Yet, according to Riefenstahl, Hitler 'almost became ecstatic' at the prospect of a film about its history.[11] Whatever his dislike of Catholicism itself, its long, vast, powerful history fascinated him; he was impressed by sprawling histories and empires of any kind. On 4 February 1942, Hitler stated that German cinema faced a 'gigantic task', namely portraying the history of the German emperors: 'for 500 years, they dominated the world'.[12] Hitler's expectations of film, art and sculpture were equally heroic, but it was film that Hitler wanted to capture grandiose historical visions of imperial power. If at times he expressed disappointment at German feature films produced in the Third Reich, despite his private enjoyment of them, and despite his public endorsements of particular films, then perhaps this was because they never produced such visions, at least not of the kind and scale he wanted. Whether any film director in her or his right mind could have taken on a grand imperial history, culminating in National Socialism, is a moot point. Certainly, thanks to Riefenstahl, Hitler was able to enjoy a visual celebration of his own imperial status – even before the Second World War had begun. Her rally films elevated him to the supreme, motivating centre of national life, directing the masses.

Hitler's rare, lofty pronouncements on film, however, contrast with the pragmatism and tactics that often characterized his interventions in film production. When Hitler watched *Victory in the West* in December 1940, Kurt Hesse noted Hitler's 'cool judgement' in assessing possible effects on the viewers.[13] This book has provided many examples of his strategic response to individual films. He decided on bans by calculating possible effects on audiences or foreign governments, and used film to justify racial and military policies – with *In Battle against the World Enemy* serving to sugar-coat the lifting of a military secret. If a film caused annoyance, he could opt to let it cause annoyance to keep the complainers in their place. During the war, he used film (*Victory in the West*) as an excuse to intensify ideological training within the army, or to deliver a lesson to his generals about the conduct he expected of them (*The Great King*). His interventions in the making of the newsreels, about which, sadly, too little is documented, reveal similar tactical motivations, though when Hitler began to ask for footage of German successes that Goebbels was no longer able to provide, wishful thinking and self-delusion became mixed with fears that audiences might lose faith in the war effort. His repeated viewing of Fanck's film about the Atlantic Wall in 1943 make one wonder if he was losing himself in seductive images of apparent inviolability. This book has shown that Hitler regarded film as another tool in his attempt to convince Germans that Nazism was all about self-defence: aggression was justified in this way in *Victims of the Past, In Battle against the World Enemy, Campaign in Poland, The Eternal Jew* and even in Riefenstahl's *Triumph of the Will*, which justifies the purge of the SA. This same dialectic characterizes many of the wartime newsreels. By the time of the making of *The Atlantic Wall*, the preoccupation with defence had become an obsession for Hitler – a defence made necessary by the very aggression he had unleashed in the name of defence. The Atlantic Wall was a pipedream, as was the idea that a film of it could strengthen the German will to resist the Allied onslaught. But, while some aspects of Hitler's film projects may have been fantastical, others were not: *Triumph of the Will*, for instance, resulted from a very shrewd awareness of how film could help to cement an impression of Nazi dominance, and this is precisely how that film was then deployed.

One of the motives for writing this book was to counteract a continuing trend. Germany has faced its past like no other country. The involvement of the German film industry in National Socialism, too, as the Bibliography shows, has been thoroughly addressed. Yet, in popular perceptions, the cinema of the Nazi period is often still imagined as one of light entertainment. Films from 1933 to 1945 are shown regularly on German television, and are easily available on the internet. Actors who took part in these films are remembered as victims or as opponents of Nazism. Gliding easily for the most part through denazification, they soon re-established their screen careers. Certainly, Riefenstahl and Veit Harlan, the most notorious directors of Nazi propaganda films, received plenty of post-war criticism and judicial attention. In 1949, Veit Harlan, the director of *Jew Süss*, was indicted on the charge of aiding and abetting crimes against humanity. But the Jury Court of Hamburg's Regional Court found him not guilty.[14] Although the British revoked the verdict, the subsequent retrial did not change the outcome. The justifications for Harlan's acquittal were that he had acted under duress and could not be held responsible for the content of the film. In essence, these were Riefenstahl's arguments, too, in relation to her rally films. Even in recent German films exploring the conduct of actors in the Third Reich, exculpatory tendencies are noticeable. Oskar Roehler's 2010 feature film *Jew Suss: Rise and Fall*, for instance, is more interested in portraying Ferdinand Marian, the actor who played Jew Süss in Harlan's 1940 film, as a philo-Semitic victim of Nazi coercion than it is in that film's appalling anti-Semitism. Joachim Lang's 2013 documentary film *George* portrays actor Heinrich George critically yet sympathetically, and more or less omits mention of his role as the Duke in *Jew Süss*.

That Hitler stood at the very heart of the world in which *all* actors and directors had moved during the Third Reich was a fact quickly forgotten after the Second World War. Yet those actors and directors knew, many of them anyway, about his obsessive interest in Third Reich film. They probably knew that a diet of evening viewings, in peace time, provided him with the distraction he needed before he plunged into the next day's politics. They knew that acting in the Third Reich meant making propaganda films for Hitler's beliefs and politics, and entertainment films to provide relief from the political pressures of living in Nazi Germany. The connection between Hitler's beliefs and a number of Nazi-period films was plain to see. That anti-Bolshevik, anti-British and war films generally, regardless of how effective or good they might have been, served Hitler's purpose was equally obvious. His interventions in particular films were only known to some, yet others were reported in the newspapers. To this day, despite critical books and articles, Germany has never really confronted the fact that the German film industry as a whole pandered to Hitler in one way or another.

Notes

Abbreviations

BAB	Bundesarchiv Berlin
BAF	Bundesarchiv Freiburg
BA FA	Bundesarchiv Filmarchiv
BAK	Bundesarchiv Koblenz
GTB	Goebbels, Joseph. *Die Tagebücher von Joseph Goebbels Online*, edited by Elke Fröhlich (Berlin, 2012), online at http://www.degruyter.com/view/db/tjgo
IfZ	Institut für Zeitgeschichte, München
LAB	Landesarchiv Berlin
LA NRW	Landesarchiv Nordrhein-Westfalen
PA AA	Politisches Archiv, Auswärtiges Amt
SAF	Staatsarchiv Freiburg
SAH	Staatsarchiv Hamburg

Introduction

1. Timothy Ryback, *Hitler's Private Library: The Books that Shaped his Life* (London, 2010).
2. See Albert Speer, *Inside the Third Reich* (London, 2003), and Sebastian Tesch, *Albert Speer: Hitlers Architekten* (Cologne, 2016).
3. Joachim Köhler, *Wagner's Hitler: The Prophet and his Disciple* (Cambridge, 2001); Brigitte Hamann, *Winifred Wagner: A Life at the Heart of Hitler's Bayreuth* (London, 2005).
4. Ines Schlenker, *Hitler's Salon: The Große Deutsche Kunstausstellung at the Haus der Deutschen Kunst in Munich 1937–1944* (Bern, 2007).
5. Birgit Schwarz, *Geniewahn: Hitler und die Kunst* (Vienna, 2011).
6. Despina Stratigakos, *Hitler at Home* (New Haven and London, 2015).
7. Frederic Spotts, *Hitler and the Power of Aesthetics* (London, 2003). Here, p. xiii.
8. Felix Moeller, *Der Filmminister: Goebbels und der Film im Dritten Reich* (Berlin, 1998).
9. David Welch, *Propaganda and the German Cinema, 1933–1945* (London and New York, 2001).

10. See, particularly, Boguslaw Drewniak, *Der Deutsche Film 1938–1945* (Düsseldorf, 1987); Erwin Leiser, *'Deutschland erwache!' Propaganda im Film des Dritten Reiches* (Hamburg, 1968); and Moeller, *Der Filmminister.*
11. See Ben Urwand, *The Collaboration: Hollywood's Pact with Hitler* (Cambridge, MA and London, 2013); also, Thomas Doherty, *Hollywood and Hitler, 1933–1939* (New York, 2013).
12. An exception is Volker Koop's study of the 'secret favourite films of the Nazi elite', which takes Hitler's film viewings seriously, but says little about his influence on Nazi film. See Volker Koop, *Warum Hitler King Kong liebte, aber den Deutschen Micky Maus verbot* (Berlin, 2015). See also Jörg Alt, 'The Dictator as Spectator: Feature Film Screenings before Adolf Hitler, 1933–39', *Historical Journal of Film, Radio and Television* 35:3 (2015), pp. 420–37.
13. Adolf Hitler, *Mein Kampf*, transl. James Murphy (London, 1939), p. 385. Online at https://archive.org/details/MeinKampf_483 (accessed 2 May 2017).
14. Spotts, *Hitler and the Power of Aesthetics*, p. 178.
15. See, for instance, Steven Bach, *Leni: The Life and Work of Leni Riefenstahl* (London, 2007); Lutz Kinkel, *Die Scheinwerferin: Leni Riefenstahl und das 'Dritte Reich'* (Hamburg and Vienna, 2002); Rainer Rother, *Leni Riefenstahl: Die Verführung des Talents* (Berlin, 2000); and Jürgen Trimborn, *Leni Riefenstahl: A Life* (New York, 2008).
16. See Joseph Goebbels, *Die Tagebücher von Joseph Goebbels Online*, ed. Elke Fröhlich (Berlin, 2012), online at http://www.degruyter.com/view/db/tjgo (hereafter *GTB*), 9 March 1934.
17. For a survey of how the Nazis cultivated German high society and created a 'strange imperial court' consisting of old elites, parvenus, 'actors, aristocrats, SS technocrats, and diplomats', see Fabrice d'Almeida, *High Society in the Third Reich* (Cambridge, 2008), quotation from back cover.
18. See, for instance, Dorothea Hollstein, *Antisemitische Filmpropaganda: Die Darstellung des Juden im nationalsozialistischen Spielfilm* (Berlin, 1971); Susan Tegel, *Jew Süss: Life, Legend, Fiction, Film* (London, 2011); and Stig Hornshøj-Møller, *'Der ewige Jude': Quellenkritische Analyse eines antisemitischen Propagandafilms* (Göttingen, 1995).
19. For a discussion of British and German media presentations of the war, see Ian Garden, *Battling with the Truth: The Contrast in the Media Reporting of World War II* (Stroud, 2015).
20. For the handling of Stalingrad in the Nazi media, see David Welch, *The Third Reich: Politics and Propaganda* (London and New York, 2006), esp. pp. 136–9.
21. See, for instance, Wolfgang Becker, *Film und Herrschaft: Organisationsprinzipien und Organisationsstrukturen der nationalsozialistischen Filmpropaganda* (Uelzen, 1973); Jana F. Bruns, *Nazi Cinema's New Women* (Cambridge and New York, 2009); Drewniak, *Der Deutsche Film 1938–1945*; Sabine Hake, *Popular Cinema of the Third Reich* (Austin, 2003); David Stewart Hull, *Film in the Third Reich* (Berkeley and Los Angeles, 1969); Klaus Kreimeier, *Die UFA-Story: Geschichte eines Filmkonzerns* (Munich, 1992); Mary-Elizabeth O'Brien, *Nazi Cinema as Enchantment: The Politics of Entertainment in the Third Reich* (Rochester, 2004); Gerhard Stahr, *Volksgemeinschaft vor der Leinwand? Der nationalsozialistische Film und sein Publikum* (Berlin, 2001); Roel Vande Winkel and David Welch, eds, *Cinema and the Swastika: The International Expansion of Third Reich Cinema* (Basingstoke, 2011); David Welch, *Propaganda and the German Cinema*; Joseph Wulf, *Theater und Film im Dritten Reich: Eine Dokumentation* (Frankfurt, Berlin and Vienna, 1983).

1 Films at the Berghof

1. BAB, R43 II/390: Meerwald to Brückner, 1 September 1937.
2. Rochus Misch, *Der Letzte Zeuge: Ich war Hitlers Telefonist, Kurier und Leibwächter* (Munich, 2009), p. 109.
3. Julius Schaub, *In Hitlers Schatten: Erinnerungen und Aufzeichnungen des persönlichen Adjutanten und Vertrauten 1925–1945* (Stegen-Ammersee, 2010), pp. 129–33.

4. Veit Harlan, *Im Schatten meiner Filme* (Gütersloh, 1966), p. 57.
5. Christa Schroeder, *Er war mein Chef* (Munich, 2002), p. 190.
6. Ernst Hanfstaengl, *Zwischen Weißem und Braunem Haus* (Munich, 1970), p. 314.
7. See Heinz Linge, *Bis zum Untergang: Als Chef des Persönlichen Dienstes bei Hitler*, ed. Werner Maser (Munich, 1980), p. 92; and Karl Wilhelm Krause, *Im Schatten der Macht: Kammerdiener bei Hitler* (Bochum, 2011), pp. 19–20.
8. See Herbert Döhring, *Hitlers Hausverwalter* (Bochum, 2013), p. 40.
9. Heinrich Hoffmann, *Hitler Was my Friend: The Memoirs of Hitler's Photographer* (London, 2011), p. 191.
10. Fritz Wiedemann, *Der Mann, der Feldherr werden wollte* (Wuppertal, 1964), p. 76.
11. Linge, *Bis zum Untergang*, p. 92.
12. Albert Speer, *Erinnerungen* (Berlin, 1995), p. 104.
13. See Oleg V. Khlevniuk, *Stalin: New Biography of a Dictator* (New Haven, 2015), pp. 2–3.
14. Speer, *Erinnerungen*, p. 104.
15. Lutz Koepnick, *Framing Attention: Windows on Modern German Culture* (Baltimore, 2007), p. 196.
16. In the Reich Chancellery, the projection unit was hidden behind a painting, the screen behind a watercolour on the opposite side of the room.
17. Krause, *Im Schatten der Macht*, p. 18.
18. Ibid., p. 19.
19. Ibid., p. 66.
20. IfZ, ZS-3135-1: Recollections of Therese Linke.
21. Anna Plaim and Kurt Kuch, *Bei Hitler: Zimmermädchen Annas Erinnerungen* (Munich, 2005), p. 77.
22. See *GTB*, 2 March 1934 and 26 May 1934.
23. See Ben Urwand, *The Collaboration: Hollywood's Pact with Hitler* (Cambridge, MA and London, 2013), p. 106.
24. See *GTB*, 18 April 1934. For Goebbels' reports on other film viewings at Hitler's various residences, see, for the year 1934 for example: *GTB*, 8 February, 24 February, 8 March, 9 April, 11 April, 16 April, 4 May, 15 May, 17 May, 19 May, 7 June, 27 June, 11 July, 18 July, 29 August, 13 September, and 15 September.
25. See BAB, NS10/49: Reichsministerium für Volksaufklärung und Propaganda (RMVP) to Adjutantur des Führers, 27 June 1939.
26. For a discussion of the reasons for this, see Chapter 2.
27. See BAB, NS10/49: Bahls to RMVP, 24 April 1939.
28. BAB, NS10/125: Overview of Hitler's activities on 19 July 1938. Goebbels was less impressed by *I Love You*: 'makes you want to throw up eventually' (*GTB*, 14 July 1938).
29. BAB, NS10/49: Bahls to Leichtenstern, 13 June 1939.
30. BAB, NS10/125: Overview of Hitler's activities on 22 June 1938.
31. BAB, R43 II/390: Ernst Seeger to Privatkanzlei des Führers, 19 April 1937.
32. See the material in BAB, R109 I/1368.
33. Hitler also admired the acting of Marlene Dietrich, while simultaneously dismissing her as a 'hyena' for having left Germany. Goebbels, with Hitler's backing, tried to lure her back – unsuccessfully – in 1936. See Guido Knopp, *Hitlers Frauen und Marlene* (Munich, 2001), pp. 374–76.
34. BAB, NS10/45: Bahls to Leichtenstern, 16 August 1938.
35. See Werner Maser, ed., *Mein Schüler Hitler: Das Tagebuch seines Lehrers Paul Devrient* (Pfaffenhofen, 1975).
36. BAB, NS10/44: Wünsche to Leichtenstern, 21 November 1938.
37. See the account by Paul Schmidt, present at the meeting as interpreter: *Statist auf diplomatischer Bühne 1923–45* (Bonn, 1949), pp. 396–97.
38. BAB, NS10/125: Overview of Hitler's activities on 15 September 1938.

39. Ibid.: Overview of Hitler's activities on 16 September 1938.
40. Ibid.: Overview of Hitler's activities on 17 September 1938. The German title of this film, *Frechdachs*, may refer to the US film *Wildcat of Arizona*, which was released in Germany as *Frechdachs von Arizona*. But, as it was not released till 1939, it is more likely it refers to the 1932 film.
41. *GTB*, 22 December 1937.
42. BAB, NS10/44: 'Verzeichnis der Archivfilme', undated, probably June 1938. See Jörg Alt, 'The Dictator as Spectator: Feature Film Screenings before Adolf Hitler, 1933–39', *Historical Journal of Film, Radio and Television* 35:3 (2015), pp. 420–37, here p. 426.
43. BAB, NS10/43: 'Aufstellung der am 15. Februar 1937 als eiserner Bestand auf dem Obersalzberg eingelagerten Filme'. The expression 'eiserner Bestand' is an economic term meaning 'base stock'; I have translated it here as 'permanent stock'. Despite the date of February 1937, the films on this list are from 1935 or earlier.
44. See Christopher Clark, *Iron Kingdom: The Rise and Downfall of Prussia, 1600–1947* (London, 2006), pp. 660–62.
45. *GTB*, 22 December 1937.
46. Ibid., 29 August 1934. Goebbels' diary also informs us that Hitler was a fan of Froelich's *The Dreamer* (*GTB*, 11 January 1936) and Harlan's *The Ruler* (*GTB*, 15 March 1937).
47. See Henry Picker, *Hitlers Tischgespräche im Führerhauptquartier* (Munich, 2003), p. 632 (18 July 1942).
48. BAB, NS10/48: Bormann to Wernicke, 30 August 1937.
49. Ibid.: Bormann to Wernicke, 21 October 1937.
50. These were *The Holy Mountain* (1926), *The Great Leap* (1927) and *The White Ecstasy* (1931).
51. For more on Gerron, see Chapter 10.
52. BAB, NS10/48: Seeger to Adjutantur des Führers, 21 July 1937.
53. For *Way Out West* and *Swiss Miss*, see BAB, NS10/125: Overview of Hitler's activities on 16 and 21 June 1938 respectively.
54. BAB, NS10/44: Wünsche to Leichtenstern, 21 November 1938.
55. Hitler no doubt approved of Hal Roach, whose studios produced all these Laurel and Hardy films: in 1937, Roach rather misguidedly formed a film company partnership with Mussolini's son. See Richard Lewis Ward, *A History of the Hal Roach Studios* (Illinois, 2006), p. 100.
56. Kate Atkinson, *Life after Life* (London, 2013), pp. 426–7.
57. See 'Did Adolf Hitler Draw Disney Characters?', *Daily Telegraph*, 23 February 2008.
58. It is possible that Hitler was being confused with the notorious SS doctor Mengele, for, while there is no real evidence Hitler was fascinated by *Snow White*, there is some in the case of Mengele. Dina Gottliebova Babbitt only survived Auschwitz because Mengele admired her drawings of *Snow White*. See Stefan Pannor, 'Comic für KZ-Künstlerin: Schneewittchen in Auschwitz', *Der Spiegel*, 15 August 2008.
59. BAB, NS10/44: 'Herrn Oberregierungsrat Dr. Zeller. Betrifft: Filmbeschaffung', 5 February 1938. Rolf Giesen and J.P. Storm claim that Hitler saw *Snow White* three weeks later, and that it became 'one of the most cherished movie treasures of his film collection'. But they provide no real evidence for either of these claims, apart from a reference to an untranscripted phone-call by one of the authors (Storm) to Hitler's former projectionist. See Giesen and Storm, *Animation under the Swastika: A History of Trickfilm in Nazi Germany, 1933–1945* (Jefferson, NC, 2003), p. 11.
60. Hanfstaengl, *Zwischen Weißem und Braunem Haus*, p. 314.
61. Volker Koop, *Warum Hitler King Kong liebte, aber den Deutschen Micky Maus verbot* (Berlin, 2015), pp. 26–7.
62. Ibid., pp. 23–4.

63. Herbert Rosendorfer, *Bayreuth für Anfänger* (Munich, 1984), p. 69f.
64. See Richard Evans, *The Third Reich in Power 1933–1939* (London, 2005), pp. 647–8.
65. See Picker, *Hitlers Tischgespräche*, p. 126 (25/26 January 1942).
66. Hans Baur, *I Was Hitler's Pilot: The Memoirs of Hans Baur* (Barnsley, 2013), Kindle Edition, Location 1923–24.
67. Koop, *Warum Hitler Kong Kong liebte*, p. 24. *King Kong* was released in early December in Germany, and recognized in the German press as a technical masterpiece. See 'Die Fabel vom King Kong', *Der Film*, 2 December 1933.
68. Robert G.L. Waite, *The Psychopathic God: Adolf Hitler* (Boston, 1993), p. 247.
69. Hoffmann, *Hitler was my Friend*, p. 191.
70. *GTB*, 31 December 1936.
71. Adolf Hitler, *Mein Kampf* (Munich, 1943 [851–5th edns]), p. 163.
72. Ibid., p. 406.
73. *GTB*, 12 May 1924.
74. Ibid., 4 November 1929. Already in 1925, Goebbels had begun to revise his view (*GTB*, 11 April 1925).
75. Ibid., 6 August 1924.
76. See 'Wiederaufführung des Fritz Lang-Films "Siegfrieds Tod" im Ufa-Palast am Zoo', *Der Film*, 27 May 1933.
77. According to the journalist and author Curt Riess, in 1933 Goebbels and Hitler wanted Fritz Lang to take over the Nazi film industry, so impressed was Hitler by Lang's films, particularly *The Nibelungs*. See Curt Riess, *Das gab's nur einmal: Das Buch der schönsten Filme unseres Lebens* (Hamburg, 1956), p. 455. Film scholar Felix Moeller, however, doubts whether Goebbels would have offered Lang such a position given that another of Lang's films, *The Testament of Dr. Mabuse*, had been banned in March 1933, not least because it appeared to constitute a critique of Hitler. See Felix Moeller, *Der Filmminister: Goebbels und der Film im Dritten Reich* (Berlin, 1998), p. 161.
78. *GTB*, 12 February and 11 April 1935.
79. Ibid., 30 December 1936.
80. Ibid., 12 September 1940.
81. Ibid., 22 November 1941.
82. Alt, 'The Dictator as Spectator', p. 432.
83. Heinz Boberach, ed., *Meldungen aus dem Reich: Die geheimen Lageberichte des Sicherheitsdienstes der SS 1938–1945, Band 12* (Herrsching, 1985), pp. 4734–5 (1 February 1943).
84. See BAB, R109 I/1033c: 'Ufa-Vorstandssitzung Nr. 1361', 28 March 1939.
85. See Urwand, *The Collaboration*, pp. 13ff.
86. Craig Brown, 'Hitlerwood: Yes, Hitler Was Obsessed by Movies – But Did He *Really* Persuade Hollywood to Collaborate with the Nazis?', *Daily Mail Online*, 16 November 2013 at http://www.dailymail.co.uk/home/event/article-2507129/Hitler-Hollywood-book-reviewed-Craig-Brown.html (accessed 29 April 2017).
87. BAB, NS10/125: Overview of Hitler's activities on 19 June 1938.
88. BAB, NS10/45, Bahls to RMVP, 4 July 1938. This only confirms the return of a translation of the film, not that Hitler requested the film or a translation of the dialogue, as Urwand claims.
89. The film was banned by the German censorship authorities precisely because it showed 'how easy it is to stop and plunder lorries in unpopulated areas'. Interestingly, the US film company Paramount, protesting against this ban, argued that the trial of the Götze brothers was bringing details of such robberies to light and therefore encouraging similar attempts (hardly, to be the fair, the purpose of the trial). See Markus Spieker, *Hollywood unterm Hakenkreuz: Der amerikanische Spielfilm im Dritten Reich* (Trier, 1999), pp. 232–4. As the ban preceded Hitler's ruling on the Götze brothers, it is unlikely he influenced it. It was upheld – despite Paramount's

protest – on 16 June 1938, three days before Hitler viewed the film (Deutsches Institut für Filmkunde: OP, Nr. 7924, 16.6.1938).

90. BAB, NS10/125: Overview of Hitler's activities on 22 June 1938.
91. *GTB*, 14 November 1935. Hitler's enthusiastic response refers to both *Mazurka* and *Frisians in Distress*.
92. Pola Negri, *Memories of a Star* (New York, 1970), p. 375.
93. BAB, NS10/125: Overview of Hitler's activities on 28 June 1938.
94. Ibid.: Overview of Hitler's activities on 28 September 1938.
95. Hitler's adjutant Max Wünsche had already seen *Alert in the Mediterranean* at Goebbels' residence in Schwanenwerder. Whether he had a hand in selecting this film for Hitler's viewing is not clear, but that Hitler's adjutants might have on occasion acted as 'previewers' is possible. See BAB, NS10/45: RMVP to Wünsche, 22 November 1938.
96. Ian Kershaw, *Hitler: 1936–1945: Nemesis* (London, 2000), p. 122.
97. Urwand, *The Collaboration*, p. 14.
98. See *GTB*, 3 October 1938.
99. Leni Riefenstahl, *Memoiren* (Cologne, 2000), p. 344.
100. Christabel Bielenberg, *The Past is Myself and The Road Ahead* (London, 2011), pp. 486–7.
101. *GTB*, 15 March 1940.
102. Wiedemann, *Der Mann, der Feldherr werden wollte*, p. 215.
103. Klaus P. Fischer, *Hitler and America* (Philadelphia, 2011), p. 10.
104. Ibid.
105. BAB, NS10/42: Seeger to Schaub, 13 May 1936.
106. Ibid.: Seeger to Schaub, 31 January 1936.
107. Wiedemann, *Der Mann, der Feldherr werden wollte*, p. 211.
108. Ernst Schramm, 'Adolf Hitler – Anatomie eines Diktators', *Der Spiegel*, 29 January 1964.
109. See Chapters 3 and 4.
110. See Wolfgang Pyta, *Hitler: Der Künstler als Politiker und Feldherr* (Munich, 2015).
111. 'Zum 50. Geburtstag Adolf Hitlers', *Film-Kurier*, 19 April 1939.
112. 'Sonderwochenschauen vom Führer-Geburtstag: Dr. Goebbels überreichte gestern dem Führer ein Geschenkwerk über den deutschen Film', *Film-Kurier*, 21 April 1939.
113. Wilhelm Brückner, 'Der Führer in seinem Privatleben', in Heinrich Hoffmann, ed., *Adolf Hitler: Bilder aus dem Leben des Führers* (Altona/Bahrenfeld, 1936), pp. 35–43, here, pp. 36–7.
114. Hitler, *Mein Kampf*, pp. 61–2.
115. Ibid., p. 279.
116. *GTB*, 18 September 1937.
117. BAB, R43 II/390: Seeger to Forum-Film, 19 August 1935.
118. BAB, NS10/125: Overview of Hitler's activities on 20 June 1938.
119. Ibid.: Overview of Hitler's activities on 30 June 1938.

2 From Bans to Commissions

1. Karl Wilhelm Krause, *Im Schatten der Macht: Kammerdiener bei Hitler* (Bochum, 2011), p. 34.
2. *GTB*, 14 November 1933.
3. At least twenty-eight German film productions from the 1933–45 period were banned. See Felix Moeller, *Der Filmminister: Goebbels und der Film im Dritten Reich* (Berlin, 1998), p. 322. See also Kraft Wetzel and Peter Hagemann, *Zensur: Verbotene deutsche Filme 1933–1945* (Berlin, 1978).
4. *GTB*, 15 November 1933.
5. See Andreas Kilb, 'Die Phantome von Lübeck', *Frankfurter Allgemeine Zeitung*, 21 December 2008.

6. *GTB*, 6 December 1933.
7. Ibid., 26 June 1937.
8. Ibid., 30 June 1937.
9. See Ibid., 11 and 13 July 1937.
10. Horn had acted in Hollywood and Britain (for instance in Thomas Bentley's 1933 film *The Love Nest*).
11. *GTB*, 14 October 1936.
12. Camilla Horn, *Verliebt in die Liebe: Erinnerungen* (Frankfurt and Berlin, 1985), p. 203.
13. Ibid., p. 205.
14. *GTB*, 26 October 1936.
15. Ibid., 18 December 1936.
16. Ibid., 24 June 1937.
17. Luis Trenker, *Alles gut gegangen: Geschichten aus meinem Leben* (Munich, 1974), p. 359.
18. *GTB*, 17 March 1937.
19. Ibid., 18 March 1937.
20. Trenker, *Alles gut gegangen*, p. 360.
21. *GTB*, 31 March 1937.
22. It was read out on Palm Sunday 1937.
23. *GTB*, 31 March 1937.
24. Trenker, *Alles gut gegangen*, pp. 360–61.
25. *GTB*, 1 April 1937.
26. Ibid., 1 April 1937.
27. Ibid., 7 and 14 January 1937.
28. Ibid., 1 May 1938.
29. BAB, NS10/125: Overview of Hitler's activities on 19 June 1938.
30. See Helga and Karlheinz Wendtland, *Geliebter Kintopp. Sämtliche deutsche Spielfilme von 1929–1945 mit zahlreichen Künstlerbiographien, Jahrgang 1935 und 1936* (Berlin, 1988).
31. Quoted in Hans Borgelt, *Das süßeste Mädel der Welt: Die Lilian Harvey Story* (Munich, 1976), p. 184.
32. Lilian Harvey's biographer, Hans Borgelt, claims that Goebbels was fed up with Harvey's demands for payment in foreign currency, and that the brothel scene in *Capriccio* caused Goebbels such indignation that he eventually ran out of patience. See Borgelt, *Das süßeste Mädel der Welt*, p. 185.
33. See BAB, NS10/125: Overview of Hitler's activities on 16 June 1938. Hitler had lunch with, among others, Goebbels, Bormann and Ribbentrop.
34. *GTB*, 1 May 1938.
35. Ibid., 12 May 1938.
36. See BAB, R43 II/390: 'Erlass des Führers 17.10.1935'.
37. See *GTB*, 24 February 1938, 25 February 1938, 24 April 1938 and 8 June 1938.
38. After the war, Hoffmann testified that Bormann had a habit of seizing on 'harmless criticism' expressed by Hitler after he had watched a film and making a note of it in his 'ominous notebook'. This usually meant, according to Hoffmann, that a particular actor was then no longer permitted to act in films, or a film could no longer be shown. See IfZ, MS 2049: Testimony of Heinrich Hoffmann.
39. See Markus Spieker, *Hollywood unterm Hakenkreuz: Der amerikanische Spielfilm im Dritten Reich* (Trier, 1999), p. 236.
40. *The Jungle Princess* had already been sent to the Berghof in December 1936, see BAB, NS10/48: Seeger to Adjutantur des Führers, 17 December 1936.
41. In January 1938, 20th Century Fox even wrote to Hitler's Adjutants Office asking 'if it would be possible to get a letter from the Führer in which he expresses his opinion about the value and effect of American films in Germany'. Hitler's chief adjutant Brückner

replied that 'the Führer up to now has on principle refused to deliver such judgments'. See BAB, NS10/48: Deutsche Fox Film to Adjutantur des Führers, 10 January 1938.

42. *GTB*, 21 June 1938.

43. Although see Chapter 7, for evidence that Hitler, during the war at least, was content to allow films to ruffle the feathers of particular professions.

44. Hitler's negative opinion of Fritz Thiery's film *Princess Sissy* and of a film about the boxer Max Schmeling did prompt Goebbels to impose bans, but, in the case of both films, Goebbels had explicitly asked for Hitler's confirmation they should be prohibited – in the case of the Max Schmeling film because 'Schmeling gets terribly beaten up' (*GTB*, 13 July 1938). See also BAB, NS10/45: Bahls to Leichtenstern, 16 July 1938.

45. See BAB, NS10/45, Bahls to Leichtenstern, 16 July 1938; and see *GTB*, 7 July 1938.

46. Moeller, *Der Filmminister*, pp. 324–25.

47. See Wetzel and Hagemann, *Zensur*, p. 90.

48. See Karl Ludwig Rost, *Sterilisation und Euthanasie im Film des 'Dritten Reichs'* (Husum, 1987), p. 65. See also BAB, NS10/64: Frercks to Hanke, 23 March 1937, and Michael Burleigh, *Death and Deliverance: Euthanasia in Germany 1900–1945* (London, 2002), p. 182.

49. See Karl Heinz Roth, 'Filmpropaganda für die Vernichtung der Geisteskranken und Behinderten im "Dritten Reich" ', in Götz Aly et al., *Reform und Gewissen, 'Euthanasie' im Dienst des Fortschritts* (Berlin, 1989), pp. 125–93, here p. 131.

50. See BA FA, B 55407-1: 'Opfer der Vergangenheit'.

51. Certainly the Propaganda Ministry sent the film to his Adjutants Office in October. See BAB, NS10/42: Seeger to Adjutantur des Führers, 26 October 1936.

52. BAB, NS10/48: Seeger to Adjutantur des Führers, 8 February 1937.

53. *GTB*, 11 February 1937.

54. BAB, NS10/64: Frercks to Hanke, 23 March 1937.

55. *The Hereditary Defective* was also shown to Foreign Organization branches of the Nazi Party, for instance in Spain. The guidelines drawn up for showing it pointed to the need to 'open the eyes' of party comrades to the 'urgent importance of soon finding a thorough solution to the hereditary health problem'. See BAB, NS9/101: 'Schmalfilm "Erbkrank", Landesgruppe Spanien', 26 March 1936.

56. BAB, NS10/64: Frercks to Hanke, 23 March 1937.

57. BAB, NS10/64: Frercks to Wiedemann, 2 April 1937.

58. BAB, NS18/901: 'Reichspropagandaleitung Amtsleitung Film an alle Gaufilmstellen der NSDAP', 8 March 1937. There was an age restriction, however; the film could only be seen by those aged 14 and over. See BAB, NS18/901: 'Rundschreiben Nr. 92/37 an alle Gaufilmstellen der NSDAP', 1 April 1937.

59. See BAB, NS18/901: 'Rundschreiben Nr. 114/37 an alle Gaufilmstellen der NSDAP', 7 May 1937.

60. Walter Groß cites this axiom in a 1937 article on *Victims of the Past*. See Walter Groß, 'Opfer der Vergangenheit', *Film-Kurier*, 8 April 1937.

61. Burleigh, *Death and Deliverance*, p. 188.

62. Gerhard Besier, *Die Kirchen und das Dritte Reich: Spaltungen und Abwehrkämpfe 1934–1937* (Munich, 2001), p. 871.

63. Ian Kershaw, *Hitler 1936–1945: Nemesis* (London, 2000), p. 256.

64. Ibid., p. 256.

65. Gerhard Engel, *Heeresadjutant bei Hitler 1938–1943: Aufzeichnungen des Majors Engel*, edited and with commentary by Hildegard von Kotze (Stuttgart, 1974), pp. 56–7.

66. For a detailed analysis of the film's structure and intent, see Paula Diehl, ' "Opfer der Vergangenheit": Konstruktion eines Feindbildes', in Sabine Moller, Miriam Rürup and Christel Trouvé, eds, *Abgeschlossene Kapitel? Zur Geschichte der Konzentrationslager und der NS-Prozesse* (Tübingen, 2002), pp. 134–44.

67. *GTB*, 4 December 1936.
68. Ibid., 10 December 1936.
69. Ibid., 11 February 1937.
70. BAB, NS10/48: Reichsministerium für Volksaufklärung und Propaganda (RMVP) to Adjutantur des Führers, 22 February 1937.
71. *GTB*, 23 February 1937.
72. In a letter of 28 April 1945, Magda Goebbels wrote that 'the world coming after the Führer and National Socialism is not worth living in'. See Anja Klabunde, *Magda Goebbels: Annäherung an ein Leben* (Munich, 1999), p. 294.
73. See 'Das Heldenlied auf die Legion Condor', *Film-Kurier*, 16 June 1939.
74. '"Pour le Merite" in Anwesenheit des Führers uraufgeführt', *Völkischer Beobachter*, 24 December 1938.
75. See Andrea Pitzer, *The Secret History of Vladimir Nabokov* (Cambridge, 2013), p. 105.
76. Ibid.
77. *GTB*, 4 December 1936.
78. Ibid., 10 January 1937.
79. Ibid., 12 January 1937.
80. According to the Spanish director Carlos Fernández Cuenca, Goebbels found Junghans' film to be 'tendentiously communist'. See Wolfgang Martin Hamdorf, *Zwischen ¡NO PASARAN! und ¡ARRIBA ESPAÑA!: Film und Propaganda im Spanischen Bürgerkrieg* (Münster, 1991), p. 107.
81. Hispano does not seem to have applied for a licence to show it in Germany at the time. See BAB, R109 I/1359a: Bavaria Filmkunst to Tobis-Tonbild-Syndikat, 10 August 1938.
82. For the negotiations between Hispano and Bavaria, see BAB, R109 I/1359b. Bavaria continued to collaborate with Hispano on the project, and a Spanish version was also made, *España heroica*.
83. '"Helden in Spanien" uraufgeführt', *Film-Kurier*, 7 October 1938. See also 'Helden in Spanien', *Licht Bild Bühne*, 7 October 1938.
84. *GTB*, 8 August 1938.
85. See BAB, NS10/48: Leichtenstern to Adjutantur des Führers, 18 February 1939.
86. Library of Congress Washington: Gerdy Troost and Paul Ludwig Troost Papers/German Documents 781/464: Schweikart to Leichtenstern, 22 December 1938.
87. A copy of *Heroes in Spain* had been recently viewed by Wehrmacht leaders as well as Hitler, and Leichtenstern indicated to Schweikart that he thought objections had come from the Wehrmacht. See Library of Congress Washington: Gerdy Troost and Paul Ludwig Troost Papers/German Documents 781/464: 'Aktennotiz (Schweikart)', 22 December 1938.
88. A list of films for Hitler's choice of viewing of 18 January 1939 includes newsreel clips about Spain, *Heroes in Spain*, and additional film material for *Heroes in Spain*. See BAB, NS10/48: 'Filmliste für 18. Januar 1939'.
89. For *Heroes in Spain*, see BA FA, K 200926-1: 'Helden in Spanien'.
90. See BAB, NS10/48: Leichtenstern to Adjutantur des Führers, 18 February 1939; and BAB, R109 I/1066: 'Protokoll über die Sitzung des Aufsichtsrates der Bavaria-Filmkunst', 27 March 1939.
91. BAB, R109 I/1066: 'Protokoll über die Sitzung des Aufsichtsrates der Bavaria-Filmkunst', 27 March 1939.
92. BAB, R109 I/1368: 'Heydenreich: Aktennotiz', 9 May 1939.
93. BAB, R109 I/1066: 'Finanzausschuss Bavaria: Bericht der Geschäftsführung'.
94. Ibid.: 'Protokoll über die Sitzung des Aufsichtsrates der Bavaria-Filmkunst', 27 March 1939.
95. See, for instance, his speech to the Reichstag of 30 January 1937 (http://research.calvin.edu/german-propaganda-archive/hitler1.htm, accessed 30 April 2017).

96. See Sozialdemokratische Partei Deutschlands (SPD), *Deutschland-Berichte der Sozialdemokratischen Partei Deutschlands (Sopade) 1934–1940, Vierter Jahrgang: 1937* (Salzhausen and Frankfurt/Main, 1980), esp. pp. 14–20.

97. See Ibid., pp. 611–16.

98. Library of Congress Washington: Gerdy Troost and Paul Ludwig Troost Papers/German Documents 781/464: Döhlemann to Winkler, 25 May 1939. There were a few 'borrowings' from *Heroes in Spain* in *In Battle against the World Enemy*, and Bavaria complained about Ritter's appropriation of material. See BAB, R109 I/1357a: 'An die Bavaria-Filmkunst Verleih', 26 June 1939.

99. From Army High Command correspondence, it is clear Hitler gave an advance order that the German public was to be informed about the Legion Condor when the time came. To prepare for this, cameramen were sent to Spain. One result of this was a short film called *German Volunteers in Spain* – exactly mirroring the subtitle of Ritter's film. It was shown in German cinemas in early June; Ritter's film premiered a few days later. See BAF, RW4/288: Oberkommando der Wehrmacht to Goebbels, 13 April 1939. See also 'Filmbericht vom Einsatz der Legion Condor', *Film-Kurier*, 3 June 1939.

100. ' "Legion Condor" heute in Hamburg', *Völkischer Beobachter*, 31 May 1939.

101. 'Das Heldenlied auf die Legion Condor', *Film-Kurier*, 16 June 1939.

102. BAB, NS10/49: Bahls to Leichtenstern, 13 June 1939.

103. BAB, R109 I/1066: 'Bavaria-Filmkunst G.m.b.H.: Anlage 1) zum Protokoll über die Aufsichtsratssitzung vom 5.8.1940'.

104. At one meeting of Bavaria's board of directors, Bavarian State Secretary Max Köglmaier said he envisaged great difficulties in solving Bavaria's financial problems given the wishes expressed by Hitler and Goebbels. See BAB, R109/1066: 'Protokoll über die Sitzung des Aufsichtsrates der Bavaria-Filmkunst', 27 March 1939.

105. BAB, NS10/35: Gauleiter Adolf Wagner to Goebbels, 31 May 1938.

106. BAB, R109 I/1066: 'Protokoll über die Sitzung des Aufsichtsrates der Bavaria-Filmkunst', 5 October 1938.

107. *GTB*, 3 June 1938.

108. Ibid., 23 June 1938.

109. According to Max Winkler. See BAB, R109 I/1066: 'Protokoll über die Sitzung des Aufsichtsrates der Bavaria-Filmkunst', 5 October 1938.

110. See BAB, R109/1066: 'Anlage II zum Protokoll über die Aufsichtsratsitzung', 5 August 1940; BAB, R55/501: Winkler to RMVP, 5 September 1940; and BAB, R2/4837: Winkler to RMVP, 16 May 1940.

111. The last reference I could trace to the project dates from June 1943; at this point, the studio was still only at planning stage. See BAB, R55/501: 'R.M.f.V.u.P. Vermerk', 30 June 1943.

112. BAB, R109 I/1066: 'Protokoll über die Sitzung des Aufsichtsrates der Bavaria-Filmkunst', 5 October 1938.

113. According to Volker Koop, *Warum Hitler King Kong liebte, aber den Deutschen Micky Maus verbot* (Berlin, 2015), p. 196.

114. See BAB, R109 I/1033a: 'Niederschrift Nr. 1302 über die Vorstandssitzung der Ufa', 12 April 1938.

115. See BAB, R109 I/1032b: 'Niederschrift Nr. 1268 über die Vorstandssitzung der Ufa', 3 November 1937.

116. Roger Moorhouse, 'Germania: Hitler's Dream Capital', *History Today* 62:3 (March 2012), online at http://www.historytoday.com/roger-moorhouse/germania-hitlers-dream-capital (accessed 30 April 2017).

117. BAB, R55/476: Deutsche Lichtspielbau G.m.b.H. to RMVP, 29 November 1940.

118. Ibid.: Deutsche Lichtspielbau G.m.b.H. to RMVP, 15 May 1941.

119. Ibid.: 'Deutsche Lichtspielbau G.m.b.H., Bericht', 23 May 1941.
120. Koop, *Warum Hitler King Kong liebte*, p. 199.
121. BAB, R55/476: Speer to all Gauleiter, 26 February 1942.
122. Ibid.: RMVP to Cautio Treuhandgesellschaft, 9 October 1944.
123. Cited in Koop, *Warum Hitler King Kong liebte*, p. 200.
124. According to Fritz Hippler, head of the Propaganda Ministry's Film Department, Hitler told Goebbels in early 1941 he wanted film studios created in Linz. See BAB, R109 I/1034b: 'Niederschrift Nr. 1452 über die Ufa-Vorstandssitzung', 8 April 1941. See also *GTB*, 18 April 1941, 30 April 1941 and 22 November 1941.
125. See BAB, R43 II/390: Bormann to the Reichsministerium des Innern, 15 September 1941. Bormann asked Lammers, in anticipation of the use of the seminary for the proposed film company, to confiscate seminary funds and transfer them to the Reichsgau Upper Danube.
126. See Paulus Nimmervoll, 'Das Zisterzienserstift Wilhering zur Zeit des Nationalsozialismus (1938–1945)', *Jahresbericht Wilhering* 60 (1969/1970), pp. 18–73. Here, p. 49.
127. BAB, R4606/2693: Speer to Körner, 13 July 1939.
128. Ibid.: 'Der Generalbauinspekteur für die Reichshauptstadt, Referent: Schelkes. Protokoll der Besprechung', 8 March 1939.
129. Ibid.: 'Schelkes: Aktennotiz: Anruf Speer', 24 June 1939.
130. Ibid.: Kötzler to Präsident der Preußischen Bau- und Finanzdirektion, 7 August 1942. For a discussion of the building plans, see Rainer Rother, *Leni Riefenstahl: Die Verführung des Talents* (Berlin, 2000), pp. 110–15.
131. See PA AA, RAV Rom (Quirinal) – Botschaft Rom 1440b, SAM 1283–84.
132. For Goebbels' discussions with Hitler about this film, see *GTB*, 15 June, 16 June, 15 July and 2 September 1941.

3 Hitler's Director

1. Leni Riefenstahl, *Memoiren* (Cologne, 2000), pp. 158–9.
2. In the late summer of 1933, the whole film branch was talking about the Greenland scandal. For material on the events in Greenland, see BAB, R9361V/109326: Arnold Fanck.
3. Riefenstahl, *Memoiren*, pp. 197–8.
4. Ibid., pp. 204–5.
5. Gunther Nickel, *Zur Diskussion: Zuckmayers 'Geheimreport'* (Göttingen, 2002), p. 220.
6. Riefenstahl, *Memoiren*, p. 332.
7. Ernst Jaeger, 'How Leni Riefenstahl Became Hitler's Girlfriend', *Hollywood Tribune*, 19 May 1939.
8. On 17 November 1932, Goebbels noted in his diary that Riefenstahl had been 'badmouthing Trenker'.
9. Trenker also tried to sell the film rights to America, but gave up when producer Paul Kohner told him that 'no interest could be aroused among the important producers in a picturization of her diary. It would of necessity have to show her in a somewhat sympathetic light and I am afraid it will be a few years before anyone in this country will have forgotten what has happened over there.' See Deutsche Kinemathek Berlin, Luis Trenker Archiv, 4.3-I98814-6: TRENKER, LUIS [VII], 3: Kohner to Trenker, 20 July 1946.
10. Riefenstahl, *Memoiren*, p. 448. Trenker began in 1946 to gather information on Eva Braun. See SAF, D180/2 Nr. 228165/1/028.
11. See Paul Tabori, ed., *The Private Life of Adolf Hitler: The Intimate Notes and Diary of Eva Braun* (New York and Tokyo, 2014), p. 71.
12. Munich's Regional Court forbade *Wochenend* from publishing details from the supposed diary. See SAF, D180/2 Nr. 228165/1/101: 'Einstweilige Verfügung des Landgerichts München I', 10 September 1948.

13. SAF, D180/2 Nr. 228165/085: Fritz Wiedemann, 'Eidesstattliche Aussage', 9 September 1948. Much material on Riefenstahl's denazification can also be found in LAB, B Rep. 031-02-01, Nr. 2654.
14. SAF, D180/2 Nr. 228165/040: Erich Kempka, 'Eidesstattliche Erklärung', 3 September 1948.
15. Ibid., Nr. 228165/038: Margarete Mittelstrasse, 'Eidesstattliche Erklärung', 3 September 1948.
16. *GTB*, 22 November 1932.
17. Although Goebbels (*GTB*, 13 January 1927) claims that Riefenstahl danced 'in natura' before a showing of *The Holy Mountain* (1927) which he attended.
18. Riefenstahl, *Memoiren*, p. 160.
19. See Despina Stratigakos, *Hitler at Home* (New Haven and London, 2015).
20. Julius Schaub, *In Hitlers Schatten* (Stegen am Ammersee, 2010), p. 140.
21. Stratigakos, *Hitler at Home*, p. 114.
22. See Brigitte Hamann, *Winifred Wagner oder Hitlers Bayreuth* (Munich and Zurich, 2002).
23. Riefenstahl, *Memoiren*, p. 158.
24. BAB, R43 II/390: 'Aufstellung über Filme, die am Heldengedenktag zugelassen werden', 22 February 1934.
25. The film scholar Siegfried Kracauer perceived in the 1920s mountain films a pre-echo of the fascist aesthetic, yet he was very positive in his assessment of *The Blue Light*, whose complexity he acknowledges. See Siegfried Kracauer, *Von Caligari zu Hitler: Eine psychologische Geschichte des deutschen Films* (Frankfurt am Main, 1979), pp. 272–3.
26. Hans Traub, *Der Film als politisches Machtmittel* (Munich, 1933), p. 27.
27. David Welch, *Propaganda and the German Cinema 1933–1945* (London and New York, 2001), pp. 37–8.
28. *GTB*, 22 October 1936.
29. 'Der Weg zum neuen deutschen Film liegt frei: Reichsminister Dr. Goebbels vor den Filmschaffenden', *Film-Kurier*, 19 May 1933.
30. Fritz Hippler, *Die Verstrickung* (Düsseldorf, 1982), p. 196.
31. According to Goebbels (*GTB*, 15 March 1937), Hitler was 'deeply moved' by *The Ruler*.
32. See Susan Tegel, *Nazis and the Cinema* (London, 2008), p. 4.
33. See Walther Schmitt, ed., 'Adolf Hitlers Rede auf der Kulturtagung der NSDAP', in *Die Reden Hitlers am Reichsparteitag 1933* (Munich, 1934), pp. 22–31.
34. David Welch argues that Hitler 'steadfastly maintained the irreconcilability of art and propaganda'. See Welch, *Propaganda and the German Cinema*, p. 35.
35. See, for instance, the protocol of an August 1949 interrogation of Riefenstahl conducted during denazification proceedings: LAB, B Rep 031-02-01 Nr. 2654/Band 8: Interrogation of Leni Riefenstahl, 8 August 1949.
36. Leni Riefenstahl, *Hinter den Kulissen des Reichsparteitages* (Munich, 1935), p. 11.
37. Thus, in August 1933, the Reich Propaganda Leadership announced that Riefenstahl was assuming the 'artistic leadership' of the Party rally film. See 'Leni Riefenstahl übernimmt künstl. Leitung des Reichsparteitag-Films', *Licht Bild Bühne*, 25 August 1933.
38. *GTB*, 3 November 1932.
39. Ibid., 12 June 1933.
40. Riefenstahl, *Memoiren*, p. 180.
41. Ibid., p. 158.
42. Jürgen Trimborn, *Leni Riefenstahl: A Life* (New York, 2008), p. 56. Trimborn cites a 1976 interview with Harry Sokal in the German weekly *Der Spiegel*. Sokal produced Riefenstahl's *The Blue Light*, but, being of Jewish background, emigrated to Britain in 1933. His relationship with Riefenstahl soured, and they fell out over the question of profits from *The Blue Light*. Given the tensions between them, his condemnation of her as anti-Semitic must be treated with caution.

43. Quoted in Steven Bach, *Leni: The Life and Work of Leni Riefenstahl* (London, 2007), p. 93.
44. See SAF, D 180/2 Nr. 228165/1/041: Frau Dr. Reuber to Leni Riefenstahl, 15 June 1949.
45. See the testimony of Walter Traut, who had worked with Riefenstahl as production leader: SAF, D 180/2 Nr. 228165/1/147. Ernst Jaeger overcame his critical attitude to Riefenstahl after the war, and also testified to the help she gave his wife, see SAF, D 180/2 Nr. 228165/1/138: Ernst Jaeger, 'Eidestattliche Versicherung', 31 July 1948. See also the Ernst Jaeger papers at the University of Southern California, which contain Jaeger's amicable post-war correspondence with Riefenstahl.
46. See the testimony of Walter Siebert, LAB, B Rep 031-02-01 Nr. 2654/Bd. 9: 'Zeuge Walter Siebert', 22 April 1952.
47. Rudolf Fichtner, a communist sympathizer whose wife was of Jewish background, was protected by Riefenstahl; see SAF, D180/2 Nr. 228165/1/150: Rudolf Fichtner, 'Eidesstattliche Erklärung', 20 April 1948.
48. Riefenstahl accused the cameraman Emil Schünemann of 'boycotting the Führer' because he refused to film under her. See Bach, *Leni*, p. 156. Original sources at BAB, R9361V/114157, provided in English in Glenn B. Infield, *Leni Riefenstahl: The Fallen Film Goddess* (New York, 1976), pp. 76–9.
49. She was denounced by a district branch of the German Labour Front (Trade Department) for shopping in a Jewish fashion store (Götz) in Berlin in March 1937. See SAF, D 180/2 Nr. 228165/1/056: Pfennig to Riefenstahl, 10 March 1937.
50. Riefenstahl, *Memoiren*, p. 204.
51. *GTB*, 17 May 1933.
52. Ibid., 12 June 1933.
53. Ibid., 14 June 1936. Goebbels also mentions discussing a film with Riefenstahl a week later (see Ibid., 20 June 1933).
54. See, for instance, Trimborn, *Leni Riefenstahl*, pp. 90ff. Audrey Salkeld, by contrast, more or less follows Riefenstahl's account; see Audrey Salkeld, *Portrait of Leni Riefenstahl* (London, 1997), Kindle Edition, Location 2286–7. For other accounts, see Bach, *Leni*, pp. 130–37; Lutz Kinkel, *Die Scheinwerferin: Leni Riefenstahl und das 'Dritte Reich'* (Hamburg and Vienna, 2002), pp. 45–51; and Rainer Rother, *Leni Riefenstahl: Die Verführung des Talents* (Berlin, 2000), pp. 52–60.
55. Riefenstahl, *Memoiren*, pp. 202–3, pp. 197–8.
56. See, for instance, *GTB*, 26 May 1933, which mentions a picnic with Hitler, Riefenstahl and others.
57. The plan to hold a rally in 1933, and to hold it in Nuremberg, did not emerge with clarity until June or July 1933; up to this point, the Nazis had been too busy with the mechanics of taking over power to give it much thought. See Siegfried Zelnhefer, *Die Reichsparteitage der NSDAP in Nürnberg* (Nuremberg, 2002), p. 64.
58. *GTB*, 27 August 1933.
59. In fact, the German artist Erwin von Osen had already written to Hitler on 30 January 1933 asking to be allowed to make a film about him; permission was refused. See BAB, R43 II/390: Erwin von Osen to Hitler, 30 January 1933.
60. Trimborn, *Leni Riefenstahl*, p. 92.
61. Ernst Jaeger claimed in his (admittedly not very reliable) series of articles for the *Hollywood Tribune* in 1939 that Riefenstahl herself suggested to Hitler she make a film about him, but he turned the idea down, before deciding later she should make the party rally film. See Ernst Jaeger, 'How Leni Riefenstahl became Hitler's Girlfriend: Part III', *Hollywood Tribune*, 12 May 1939.
62. Riefenstahl, *Memoiren*, p. 204.
63. See, for instance, 'Leni Riefenstahl übernimmt künstl. Leitung des Reichsparteitag-Filmes', *Licht Bild Bühne*, 25 August 1933.

64. See Karin Wieland, *Dietrich und Riefenstahl: Der Traum von der neuen Frau* (Munich, 2011), p. 300. Raether was responsible, for instance, for the 1933 Nazi film *Germany Awakens!*, a dull overview of the events leading to the Nazi success, notable for the awkward, stiffly delivered statements to camera given by Goebbels and Göring.

65. Picking up on a potentially damaging rumour he had heard about Riefenstahl having a Jewish mother, Raether triggered an investigation into her racial credentials, but it only confirmed her 'Aryan' background. The rumour would seem to have been started by the scriptwriter Rudolf Katscher, who passed it on to Ufa's chief dramaturgist Fritz Podehl. See BAB, R9361 V/24931/1: Lange to Allwörden, 28 August 1933. See also SAF, D180/2 Nr. 228165. More details of the dispute over Riefenstahl's ancestry can be found both in BAB, R9361 V/124931 and R9361 V/114157.

66. See, for instance, 'Der Reichsparteitag 1933 der NSDAP im Film', *Licht Bild Bühne*, 30 August 1933, which omits all reference to Riefenstahl, as does 'Filmaufnahmen vom Parteitag', *Film-Kurier*, 31 August 1933. But she is mentioned in 'Die Filmarbeit in Nürnberg beginnt', *Film-Kurier*, 1 September 1933.

67. Quoted in Jürgen Trimborn, 'Ein Meister der subjektiven Kamera: Karriere im Windschatten Leni Riefenstahls', in Hans Georg Hiller von Gaertringen, ed., *Das Auge des Dritten Reiches: Walter Frentz – Hitlers Kameramann und Fotograf* (Augsburg, 2009), pp. 69–81, here p. 71.

68. Riefenstahl, *Memoiren*, p. 207.

69. Ibid., p. 208.

70. Ibid., p. 209.

71. Raether, as it happened, had been arrested on the charge of spying, only to be released on the day Riefenstahl voiced her complaint.

72. *GTB*, 21 September 1933.

73. Ibid., 23 September 1933.

74. Ibid., 16 October 1933. The impression given by Goebbels' diaries is that relations between him and Riefenstahl were good in October, see e.g. Ibid., 9 October 1933.

75. Riefenstahl, *Memoiren*, p. 210.

76. SAF, D180/2 Nr. 228165: Rudolf Diels, 'Erklärung betr. Frau Leni Riefenstahl', 29 June 1949.

77. See Rother, *Leni Riefenstahl*, pp. 62–3.

78. Riefenstahl, *Memoiren*, p. 212.

79. See 'Imposante Wochenschauberichte', *Licht Bild Bühne*, 6 September 1933.

80. See Bach, *Leni*, p. 144; and Kinkel, *Die Scheinwerferin*, pp. 56–7.

81. *GTB*, 29 November 1933.

82. Ibid., 2 December 1933.

83. Quoted in Kinkel, *Die Scheinwerferin*, p. 60.

84. 'Sieg des Glaubens, der Reichsparteitagfilm 1933', *Licht Bild Bühne*, 7 November 1933.

85. 'Imposante Wochenschauberichte.'

86. Although it seems likely one or two of the speakers – notably Hess – had to be rerecorded in a studio because of the poor quality of the original recordings. See Peter Reichelt, 'Der Sieg des Glaubens 1933: Der Nachdreh oder: Wie wichtige Reden des Reichsparteitages 1933 in Nürnberg durch die Regisseurin Riefenstahl in einem Berliner Filmstudio für das Kino neu inszeniert wurden', in Ina Brockmann and Peter Reichelt, eds, *Leni Riefenstahl* (Mannheim, 2012), pp. 56–64.

87. For the rally speeches, see Julius Streicher, ed., *Reichstagung in Nürnberg 1933* (Berlin, 1934).

4 Celebrating Hitler

1. Leni Riefenstahl, *Memoiren* (Cologne, 2000), p. 208.

2. LAB, B Rep 031-02-01 Nr. 2654/Bd. 8: Interrogation of Leni Riefenstahl by the US Department of Justice, Overseas Branch, 8 August 1949.

3. According to a Ufa board meeting, this letter was issued on 19 April 1934. See Jürgen Trimborn, *Leni Riefenstahl: A Life* (New York, 2008), p. 110.
4. Riefenstahl, *Memoiren*, p. 217.
5. Ibid., p. 222.
6. LAB, B Rep 031-02-01 Nr. 2654/Bd. 8: Interrogation of Leni Riefenstahl by the US Department of Justice, Overseas Branch, 8 August 1949.
7. Riefenstahl, *Memoiren*, p. 217.
8. 'Reichsparteitag-Film im Ufaverleih', *Licht Bild Bühne*, 31 August 1934.
9. Trimborn, *Leni Riefenstahl*, p. 109.
10. According to the minutes of a Ufa board meeting, see BAB, 109 I/1029b. Quoted in Trimborn, *Leni Riefenstahl*, p. 110.
11. BAB, R2/20619: 'Vermerk: Fräulein Riefenstahl erschien am 26.11.1935 in Begleitung ihres Steuerberaters', 6 December 1935. The sum mentioned here, however, is 200,000 Reichsmarks.
12. LAB, B Rep 031-02-01 Nr. 2654/Bd. 8: Interrogation of Leni Riefenstahl by the US Department of Justice, Overseas Branch, 8 August 1949.
13. Ibid.: Additional Interrogation of Leni Riefenstahl, 10 August 1949.
14. Ibid.: Interrogation of Hans Saupert, 23 August 1949.
15. Ibid.: Interrogation of Hans Saupert, 24 August 1949.
16. Ibid.: Interrogation of Albert Miller, 6 October 1949.
17. Ibid.: Interrogation of Alfred Leitgen, 12 October 1949.
18. Ibid.: Interrogation of Hugo Fischer, 18 October 1949.
19. BAB, R2/20619: 'Referat III/8: Vermerk', 10 October 1935.
20. See, for instance, 'Kamera-Stab für Nürnberg gerüstet', *Film-Kurier*, 29 August 1934. Even after the rally was over and Riefenstahl began putting her film together, some newspapers reported that it was Ruttmann who was the overall director of the project (e.g. ' "Triumph des Willens" im Neubabelsberger Atelier', *Licht Bild Bühne*, 2 October 1934).
21. Although there is some evidence it continued to be viewed at 'special events'. See 'Was der Reichsparteitagfilm zeigen soll', *Licht Bild Bühne*, 24 August 1934.
22. 'Aufruf der Kulturschaffenden', *Völkischer Beobachter*, 18 August 1934.
23. Leni Riefenstahl, *Hinter den Kulissen des Reichsparteitag-Films* (Munich, 1935), p. 3.
24. Steven Bach, *Leni: The Life and Work of Leni Riefenstahl* (London, 2007), p. 157.
25. 'Leni Riefenstahl in der Lessing-Hochschule: Was der Reichsparteitagfilm kostet', *Licht Bild Bühne*, 4 April 1935.
26. Riefenstahl, *Memoiren*, p. 224.
27. LAB, B Rep 031-02-01 Nr. 2654/Bd. 8: Interrogation of Alfred Leitgen, 12 October 1949.
28. *GTB*, 26 August 1934.
29. Ibid., 17 October 1934.
30. Ibid., 22 November 1934.
31. See Siegfried Zelnhefer, *Die Reichsparteitage der NSDAP in Nürnberg* (Nuremberg, 2002), p. 226.
32. According, at least, to one contemporary newspaper report; see 'Was der Reichsparteitagfilm zeigen soll', *Licht Bild Bühne*, 24 August 1934.
33. 'Großfilm vom Reichsparteitag 1934', *Licht Bild Bühne*, 22 August 1934.
34. 'Des Führers Interesse am "Triumph des Willens" ', *Film-Kurier*, 27 September 1934.
35. 'Der Führer bei den Schneide-Arbeiten Leni Riefenstahls für "Triumph des Willens" ', *Film-Kurier*, 7 December 1934.
36. See 'Leni Riefenstahl berichtet: Triumph des Willens', *Licht Bild Bühne*, 26 March 1935.
37. 'Des Führers Interesse am "Triumph des Willens" '.

38. Jaeger claimed he wrote the book because Riefenstahl rescued him from incarceration in a concentration camp. See Heinrich Lewinski, 'Eine biographische Skizze', in Rolf Aurich and Wolfgang Jacobsen (eds), *Ernst Jäger. Filmkritiker* (Berlin, 2006), pp. 10–75, p. 41.

39. 'Ein Vorwort des Führers – zum Buch über das Entstehen des Reichsparteitagfilms', *Film-Kurier*, 18 March 1935.

40. Riefenstahl, *Hinter den Kulissen*, p. 3.

41. 'Leni Riefenstahl in der Lessing-Hochschule', *Licht Bild Bühne*, 4 April 1935.

42. 'Triumph über die Herzen – "Triumph des Willens"', *Film-Kurier*, 29 March 1935.

43. See 'Vorbereitungen zum Parteitag-Film', *Licht Bild Bühne*, 31 August 1934.

44. See LAB, B Rep 031-02-01 Nr. 2654/Bd. 9: Letter from Riefenstahl's lawyer to the Appeals Commission, 15 February 1950.

45. 'Triumph über die Herzen – "Triumph des Willens"'.

46. Cited in Karin Wieland, *Dietrich and Riefenstahl: Der Traum von der neuen Frau* (Munich, 2011), p. 324.

47. Within two weeks of the film opening in Berlin, it was being screened in over sixty German cities. See 'Rekorderfolg des Reichsparteitagfilms', *Licht Bild Bühne*, 11 April 1935.

48. *GTB*, 26 March 1935.

49. Cited in 'Triumph des Willens erhält Staatspreis', *Licht Bild Bühne*, 2 May 1935.

50. 'Die Uraufführung des Parteitagfilms "Triumph des Willens": Der Standardfilm der nationalsozialistischen Bewegung', *Völkischer Beobachter*, 30 March 1935.

51. See particularly 'Triumph über die Herzen – "Triumph des Willens"'.

52. Riefenstahl, *Memoiren*, pp. 227–29.

53. Quoted in *Filmkritik* Nr. 188 (August 1972). See Manfred Hobsch, *Film im 'Dritten Reich', Band 2* (Berlin, 2010), p. 572.

54. See David Culbert and Martin Loiperdinger, 'Leni Riefenstahl's "Tag der Freiheit": The 1935 Nazi Party Rally Film', *Historical Journal of Film, Radio and Television* 12:1 (1992), pp. 3–40.

55. Riefenstahl, *Memoiren*, pp. 245–6.

56. Kinkel, Lutz, *Die Scheinwerferin: Leni Riefenstahl und das 'Dritte Reich'* (Hamburg and Vienna, 2002), p. 93.

57. Riefenstahl, *Memoiren*, p. 246.

58. BAB, R109 I/1031a: 'Niederschrift Nr. 1126 über die Vorstandssitzung vom 29. November 1935'.

59. Culbert and Loiperdinger, 'Leni Riefenstahl's "Tag der Freiheit"', pp. 12–13.

60. SAF, D 180/2 Nr. 228165/1/022: 'Protokoll der Sitzung vom 6. Juli 1949. Zur Person: Leni Riefenstahl, Filmschauspielerin'.

61. Riefenstahl, *Memoiren*, pp. 236–7. She also claims in her memoirs (p. 251) that Hitler did not know she was to make a film of the Olympics until she told him on 24 December 1935.

62. *GTB*, 17 August 1935 and 5 October 1935.

63. See David Clay Large, *Nazi Games: The Olympics of 1936* (New York and London, 2007), especially pp. 69–109.

64. Ian Buruma, *Theater of Cruelty: Art, Film, and the Shadows of War* (New York, 2014).

65. Riefenstahl, *Memoiren*, pp. 239–40.

66. BAB, R2/4788: 'Vermerk zur gestrigen Vorlage betr. Großfilmaufnahme der Sommerolympiade', October 1935.

67. Ibid.: 'Betrifft Olympiade-Film', October 1935.

68. 'Anforderung neuer Mittel für Werbung zur Olympiade 1936', 15 October 1935. Cited in Erwin Leiser, *'Deutschland erwache!' Propaganda im Film des Dritten Reichs* (Hamburg, 1968), pp. 126–8.

69. See *GTB*, 7 November 1935, also 13 October 1935.

70. Letter from Karl Ott (Finance Department of the Propaganda Ministry) to the Berlin-Charlottenburg Court, quoted in Hans Barkhausen, 'Footnote to the History of Riefenstahl's "Olympia" ', *Film Quarterly* 28:1 (autumn 1974), pp. 8–12, here p. 10.
71. BAB, R109 I/5007: Tobis to Olympia-Film GmbH, 19 May 1936.
72. BAB, R55/503: 'Bericht über die in der Zeit vom 3. bis zum 8. Oktober 1936 stattgefundenen Kassen- und Rechnungsprüfung bei der Olympia-Film GmbH', 16 October 1936.
73. BAB, R55/503: Ott to Hanke, 19 October 1936.
74. Ibid.: 'Vorgeladen erscheint Herr Bühnenmeister Wilhelm Lipke', 12 November 1936.
75. Ibid.: Präsident der Reichsfilmkammer to RMVP (Reichsministerium für Volksaufklärung und Propaganda), 8 March 1937.
76. Ibid.: Präsident der Reichsfilmkammer to RMVP, 18 May 1937.
77. See BAB, R55/1327: 'Die Olympia-Filme sind finanziert worden', 23 November 1938.
78. See Ibid.: Pfennig to Olympia-Film (complaining about the fact that no permission had been sought for making the short film *Wild Waters*), 20 December 1938.
79. Ibid.: Pfennig to Olympia-Film, 20 December 1938.
80. Ibid.: 'R.M.f.V.u.P, Vermerk', 14 January 1943. The exact sum was 114,066.45 Reichsmarks. Also cited in Leiser, '*Deutschland erwache!*', p. 129.
81. Ibid.: 'Die Olympia-Filme sind finanziert worden', Berlin, 23 November 1938.
82. Trimborn, *Leni Riefenstahl*, p. 134. Goebbels, following the success of the film, transferred 'another 100,000' to Riefenstahl, which made her 'very happy' (*GTB*, 22 April 1938).
83. *GTB*, 6 August 1936.
84. Riefenstahl, *Memoiren*, p. 270.
85. SAF, D180/2 Nr. 228165/1/148: Friedrich A. Mainz, 'Eidesstattliche Erklärung', 15 April 1948.
86. Ibid. Nr. 228165/1/144: Hans Ertl, 'Eidesstattliche Erklärung', 29 August 1948.
87. *GTB*, 18 September 1936.
88. SAF, D180/2 Nr. 228165/2/064: 'Abschrift: Aktenzeichen: 7 Bs 6920693: Urteil', 30 November 1949.
89. Ibid. Nr. 228165/2/110: 'Anlage: Tatbestand und Entscheidungsgründe', no date (probably 1949).
90. See the material in BAB, R55/1327.
91. SAF, D180/2 Nr. 228165/1/032: Julius Schaub, 'Eidesstattliche Erklärung', 28 June 1949.
92. Ibid. Nr. 228165/1/037: Julius Schaub, 'Eidesstattliche Aussage', 9 September 1948.
93. *GTB*, 17 June 1937.
94. Trimborn, *Leni Riefenstahl*, p. 143.
95. *GTB*, 24 November 1937.
96. Ibid., 26 November 1937.
97. Ibid., 22 December 1937.
98. Cooper C. Graham, *Leni Riefenstahl and Olympia* (London, 1986), pp. 179–80.
99. Hitler was in Innsbruck on 5 and 6 April, see Harald Sandner, *Hitler: Das Itinerar. Aufenthaltsorte und Reisen von 1889 bis 1945, Band 3* (Berlin, 2016), pp. 1521–2.
100. Riefenstahl, *Memoiren*, p. 305.
101. See, for instance, 'Uraufführung des Olympiafilms', *Film-Kurier*, 31 March 1938.
102. See 'Leni Riefenstahl zum 10. April', *Film-Kurier (Beiblatt)*, 9 April 1938.
103. *Triumph of the Will* had also been shown in Garmisch-Partenkirchen during the Winter Olympics. See BAB R56 VI/9: Gauleitung München-Oberbayern to Hans Weidemann, 18 January 1936.

104. 'Nationalsozialistische Filme begeistern in Oesterreich', *Film-Kurier*, 29 March 1938.
105. 'Begeisterte Aufnahme des Olympia-Films', *Film-Kurier*, 21 April 1938.
106. See 'Festliche Uraufführung des Olympiafilms', *Völkischer Beobachter*, 22 April 1938.
107. Bach, *Leni*, pp. 178–81.
108. For these reports, see BAB, NS10/51.
109. 'The Jews in Austria', *Guardian*, 13 April 1938.
110. 'The Fate of the Jews in Austria', *Guardian*, 20 April 1938.
111. For the original version of the film, see BA FA, K 139295-3: *Olympia*.
112. 'Olympia-Film für den Duce', *Licht Bild Bühne*, 6 May 1938.
113. *GTB*, 8 July 1938.
114. Ibid., 21 October 1938.
115. 'Triumph des Willens vor der Kölner Jugend', *Film-Kurier*, 13 May 1935.

5 The Führer at the Movies

1. Quoted in Manfred Hobsch, *Film im 'Dritten Reich'. Alle deutschen Spielfilme von 1933 bis 1945, Band 4* (Berlin, 2010), p. 219.
2. See '"*Morgenrot*" im Unterhaus', *Film-Kurier*, 14 February 1933.
3. See, for instance, 'Germany and Arms', *The Times*, 22 February 1934, which makes clear that German and British official statements on the progress of the talks were vague, if generally positive.
4. See Earl of Avon, *The Eden Memoirs: Facing the Dictators* (London, 1962), p. 64.
5. See the quotation from the *Völkischer Beobachter* in Hobsch, *Film im 'Dritten Reich', Band 4* (pp. 266–7).
6. *GTB*, 15 June 1933.
7. Ibid., 7 October 1933.
8. Recreating the street conflicts of the Weimar Republic period between Nazis and communists had, in the case of *Horst Wessel* at least, almost risked triggering these off again. The script for *Horst Wessel* asked for local residents to heckle the SA groups participating in the film, so that a sense of the conflict between communists and Nazis could be recreated. The heckling turned into violence, and one young Nazi suffered from a broken skull. See '"Horst Wessel" bekommt ein neues Gesicht', *Film-Kurier*, 27 July 1933.
9. This description of the premiere is provided by the German film producer Oskar Kalbus, quoted in Rolf Giesen and Manfred Hobsch, eds, *Hitlerjunge Quex, Jud Süss und Kolberg: Die Propagandafilme des Dritten Reichs* (Berlin, 2005), pp. 32–3.
10. See 'Adolf Hitler bei der Uraufführung "SA-Mann Brand"', *Film-Kurier*, 15 June 1933.
11. *Reichsfilmblatt*, 1933, quoted in Giesen and Hobsch, *Hitlerjunge Quex*, pp. 33–4.
12. Peter Longerich, *Hitler: Biographie* (Munich, 2015), Kindle Edition, Location 13824.
13. BAB, NS10/49: Bahls to Fink, 24 April 1939.
14. BAB, NS10/48: Programme for Hitler's cinema visit.
15. See 'Festaufführung im Ufa-Palast', *Film-Kurier*, 20 April 1937.
16. *GTB*, 20 April 1937.
17. 'Deutsch-italienisches Filmabkommen', *Film-Kurier*, 12 April 1937.
18. Hitler's attendance of individual film premieres also had the effect of advertising these films. In 1934, the Nazi *Film-Kurier* warned against interpreting Hitler's presence at the premiere of a film or new theatre production as an endorsement (see 'Zu den Besuchen des Führers in Theatern und Film-Theatern', *Film-Kurier*, 15 January 1934). Yet it was inevitable that the public would interpret such visits as conferring a seal of approval upon the productions concerned.
19. 'Die Lichtspielhäuser am 1. Mai', *Film-Kurier*, 19 April 1933.
20. 'Die Führer-Rede in den Filmtheatern', *Film-Kurier*, 18 May 1935. See also 'Gemeinschaftsempfang der Führerrede', *Film-Kurier*, 21 May 1935.
21. 'Der Führer hat gesprochen', *Film-Kurier*, 22 May 1935.

22. 'Mit dem Tonfilmwagen auf Wahlpropaganda', *Film-Kurier*, 13 November 1933.
23. 'Hindenburg-Gedenk-Film der Ufa', *Film-Kurier*, 3 August 1934.
24. 'Ein Film vom Führer', *Film-Kurier*, 13 August 1934.
25. 'Gaufilmstelle Pommern eröffnert den Wahlkampf', *Film-Kurier*, 16 August 1934.
26. 'Filmtheater im Dienst der Wahl', *Film-Kurier*, 28 March 1938.
27. 'Generalappell des deutschen Volkes', *Film-Kurier*, 5 April 1938.
28. Curt Belling, 'Der Dank des deutschen Films an den Führer', *Licht Bild Bühne*, 7 May 1938.
29. The German words 'Wiedererhebung', which I have rendered as 'rebirth', and 'Wiederaufrichtung', which I have translated as 're-emergence', are difficult to capture precisely in English, but certainly carry messianic associations.
30. See Jean-Pierre Hombach, *Serdar Somuncu: 'Der neue Deutsche Kafka?'* (Hombach, 2010), p. 206.
31. See Richard Taylor, *Film Propaganda: Soviet Russia and Nazi Germany* (London and New York, 2006), p. 147.
32. For a succinct overview of the history of the Nazi newsreels, see David Welch, *Propaganda and the German Cinema, 1933–1945* (London, 2001), p. 163.
33. Fox Tönende Wochenschau, 22 (October 1936).
34. Ibid., 18 (May 1939).
35. One of the longer excerpts from a Hitler speech is provided in ibid., 40, September 1937. The newsreel reports on Mussolini's visit to Berlin.
36. Deulig Tonwoche, 83 (August 1933). For more details of the speech, see Max Domarus, *Hitler: Reden 1932 bis 1945, Band 1* (Wiesbaden, 1973), p. 291.
37. Deulig Tonwoche, 98 (November 1933).
38. Ufa-Tonwoche, 237 (March 1935).
39. *GTB*, 24 April 1937.
40. Ibid., 7 August 1937.
41. See BAB, NS10/44: Draft letter from the Adjutantur des Führers to RMVP (Reichsministerium für Volksaufklärung und Propaganda), 1 June 1938. See also Felix Moeller, *Der Filmminister: Goebbels und der Film im Dritten Reich* (Berlin, 1998), p. 368.
42. Ufa-Tonwoche, 420 (21 September 1938). I am grateful to Michael Schwartz of the Institute for Contemporary History, Munich, for providing information on the situation in the Sudetenland in September 1938.
43. Ufa-Tonwoche, 422 (5 October 1938).
44. Fox Tönende Wochenschau, 42 (October 1938).
45. Ibid., 28 (August 1934).
46. For a detailed discussion of the film, see Welch, *Propaganda and the German Cinema 1933–1945*, pp. 134–8.
47. See Veit Harlan, *Im Schatten meiner Filme* (Gütersloh, 1966), p. 38.
48. 'Der Herrscher: Ufa-Palast am Zoo', *Film-Kurier*, 18 March 1937.
49. 'Diskussion um den "Herrscher"', *Film-Kurier*, 22 April 1937.
50. *GTB*, 10 April 1937.
51. See BAB, NS18/905: 'Filme, die im Winterhalbjahr 1938/39 (Oktober bis Mai) in den Jugendfilmstunden eingesetzt wurden'. Topping the list of films shown is Karl Ritter's *Pour le Mérite*, with *The Ruler* in 13th place.
52. See Axel Marquardt and Heinz Rathsack, eds, *Preußen im Film: Eine Retrospektive der Stiftung Deutsche Kinemathek* (Hamburg, 1981).
53. Carl Schmitt, 'Der Führer schützt das Recht', *Deutsche Juristen-Zeitung* 15 (1 August 1934), pp. 945–50, here pp. 946–7.
54. 'Der alte und der junge König', *Licht Bild Bühne*, 6 February 1935.
55. *GTB*, 23 January 1937.
56. Heinz Boberach, ed., *Meldungen aus dem Reich: Die geheimen Lageberichte des Sicherheitsdienstes der SS 1938–1945, Band 3* (Herrsching, 1984), p. 527 (4 December 1939).
57. BAB, R9361 V/113118: Steinhoff to Hitler, undated.

58. BAB, NS10/45: Leichtenstern to Wiedemann, 6 December 1938.

59. See the list and table of contents in BAB, NS10/45.

60. After the war was over, Herbert St Goar of the 196th Field Artillery's Intelligence Branch acquired Baur's Hitler films (Baur had filmed Hitler from 1935 to 1940). It seems Baur had buried them in a flower-bed, where Goar found them. He kept them at his home in Chattanooga, perhaps even forgot all about them – until he decided to release them into the public realm in 1998. See Sebastian Knauer and Michael Kloft, 'Hitler in Agfacolor', *Der Spiegel* 44 (1998), pp. 84–90.

61. See, for instance, the Deulig Tonwoche, 370, 7 February 1939. Certainly, Goebbels could be seen in the newsreels railing against Jews; see for instance the excerpt from a 1935 Ufa-Tonwoche at https://www.ushmm.org/online/film/display/detail.php?file_num=4973 (accessed 6 May 2017).

6 Holding Court

1. BAB, NS10/43: 'Gästeliste für die Abendeinladung am 29. Oktober 1937'.

2. Julius Schaub, *In Hitlers Schatten* (Stegen-Ammersee, 2010), p. 110.

3. IfZ, ZS-0287: 'Niederschrift der Unterredung mit Fräulein Antonie Reichert', 9 September 1952.

4. Anna Plaim and Kurt Kuch, *Bei Hitler: Zimmermädchen Annas Erinnerungen* (Munich, 2005), p. 79.

5. BAB, NS10/43: Letter to Adjutantur des Führers, 28 May 1937.

6. BAB, NS10/591: 'Terminkalender und Telefonbuch Hitlers. – geführt von Max Wünsche, 1939. Ordonnanzoffizier und Adjutant Hitlers 07. Okt. 1939–09. Jan 1940'.

7. BAB, R9361 V/113401: 'Rücksprache mit Frau Olga Tschechowa, 15 March 1946; Vernehmung von Frau Tschechowa', 6 June 1946. Chekhova made no mention of her possible involvement in a Soviet espionage attempt to assassinate Hitler, which might have shed a different light on her attendance at such occasions. See Anthony Beevor, *The Mystery of Olga Chekhova* (London, 2005).

8. Camilla Horn, *Verliebt in die Liebe* (Frankfurt and Berlin, 1990), p. 178.

9. Max Schmeling, *Erinnerungen* (Frankfurt and Berlin, 1977), p. 263.

10. Veit Harlan, *Im Schatten meiner Filme* (Gütersloh, 1966), pp. 40–51.

11. Johannes Heesters, *Ich bin gottseidank nicht mehr jung* (Munich, 1993), p. 117.

12. Marika Rökk, *Herz mit Paprika* (Munich, 1976), pp. 100–101.

13. Paul Hörbiger, *Ich hab für Euch gespielt* (Frankfurt and Berlin, 1989), p. 230.

14. Zarah Leander, *Es war so wunderbar! Mein Leben* (Hamburg, 1973), p. 179.

15. Olga Tschechowa, *Meine Uhren gehen anders* (Munich and Berlin, 1973), p. 164.

16. Ibid., pp. 145–6.

17. The Reich Film Chamber and Propaganda Ministry kept lists of Jewish and 'half-Jewish' actors. See BAB, R55/21306: 'Liste der Filmschaffenden, die nicht arisch sind bzw. mit einem Nichtarier verheiratet sind'.

18. These included Gustaf Gründgens, Oskar Sima, Viktor de Kowa, Veit Harlan and Willi Forst. See 'Die deutsche Kunst dankt dem Führer', *Licht Bild Bühne*, 8 April 1938.

19. 'Wiener Künstler zum 10. April', *Neues Wiener Journal*, 7 April 1938.

20. *GTB*, 2 April 1933.

21. See, for instance, Hitler's 'list of presents' for 1935 and 1936, in Anton Joachimsthaler, *Hitlers Liste: Ein Dokument persönlicher Beziehungen* (Munich, 2003), pp. 12–15. The list refers to a present of perfume for the actress Marianne Hoppe, and a porcelain bonbon-nière for Jenny Jugo.

22. See Chapter 5.

23. BAB, R9361 V/110430: Telegram from Jannings to Hitler, 18 August 1938.

24. BAB, NS10/111: Marika Rökk, letter to 'Mein Führer', 22 March 1937.

25. Luise Ullrich, *Komm auf die Schaukel, Luise: Balance eines Lebens* (Munich, 1990), p. 123.
26. See BAB, R9361 V/119997: Letter from Ullrich to Hitler, 20 January 1938.
27. BAB, NS10/111: Letter from Erika von Thellmann to Hitler, 18 April 1937.
28. Axel von Ambesser, *Nimm einen Namen mit A.* (Frankfurt and Berlin, 1985), pp. 151–3.
29. Luis Trenker, *Alles gut gegangen: Geschichten aus meinem Leben* (Munich, 1974), p. 303.
30. Berta Drews, *Wohin des Wegs* (Munich and Vienna, 1986), p. 169.
31. Hörbiger, *Ich habe für Euch gespielt*, p. 232.
32. Ibid., p. 232.
33. Ibid., p. 231.
34. See Henrik Eberle and Matthias Uhl, eds, *Das Buch Hitler: Geheimdossier des NKWD für Josef W. Stalin* (Cologne, 2005), p. 36
35. Schmeling, *Erinnerungen*, p. 263.
36. See, for instance, 'Große Summen – Große Pläne – aber auch ein großer Geist?', *Der Film*, 19 May 1935, and 'Ruhm in Zahlen', *Der Film*, 19 October 1935.
37. Eventually, under the financial pressures of war, Hitler did ask Bormann to instruct Goebbels to prevent further increases in fees in the worlds of opera and theatre. See BAB, NS18/748: Bormann to Goebbels, 14 April 1942.
38. *GTB*, 15 December 1937. See also *GTB*, 20 February 1938.
39. Lists are provided in BAB, R55/123.
40. Ibid.: Reichsminister der Finanzen to the Reichsminister und Chef der Reichskanzlei, 18 June 1938. See also the material in BAB, R2/56522.
41. BAB, R55/123: 'Der Reichsminister der Finanzen. Betrifft: Besteuerung prominenter Künstler', 28 November 1938.
42. Ibid.: Reichsminister der Finanzen to the Reichsminister und Chef der Reichskanzlei, 18 June 1938.
43. BAB, R2/56522: Reichsminister der Finanzen to the Reichsminister und Chef der Reichskanzlei, May 1942.
44. On 3 March 1937, Goebbels noted in his diary that Hitler would decide whether this was to be funded by Reich subsidies or by a small levy on theatre ticket prices. See Alan E. Steinweis, *Art, Ideology, and Economics in Nazi Germany: The Reich Chambers of Music, Theater, and the Visual Arts* (Chapel Hill and London, 1993), pp. 100–1.
45. See *GTB*, 8 March 1937.
46. 'Der Führer im Harnack-Haus', *Deutsches Nachrichtenbüro*, 5 February 1935.
47. See *GTB*, 1 May 1939.
48. BAB, R43 II/90: Telegram from Froelich to Hitler, 2 May 1935.
49. See, for instance, BAB, R9361 V/110305: Carl Auen to Marianne Hoppe, 18 November 1937.
50. See Benjamin George Martin, '"European Cinema for Europe!" The International Film Chamber, 1935–42', in Roel Vande Winkel and David Welch (eds), *Cinema and the Swastika: The International Expansion of Third Reich Cinema* (Basingtoke, 2011), pp. 25–41. Also 'Dem Wohl des völkerverbindenden Films zu dienen!', *Der Film*, 27 April 1935.
51. The Reich Film Chamber sent out letters to actors to this effect, see BAB, R9361 V/110204: Reichsfachschaft Film to Werner Hinz, 6 April 1935.
52. BAB, R43/390: Adjutantur des Führers to Reichsminister Lammers, 30 May 1938.
53. *GTB*, 8 January 1938, 11 January 1938 and 2 December 1938.
54. Though in the midst of the scandal surrounding his affair, he did make an effort to reduce the number of non-Germans in films; see *GTB*, 13 December 1938.
55. See Gerd Albrecht, *Nationalsozialistische Filmpolitik: Eine soziologische Untersuchung über die Spielfilme des Dritten Reichs* (Stuttgart, 1969), pp. 108–9.
56. See ibid., pp. 108–09.
57. One example being the 1934 film *Gold*, which Albrecht classifies as an action film – despite its strong anti-British animus and the thematic focus on the manufacture of

artificial gold, a theme which chimed perfectly with the Nazi emphasis on synthetic products. See ibid., p. 352.

58. Ibid., pp. 194–7.

59. Schmeling, *Erinnerungen*, p. 263.

60. Interview with Zeissler [sic], 24 June 1943, at http://www.nizkor.org/ftp.py?people/h/hitler.adolf/oss-papers/text/oss-sb-zeissler (accessed 2 December 2014).

61. See Uwe Klöckner-Draga, *Renate Müller: Ihr Leben, ein Drahtseilakt* (Bayreuth, 2006).

62. See, for instance, https://www.jewishvirtuallibrary.org/jsource/Holocaust/women.html (accessed 6 May 2017).

63. Pauline Kohler (John Beevor), *I Was Hitler's Maid* (London, 1940).

64. See Carola Stern, *Auf den Wassern des Lebens: Gustaf Gründgens und Marianne Hoppe* (Cologne, 2005), p. 105.

65. For the Hoppe anecdote, see Johannes Steinhoff (ed.), *Deutsche im Zweiten Weltkrieg: Zeitzeugen sprechen* (Munich, 1989), p. 75. See also Volker Elis Pilgrim, *Hitler 1 und Hitler 2* (Hamburg, 2017), and Erich Fromm, *The Anatomy of Human Destructiveness* (New York, 2013), p. 459. In the scene to which Hoppe refers, French soldiers are shown being struck by boulders hurled from above by Tyrolean freedom-fighters during the Napoleonic wars. However, that Hitler clasped his knees during a suspenseful scene where the 'baddies' get their comeuppance is hardly a form of 'orgasm'; it is something many of us might do at such moments. Hoppe's tale is an example of actors, after the war, presenting Hitler as abnormal; the more perverted he appears, the more moral and decent actors could appear by contrast – all in the interests of dissociating themselves from a dictator under whose regime they made films.

66. Pola Negri, *Memories of a Star* (New York, 1970), p. 375.

67. See Géza von Cziffra, *Es war eine rauschende Ballnacht* (Munich and Berlin, 1985), p. 185.

68. Kuno Kruse, *Dolores and Imperio: Die drei Leben des Sylvin Rubinstein* (Cologne, 2003), p. 39.

69. Jefferson Adams, *Historical Dictionary of German Intelligence* (Lanham, Toronto and Plymouth, 2009), p. 429.

70. *GTB*, 18 February 1935.

71. Ibid., 19 January 1936.

72. BAB, R9361 V/111760: State Secretary Funk to Niako, 24 July 1936.

73. Ibid.: Albrecht to Niako, 19 October 1939.

74. Ibid.: Leichtenstern to Albrecht, 12 October 1939.

75. Ibid.: Albrecht to Niako, 19 October 1939.

76. Ibid.: 'Albrecht, Die Tänzerin Lea Niako', 13 October 1939.

77. BAB, R9361 V/112148: Ralph to Hitler, 12 May 1939.

78. For the correspondence, see ibid.

79. BAB, R55/120150: Letter from Scherler (Department T) to Goebbels, 4 October 1939.

80. Ibid.: Hilpert to Schlösser, 26 March 1940.

81. For the correspondence between Brückner and Schneider, see BAB, R9361 V/112854.

82. For a lively discussion of the social functions of Hitler's personal adjutants, see Fabrice d'Almeida, *High Society in the Third Reich* (Cambridge, 2008).

83. The assumption that Hitler would simply hand out acting roles to those who stressed their loyalty to the party was misguided. Actress Leni Morel turned to Hitler's half-sister, Angela Raubal, in 1935 hoping that Raubal would intervene with Hitler on her behalf. The matter reached the desk of the Reich Theatre Chamber, who wrote to Morel saying they were unable to provide her with an acting certificate ('Bühnennachweis'). While the chamber recognized that she had been an early member of the League of German Girls, this could not be deemed more important than her artistic abilities. See BAB, R9361 V/114099: Benno von Arent to Leni Morel, 22 June 1935.

84. See 'Der Führer in Neubabelsberg', *Film-Kurier*, 5 January 1935. See also *GTB*, 6 January 1935.

85. Lída Baarová, *Die süße Bitterkeit meines Lebens* (Koblenz, 2001), pp. 56–7.

86. See Peter Conradi, 'Goebbels' Mistress Tells Tales from the Grave', *Sunday Times*, 21 January 2001.
87. See Baarová, *Die süße Bitterkeit*, pp. 60–1.
88. Gustav Fröhlich, *Waren das Zeiten: Mein Film-Heldenleben* (Munich and Berlin, 1983), p. 364.
89. Ibid., p. 365.
90. Baarová, *Die süße Bitterkeit*, pp. 113–14.
91. Ibid., p. 109.
92. According to Graf von Helldorff, at the time Police President of Berlin. See Stanislav Motl, *Lída Baarová, Joseph Goebbels: Die verfluchte Liebe einer tschechischen Schauspielerin und des Stellvertreters des Teufels* (Prague, 2009), p. 105.
93. *GTB*, 24 October 1938.
94. Baarová, *Die süße Bitterkeit*, p. 144.
95. See ibid., p. 142.
96. See ibid., p. 149.
97. Ibid., p. 151; Motl, *Lída Baarová, Joseph Goebbels*, p. 108. The film director Géza von Cziffra gives a different account. According to Cziffra, an inebriated Schaub insisted that she leave Berlin – 'the Führer wants it, and so do the people' (Géza von Cziffra, *Es war eine rauschende Ballnacht*, p. 150).
98. According to Motl, *Lída Baarová, Joseph Goebbels*, pp. 141–2.
99. Baarová, *Die süße Bitterkeit*, p. 175.
100. Czech National Archives, 642 sg. 110-4/490: Karl Hermann Frank to Ernst Kaltenbrunner, 6 July 1944.
101. Ibid.
102. Czech National Archives, 1709 sg. 109/4/1464: 'Der Abteilungsleiter IV W/Kt: Vermerk: Lida Baarová', 25 June 1942.
103. Czech National Archives, 642 sg. 110-4/490: Karl Hermann Frank to Ernst Kaltenbrunner, 23 November 1944. According to Frank, Reich Film Superintendent Fritz Hippler had been refusing to grant her permission (see Czech National Archives, 642 sg. 110-4/490: Karl Hermann Frank to Ernst Kaltenbrunner, 6 July 1944). Hippler, however, had been removed from his post by Goebbels in April 1943 following a bout of binge-drinking and womanizing in Prague. See Czech National Archives, 1734 sg. 109-4/1489, and *GTB*, 28 February 1943.
104. Czech National Archives, 642 sg. 110-4/490: 'Vermerk. Betr.: Gespräch von SS-Gruppenführer Ministerialdirektor Hinkel mit Frau Lida Baarová anlässlich seines Aufenthaltes in Prag am 20. Juni 1944'.
105. Baarová, *Die süße Bitterkeit*, p. 151.
106. Czech National Archives, 642 sg. 110-4/490: 'Vermerk. Betr.: Gespräch von SS-Gruppenführer Ministerialdirektor Hinkel mit Frau Lida Baarová anlässlich seines Aufenthaltes in Prag am 20. Juni 1944'.
107. See Motl, *Lída Baarová, Joseph Goebbels*, pp. 128–34.
108. As of 1941, she was also effectively banned from Czech films.
109. See Jürgen Matthäus and Frank Bajohr (eds), *Alfred Rosenberg: Die Tagebücher von 1934 bis 1944* (Frankfurt am Main, 2015), pp. 266–7.
110. See, for instance, von Cziffra, *Es war eine rauschende Ballnacht*, p. 142.
111. In 1940, the actress Manja Behrens began a relationship with Hitler's private secretary, Martin Bormann. The relationship was tolerated by Bormann's wife.
112. That Baarová tried to commit suicide is claimed in a number of actors' autobiographies; see for instance Albrecht Schoenhals and Anneliese Born, *Immer zu zweit: Erinnerungen* (Wiesbaden and Munich, 1977), p. 179.
113. BAB, R9361 V/110812: Körber to Hitler, 14 March 1939.
114. Guido Knopp, *Hitlers nützliche Idole: Wie Medienstars sich in den Dienst der NS-Propaganda stellten* (Munich, 2007).

115. See 'Großdeutschlands Reichskanzlei', *Völkischer Beobachter*, 13 January 1939.
116. Paul Bruppacher, *Adolf Hitler und die Geschichte der NSDAP: Eine Chronik. Teil 2: 1938–1945* (Norderstedt, 2013), here p. 100.
117. Anneliese Uhlig, *Rosenkavaliers Kind: Eine Frau und drei Karrieren* (Munich, 1977), p. 87.

7 Watching over War

1. See Helmut Heiber and David M. Glantz, *Hitler and his Generals: Military Conferences 1942–1945* (New York, 2002), 31 August 1944, p. 467.
2. Karl Wilhelm Krause, *Im Schatten der Macht: Kammerdiener bei Hitler* (Bochum, 2011), p. 34.
3. IfZ, ZS-0638: Hans Baur, 'Die letzten Tage in der Reichskanzlei', 1962/1963.
4. Julius Schaub, *In Hitlers Schatten: Erinnerungen und Aufzeichnungen des persönlichen Adjutanten und Vertrauten 1925–1945* (Stegen-Ammersee, 2010), p. 132.
5. Traudl Junge, *Bis zur letzten Stunde* (Munich, 2003), p. 219 (footnote).
6. *GTB*, 4 October 1942.
7. Henrik Eberle and Matthias Uhl, eds, *Das Buch Hitler: Geheimdossier des NKWD für Josef W. Stalin* (Cologne, 2005), p. 202.
8. BAB, NS10/591: 'Terminkalender und Telefonbuch Hitlers. – geführt von Max Wünsche, Ordonnanzoffizier und Adjutant Hitlers, 07. Okt. 1939–09. Jan. 1940'.
9. See 'Der Feldzug in Polen', *Film-Kurier*, 9 October 1939.
10. It was probably the role of the army leaders that was felt to be inadequately reflected. See BAF, RW4/295: Kurt Hesse (WPr V (Heer)) to WPr Abteilungschef, 4 December 1940.
11. BAB, NS10/591: 'Terminkalender und Telefonbuch Hitlers', 8 October 1939.
12. *GTB*, 28 October and 2 November 1939.
13. Ibid., 10 December 1939.
14. BAB, NS10/591: 'Terminkalender und Telefonbuch Hitlers', 11 December 1939; see also *GTB*, 13 December 1939.
15. BAB, NS10/49: Albrecht to Hippler, 14 December 1939.
16. Jürgen Trimborn, *Leni Riefenstahl: A Life* (New York, 2008), p. 176.
17. BAF, RW4/185: 'Reichsministerium für Volksaufklärung und Propaganda. Betrifft: Film-Sondertrupp Riefenstahl', 10 September 1939.
18. Trimborn, *Leni Riefenstahl*, p. 176.
19. Leni Riefenstahl, *Memoiren* (Cologne, 2000), p. 349.
20. See Trimborn, *Leni Riefenstahl*, p. 286.
21. See, for instance, Riefenstahl, *Memoiren*, p. 351.
22. See BAF, RW4/185: 'Reichsministerium für Volksaufklärung und Propaganda. Betrifft: Film-Sondertrupp Riefenstahl', 10 September 1939; and BAF, RW4/261: 'Tätigkeitsbericht WPr v. 29.9.39'.
23. See Steven Bach, *Leni: The Life and Work of Leni Riefenstahl* (London, 2007), p. 229.
24. See 'Feldzug in Polen', *Film-Kurier*, 9 October 1939, and, for the original version of the film, BA FA, K89890-6: 'Feldzug in Polen'.
25. Heinz Boberach, *Meldungen aus dem Reich: Die geheimen Lageberichte des Sicherheitsdienstes der SS 1938–1945. Band 3* (Herrsching, 1984), p. 846 (6 March 1940)
26. *GTB*, 13 February 1940. See also Frank Maraun, 'Der Feldzug in Polen – filmisch gestaltet', *Der Deutsche Film* 4:7 (January 1940), pp. 138–40.
27. Heinz Boberach, *Meldungen aus dem Reich, Band 3*, p. 759 (14 February 1940).
28. See Max Domarus, *Hitler: Reden 1932 bis 1945, Band 3* (Wiesbaden, 1973), pp. 1354–66.
29. For a discussion of *Baptism of Fire*, see David Welch, *Propaganda and the German Cinema, 1933–1945* (London and New York, 2001), pp. 172–83.
30. See the report on the film's production in BAF, RH26/123–140: 'WPr (Heer) Gruppenleiter. Betr.: Aufbau des Heeresdokumentarfilmes', November 1940.

31. At least according to the draft of a Brauchitsch letter responding to a Goebbels' letter in BAF, RH1/54: 'Entwurf', undated (probably May 1940).
32. BAF, RW4/295: OKW W Pr. IIIc to In 4, In 5, In 6, 22 November 1940.
33. Ibid.: W Pr. IIIc to W Pr. V, 22, November 1940. Hitler also objected to scenes showing 'tanks on the attack' in the film, see ibid.: 'Betr.: Manuskript "Achtung Panzer!" ', 7 April 1941.
34. Ibid.: 'W Pr V (Heer): Betr.: Film der Reichspropagandaleitung "Auf den Strassen des Sieges" ', 4 December 1940. Goebbels probably viewed this film in November (see *GTB*, 23 November 1940).
35. *GTB*, 22 December 1940.
36. Ibid.
37. Kurt Hesse, *Der Geist von Potsdam* (Mainz, 1967), p. 184.
38. Cited in Cooper C. Graham, ' "Sieg im Westen" (1941): Interservice and Bureaucratic Propaganda Rivalries in Nazi Germany', *Historical Journal of Film, Radio and Television* 9:1 (1989), pp. 19–45, here p. 25.
39. *GTB*, 22 January 1941.
40. Willi A. Boelcke, ed., *Kriegspropaganda 1939–1941: Geheime Ministerkonferenzen im Reichspropagandaministerium* (Stuttgart, 1966), p. 610.
41. See Daniel Uziel, *The Propaganda Warriors: The Wehrmacht and the Consolidation of the German Home Front* (Berne, 2008).
42. For the dispute between Goebbels and Brauchitsch, see *GTB*, 27 February, 8 March and 12 March 1941.
43. See Wolfgang Pyta, *Hitler: Der Künstler als Politiker und Feldherr* (Munich, 2015), pp. 295–6.
44. See BAF, RH1-81: 'Oberkommando der Wehrmacht. Betrifft: Arbeitsabkommen', 23 December 1940.
45. Ibid.: 'Arbeitsabkommen zwischen dem Beauftragten des Führers [. . .] und dem Chef des Oberkommandos der Wehrmacht', 9 November 1940. Brauchitsch, predictably, complained about this agreement, objecting to the 'political control' it would allow Rosenberg to exercise. See ibid.: 'Vortrags-Notiz über das Arbeitsabkommen zwischen dem Beauftragten des Führers, Reichsleiter Rosenberg und dem O.K.W.', 19 January 1941.
46. Full English citation in Graham, ' "Sieg im Westen" (1941)', p. 31.
47. See BAF, RW4/295: 'W Pr V (Heer): Betr.: Aufbau des Heeresdokumentarfilms', November 1940.
48. Pyta, *Hitler*, p. 296.
49. See Marianne Feuersenger, *Mein Kriegstagebuch: Führerhauptquartier und Berliner Wirklichkeit* (Freiburg, Basle and Vienna, 1982), p. 97.
50. The Armed Forces' High Command did oversee the making of a film about the *Battle for Norway* (1940), but it was never shown. The propaganda film *Campaign in the East* (1942) was simply a compilation of newsreel material, and was in any case not designed for public viewing, although the Armed Forces' High Command did agree to it being shown in Norway. See BAB, NS18/348: 'Notiz für Pg. Dr. Hippler, Betr.: Filmwerk "Feldzug im Osten" ', 16 June 1942.
51. IfZ, Bestand Adolf Hitler F19/4: 'SS-Hauptsturmführer Heinz Linge und SS-Obersturmführer Hans Junge: Hitlers Terminkalender', March–June 1943 and August–December 1943.
52. See SAF, D180/9 182187: 'Arnold Fanck, Anmerkungen zu meinem Fragebogen', 5 November 1946.
53. For a report on the film *Westwall*, see 'Der Westwall', *Film-Kurier*, 11 August 1939.
54. See, for instance, Ufa-Tonwoche, 654 (17 March 1943), 705 (8 March 1944) and 715 (17 May 1944).

55. BAB, R109 I/1034b: 'Niederschrift über die Ufa-Vorstandssitzung Nr. 1443', 22 January 1941.
56. BAB, R43 II/389: Speer to Lammers, 11 May 1940.
57. Ibid.
58. BAB, R4606/4838: Verwaltungsamt B 13/3 to R.M.f.R.u.K., 12 December 1944.
59. Trimborn, *Leni Riefenstahl: A Life*, p. 197.
60. BAB, R4606/4838: 'RM.F.B.u.M: Vermerk', 7 August 1943.
61. Ibid.: R.M.f.R.u.K. to Hauptamt Verwaltung und Wirtschaft, 26 November 1944. See also Bach, *Leni*, pp. 234–35.
62. BAB, R4606/4341: H. Tenz to Generalbauinspekteur für die Reichshauptstadt, 14 February 1942.
63. Anna Plaim and Kurt Kuch, *Bei Hitler: Zimmermädchen Annas Erinnerungen* (Munich, 2005), p. 79.
64. Eberle and Uhl, *Das Buch Hitler*, p. 204.
65. BAB, NS10/591: 'Terminkalender und Telefonbuch Hitlers'.
66. IfZ, Bestand: Hitler, Adolf: F19/4: 'Hitlers Terminkalender'.
67. Peter Witte, Michael Wildt, Martina Voigt et al., eds, *Der Dienstkalender Heinrich Himmlers 1941/42* (Hamburg, 1999), p. 487.
68. Ibid., p. 367.
69. *GTB*, 20 March 1942.
70. Ibid., 12 June 1943.
71. Ibid., 2 September 1942.
72. According to ibid., 27 April 1943, the film was poorly directed, stiff and unconvincing.
73. See ibid., 24 June 1943.
74. See, for instance, ibid., 4 October 1942.
75. Ibid., 21 March 1941.
76. Ibid., 1 April 1941.
77. Herbert Döhring, *Hitlers Hausverwalter* (Bochum, 2013), p. 40.
78. Heinrich Hoffmann, *Hitler was my Friend: The Memoirs of Hitler's Photographer* (London, 2011), p. 191.
79. *GTB*, 30 July 1940.
80. Rochus Misch, *Der Letzte Zeuge: Ich war Hitlers Telefonist, Kurier und Leibwächter* (Munich, 2009), p. 109.
81. See, for instance, David Bret, *Clark Gable: Tormented Star* (New York, 2007), p. 190.
82. In addition to intervening in the films discussed in this chapter, during the war Hitler influenced the fate of other films, but I was unable to find enough detailed information on the precise circumstances. One of these films was Karl Ritter's *Above All Else in the World* (1941), a film about the persecution of Germans abroad after the start of the war. According to Goebbels, Martin Bormann agitated against the film, but Hitler decided it should be shown. See *GTB*, 22 March 1941 and 23 March 1941.
83. BAB, NS18/501: 'Abschrift: Betreff: Verächtlichmachung des Erzieherstandes im Film'.
84. BAB, NS18/349: Reichspropagandaleitung to the Deutsche Apothekerschaft, 27 April 1943.
85. *GTB*, 23 May 1942.
86. SAH, Bestandsnummer 213–11, Signatur Staatsanwaltschaft Hamburg – Strafsachen 21249/50 Band 2, pp. 304–10. See also Veit Harlan, *Im Schatten meiner Filme* (Gütersloh, 1966), p. 133.
87. BAB, R55/412: President of Reich Film Chamber to Propaganda Ministry, 14 October 1941.
88. *GTB*, 2 March 1942, 3 March 1942.
89. Ibid., 20 March 1942.
90. Ibid., 3 March 1942.
91. Ibid., 20 January 1942.

92. See Pyta, *Hitler*, pp. 638–9.
93. *GTB*, 20 March 1942.
94. See Joseph Goebbels, 'Führergeburtstag 1942: Rundfunkrede zum Geburtstag des Führers', in Goebbels, *Das eherne Herz: Reden und Aufsätze aus den Jahren 1941/42* (Munich, 1942), pp. 285–94, here p. 289 and p. 286. Also *GTB*, 20 April 1942.
95. Max Domarus, *Hitler: Reden 1932–1945, Band 4*, p. 1867.
96. Emil Jannings, 'Bismarck in dieser Zeit', *Völkischer Beobachter*, 4 October 1942.
97. PA AA, R 26808: 'Betrifft: Den Jannings-Film der Tobis Filmkunst G.m.b.H. "Die Entlassung"', 9 February 1942.
98. Ibid.: 'Zu Inf. 1148: Berlin, den 10. Februar 1942, Sofort!'
99. *GTB*, 1 December 1941.
100. Ibid., 3 February 1942.
101. Ibid., 28 June 1942.
102. Ibid., 7 August 1942.
103. Ibid., 20 August 1942.
104. Ibid., 16 September 1942.
105. Ibid., 4 October 1942.
106. Ibid., 25 October 1942.
107. Ibid., 13 December 1942.
108. BAB, NS18/283: Walter Tießler, 'Vorlage für den Herrn Minister: Betr.: Beurteilung des Films "Die Entlassung" durch Reichsleiter Rosenberg', 24 September 1942.
109. See, for instance, *GTB*, 23 January 1939. Goebbels writes of Hitler's hatred for the Habsburgs and his low opinion of Wilhelm ('a deserter').
110. BAB, NS18/282: 'Betrifft: "Die Entlassung": Bericht und Auszug aus den eingelangten Beurteilungen', 27 July 1942.
111. Ibid.: Bacmeister to State Secretary Gutterer, 13 August 1942.
112. Heinz Rühmann, *Das war's: Erinnerungen* (Frankfurt am Main, 1995), pp. 154–6.
113. *GTB*, 25 January 1944.
114. 'Die Feuerzangenbowle', *Film-Kurier*, 28 January 1944.
115. BAB, R9361 V/155032. 'Aus dem Protokoll vom 4.3.1946: Rücksprache mit Herrn Rühmann'.
116. IfZ, ZS-0137: 'Vernehmung von Julius Schaub in Nürnberg am 7. Dezember 1946'.
117. Eberle and Uhl, *Das Buch Hitler*, p. 202.
118. E.g. *GTB*, 20 August 1942.
119. 'Statut für das Reichsfilmarchiv', *Film-Kurier*, 4 February 1934.
120. See Volker Koop, *Warum Hitler King Kong liebte, aber den Deutschen Micky Maus verbot* (Berlin, 2015), p. 186.
121. *GTB*, 4 October 1942.
122. According to Hans Barkhausen; see Andreas-Michael Velten and Matthias Klein, eds, *Chaplin und Hitler: Materialien zu einer Ausstellung* (Munich, 1989), p. 120.
123. A short sequence asserting Chaplin's Jewishness was included in the film *The Eternal Jew* (1940).
124. Quoted in Velten and Klein, *Chaplin und Hitler*, p. 120.
125. BAB, R43 II/389: Goebbels to Lammers, 7 January 1943.
126. Koop, *Warum Hitler King Kong liebte*, p. 188.
127. Ibid., p. 189–95. Actors and directors were usually able to get access to British and American films by claiming they needed to watch them to prepare for their own films.
128. BAB, R43 II/389: Goebbels to Lammers, 26 March 1943.
129. Ibid.: Rosenberg to Lammers, 15 April 1943.
130. Ibid.: 'Betrifft: Ausländische Filme. Vermerk', 3 May 1943.
131. *GTB*, 27 May 1940.

132. BAF, RW4/296: Reichsministerium für Volksaufklärung und Propaganda to the Oberkommando der Wehrmacht, 12 July 1940.
133. Ibid.: Chef des Oberkommandos der Wehrmacht to the Reichsministerium für Volksaufklärung und Propaganda, 3 June 1940.
134. Ibid.: 'An das OKW Abtlg. Film', 1 June 1940.
135. Cited in Koop, *Warum Hitler King Kong liebte*, p. 188.
136. BAB, R56 I/20: Bormann to Goebbels, 2 July 1941.
137. Ibid.: Goebbels to Bormann, 8 August 1941.
138. Ibid.: Müller-Goerne to Deutsche Arbeitsfront, 12 January 1942.
139. Ibid.: Deutsche Arbeitsfront to Reichskulturkammer, 23 July 1942.
140. Ibid.: Reichskulturkammer to Reichsfilmkammer, 31 July 1942.
141. Ibid.: 'Reichsverfügungsblatt: Anordnung A 7/42', 20 February 1942.
142. 'Erlaß des Führers über die Rechtsstellung der Nationalsozialistischen Deutschen Arbeiterpartei vom 12 Dezember 1942', *Reichsgesetzblatt 1942* (Teil I, 131), pp. 733–4.
143. BAB, R56 I/20: Reichspropagandaleitung (Tießler) to Reichskulturkammer, 25 March 1943.
144. BAB, R43 II/390a: Goebbels to the Reichsfilmkammer, 28 September 1943. In a 23 July 1943 diary entry, Goebbels had made clear he finds it quite acceptable that local communities should own cinemas, and that it was Max Winkler who resisted this idea. However, the September ruling shows equally clearly that Goebbels was not in favour of 'Gemeinden' expanding their ownership at the expense of Reich-owned or private cinemas.
145. BAB, R43 II/390a: Bormann to Goebbels, 9 March 1944.
146. BAB, R55/663: Goebbels to the President of the Film Chamber, quoted in draft letter from Parbel (Reich Propaganda Office) to State Secretary Hayler (Reich Ministry of Economics), September 1944.
147. Jürgen Matthäus and Frank Bajohr, eds, *Alfred Rosenberg: Die Tagebücher von 1934 bis 1944* (Frankfurt, 2015), p. 303 (11 December 1939). Hitler had also complained about films overfocusing on professional problems in 1938 (see *GTB*, 21 June 1938).
148. *GTB*, 12 December 1939.
149. Hitler banned a Rosenberg film about the Autobahn project in 1937 (see *GTB*, 22 August 1937). For a discussion of Nazi documentary films about the Autobahn, see Karlheinz Hoffmann, '"Strassen der Zukunft": Die Reichsautobahnen', in Peter Zimmermann and Karlheinz Hoffmann, eds, *Geschichte des dokumentarischen Films in Deutschland. Band 3: Drittes Reich, 1933–1945* (Stuttgart, 2005), pp. 276–86.
150. Picker, *Hitlers Tischgespräche im Führerhauptquartier* (Munich, 2003), p. 632.
151. See, for instance, *GTB*, 20 June 1939.
152. See ibid., 7 March 1938, 30 May 1938, 30 January 1939, 22 February 1939 and 30 September 1939, 20 March 1940, 23 May 1940.
153. See Felix Moeller, *Der Filmminister: Goebbels und der Film im Dritten Reich* (Berlin, 1998), pp. 219ff.
154. *GTB*, 12 December 1939.
155. BAB, NS10/591: 'Terminkalender und Telefonbuch Hitlers', entry for 11 December 1939.
156. *GTB*, 20 January 1942.
157. Goebbels relates that Bormann objected to Ritter's film *Above All Else in the World*; see note 82 and *GTB*, 22 March 1941.
158. *GTB*, 10 May 1943.

8 Preparing Genocide

1. 'Juden demonstrieren in Berlin', *Der Angriff*, 15 July 1935.
2. See the excerpt from a 1935 Ufa-Tonwoche at https://www.ushmm.org/online/film/display/detail.php?file_num=4973 (accessed 6 May 2017).

3. BAB, R43/3546: P.V. Rasmussen to the Dänische Gesandtschaft, Berlin, 15 July 1935.
4. Gerhard Stahr, *Volksgemeinschaft vor der Leinwand? Der nationalsozialistische Film und sein Publikum* (Berlin, 2001), p. 157.
5. See, for instance, 'Juden demonstrieren in Berlin'.
6. *GTB*, 28 September 1934.
7. Erika Fries, 'Warum ist "Pettersson & Bendel" ein Erfolg in Deutschland?', *Beiblatt zum Film-Kurier*, 24 August 1935.
8. *GTB*, 12 February 1937.
9. Ibid., 23 May 1939.
10. See Manfred Hobsch, *Film im 'Dritten Reich', Band 2* (Berlin, 2010), p. 429.
11. SAH, Bestandsnummer 213–11, Signatur Staatsanwaltschaft Hamburg – Strafsachen 21249/50 Band 3: 'Der Oberstaatsanwalt bei dem Landgericht Hamburg, Anklageschrift gegen den Filmregisseur Veit Harlan, Az.: 1 Js 1/48, 15.7.48'.
12. Ibid. – Strafsachen 21249/50 Band 5: Alf Teichs Testimony.
13. 'Der Text des Gerichtsurteils über Veit Harlan', published in *Filmpress*, 22 July 1950. See BAB, R 109 I/1564.
14. For a good overview, see Peter Longerich, *Goebbels: Biographie* (Munich, 2012), pp. 393–9.
15. *GTB*, 18 November 1938.
16. 'Juden ohne Maske', *Licht Bild Bühne*, 26 November 1938.
17. 'Juden dürfen keine Kinos mehr besuchen', *Film-Kurier*, 14 November 1938. See also *GTB*, 12 November 1938.
18. 'Pettersson & Bendel', *Licht Bild Bühne*, 3 December 1938. On 14 December 1938, Ufa's board of directors approved a poster for the showing of *Pettersson & Bendel* in Ufa theatres on Kurfürstendamm and Friedrichsstrasse for four days. See BAB, R109 I/1033b: 'Niederschrift Nr. 1346 über die Vorstandssitzung der Ufa vom 14. Dezember 1938'.
19. See Peter Longerich, *Hitler: Biographie* (Munich, 2015), Kindle Edition, Location 13391.
20. See Max Domarus, ed., *Hitler: Reden 1932 bis 1945, Band 2* (Wiesbaden, 1973), pp. 1047–73.
21. 'Unter dem Eindruck der Führer-Rede', *Film-Kurier*, 31 January 1939.
22. Jürgen Matthäus and Frank Bajohr, eds, *Alfred Rosenberg: Die Tagebücher von 1934 bis 1944* (Frankfurt, 2015), p. 303 (11 December 1939).
23. For a history of the film's production, see Susan Tegel, *Jew Süss: Life, Legend, Fiction, Film* (London, 2011), pp. 151–67.
24. This was later confirmed by Reich Film Superintendent Fritz Hippler, see LAB, B Rep. 031-02-01 Nr. 12496: 'Urteil im Namen des Rechts in dem Spruchgerichtsverfahren gegen den ehemaligen Zivilinternierten Dr. Fritz Hippler, 28/29 September 1948'.
25. Veit Harlan, *Im Schatten meiner Filme* (Gütersloh, 1966), p. 220.
26. SAH, Bestandsnummer 213–11, Signatur Staatsanwaltschaft Hamburg – Strafsachen 21249/50 Band 4.1: Letter from Annie Rosar to Spruchkammer, 28 February 1949.
27. *GTB*, 9 November 1939.
28. Ibid., 5 December 1939.
29. Ibid., 15 December 1939.
30. 'Nun auch noch Harlan', *Tägliche Rundschau*, 18 December 1948.
31. These scripts can be found in the Deutsche Kinemathek in Berlin. For the earlier version, see A621: 'Jud Süß: Endgültige Fassung! Ein Historischer Film von Eberhard Wolfgang Möller und Ludwig Metzger. Regie: Dr. Peter Paul Brauer'; and for the Harlan version, see A623: 'Jud Süß: Ein historischer Film. Regie: Veit Harlan'.
32. For a discussion of the smith Bogner, a figure added by Harlan whose house is half demolished at Süss's orders and who is then hung for protesting, see Tegel, *Jew Süss*, p. 171.
33. Matthäus and Bajohr, *Alfred Rosenberg*, p. 290.

34. Matthäus and Bajohr, *Alfred Rosenberg*, p. 303.
35. See Harlan, *Im Schatten meiner Filme*, pp. 96–9.
36. See the testimony by Wolff von Gordon in LAB, E Rep. 400–31 Nr. 6: 'Weiterverhandelt am 16. Februar 1948: In der Ermittlungssache gegen Harlan, 9 April 1948'. There is no ghetto scene in the original Metzger–Moeller script, see Deutsche Kinemathek Berlin, A621.
37. See the post-war testimony by German film director Erich Engel, LAB, E Rep. 400–31 Nr. 6: 'Betrifft: Veit Harlan'. From *GTB*, 5 January 1940, it is clear that Marian was reluctant, and that Goebbels also applied pressure.
38. See the testimony of Otto Lehmann, LAB, E Rep. 400–31 Nr. 6: 'Weiterverhandelt am 16. Februar 1948'. See also 'Wie "Der ewige Jude" in Polen gefilmt wurde', *Film-Kurier*, 27 November 1940.
39. Harlan, *Im Schatten meiner Filme*, p. 106.
40. See 'Die Spruchkammerakte Werner Krauß', in Carl Zuckmayer, *Briefe an Hans Schiebelhuth 1921–1936* (Göttingen, 2003), p. 275.
41. Thus the literary critic Elisabeth Frenzel praised Krauß for seeking, as she saw it, to represent the 'unity of the [Jewish] race' by acting all the smaller roles. See 'Die Darstellung des Juden im Film', *Hamburger Tageblatt*, 2 March 1940. Harlan himself did more than hint at this motive in an interview with *Der Film* of 20 January 1940, when he said that the temperaments and characters represented by Krauß 'stem from one and the same root'. Quoted in Erwin Leiser, *'Deutschland, Erwache!' Propaganda im Film des Dritten Reiches* (Reinbek bei Hamburg, 1968), p. 142.
42. See SAH, Bestandsnummer 213–11, Signatur Staatsanwaltschaft Hamburg – Strafsachen 21249/50 Band 4.2: Conny Carstennsen Testimony.
43. Harlan, *Im Schatten meiner Filme*, p. 116.
44. For an in-depth study of the Lublin area under Nazi rule, see Bogdan Musial, *Deutsche Zivilverwaltung und Judenverfolgung im Generalgouvernement: Eine Fallstudie zum Distrikt Lublin 1939–1944* (Wiesbaden, 1999).
45. 'Die Fratze des Juden: Gespräch mit Veit Harlan', *Lodscher Zeitung*, 31 January 1940.
46. SAH, Bestandsnummer 213-11, Signatur Staatsanwaltschaft Hamburg – Strafsachen 21249/50 Band 1: 'Aktenauszug'.
47. Ibid. – Strafsachen 21249/50 Band 4.1: Fritz Hippler Testimony, 27 April 1948.
48. The interview was published in the *Völkischer Beobachter* on 5 May 1933 and is reproduced in SAH, Bestandsnummer 213-11, Signatur Staatsanwaltschaft Hamburg – Strafsachen 21249/50, Band 1: 'Aktenauszug'.
49. Adolf Hitler, *Mein Kampf* (Munich, 1943), p. 341.
50. Ibid., p. 342.
51. Ibid., p. 357.
52. Figure given in Christian Adam, *Lesen unter Hitler: Autoren, Bestseller, Leser im Dritten Reich* (Frankfurt, 2013), p. 116.
53. BAB, R43 II/389: Joseph Goebbels, 'Bericht von der deutsch-französischen Filmwoche in Venedig'.
54. Ibid.: Goebbels to Lammers, 19 September 1940.
55. *GTB*, 25 September 1940.
56. Ibid., 26 September 1940.
57. BAB, R55/21306: Report of 13 November 1944.
58. *Film-Kurier*, 28 November 1940.
59. '100.000. Besucher bei "Jud Süß" in Königsberg', *Film-Kurier*, 29 November 1940.
60. Tegel, *Jew Süss*, pp. 186ff.
61. Claude Singer, *Le Juif Süss et la Propagandie nazie* (Paris, 2003), pp. 228–30.
62. SAH, Bestandsnummer 213-11, Signatur Staatsanwaltschaft Hamburg – Strafsachen 21249/50 Band 3: Otto Froböse, 'Betr.: Prozess gegen den Filmregisseur Veit Harlan'.

63. 'Die Erfolgsfilme 1941', *Deutsche Allgemeine Zeitung*, 8 January 1942.
64. See Jeffrey Herf, *The Jewish Enemy: Nazi Propaganda during World War II and the Holocaust* (Cambridge, 2008).
65. Quoted in Otto Dov Kulka and Eberhard Jäckel, eds, *Die Juden in den geheimen SS-Stimmungsberichten 1933–1945* (Düsseldorf, 2004), p. 435.
66. Ralph Giordano, *Erinnerung eines Davongekommenen: Die Autobiographie* (Cologne, 2007), p. 159.
67. BAB, R9361 V/154966: Helene Rothenberg Testimony, 1 April 1948.
68. SAH, Bestandsnummer 213-11, Signatur Staatsanwaltschaft Hamburg – Strafsachen 21249/50 Band 2: 'Vernehmung in der Ermittlungssache gegen Veit Harlan', 30 April 1948.
69. See Edith Raim, *Zwischen Diktatur und Demokratie* (Munich, 2013), p. 707.
70. See Heinz Boberach, ed., *Meldungen aus dem Reich: Die geheimen Lageberichte des Sicherheitsdienstes der SS 1938–1945, Band 6* (Herrsching, 1984), p. 1801 (25 November 1940).
71. Dorothea Hollstein, *Antisemitische Filmpropaganda: Die Darstellung des Juden im nationalsozialistischen Spielfilm* (Berlin, 1971), p. 76.
72. SAH, Bestandsnummer 213-11, Signatur Staatsanwaltschaft Hamburg – Strafsachen 21249/50 Band 3: Emil Oestreicher Testimony.
73. BAB, R43 II/389: Hadamovsky to Lammers, 31 March 1941.
74. See Michele Sarfatti, *The Jews in Mussolini's Italy: From Equality to Persecution* (Madison, 2006), p. 139.
75. See Armin Nolzen, ' "Hier sieht man den Juden, wie er wirklich ist . . .": Die Rezeption des Filmes Jud Süß in der deutschen Bevölkerung', in Alexandra Przyrembel and Jörg Schönert, eds, *'Jud Süß': Hofjude, literarische Figur, antisemitisches Zerrbild* (Frankfurt and New York, 2006), pp. 245–62, here p. 259.
76. SAH, Bestandsnummer 213-11, Signatur Staatsanwaltschaft Hamburg – Strafsachen 21249/50 Band 2: 'In der Sache gegen Veit Harlan erklärt der Zeuge Dr. Angyal Bela', 25 March 1948.
77. Rudy Rosenberg, *And Somehow We Survive* (Bloomington, IN, 2008), pp. 33–4.
78. BAB, NS10/84: Himmler letter of 30 September 1940.
79. 'Vorführung des Filmes "Jud Süß": Runderlaß des Reichsführers SS und Chef der Deutschen Polizei v. 15.11.1940', in Andrea Löw, ed., *Die Verfolgung und Ermordung der europäischen Juden durch das nationalsozialistische Deutschland 1933–1945: Deutsches Reich und Protektorat, September 1939–September 1941* (Munich, 2012), pp. 309–10.
80. BAF, RS4/903: 'SS u. Polizeiführer im Distrikt Lublin', 22 November 1940.
81. See Wolf Gruner, *Jewish Forced Labour under the Nazis: Economic Needs and Racial Aims, 1938–1944* (Cambridge, 2008), esp. pp. 238ff.
82. Gedenkstätte Buchenwald, ed., *Buchenwald Concentration Camp, 1937–1945: A Guide to the Permanent Historical Exhibition* (Frankfurt, 2004), p. 37.
83. Simone Erpel et al., eds, *Im Gefolge der SS: Aufseherinnen des Frauen-KZ Ravensbrück. Begleitband zur Ausstellung* (Berlin, 2007), p. 176.
84. SAH, Bestand 213-11, Staatsanwaltschaft Hamburg – Strafsachen, 21249/50 Band 3: Max Durner to the Oberstaatsanwalt beim Landgericht Hamburg, 14 March 1939.
85. SAH Hamburg, Bestandsnummer 213-11, Signatur Staatsanwaltschaft Hamburg – Strafsachen 21249/50 Band 2: Walter Preisser Testimony.
86. Ibid. – Strafsachen 21249/50 Band 6: Paul Wilhelm Rass Testimony.
87. Ibid. – Strafsachen 21249/50 Band 5: Helmut Bickel Testimony. See also the references to Stefan Baretzki's Auschwitz Testimony, in Tegel, *Jew Süss*, p. 187.
88. Thus members of the Union of Persecutees of the Nazi Regime (VVN) were unable to confirm the Sachsenhausen testimony of Helmut Bickel, while the Auschwitz testimony of

Baretzki, an ethnic German former camp guard, was also regarded with scepticism. Bickel and Baretzki may have been trying to make a favourable impression given that they themselves stood accused of various criminal dealings.

89. See Jürgen Trimborn, *Der Herr im Frack: Johannes Heesters* (Berlin, 2003), p. 465.
90. BAF, RW4/292: Oberkommando der Wehrmacht to the Reichspropagandaleitung, Hauptamt Film, 13 November 1940.
91. See SAH, Bestand 213-11, Staatsanwaltschaft Hamburg – Strafsachen, 21249/50 Band 6: Dr Erich Masur, Landgerichtspräsident Itzehoe (Holstein) to Herrn Oberstaatsanwalt b.d. Staatsgericht Hamburg, 14 April 1950.
92. BAB, NS10/74: Greiser to Brückner, October 1939.
93. Harlan, *Im Schatten meiner Filme*, p. 97.
94. See Wolfgang Benz, *'Der Ewige Jude': Metaphern und Methoden nationalsozialistischer Propaganda* (Berlin, 2010).
95. Goebbels also attended a showing of *Jews Unmasked*; see 'Dr. Goebbels bei einer Gaufilm-Veranstaltung', *Licht Bild Bühne*, 15 December 1938.
96. *GTB*, 5 November 1937.
97. Ibid., 5 October 1939.
98. Ibid., 6 October 1939.
99. Ibid., 7 October 1939.
100. Fritz Hippler, *Die Verstrickung* (Düsseldorf, 1981), p. 187.
101. See Felix Moeller, *Der Filmminister: Goebbels und der Film im Dritten Reich* (Berlin, 1998), p. 241.
102. *GTB*, 6 October 1939.
103. BAF, RW4/241: 'Propagandaanweisung des Reichspropagandaministers für den 2. Oktober 1939'.
104. Ibid.: 'Propagandaanweisung des Reichspropagandaministers für den 6. Oktober 1939'.
105. Ibid.: 'An AOK 8 Ic: Zur Erledigung von Sonderaufgaben werden vom Reichpropaganda-Ministerium entsandt, 7 October 1939'. Teams of four cameramen respectively were sent to Łódź and Cracow.
106. See ibid.: 'Propagandaanweisung des Reichspropagandaministers für den 6. Oktober 1939'.
107. See Daniel Uziel, 'Wehrmacht Propaganda Troops and the Jews', Shoah Resource Centre, Yad Vashem at http://www.yadvashem.org/odot_pdf/Microsoft%20Word%20-%20 2021.pdf (accessed 30 April 2017).
108. See, for instance, 'Wie "Der ewige Jude" in Polen gefilmt wurde: Dr. Hippler über seinen neuen großen Dokumentarfilm', *Film-Kurier*, 27 November 1940.
109. *GTB*, 17 October 1939.
110. Ibid., 18 November 1939.
111. Ibid., 19 November 1939.
112. Ibid., 25 November 1939.
113. Ibid., 28 November 1939.
114. Ibid., 18 December 1939.
115. Ibid., 12 January 1940.
116. See 'Symphonie des Ekels', *Der Deutsche Film* 8:4 (February 1940), pp. 156–8.
117. LA NRW, 1069-Katg. IV 26: Hans Hinkel, 'Äußerungen zu dem Film "Der ewige Jude" anläßlich der Vorführung vor einem geschlossenen Kreis von etwa 120 Personen am 1. März 1940'.
118. *GTB*, 4 April 1940.
119. Ibid., 9 May 1940.
120. Ibid., 6 June 1940.
121. Ibid., 3 September 1940.

122. See Yizhak Ahren and Stig Hornshøj-Møller, '*Der Ewige Jude*' *oder wie Goebbels hetzte* (Aachen, 1990), pp. 21–2; and Willi A. Boelcke, *Kriegspropaganda 1939–1941: Geheime Ministerkonferenzen im Reichspropagandaministerium* (Stuttgart, 1966), p. 487.

123. Matthäus and Bajohr, *Alfred Rosenberg*, p. 334.

124. *GTB*, 9 May 1940.

125. Similar vacillations in Nazi attitudes to Britain may have been responsible for the withdrawal of the anti-British *The Rothschilds* shortly after its July 1940 premiere; see David Welch, *Propaganda and the German Cinema 1933–1945* (London and New York, 2001), pp. 226–7.

126. See Boelcke, *Kriegspropaganda 1939–1941*, pp. 259–63.

127. See Peter Longerich, *The Unwritten Order: Hitler's Role in the Final Solution* (Stroud, 2001), p. 55.

128. See Boelcke, *Kriegspropaganda 1939–1941*, p. 332.

129. Stig Hornshøj-Møller, '*Der ewige Jude*': *Quellenkritische Analyse eines antisemitischen Propagandafilms* (Göttingen, 1995), p. 3.

130. For a good discussion of these two films, see Stefan Mannes, *Antisemitismus im nationalsozialistischen Propagandafilm: Jud Süß und Der Ewige Jude* (Cologne, 1999). See also Susan Tegel, *Nazis and the Cinema* (London, 2007), esp. Chapters 10 and 11.

131. Peter Bucher, 'Die Bedeutung des Films als historische Quelle: "Der Ewige Jude" (1940)', in Heinz Duchhardt and Manfred Schlenke, eds, *Festschrift für Eberhard Kessel zum 75. Geburtstag* (Munich, 1982), pp. 300–329, here p. 317.

132. Boberach, *Meldungen aus dem Reich, Band 6*, pp. 1917–19, 20 January 1941.

133. See, for instance, Bucher, 'Die Bedeutung des Films als historische Quelle', p. 318.

134. Saul Friedländer, *Nazi Germany and the Jews, 1939–1945: The Years of Extermination* (New York, 2007), p. 102.

135. See Kathrin Engel, *Deutsche Kulturpolitik im besetzten Paris 1940–1944: Film und Theater* (Munich, 2003), p. 384.

136. Hans Hohenstein, 'Ahasver ohne Maske', *Völkischer Beobachter*, 30 November 1940.

137. Dirk Rupnow, *Vernichten und Erinnern: Spuren nationalsozialistischer Gedächtnispolitik* (Göttingen, 2005), p. 247.

9 From Hero to Camera-shy

1. See, for instance, *GTB*, 29 July 1940, and 19 May 1941.

2. Ibid., 17 December 1938.

3. Ibid., 28 January 1939.

4. Ibid., 1 February 1939.

5. Ibid., 12 December 1939.

6. Jürgen Matthäus and Frank Bajohr, eds, *Alfred Rosenberg: Die Tagebücher von 1934 bis 1944* (Frankfurt am Main, 2015), pp. 302–03 (11 December 1939).

7. See Daniel Uziel, *The Propaganda Warriors: The Wehrmacht and the Consolidation of the German Home Front* (Berne, 2008), pp. 186f.

8. For Hitler's complaints about the Wochenschau, see *GTB*, 4 September 1940, 14 January 1941, 5 July 1941, 3 June 1942 and 3 October 1942.

9. Ibid., 20 August 1942.

10. For an excellent overview of the coordination of propaganda within the Wehrmacht, see BAF, Nachlass Kurt Hesse, N558/6: 'Die Deutsche Wehrmachtpropaganda im Zweiten Weltkrieg'.

11. See Willi A. Boelcke, ed., *Kriegspropaganda 1939–1941: Geheime Ministerkonferenzen im Reichspropagandaministerium* (Stuttgart, 1933), p. 131.

12. Three of these accompanying texts, along with Hippler's letters to Hitler's Adjutants Office, can be found in BAB, NS10/49. They date from 1940, and relate to newsreels 510, 512 and 513.

13. For Goebbels' discussions with Hitler about the Wochenschau, see, for instance, his diary entries of 28 November 1939, 14 February 1940, 20 March 1940, 17 April 1940, 29 May 1940, 16 August 1940, 14 January 1941, 19 April 1941, 29 April 1941, 16 June 1941, 7 July 1941, 5 August 1941, 26 September 1941, 18 November 1941, 13 January 1942, 24 February 1942, 21 April 1942, 24 May 1942, 10 June 1942, 25 August 1942, 4 October 1942, 13 October 1942, 12 January 1943, 29 April 1943, 25 January 1944, 27 April 1944 and 6 June 1944.

14. BAB, NS10/591: 'Terminkalender und Telefonbuch Hitlers. – geführt von Max Wünsche, Ordonnanzoffizier und Adjutant Hitlers 07. Okt. 1939–09. Jan 1940', entries for 9, 19 and 25 October 1939.

15. For instance on 27 September, 11 and 25 October, and 1, 15 and 29 November. See IfZ, Bestand Adolf Hitler: F19/4: 'Hitlers Terminkalender'.

16. Henrik Eberle and Matthias Uhl, eds, *Das Buch Hitler: Geheimdossier des NKWD für Josef W. Stalin* (Cologne, 2005), p. 208.

17. Karl Wilhelm Krause, *Im Schatten der Macht: Kammerdiener bei Hitler* (Bochum, 2011), p. 34.

18. See BAB, NS10/49: Wochenschau text for newsreel 513 (p. 144).

19. See ibid.: Wochenschau text for newsreel 512 (pp. 168 and 178).

20. IfZ, ZS-0638: Lecture given by Baur, 'Die letzten Tage in der Reichskanzlei', to the Deutsche Gemeinschaft in 1962.

21. *GTB*, 12 May 1940.

22. BAF, RW4/296: Oberkommando der Wehrmacht to RMVP (Reichsministerium für Volksaufklärung und Propaganda), 11 June 1940.

23. BAF, RW4/449: 'Aktennotiz. Betrifft: Filmzensur', 26 April 1939.

24. Werner Jochmann, *Adolf Hitler: Monologe im Führerhauptquartier 1941–1944: Die Aufzeichnungen Heinrich Heims* (Hamburg, 1980), p. 217 (28 March 1942).

25. BAF, RW4/289: 'Der Chef des Oberkommandos der Wehrmacht an OKM/M Wa II, 2. April 1940. Betrifft: Filmaufnahmen in Rüstungsbetrieben'.

26. See *GTB*, 24 May 1942.

27. See BAB, R55/663: 'Führerentscheid über die Freigabe von V1 für die Deutsche Wochenschau', 4 July 1944 and 6 July 1944.

28. *GTB*, 7 July 1941.

29. Ibid., 29 April 1941.

30. This complaint was dismissed by Armed Forces Chief, Wilhelm Keitel. See BAB, R43 II/389: Keitel to Lammers, 29 September 1943.

31. BAB, R55/663: Hinkel to Goebbels, 7 December 1944.

32. *GTB*, 3 October 1942.

33. See Eberle and Uhl, *Das Buch Hitler*, p. 208.

34. Jochmann, *Adolf Hitler: Monologe*, p. 77 (entry for 25/26 September 1941).

35. *GTB*, 3 June 1942.

36. Ibid., 5 July 1941.

37. See David Welch, *Propaganda and the German Cinema, 1933–1945* (London, 2001), p. 38.

38. See BAB, NS10-464: Olympia-Film-Gesellschaft to Sturmbannführer Wernicke, 31 July 1939.

39. Frentz filmed material of Hitler for the newsreels from early September 1939 through to March 1945 (according to a list of Frentz's Wochenschau contributions put together by the Bundesarchiv).

40. See Hans Georg Hiller von Gaertringen, ed., *Das Auge des Dritten Reiches: Walter Frentz – Hitlers Kameramann und Fotograf* (Munich, 2006).

41. Ufa-Tonwoche, 492 (7 February 1940).

42. See ibid., 471 (14 September 1939) and 472 (21 September 1939).

43. Ibid., 471 (14 September 1939).
44. Ibid., 492 (7 February 1940).
45. Ibid., 471 (14 September 1939), 472 (21 September 1939) and 474 (4 October 1939).
46. Ibid., 472 (21 September 1939).
47. Ibid., 497 (14 March 1940).
48. Ibid., 510 (13 June 1940).
49. Heinz Boberach, *Meldungen aus dem Reich: Die geheimen Lageberichte des Sicherheitsdienstes der SS 1938–1945, Band 4* (Herrsching, 1984), pp. 1222–3 (6 June 1940).
50. 'Sondervorführungen der Wochenschau', *Film-Kurier*, 21 September 1939.
51. *GTB*, 17 May 1940.
52. Boberach, *Meldungen aus dem Reich, Band 4*, pp. 1283–4 (20 June 1940).
53. Ufa-Tonwoche, 514 (10 July 1940).
54. Such as the crowds cheering on Hitler at Munich station in 1940 as he sets off to meet Mussolini at the Brenner Pass, see Deutsche Wochenschau, 527 (9 October 1940).
55. Deutsche Wochenschau, 550 (19 March 1941) and 602 (18 March 1942).
56. Ibid., 533 (20 November 1940) and 537 (18 December 1940).
57. Ibid., 612 (27 May 1942) and 712 (26 April 1944).
58. Ibid., 497 (14 March 1940), 550 (19 March 1941), 602 (18 March 1942), 655 (24 March 1943).
59. Ibid., 557 (7 May 1941) and 608 (29 April 1942).
60. Ibid., 584 (12 November 1941), 637 (19 November 1942) and 689 (19 November 1943).
61. Ibid., 544 (5 February 1941), 586 (26 November 1941) and 587 (3 December 1941).
62. Ibid., 598 (18 February 1942).
63. Ibid., 615 (18 June 1942). See Robert Gerwarth, *Hitler's Hangman: The Life of Heydrich* (New Haven, 2012).
64. In May 1943, Hitler was also shown at the funeral of Viktor Lutze, the loyal SA leader who had taken over from Ernst Röhm following the 'Night of the Long Knives' in 1934. See Deutsche Wochenschau, 662 (12 May 1943).
65. Usually, the heroic music accompanying such newsreel reports was 'Siegfried's Death' from Wagner's *Twilight of the Gods*. Given that Siegfried did not fall in battle, but was killed through Hagen's treachery, one wonders at this choice.
66. See, for instance, Deutsche Wochenschau, 579 (8 October 1941).
67. Boberach, *Meldungen aus dem Reich, Band 4*, p. 1222 (6 June 1940).
68. Ibid., *Band 6*, p. 1813 (28 November 1940).
69. Ibid., *Band 6*, pp. 2045–6 (27 February 1941). See also ibid., *Band 6*, p. 1908 (16 January 1941), p. 2153 (27 March 1941) and p. 2190 (7 April 1941).
70. Ibid., *Band 7*, p. 2537 (17 July 1941), pp. 2595–6 (31 July 1941) and p. 2623 (7 August 1941).
71. Ibid., *Band 7*, p. 2649 (14 August 1941).
72. See Ibid., *Band 8*, p. 2725 (11 September 1941) and p. 2775 (18 September 1941); *Band 9*, p. 3225 (29 January 1942), p. 3300 (12 February 1942); *Band 10*, p. 3629 (16 April 1942), p. 3691 (30 April 1942); *Band 11*, p. 4191 (10 September 1942); *Band 12*, p. 4457 (12 November 1942); *Band 13*, p. 5038 (1 April 1943), p. 5192 (29 April 1943). See also BAB, R109/II 67: 'Zur Aufnahme der Wochenschau vom 30. Mai bis zum 5. Juni 1944'.
73. BAB, NS18/341: 'Vorlage für den Herrn Minister. Betrifft: Der Führer in der Wochenschau, Berlin', 1 April 1943.
74. See *GTB*, 3 November 1943.
75. Eberle and Uhl, *Das Buch Hitler*, p. 208.
76. Deutsche Wochenschau, 678 (1 September 1943) and 680 (15 September 1943).
77. Ibid., 742 (23 November 1944).
78. Eberle and Uhl, *Das Buch Hitler*, p. 208.

79. *GTB*, 7 April 1943.
80. Deutsche Wochenschau, 655 (24 March 1943).
81. *GTB*, 10 June 1942.
82. Deutsche Wochenschau, 611 (20 May 1942), 675 (4 August 1943) and 679 (8 September 1943).
83. *GTB*, 14 March 1944.
84. See Hans-Joachim Neumann and Henrik Eberle, *War Hitler krank: Ein abschließender Befund* (Cologne, 2009), esp. pp. 217ff.
85. Ellen Gibbels, 'Hitlers Parkinson-Syndrom: Eine posthume Motilitätsanalyse in Filmaufnahmen der Deutschen Wochenschau', *Der Nervenarzt* 59 (1988), 521–8, here p. 521. The article bears the English translation 'Hitler's Parkinsonian Syndrome: A Posthumous Analysis of Motility in German Newsreels, 1940–1945'.
86. According to Henry Picker, during the war SS doctor Max de Crinis had already come to the conclusion that Hitler had Parkinson's disease on the basis of the Wochenschau and photographs. See Henry Picker, *Tischgespräche im Führerhauptquartier 1941–1942* (Stuttgart, 1963), p. 110.
87. Deutsche Wochenschau, 726 (3 August 1944).
88. Ibid., 731 (7 September 1944).
89. Gibbels, 'Hitlers Parkinson-Syndrom', p. 521. See also Ellen Gibbels, 'Hitlers Nervenkrankheit', *Vierteljahreshefte für Zeitgeschichte* 42:2 (April 1994), pp. 155–220.
90. Boberach, *Meldungen aus dem Reich, Band 13*, p. 5038 (1 April 1943).
91. Ibid., *Band 13*, pp. 4892ff. (4 March 1943).
92. Ibid., *Band 13*, p. 5038 (1 April 1943).
93. See ibid., *Band 7*, p. 2276 (8 May 1941); *Band 8*, p. 2750 (11 September 1941).

10 The Divinely Gifted

1. IfZ, ED-100 79 (Hewel papers).
2. BAB, NS10/591: 'Terminkalender und Telefonbuch Hitlers', 3 November 1939.
3. BAB, Berlin NS26/2459: 'Führers Tagebuch 1934–1943', 11 October 1942.
4. See the photographs in Robert Amos, *Mythos Romy Schneider* (Munich, 2000), p. 69.
5. BAB, R9361 V/110482: Jugo to Hitler, 15 February 1940.
6. See, for instance, BAB, R9361 V/111399: Oswald Lehnich to Ferdinand Marian, 17 April 1939; and BAB, R9361 V/108955: Lehnich to Lil Dagover, 25 May 1939.
7. See Boguslaw Drewniak, *Das Theater im NS-Staat: Szenarium deutscher Zeitgeschichte 1933–1945* (Düsseldorf, 1983), p. 350. For a good discussion of the privileges accorded to those working in the arts in Nazi Germany, see Oliver Rathkolb, *Führertreu und Gottbegnadet: Künstlereliten im Dritten Reich* (Vienna, 1991).
8. BAB, R109 II/33: Bavaria-Filmkunst to Reichsfilmintendant, 8 July 1944.
9. See *GTB*, 22 November 1941.
10. See BAB, R55/20251a: 'Liste der Schauspieler, die für die Filmproduktion benötigt werden'.
11. The list of actors cited by Oliver Rathkolb, for instance, as the List of the Divinely Gifted is – to my knowledge – actually another list of actors and actresses deferred from military service by the Propaganda Ministry ('weitere uk-gestellte Einzelkünstler'). Ernst Klee in his lexicon on culture in the Third Reich also may have confused the latter list with the former. See Rathkolb, *Führertreu und Gottbegnadet*, pp. 176–8, and Ernst Klee, *Kulturlexikon zum Dritten Reich: Wer war was vor und nach 1945* (Frankfurt, 2009). For the original lists, see BAB, R55/20252a and R56 I/33.
12. Other surviving lists complicate the picture even more. Thus the Propaganda Ministry issued production chiefs with a list known as the 'II+List'. On it, for instance, were the names of film actors regarded as suitable for more than five days of shooting. See BAB,

R109 I/2140: 'Richtlinien zur Stoff- und Personenauswahl in der deutschen Filmproduktion', 30 July 1943.
13. BAB, R55/20252a: 'Liste der Schauspieler, die für die Filmproduktion benötigt werden'.
14. Ibid.: '1. Gottbegnadeten-Liste. [. . .] B. Alle übrigen'.
15. Ibid.: '2. Weitere uk-gestellte Einzelkünstler A. Filmliste'.
16. BAB, R55/174: Hinkel to Goebbels, 3 May 1943.
17. See Werner Maser, *Heinrich George: Mensch aus Erde gemacht* (Berlin, 1998); and Wolfgang Noa, *Paul Wegener* (Berlin, 1964).
18. For the Allied denazification case relating to Ilse Werner – also suspected of having a relationship with Hermann Fegelein, who married Eva Braun's sister – see the material in BAB, R9361 V/155073, and BAB, R9361 V/113742.
19. See Jürgen Trimborn, *Romy und ihre Familie* (Munich, 2008), pp. 122–5.
20. See *GTB*, 25 January 1939, 19 January 1940 and 12 February 1941.
21. For criticism of his conduct under Nazism, see the denazification material in BAB, R9361 V/154985.
22. In the case of *White Slaves*, at least, this was true (see Chapter 2).
23. BAB, R9361 V/143991: Werner Hinz to Direktor Herzberg, 12 May 1947.
24. Ibid.: 'Major Lovell: Subject: Werner Hinz', 22 December 1945.
25. *GTB*, 27 December 1939.
26. See Manfred Hobsch, *Film im 'Dritten Reich': Alle deutschen Spielfilme von 1933 bis 1945, Band 4* (Berlin, 2010), pp. 257–8.
27. See LA NRW, Abt. R: NW 1002 AD 29593: 'Abschrift Nr. 7 Jahr 1946 des Notariatsregisters, verhandelt zu Berlin am 16. Januar 1946'.
28. 'Goebbels über die nationale Aufgabe des Films', *Film-Kurier*, 13 October 1941.
29. See Roel Vande Winkel and David Welch, eds, *Cinema and the Swastika: The International Expansion of Third Reich Cinema* (Basingstoke, 2011).
30. BAB, R109 II/14: 'Betrifft: Einsatz von Filmen soldatischen und nationalen Charakters', 24 November 1944.
31. See BAB, R9361 V/111412: 'Aktenvermerk Fachschaft Film', 12 May 1944.
32. See BAB, R9361 V/118601: 'Betrifft: Film-Fachdarsteller Karl Etlinger', 11 April 1938.
33. See the documents in ibid.
34. Heinz Rühmann, *Das war's: Erinnerungen* (Frankfurt and Berlin, 1995), p. 132.
35. Rühmann was able to provide proof of financial payments to his former wife to the denazification authorities after the war, see BAB, R9361 V/155032: 'Rechtsabteilung: Rücksprache mit Herrn Heinz Rühmann', 26 January 1946.
36. See Felix Moeller, *Der Filmminister: Goebbels und der Film im Dritten Reich* (Berlin, 1998), pp. 295–9, 309–12, p. 414.
37. See, for instance, BAB, R56 I/29: 'Liste der aus der Reichstheaterkammer ausgeschlossenen Nichtarier bezw. mit Volljuden verheiratete (Februar bis April 1939)'.
38. Thus he praised Moser's performance in *Little County Court* (1938), see BAB, NS10/45: Wünsche to Leichtenstern, 21 November 1938.
39. Moser's letter is printed in *exilOgraph* 5 (2000), p. 1 (online at https://www.exilforschung.uni-hamburg.de/forschung/publikationen/exilograph/pdf/exilograph05.pdf, accessed 30 April 2017).
40. Although historian Oliver Rathkolb claims Moser's letter never reached Hitler. See Angelika Hager, 'Wie österreichische Publikumslieblinge sich mit dem NS-Regime arrangierten', *profil*, 23 February 2010 (http://www.profil.at/home/wie-publikumslieblinge-ns-regime-262724, accessed 30 April 2017).
41. See BAB, R9361 V/112057: Porten to Schaub, 3 August 1939.
42. *GTB*, 10 August 1943.
43. BAB, NS10/42: 'Aufstellung der am 15. Februar 1937 als eiserner Bestand auf dem Obersalzberg eingelagerten Filme'.

44. *GTB*, 25 January 1944.
45. BAB, R9361 V/136935: Hinkel to Goebbels, 25 January 1945.
46. See Maser, *Heinrich George*, pp. 283–4.
47. BAB, R9361 V/114058: Hilleke to Goebbels, 27 November 1942.
48. For a good account of inconsistencies in the application of Nazi anti-Semitic policy, see John M. Steiner and Jobst Freiherr von Cornberg, 'Willkür in der Willkür: Befreiungen von den antisemitischen Nürnberger Gesetzen', *Vierteljahreshefte für Zeitgeschichte* 46: 2 (April 1998), pp. 143–88.
49. BAB, R9361 V/154969: Paul Henckels, 'Lebenslauf und Darstellung meiner besonderen Situation in den Jahren 1933/45'.
50. See Lale Andersen, *Der Himmel hat viele Farben* (Munich, 1974), pp. 162–4.
51. BAB, R55/20251a: 'Liste der Schauspieler, die für die Filmproduktion benötigt werden'.
52. *GTB*, 14 August 1943.
53. Ibid., 23 September 1943.
54. Ibid., 4 March 1942.
55. Ibid., 27 April 1942.
56. Ibid., 14 August 1943.
57. Ibid., 29 October 1943. A comparable case is that of the film director Herbert Selpin, who was found hung in a Gestapo prison on 1 August 1942 following his arrest for making critical comments about the Wehrmacht. See Friedemann Beyer, *Der Fall Selpin: Chronik einer Denunziation* (Munich, 2011).
58. See BAB, R109 II/29: 'Besetzungsschwierigkeiten der Berliner Produktion', 15 July 1944.
59. BAB, R109 II/06: 'Niederschrift über die 4. Sitzung der Produktionschefs im Produktionsjahr 1944/45', 21 July 1944.
60. *GTB*, 29 February 1944.
61. For Hitler's and Goebbels' disgust at Jannings' 'cowardice', see ibid., 29 February 1944, 14 March 1944, 27 April 1944 and 2 December 1944.
62. Ibid., 27 April 1944.
63. BAB, R109 II/55: Anonymous letter to Magda Goebbels, 9 August 1944.
64. See 'Geschichten zwischen Gestapo-Keller und Buchenwald', *Die Welt*, 3 January 1998 (http://www.welt.de/print-welt/article595904/Geschichten-zwischen-Gestapo-Keller-und-Buchenwald.html, accessed 30 April 2017).
65. BAB, R9361 V/136935: Hinkel to Goebbels, 20 December 1944. See also BAB, R9361 V/136935: Hinkel to Goebbels, 9 January 1945, 18 January 1945, 25 January 1945 and 22 February 1945.
66. See BAB, R9361 V/154992: Denazification testimony given by Wolfgang Harich in support of de Kowa, 20 May 1946.
67. See BAB, R9361 V/128787: Hinkel to Goebbels, 16 February 1945. For a lexicon of artists persecuted under Hitler, which also provides details of those involved in anti-Nazi resistance, see the excellent book by Kay Weniger, *Zwischen Bühne und Baracke: Lexikon der verfolgten Theater-, Film- und Musikkünstler 1933–1945* (Berlin, 2008).
68. This was recently rumoured to be the case with Marika Rökk, who allegedly spied for the Soviets while making films for Hitler. If she did spy for the Soviets, then this was not necessarily to resist Hitler, but to be able to exonerate herself in the event of the Nazis losing the war. As it was, after the war she was accused of spying for the Nazis. See Kate Connolly, 'Star of Postwar German Cinema was Soviet Spy, Declassified Files Show', *Guardian*, 20 February 2017.
69. Hinkel refers to Pfitzner's reply in a letter to Goebbels, see BAB, R9361-V/135943: Hinkel to Goebbels, 1 December 1944.
70. See BAB, R9361 V/135943: Hinkel to Goebbels, 16 November 1944.
71. See ibid.: Hinkel to Goebbels, 1 December 1944.
72. See IfZ, MA 103: '1. Gottbegnadeten-Liste [. . .] B. Alle übrigen, d) Theater'.

73. BAB, R9361 V/135943: Hinkel to Goebbels, 13 December 1944.

74. In his diary on 24 January 1944, Goebbels noted that he was having 'problems' as a result of the fact that artists married to Jews were in desperate straits since the introduction of more severe measures against Jews. Goebbels indicates that these problems pertain particularly to those in film and theatre. 'Artists are extraordinarily sensitive in these matters,' he writes, 'so that we must proceed with particular care.' This suggests that there had already been complaints within the film industry about the disadvantaged position of actors in mixed marriages, and that Goebbels was prepared to listen to these complaints.

75. 'Wiener Künstler zum 10. April', *Neues Wiener Journal*, 7 April 1938.

76. CI-TB, 12 November 1944, and 2 December 1944.

77. BAB, R9361 V/137223: Hinkel to Goebbels, 13 December 1944.

78. Ibid.

79. *GTB*, 3 December 1944.

80. Following claims that he had not opted for Germany when the ethnic German population of South Tyrol had to decide whether they wanted to remain in Italy or emigrate to Germany, Luis Trenker wrote to Hitler on 27 February 1940 explicitly stating his commitment to fostering links between Mussolini and Germany (see BAB, R9361 V/113388: Trenker to Hitler, 27 February 1940).

81. BAB, R9361 V/137223: Hinkel to Goebbels, 1 December 1944.

82. See Karl Heinz Roth, 'Filmpropaganda für die Vernichtung der Geisteskranken und Behinderten im Dritten Reich', in Götz Aly et al., eds, *Reform und Gewissen: 'Euthanasie' im Dienst des Fortschritts* (Berlin, 1989), pp. 125–93. Plans for a documentary film continued after *I Accuse* had been shown. Herman Schweninger, one of those involved in the euthanasia programme, submitted a draft for such a film in 1942, in which he presented gassing as a painless way to die. See BAB, N2503/1123: 'Geheime Reichssache! Entwurf für den wissenschaftlichen Dokumentarfilm G.K.', 29 October 1942.

83. Cited in Roth, 'Filmpropaganda', p. 125.

84. Ibid., p. 126.

85. Goebbels, according to his diary on 15 August 1941, had wanted to talk to Hitler about using the film to trigger discussion of euthanasia, but then decided it was not a good idea – presumably in the light of the effect of van Galen's sermon.

86. Hitler had planned to implement a law on 'assisted dying', but decided in late 1940 to postpone it until after the war. See Karl Heinz Roth, ' "Ich Klage an": Aus der Entstehungsgeschichte eines Propaganda-Films', in Götz Aly, ed., *Aktion T4 1939–1945: Die 'Euthanasie'-Zentrale in der Tiergartenstraße 4* (Berlin, 1989), pp. 92–119.

87. There were reports, however, of the Church's resistance to the film's message, and of the fact that intellectuals and middle-class women also proved unreceptive. For comments on reactions to the film, see e.g. BAB, NS18/348: 'Gauleitung: Ost Hannover. Fernschreiber-Kurzbericht an die Partei-Kanzlei vom 10. Januar 1942'; and BAB, NS18/348: 'Gauleitung: Bayerische Ostmark: Fernschreiber-Kurzbericht an die Partei-Kanzlei vom 17. Februar 1942'.

88. After the war, director Wolfgang Liebeneiner claimed that the film helped to end the killing of the mentally ill, and triggered a discussion which made possible Clemens August von Galen's sermon against euthanasia. Neither of these claims is true: both von Galen's sermon and Hitler's decision to end the euthanasia campaign preceded the showing of *I Accuse*. See 'Ein Brief von Wolfgang Liebeneiner, 16. März 1965', in Erwin Leiser, *'Deutschland, erwache!' Propaganda im Film des Dritten Reichs* (Hamburg, 1968), pp. 139–41.

89. *GTB*, 20 August 1941.

90. 'Film der Nation "Heimkehr" vor Soldaten und Rüstungsarbeitern', *Film-Kurier*, 24 October 1941.

91. C.B., ' "Heimkehr" vor den Soldaten der Ostfront', *Film-Kurier*, 8 November 1941.

92. It thus helped to reinforce the impact of the Nazi newsreels, which had reported on the atrocities committed against Ukrainians by the Soviets in Lemberg in July 1941 (Deutsche Wochenschau, 566). For a good discussion of *Homecoming*, see David Welch, *Propaganda and the German Cinema 1933–1945* (London, 2001), p. 110–16.

93. See Hobsch, *Film im 'Dritten Reich', Band 2*, p. 466.

94. See Maria Steiner, *Paula Wessely: Die verdrängten Jahre* (Vienna, 1996).

95. See BAB, R 109 II/29: Reichsfilmintendanz (Müller-Goerne) to Leiter Film, 18 July 1944.

96. BAB, R109 II/14: Leiter F/Reichsfilmintendant to Goebbels, 15 November 1944.

97. BAB, R109 II/27: 'Nachrichtenblatt des Reichsministeriums für Volksaufklärung und Propaganda', 13 September 1944.

98. See 'Für die Mitglieder der Fachgruppe Kultur- und Werbefilm', *Film-Kurier*, 8 August 1944.

99. 'Gesetze des Krieges für den deutschen Film', *Film-Kurier*, 15 August 1944.

100. BAB, R109 I/1716: 'Niederschrift Nr. 1569 über die Ufa-Vorstandssitzung vom 28.6.1944 in Berlin'.

101. BAB, R55/1231: 'Betr.: Besuch von Kino- und Theaterveranstaltungen durch ausländische Arbeitskräfte', 16 June 1944.

102. See, for instance, BAB, R55/21333: Reichspropagandaamt Mark Brandenburg to RMVP, 7 June 1944.

103. BAB, R109 II/14: Leiter F/Reichsfilmintendant to Herrn Staatssekretär, 8 December 1944.

104. See the correspondence between Bormann, Funk, Hans Heinrich Lammers and Riefenstahl-Film in BAB, R43 II/8106.

105. Jürgen Trimborn, *Leni Riefenstahl: A Life* (New York, 2008), p. 202.

106. Leiser, *'Deutschland Erwache'*, p. 83.

107. For material relating to the film, see Wiener Library 1621/1, 1621/2, 1621/3 and 1621/4.

108. Frowein refers to 'Harlan's plan' to make a film about *The Merchant of Venice*. See BAB, R109 II/14: Frowein to Goebbels, 12 October 1944. For evidence that Harlan definitely set about preparing this film, see the material in BAB, R109 II/50, for instance Harlan to Reichsfilmkammer (Müller-Goerne), 28 October 1944. See also LAB, E Rep. 400–31, Nr. 6.

109. BAB, R109 II/15: Leiter F, Reichsfilmintendant to Goebbels, 12 December 1944.

110. See Hans-Christoph Blumenberg, *Das Leben geht weiter. Der letzte Film des Dritten Reichs* (Berlin, 1993). See also the material in BAB, R109 II/53.

111. 'Morden, Plündern, Schänden, Sengen', *Völkischer Beobachter*, 8 March 1945.

112. 'Neujahrsaufruf des Führers an das deutsche Volk: Wir werden den Sieg erzwingen!', *Völkischer Beobachter*, 2 January 1945.

113. The letter is reproduced in Veit Harlan, *Im Schatten meiner Filme* (Gütersloh, 1966), p. 183. See also Haus-, Hof- und Staatsarchiv Vienna, AT-OeStA/HHStA HA Burg SR 11-30: Goebbels to Harlan, 1 June 1943.

114. For good accounts of the history and deployment of *Kolberg*, see Rolf Giesen, *Nazi Propaganda Films: A History and Filmography* (Jefferson, NC, 2003), pp. 163–84; and Moeller, *Der Filmminister*, pp. 295–9, 309–12.

115. See 'Funkspruch Dr. Goebbels' an den Festungskommandanten', *Völkischer Beobachter*, 1 February 1945.

116. Harlan, *Im Schatten meiner Filme*, p. 183.

117. SAH, Bestandsnummer 213–11, Signatur Staatsanwaltschaft Hamburg – Strafsachen 21249/50 Band 4.2: Testimony of Fritz Hippler, 27 April 1948.

118. Max Domarus, *Hitler: Reden 1932 bis 1945. Band IV: 1941–1945* (Wiesbaden, 1973), pp. 2194–8.

119. 'Funkspruch Dr. Goebbels' an den Festungskommandanten'.
120. Harlan, *Im Schatten meiner Filme*, p. 182.

Epilogue

1. *Swiss Miss* had been banned by the Nazi censorship authorities on the grounds that it was 'artistically inferior'. See Markus Spieker, *Hollywood unterm Hakenkreuz: Der amerikanische Spielfilm im Dritten Reich* (Trier, 1999), p. 232.
2. BAB, NS10/125: Overview of Hitler's activities on 21 June 1938.
3. Max Domarus, *Hitler: Reden 1932 bis 1945, Band 2* (Wiesbaden, 1973), p. 875
4. Leni Riefenstahl, *Memoiren* (Cologne, 2000), p. 367.
5. Ibid., p. 367.
6. Ibid., p. 367.
7. The script can be found at BAB, R1/92: 'Film der NSDAP: "Ich aber beschloss, Politiker zu werden"', dated 1943.
8. See BAB, NS18/1235: 'Betrifft: Archiv der Persönlichkeiten'.
9. Werner Jochmann, ed., *Adolf Hitler: Monologe im Führerhauptquartier 1941–1944: Die Aufzeichnungen Heinrich Heims* (Hamburg, 1980), p. 355.
10. Henry Picker, *Hitlers Tischgespräche im Führerhauptquartier* (Munich, 2003), p. 480.
11. Riefenstahl, *Memoiren*, p. 367.
12. Jochmann, *Adolf Hitler*, p. 265.
13. Kurt Hesse, *Der Geist von Potsdam* (Mainz, 1967), p. 184.
14. For an overview of the verdict, see BAB, R109 I/1564: 'Filmpress: Der Text des Gerichtsurteils über Veit Harlan', 22 July 1950.

Bibliography

Archival Sources

Bundesarchiv Berlin (BAB)
Bundesarchiv Filmarchiv (BA FA)
Bundesarchiv Freiburg (BAF)
Bundesarchiv Koblenz (BAK)
Czech National Archives
Deutsche Kinemathek Berlin
Goebbels' Diaries (*GTB*, see Published Sources)
Haus-, Hof- und Staatsarchiv Wien
Institut für Zeitgeschichte, München (IfZ)
Landesarchiv Berlin (LAB)
Landesarchiv Nordrhein-Westfalen (LA NRW)
Library of Congress Washington
Politisches Archiv, Auswärtiges Amt (PA AA)
Staatsarchiv Freiburg (SAF)
Staatsarchiv Hamburg (SAH)
Staatsarchiv Wien
University of Southern California
Wiener Library

Published Sources

Adam, Christian. *Lesen unter Hitler: Autoren, Bestseller, Leser im Dritten Reich*. Frankfurt am Main, 2013.

Adams, Jefferson. *Historical Dictionary of German Intelligence*. Lanham, Toronto and Plymouth, 2009.

Ahren, Yizhak and Stig Hornshøj-Møller. *'Der Ewige Jude' oder wie Goebbels hetzte*. Aachen, 1990.

Albrecht, Gerd. *Nationalsozialistische Filmpolitik: Eine soziologische Untersuchung über die Spielfilme des Dritten Reichs*. Stuttgart, 1969.

d'Almeida, Fabrice. *High Society in the Third Reich*. Cambridge, 2008

Alt, Jörg. 'The Dictator as Spectator: Feature Film Screenings before Adolf Hitler, 1933–39.' *Historical Journal of Film, Radio and Television* 35:3 (2015), 420–37.

Ambesser, Axel von. *Nimm einen Namen mit A*. Frankfurt am Main and Berlin, 1985.

Amos, Robert. *Mythos Romy Schneider*. Munich, 2000.

Andersen, Lale. *Der Himmel hat viele Farben*. Munich, 1974.

Atkinson, Kate. *Life after Life*. London, 2013.

August, Wolf-Eberhard. *Die Stellung der Schauspieler im Dritten Reich*. Munich: PhD Dissertation, 1973.

Aurich, Rolf and Wolfgang Jacobsen, eds. *Ernst Jäger. Filmkritiker*. Berlin, 2006.

Avon, the Earl of. *The Eden Memoirs: Facing the Dictators*. London, 1962

Baarová, Lída. *Die süße Bitterkeit meines Lebens*. Koblenz, 2001.

Bach, Steven. *Leni: The Life and Work of Leni Riefenstahl*. London, 2007.

Barkhausen, Hans. 'Footnote to the History of Riefenstahl's "Olympia".' *Film Quarterly* 28:1 (1974), 8–12.

Barkhausen, Hans. *Filmpropaganda für Deutschland im Ersten und Zweiten Weltkrieg*. Hildesheim, Zurich and New York, 1982.

Bartov, Omer. *The 'Jew' in Cinema*. Bloomington and Indianapolis, 2005.

Baur, Hans. *I Was Hitler's Pilot: The Memoirs of Hans Baur*. Barnsley, 2013. Kindle Edition.

Becker, Wolfgang. *Film und Herrschaft: Organisationsprinzipien und Organisationsstrukturen der nationalsozialistischen Filmpropaganda*. Uelzen, 1973.

Beevor, Anthony. *The Mystery of Olga Chekhova*. London, 2005.

Belach, Helga. *Henny Porten: Der erste deutsche Filmstar 1890–1960*. Berlin, 1986.

Benz, Wolfgang. *'Der Ewige Jude': Metaphern und Methoden nationalsozialistischer Propaganda*. Berlin, 2010.

Besier, Gerhard. *Die Kirchen und das Dritte Reich: Spaltungen und Abwehrkämpfe 1934–1937*. Munich, 2001.

Beyer, Friedemann. *Schöner als der Tod: Das Leben der Sybille Schmitz*. Munich, 1998.

Beyer, Friedemann. *Der Fall Selpin: Chronik einer Denunziation*. Munich, 2011.

Bielenberg, Christabel. *The Past is Myself and The Road Ahead*. London, 2011.

Blumenberg, Hans-Christoph. *Das Leben geht weiter. Der letzte Film des Dritten Reichs*. Berlin, 1993.

Boberach, Heinz, ed. *Meldungen aus dem Reich: Die geheimen Lageberichte des Sicherheitsdienstes der SS 1938–1945*. Herrsching, 1984.

Boelcke, Willi A., ed. *Kriegspropaganda 1939–1941: Geheime Ministerkonferenzen im Reichspropagandaministerium*. Stuttgart, 1966.

Borgelt, Hans. *Das süßeste Mädel der Welt: Die Lilian Harvey Story*. Munich, 1976.

Bret, David. *Clark Gable: Tormented Star*. New York, 2007.

Brockmann, Ina and Peter Reichelt. *Leni Riefenstahl*. Mannheim, 2012.

Brückner, Wilhelm. 'Der Führer in seinem Privatleben.' In *Adolf Hitler: Bilder aus dem Leben des Führers*, edited by Heinrich Hoffmann. Altona/Bahrenfeld, 1936.

Bruns, Jana F. *Nazi Cinema's New Women*. Cambridge and New York, 2009.

Bruppacher, Paul. *Adolf Hitler und die Geschichte der NSDAP: Eine Chronik*. Norderstedt 2013.

Bucher, Peter. 'Die Bedeutung des Films als historische Quelle: "Der Ewige Jude" (1940).' In *Festschrift für Eberhard Kessel zum 75. Geburtstag*, edited by Heinz Duchhardt and Manfred Schlenke. 300–329. Munich, 1982.

Bucher, Peter. 'Goebbels und die Deutsche Wochenschau: Nationalsozialistische Filmpropaganda im Zweiten Weltkrieg, 1939–1945.' *Militärgeschichtliche Mitteilungen* 15:2 (1986), 53–69.

Burleigh, Michael. *Death and Deliverance: Euthanasia in Germany 1900–1945*. London, 2002.

Buruma, Ian. *Theater of Cruelty: Art, Film, and the Shadows of War*. New York, 2014.

Carr, Jonathan. *The Wagner Clan*. London, 2009.

Clark, Christopher. *Iron Kingdom: The Rise and Downfall of Prussia, 1600–1947*. London, 2006.

Clay Large, David. *Nazi Games: The Olympics of 1936*. New York and London, 2007.

Culbert, David and Martin Loiperdinger. 'Leni Riefenstahl's "Tag der Freiheit": the 1935 Nazi Party Rally Film.' *Historical Journal of Film, Radio and Television* 12:1 (1992), 3–40.

Cziffra, Géza von. *Es war eine rauschende Ballnacht*. Munich and Berlin, 1985.

Diehl, Paula. 'Opfer der Vergangenheit: Konstruktion eines Feindbildes'. In *Abgeschlossene Kapitel? Zur Geschichte der Konzentrationslager und der NS-Prozesse*, edited by Sabine Moller, Miriam Rürup, Christel Trouvé. 134–44. Tübingen, 2002.

Doherty, Thomas. *Hollywood and Hitler, 1933–1939*. New York, 2013.

Döhring, Herbert. *Hitlers Hausverwalter*. Bochum, 2013.

Domarus, Max. *Hitler: Reden 1932 bis 1945*. Wiesbaden, 1973.

Drewniak, Boguslaw. *Das Theater im NS-Staat: Szenarium deutscher Zeitgeschichte 1933–1945*. Düsseldorf, 1983.

Drewniak, Boguslaw. *Der deutsche Film 1938–1945*. Düsseldorf, 1987.

Drews, Berta. *Wohin des Wegs*. Munich and Vienna, 1986.

Eberle, Henrik and Matthias Uhl, eds. *Das Buch Hitler: Geheimdossier des NKWD für Josef W. Stalin*. Cologne, 2005.

Ebermayer, Erich. *'Denn heute gehört uns Deutschland . . .': Persönliches und politisches Tagebuch*. Hamburg and Vienna, 1959.

Ebermayer, Erich. *'. . . und morgen die ganze Welt': Erinnerungen an Deutschlands dunkle Zeit*. Bayreuth, 1966.

Eeghen, Isa van. '"*Lieux de mémoire*" Recycled: the Denazification of German Feature Films with a Historical Subject.' *European Review of History* 4:1 (1997), 45–71.

Engel, Gerhard. *Heeresadjutant bei Hitler 1938–1943: Aufzeichnungen des Majors Engel*, edited by Hildegard von Kotze. Stuttgart, 1974.

Engel, Kathrin. *Deutsche Kulturpolitik im besetzten Paris 1940–1944: Film und Theater*. Munich, 2003.

Erpel, Simone et al., eds. *Im Gefolge der SS: Aufseherinnen des Frauen-KZ Ravensbrück. Begleitband zur Ausstellung*. Berlin, 2007.

Evans, Richard. *The Third Reich in Power 1933–1939*. London, 2005.

Feuersenger, Marianne. *Mein Kriegstagebuch: Führerhauptquartier und Berliner Wirklichkeit*. Freiburg, Basle and Vienna, 1982.

Finck, Werner. *Der brave Soldat Finck*. Munich and Berlin, 1975.

Fischer, Klaus P. *Hitler and America*. Philadelphia, 2011.

Friedländer, Saul. *Nazi Germany and the Jews 1939–1945: The Years of Extermination*. New York, 2007.

Fröhlich, Gustav. *Waren das Zeiten: Mein Film-Heldenleben*. Munich and Berlin, 1983.

Fromm, Erich. *The Anatomy of Human Destructiveness*. New York, 2013.

Gaertringen, Hans Georg Hiller von. *Das Auge des Dritten Reiches: Walter Frentz – Hitlers Kameramann und Fotograf*. Berlin and Munich, 2006.

Garden, Ian. *Battling with the Truth: The Contrast in the Media Reporting of World War II*. Stroud, 2015.

Gedenkstätte Buchenwald, ed., *Buchenwald Concentration Camp, 1937–1945: A Guide to the Permanent Historical Exhibition*. Frankfurt am Main, 2004.

Gerwarth, Robert. *Hitler's Hangman: The Life of Heydrich*. New Haven, 2012.

Gibbels, Ellen. 'Hitlers Parkinson-Syndrom: Eine posthume Motilitätsanalyse in Filmaufnahmen der Deutschen Wochenschau.' *Der Nervenarzt* 59 (1988), 521–8.

Gibbels, Ellen. 'Hitlers Nervenkrankheit.' *Vierteljahreshefte für Zeitgeschichte* 42:2 (April 1994), 155–220.

Giesen, Rolf. *Nazi Propaganda Films: A History and Filmography.* Jefferson, NC, 2003.

Giesen, Rolf and J.P. Storm. *Animation under the Swastika: A History of Trickfilm in Nazi Germany, 1933–1945.* Jefferson, NC, 2012.

Giesen, Rolf and Manfred Hobsch. *Hitlerjunge Quex, Jud Süss und Kolberg: die Propagandafilme des Dritten Reiches. Dokumente und Materialien zum NS-Film.* Berlin, 2005.

Giordano, Ralph. *Erinnerung eines Davongekommenen: Die Autobiographie.* Cologne, 2007.

Goebbels, Joseph. *Das eherne Herz: Reden und Aufsätze aus den Jahren 1941/42.* Munich, 1942.

Goebbels, Joseph. *Die Tagebücher von Joseph Goebbels Online,* edited by Elke Fröhlich. Berlin, 2012. Online at http://www.degruyter.com/view/db/tjgo. Abbreviated in the text as *GTB.*

Graham, Cooper C. *Leni Riefenstahl and Olympia.* London, 1986.

Graham, Cooper C. '"Sieg im Westen" (1941): Interservice and Bureaucratic Propaganda Rivalries in Nazi Germany.' *Historical Journal of Film, Radio and Television* 9:1 (1989), 19–45.

Gruner, Wolf. *Jewish Forced Labour under the Nazis: Economic Needs and Racial Aims, 1938–1944.* Cambridge, 2008.

Hachmeister, Sylke. *Kinopropaganda gegen Kranke: Die Instrumentalisierung des Spielfilms 'Ich klage an' für das nationalsozialistische 'Euthanasieprogramm'.* Baden-Baden, 1992.

Hachtmann, Rüdiger. 'Arbeit und Arbeitsfront: Ideologie und Praxis.' In *Arbeit im Nationalsozialismus,* edited by Marc Buggeln und Michael Wildt. 87–106. Munich, 2014.

Hake, Sabine. *Popular Cinema of the Third Reich.* Austin, 2003.

Hamann, Brigitte. *Winifred Wagner oder Hitlers Bayreuth.* Munich and Zurich, 2002.

Hamann, Brigitte. *Winifred Wagner: A Life at the Heart of Hitler's Bayreuth.* London, 2005.

Hamburger Arbeitsstelle für deutsche Exilliteratur. 'Das Institut der "Spielerlaubnis mit Sondergenehmigung" im NS-Staat.' *exilOgraph* 5 (2000).

Hamdorf, Wolfgang Martin. *Zwischen ¡NO PASARAN! und ¡ARRIBA ESPAÑA!: Film und Propaganda im Spanischen Bürgerkrieg.* Münster, 1991.

Hanfstaengl, Ernst. *Zwischen Weißem und Braunem Haus.* Munich, 1970.

Harlan, Veit. *Im Schatten meiner Filme.* Gütersloh, 1966.

Haus der Geschichte Baden-Württemberg, ed. *'Jud Süss': Propagandafilm im NS-Staat.* Stuttgart, 2007.

Heesters, Johannes. *Ich bin gottseidank nicht mehr jung.* Munich, 1993.

Heiber, Helmut and David M. Glantz. *Hitler and his Generals: Military Conferences 1942–1945.* New York, 2002.

Hein, Bastian. *Volk und Führer? Die Allgemeine SS und ihre Mitglieder.* Munich, 2012.

Herf, Jeffrey. *The Jewish Enemy: Nazi Propaganda during World War II and the Holocaust.* Cambridge, 2008.

Herzstein, Robert Erwin. *The War that Hitler Won: The Most Infamous Propaganda Campaign in History.* New York, 1978.

Hesse, Kurt. *Der Geist von Potsdam.* Mainz, 1967.

Hiller von Gaertringen, Hans Georg, ed. *Das Auge des Dritten Reiches: Walter Frentz – Hitlers Kameramann und Fotograf.* Munich, 2006.

Hippler, Fritz. *Die Verstrickung.* Düsseldorf, 1981.

Hitler, Adolf. *Die Reden Hitlers am Reichsparteitag 1933.* Munich, 1934.

Hitler, Adolf. *Mein Kampf.* Translated by James Murphy. London, 1939.

Hitler, Adolf. *Mein Kampf.* Munich, 1943.

Hobsch, Manfred. *Film im 'Dritten Reich'.* Berlin, 2010.

Hoffmann, Heinrich. *Hitler Was My Friend: The Memoirs of Hitler's Photographer.* London, 2011.

Hoffmann, Karl-Heinz. '"Strassen der Zukunft": Die Reichsautobahnen.' In *Geschichte des dokumentarischen Films in Deutschland. Band 3: Drittes Reich, 1933–1945,* edited by Peter Zimmermann and Karlheinz Hoffmann. 276–86. Stuttgart, 2005.

Hollstein, Dorothea. *Antisemitische Filmpropaganda: Die Darstellung des Juden im national-sozialistischen Spielfilm.* Berlin, 1971.

Hombach, Jean-Pierre. *Serdar Somuncu 'Der neue Deutsche Kafka?'*. 2012.

Hörbiger, Paul. *Ich habe für Euch gespielt*. Frankfurt am Main and Berlin, 1989.

Horn, Camilla. *Verliebt in die Liebe: Erinnerungen*. Berlin, 1985.

Hornshøj-Møller, Stig. *'Der ewige Jude': Quellenkritische Analyse eines antisemitischen Propagandafilms*. Göttingen, 1995.

Hubmann, Hans. *Augenzeuge 1933–1945*. Munich and Berlin, 1980.

Hull, David Stewart. *Film in the Third Reich*. Berkeley and Los Angeles, 1969.

Infield, Glenn B. *Leni Riefenstahl: The Fallen Film Goddess*. New York, 1976.

Joachimsthaler, Anton. *Hitlers Liste: Ein Dokument persönlicher Beziehungen*. Munich, 2003.

Jochmann, Werner, ed. *Adolf Hitler: Monologe im Führerhauptquartier 1941–1944: Die Aufzeichnungen Heinrich Heims*. Hamburg, 1980.

Junge, Traudl. *Bis zur letzten Stunde*. Munich, 2003.

Kershaw, Ian. *Hitler: 1936–1945: Nemesis*. London, 2000.

Khlevniuk, Oleg V. *Stalin: New Biography of a Dictator*. New Haven, 2015.

Kinkel, Lutz. *Die Scheinwerferin: Leni Riefenstahl und das 'Dritte Reich'*. Hamburg and Vienna, 2002.

Kirkpatrick, Ivone. *The Inner Circle*. New York, 1959.

Klabunde, Anja. *Magda Goebbels: Annäherung an ein Leben*. Munich, 1999.

Klee, Ernst. *Kulturlexikon zum Dritten Reich: Wer war was vor und nach 1945*. Frankfurt am Main, 2009.

Kleinhans, Bernd. *Ein Volk, ein Reich, ein Kino*. Cologne, 2003.

Klöckner-Draga, Uwe. *Renate Müller: Ihr Leben, ein Drahtseilakt*. Bayreuth, 2006.

Knopp, Guido. *Hitlers Frauen und Marlene*. Munich, 2003.

Knopp, Guido. *Hitlers nützliche Idole: Wie Medienstars sich in den Dienst der NS-Propaganda stellten*. Munich, 2007.

Koepnick, Lutz. *Framing Attention: Windows on Modern German Culture*. Baltimore, 2007.

Köhler, Joachim. *Wagner's Hitler: The Prophet and his Disciple*. Cambridge, 2001.

Kohler, Pauline (John Beevor). *I Was Hitler's Maid*. London, 1940.

Koop, Volker. *Warum Hitler King Kong liebte, aber den Deutschen Micky Maus verbot: die geheimen Lieblingsfilme der Nazi-Elite*. Berlin, 2015.

Kracauer, Siegfried. *Von Caligari zu Hitler: Eine psychologische Geschichte des deutschen Films*. Frankfurt am Main, 1979.

Krause, Karl Wilhelm. *Im Schatten der Macht: Kammerdiener bei Hitler*, Bochum, 2011.

Kreimeier, Klaus. *Die UFA-Story: Geschichte eines Filmkonzerns*. Munich, 1995.

Kruse, Kuno. *Dolores and Imperio: Die drei Leben des Sylvin Rubinstein*. Cologne, 2003.

Kulka, Otto Dov and Eberhard Jäckel, eds. *Die Juden in den geheimen SS-Stimmungsberichten 1933–1945*. Düsseldorf, 2004.

Lang, Jochen von. *Der Sekretär: Martin Bormann, der Mann, der Hitler beherrschte*. Frankfurt am Main, 1980.

Larsen, Stein Ugelvik, Beatrice Sandberg and Volker Dahm, eds. *Meldungen aus Norwegen 1940–1945: Die geheimen Lageberichte des Befehlshabers der Sicherheitspolizei und des SD in Norwegen*. Munich, 2008.

Leander, Zarah. *Es war so wunderbar! Mein Leben*. Hamburg, 1973.

Leiser, Erwin. *'Deutschland erwache!' Propaganda im Film des Dritten Reichs*. Hamburg, 1968.

Lewinski, Heinrich. *'Eine biographische Skizze.'* In *Ernst Jäger. Filmkritiker*, edited by Rolf Aurich and Wolfgang Jacobsen. Berlin, 2006.

Linge, Heinz. *Bis zum Untergang: Als Chef des Persönlichen Dienstes bei Hitler*, edited by Werner Maser. Munich, 1980.

Loiperdinger, Martin, ed. *Märtyrerlegenden im NS-Film*. Opladen, 1991.

Longerich, Peter. *The Unwritten Order: Hitler's Role in the Final Solution*. Stroud, 2001.

Longerich, Peter. *Goebbels: Biographie*. Munich, 2012.

Longerich, Peter. *Hitler: Biographie*. Munich, 2015. Kindle Edition.

Löw, Andrea, ed. *Die Verfolgung und Ermordung der europäischen Juden durch das nationalsozialistische Deutschland 1933–1945: Deutsches Reich und Protektorat, September 1939–September 1941*. Munich, 2012.

Maiwald, Klaus-Jürgen. *Filmzensur im NS-Staat*. Dortmund, 1983.

Mannes, Stefan. *Antisemitismus im nationalsozialistischen Propagandafilm: Jud Süß und Der Ewige Jude*. Cologne, 1999.

Marquardt, Axel and Heinz Rathsack, eds. *Preußen im Film: Eine Retrospektive der Stiftung Deutsche Kinemathek*. Hamburg, 1981.

Martin, Benjamin George. ' "European Cinema for Europe!" The International Film Chamber, 1935–42.' In *Cinema and the Swastika: The International Expansion of Third Reich Cinema*, edited by Roel Vande Winkel and David Welch. 25–14. Basingtoke, 2011.

Maser, Werner. *Hitlers Briefe und Notizen. Sein Weltbild in handschriftlichen Dokumenten*. Düsseldorf and Vienna, 1973.

Maser, Werner, ed. *Mein Schüler Hitler: Das Tagebuch seines Lehrers Paul Devrient*. Pfaffenhofen, 1975.

Maser, Werner. *Heinrich George: Mensch aus Erde gemacht*. Berlin, 1998.

Matthäus, Jürgen and Frank Bajohr, eds. *Alfred Rosenberg: Die Tagebücher von 1934 bis 1944*. Frankfurt am Main, 2015.

Misch, Rochus. *Der Letzte Zeuge: Ich war Hitlers Telefonist, Kurier und Leibwächter*. Munich, 2009.

Moeller, Felix. *Der Filmminister: Goebbels und der Film im Dritten Reich*. Berlin, 1998.

Moeller, Felix. *The Film Minister: Goebbels and the Cinema in the Third Reich*. Stuttgart and London, 2000.

Moltke, Johannes von. *No Place Like Home: Locations of Heimat in German Cinema*. Berkeley, Los Angeles and London, 2005.

Moorhouse, Roger. *Killing Hitler: The Third Reich and the Plots against the Führer*. London, 2006.

Motl, Stanislav. *Lída Baarová, Joseph Goebbels: Die verfluchte Liebe einer tschechischen Schauspielerin und des Stellvertreters des Teufels*. Prague, 2009.

Musial, Bogdan. *Deutsche Zivilverwaltung und Judenverfolgung im Generalgouvernement: Eine Fallstudie zum Distrikt Lublin 1939–1944*. Wiesbaden, 1999.

Negri, Pola. *Memories of a Star*. New York, 1970.

Neumann, Hans-Joachim and Henrik Eberle. *War Hitler krank: Ein abschließender Befund*. Cologne, 2009.

Nickel, Gunther. *Zur Diskussion: Zuckmayers 'Geheimreport'*. Göttingen, 2002.

Nielsen, Asta. *Die schweigende Muse: Das leidenschaftlich bewegte Leben des großen Stummfilmstars*. Munich, 1979.

Nimmervoll, Paulus. 'Das Zisterzienserstift Wilhering zur Zeit des Nationalsozialismus (1938–1945).' *Jahresbericht Wilhering* 60 (1969/70), 18–73.

Noa, Wolfgang. *Paul Wegener*. Berlin, 1964.

Nolzen, Armin. ' "Hier sieht man den Juden, wie er wirklich ist . . .": Die Rezeption des Filmes Jud Süß in der deutschen Bevölkerung.' In *'Jud Süß': Hofjude, literarische Figur, antisemitisches Zerrbild*, edited by Alexandra Przyrembel and Jörg Schönert. 245–262. Frankfurt am Main and New York, 2006.

O'Brien, Mary-Elizabeth. *Nazi Cinema as Enchantment: The Politics of Entertainment in the Third Reich*. Rochester, 2004.

Pages, Neil Christian, Mary Rhiel and Ingeborg Majer-O'Sickey. *Riefenstahl Screened: An Anthology of New Criticism*. New York and London, 2008.

Picker, Henry. *Hitlers Tischgespräche im Führerhauptquartier*. Munich, 2003.

Pilgrim, Volker Elis, *Hitler 1 und Hitler 2*. Hamburg, 2017.

Pitzer, Andrea. *The Secret History of Vladimir Nabokov*. Cambridge, 2013.

Plaim, Anna and Kurt Kuch. *Bei Hitler: Zimmermädchen Annas Erinnerungen*. Munich, 2005.

Preston, Paul. *The Spanish Civil War: Reaction, Revolution and Revenge*. London and New York, 2006.

Przyrembel, Alexandra and Jörg Schönert, eds. *'Jud Süß': Hofjude, literarische Figur, antisemitisches Zerrbild*. Frankfurt am Main and New York, 2006.

Pyta, Wolfgang. *Hitler: Der Künstler als Politiker und Feldherr*. Munich, 2015.

Raim, Edith. *Zwischen Diktatur und Demokratie*. Munich, 2013.

Rathkolb, Oliver. *Führertreu und Gottbegnadet: Künstlereliten im Dritten Reich*. Vienna, 1991.

Reichelt, Peter. 'Der Sieg des Glaubens 1933: Der Nachdreh oder: Wie wichtige Reden des Reichsparteitages 1933 in Nürnberg durch die Regisseurin Riefenstahl in einem Berliner Filmstudio für das Kino neu inszeniert wurden.' In *Leni Riefenstahl*, edited by Ina Brockmann and Peter Reichelt. 56–64. Mannheim, 2012.

Riefenstahl, Leni. *Hinter den Kulissen des Reichsparteitages*. Munich, 1935.

Riefenstahl, Leni. *Memoiren*. Cologne, 2000.

Riess, Curt. *Das gab's nur einmal: Das Buch der schönsten Filme unseres Lebens*. Hamburg, 1956.

Rökk, Marika. *Herz mit Paprika*. Munich, 1976.

Rosenberg, Alfred. *Die Tagebücher von 1934 bis 1944*, edited by Jürgen Matthäus and Frank Bajohr. Frankfurt am Main, 2015.

Rosenberg, Rudy. *And Somehow We Survive*. Bloomington, IN, 2008.

Rosendorfer, Herbert. *Bayreuth für Anfänger*. Munich, 1984.

Rost, Karl Ludwig. *Sterilisation und Euthanasie im Film des 'Dritten Reichs'*. Husum, 1987.

Roth, Karl Heinz. 'Filmpropaganda für die Vernichtung der Geisteskranken und Behinderten im Dritten Reich.' In *Reform und Gewissen, 'Euthanasie' im Dienst des Fortschritts*, edited by Götz Aly et al. 125–93. Berlin, 1989.

Roth, Karl Heinz. ' "Ich Klage an": Aus der Entstehungsgeschichte eines Propaganda-Films.' In *Aktion T4 1939–1945: Die 'Euthanasie'-Zentrale in der Tiergartenstraße 4*, edited by Götz Aly. 92–119. Berlin, 1989.

Rother, Rainer. *Leni Riefenstahl: Die Verführung des Talents*. Berlin, 2000.

Rühmann, Heinz. *Das war's: Erinnerungen*. Frankfurt am Main, 1995.

Rupnow, Dirk. *Vernichten und Erinnern: Spuren nationalsozialistischer Gedächtnispolitik*. Göttingen, 2005.

Ryback, Timothy. *Hitler's Private Library: The Books that Shaped his Life*. London, 2010.

Salkeld, Audrey. *Portrait of Leni Riefenstahl*. London, 1997.

Sandner, Harald. *Hitler: Das Itinerar. Aufenthaltsorte und Reisen von 1889 bis 1945*. Berlin, 2016.

Sarfatti, Michele. *The Jews in Mussolini's Italy: From Equality to Persecution*. Madison, 2006.

Sarkowicz, Hans, ed. *Hitlers Künstler: Die Kultur im Dienst des Nationalsozialismus*. Frankfurt am Main and Leipzig, 2004.

Schaub, Julius. *In Hitlers Schatten: Erinnerungen und Aufzeichnungen des persönlichen Adjutanten und Vertrauten 1925–1945*. Stegen-Ammersee, 2010.

Schlenker, Ines. *Hitler's Salon: The Große Deutsche Kunstausstellung at the Haus der Deutschen Kunst in Munich 1937–1944*. Bern, 2007.

Schmeling, Max. *Erinnerungen*. Frankfurt am Main and Berlin, 1977.

Schmidt, Paul. *Statist auf diplomatischer Bühne 1923–45*. Bonn, 1949.

Schmitt, Carl. 'Der Führer schützt das Recht.' *Deutsche Juristen-Zeitung* 15 (1934), 945–50.

Schmitt, Walther, ed. *Die Reden Hitlers am Reichsparteitag 1933*. Munich, 1934.

Schoenhals, Albrecht and Anneliese Born. *Immer zu zweit: Erinnerungen*. Wiesbaden and Munich, 1977.

Schroeder, Christa. *Er war mein Chef*. Munich, 2002.

Schwarz, Birgit. *Geniewahn: Hitler und die Kunst*. Vienna, 2011.

Semler, Daniel. *Brigitte Helm: Der Vamp des deutschen Films*. Munich, 2008.

Short, K.R.M. and Stephan Dolezel. *Hitler's Fall: The Newsreel Witness*. London, New York and Sydney, 1988.

Singer, Claude. *Le Juif Süss et la Propagandie nazie*. Paris, 2003.

Sozialdemokratische Partei Deutschlands (SPD). *Deutschland-Berichte der Sozialdemokratischen Partei Deutschlands (Sopade) 1934–1940*. Salzhausen and Frankfurt am Main, 1980.

Speer, Albert. *Erinnerungen*. Berlin, 1995.

Speer, Albert. *Inside the Third Reich*. London, 2003.

Spieker, Markus. *Hollywood unterm Hakenkreuz: Der amerikanische Spielfilm im Dritten Reich.* Trier, 1999.

Spotts, Frederic. *Hitler and the Power of Aesthetics*. London, 2003.

Stahr, Gerhard. *Volksgemeinschaft vor der Leinwand? Der nationalsozialistische Film und sein Publikum*. Berlin, 2001.

Steiner, John M. and Jobst Freiherr von Cornberg. 'Willkür in der Willkür: Befreiungen von den antisemitischen Nürnberger Gesetzen.' *Vierteljahreshefte für Zeitgeschichte* 46:2 (April 1998), 143–88.

Steiner, Maria. *Paula Wessely: Die verdrängten Jahre*. Vienna, 1996.

Steinhoff, Johannes, ed. *Deutsche im Zweiten Weltkrieg: Zeitzeugen sprechen*. Munich, 1989.

Steinweis, Alan E. *Art, Ideology, and Economics in Nazi Germany: The Reich Chambers of Music, Theater, and the Visual Arts*. Chapel Hill and London, 1993.

Stern, Carola. *Auf den Wassern des Lebens: Gustaf Gründgens und Marianne Hoppe*. Cologne, 2005.

Stratigakos, Despina. *Hitler at Home*. New Haven and London, 2015.

Streicher, Julius, ed. *Reichstagung in Nürnberg 1933*. Berlin, 1934.

Tabori, Paul, ed. *The Private Life of Adolf Hitler: The Intimate Notes and Diary of Eva Braun*. New York and Tokyo, 2014.

Taylor, Richard. *Film Propaganda: Soviet Russia and Nazi Germany*. London and New York, 2006.

Tegel, Susan. 'Veit Harlan and the Origins of "Jud Süss".' *Historical Journal of Film, Radio and Television* 16:4 (1996), 515–31.

Tegel, Susan. *Nazis and the Cinema*. London, 2008.

Tegel, Susan. *Jew Süss: Life, Legend, Fiction, Film*. London, 2011.

Tesch, Sebastian. *Albert Speer: Hitlers Architekten*. Cologne, 2016.

Traub, Hans. *Der Film als politisches Machtmittel*. Munich, 1933.

Trenker, Luis. *Alles gut gegangen: Geschichten aus meinem Leben*. Munich, 1974.

Trimborn, Jürgen. *Der Herr im Frack: Johannes Heesters*. Berlin, 2003.

Trimborn, Jürgen. *Leni Riefenstahl: A Life*. New York, 2008.

Trimborn, Jürgen. *Romy und ihre Familie*. Munich, 2008.

Trimborn, Jürgen. 'Ein Meister der subjektiven Kamera: Karriere im Windschatten Leni Riefenstahls.' In *Das Auge des Dritten Reiches: Walter Frentz – Hitlers Kameramann und Fotograf*, edited by Hans Georg Hiller von Gaertringen. 69–81. Augsburg, 2009.

Tschechowa, Olga. *Meine Uhren gehen anders*. Munich and Berlin, 1973.

Uhlig, Anneliese. *Rosenkavaliers Kind: Eine Frau und drei Karrieren*. Munich, 1977.

Ullrich, Luise. *Komm auf die Schaukel, Luise: Balance eines Lebens*. Munich, 1990.

Urwand, Ben. *The Collaboration: Hollywood's Pact with Hitler*. Cambridge, MA, and London, 2013.

Uziel, Daniel. *The Propaganda Warriors: The Wehrmacht and the Consolidation of the German Home Front*. Berne, 2008.

Uziel, Daniel. 'Wehrmacht Propaganda Troops and the Jews.' Shoah Resource Centre at http://www.yadvashem.org/odot_pdf/Microsoft%20Word%20-%202021.pdf (accessed 1 May 2017).

Vande Winkel, Roel and David Welch, eds. *Cinema and the Swastika: The International Expansion of Third Reich Cinema*. Basingstoke, 2011.

Velten, Andreas-Michael and Matthias Klein, eds. *Chaplin und Hitler: Materialien zu einer Ausstellung*. Munich, 1989.

Waite, Robert G. L. *The Psychopathic God: Adolf Hitler*. Boston, 1993.

Ward, Richard Lewis. *A History of the Hal Roach Studios*. Illinois, 2006.

Welch, David. *Propaganda and the German Cinema 1933–1945*. London and New York, 2001.

Welch, David. *The Third Reich: Politics and Propaganda*. London and New York, 2006.

Wendtland, Helga and Karl-Heinz Wendtland. *Geliebter Kintopp. Sämtliche deutsche Spielfilme von 1929–1945 mit zahlreichen Künstlerbiographien*. Berlin, 1988.

Weniger, Kay. *Zwischen Bühne und Baracke: Lexikon der verfolgten Theater-, Film- und Musikkünstler 1933–1945*. Berlin, 2008.

Werner, Ilse. *So wird's nie wieder sein: Ein Leben mit Pfiff!* Kiel, 1991.

Wetzel, Kraft and Peter Hagemann. *Zensur: Verbotene deutsche Filme 1933–1945*. Berlin, 1978.

Wiedemann, Fritz. *Der Mann, der Feldherr werden wollte*. Wuppertal, 1964.

Wieland, Karin. *Dietrich und Riefenstahl: Der Traum von der neuen Frau*. Munich, 2011.

Witte, Karsten. *Lachende Erben, Toller Tag: Filmkomödie im Dritten Reich*. Berlin, 1995.

Witte, Karsten. 'Film im Nationalsozialismus.' In *Geschichte des deutschen Films. Zweite Auflage*, edited by Wolfgang Jacobsen, Anton Kaes and Hans Helmut Prinzler. 119–71. Stuttgart, 2004.

Witte, Peter, Michael Wildt, Martina Voigt et al., eds. *Der Dienstkalender Heinrich Himmlers 1941/42*. Hamburg, 1999.

Wulf, Joseph. *Theater und Film im Dritten Reich: Eine Dokumentation*. Frankfurt am Main, Berlin and Vienna, 1983.

Zelnhefer, Siegfried. *Die Reichsparteitage der NSDAP in Nürnberg*. Nuremberg, 2002.

Zimmermann, Peter and Kay Hoffmann. *Geschichte des dokumentarischen Films in Deutschland: 'Drittes Reich', 1933–1945*. Stuttgart, 2005.

Zöberlein, Hans. *Der Glaube an Deutschland*. Munich, 1931.

Zuckmayer, Carl. *Briefe an Hans Schiebelhuth 1921–1936*. Göttingen, 2003.

Filmography

Abel with the Mouth Organ (*Abel mit der Mundharmonika*). 1933. Dir. Erich Waschneck. Germany.

Above All Else in the World (*Über alles in der Welt*). 1941. Dir. Karl Ritter. Germany.

Alarm in Peking. 1937. Dir. Herbert Selpin. Germany.

Alert in the Mediterranean (*Alerte en Méditerranée*). 1938. Dir. Léo Joannon. France.

A Mad Idea (*Ein toller Einfall*). 1932. Dir. Kurt Gerron. Germany.

And Sudden Death. 1936. Dir. Charles Barton. United States.

Annelie. 1941. Dir. Josef von Báky. Germany.

Baptism of Fire (*Feuertaufe*). 1940. Dir. Hans Bertram. Germany.

Barcarole. 1935. Dir. Gerhard Lamprecht. Germany.

Bengasi. 1942. Dir. Augusto Genina. Italy.

Bismarck. 1940. Dir. Wolfgang Liebeneiner. Germany.

Block-Heads. 1938. Dir. John G. Blystone. United States.

Bluebeard's Eighth Wife. 1938. Dir. Ernst Lubitsch. United States.

Border Fire (*Grenzfeuer*). 1939. Dir. Luis Trenker. Germany.

Breakfast in Bed. 1930. Dir. Fred Guiol. United States.

By a Silken Thread (*Am seidenen Faden*). 1938. Dir. Robert A. Stemmle. Germany.

Cadets (*Kadetten*). 1939. Dir. Karl Ritter. Germany.

Camille (*Die Kameliendame*). 1936. Dir. George Cukor. United States.

Campaign in Poland (*Feldzug in Polen*). 1940. Dir. Fritz Hippler. Germany.

Capriccio. 1938. Dir. Karl Ritter. Germany.

Captain January. 1936. Dir. David Butler. United States.

Carl Peters. 1941. Dir. Herbert Selpin. Germany.

Cavalcade. 1933. Dir. Frank Lloyd. USA.

Cheeky Devil (*Der Frechdachs*). 1932. Dir. Carl Boese and Heinz Hille. Germany.

Condottieri. 1937. Dir. Luis Trenker. Germany.

Dance on the Volcano (*Tanz auf dem Vulkan*). 1938. Dir. Hans Steinhoff. Germany.

Dawn (*Morgenrot*). 1933. Dir. Gustav Ucicky. Germany.

281

Day of Freedom: Our Wehrmacht (*Tag der Freiheit: Unsere Wehrmacht*). 1935. Dir. Leni Riefenstahl. Germany.

Detours to Happiness (*Umwege zum Glück*). 1939. Dir. Fritz Peter Buch. Germany.

Doctor Crippen. 1942. Dir. Erich Engels. Germany.

Don't Lose Heart, Suzanne (*Nur nicht weich werden, Susanne!*). 1935. Dir. Arzén von Cserépy. Germany.

Emil and the Detectives (*Emil und die Detektive*). 1931. Dir. Gerhard Lamprecht. Germany.

Faded Melody (*Verklungene Melodie*). 1938. Dir. Viktor Tourjansky. Germany.

Faust. 1926. Dir. F.W. Murnau. Germany.

Festive Nuremberg (*Festliches Nürnberg*). 1937. Dir. Hans Weidemann. Germany.

Fools in the Snow (*Narren im Schnee*). 1938. Dir. Hans Deppe. Germany.

Four Apprentices (*Die vier Gesellen*). 1938. Dir. Carl Froelich. Germany.

Fridericus. 1937. Dir. Johannes Meyer. Germany.

Friedrich Schiller – The Triumph of a Genius (*Friedrich Schiller – Der Triumph eines Genies*). 1940. Dir. Herbert Maisch. Germany.

Frisians in Distress (*Friesennot*). 1935. Dir. Peter Hagen. Germany.

Fury. 1936. Dir. Fritz Lang. United States.

Gabriel over the White House. 1933. Dir. Gregory La Cava. USA.

George. 2013. Dir. Joachim A. Lang. Germany.

Germanin: The Story of a Colonial Deed (*Germanin: Die Geschichte einer kolonialen Tat*). 1943. Dir. Max W. Kimmich. Germany.

Germany Awakens! (*Deutschland erwacht!*). 1933. Dir. Arnold Raether. Germany.

Girls in Uniform (*Mädchen in Uniform*). 1931. Dir. Leontine Sagan and Carl Froelich. Germany.

Give Us This Night. 1936. Dir. Alexander Hall. United States.

Gold. 1934. Dir. Karl Hartl. Germany.

Gone with the Wind. Dir. Victor Fleming, George Cukor, and Sam Wood. 1939. United States.

Hans Westmar. 1933. Dir. Franz Wenzler. Germany.

Hello Janine (*Hallo Janine!*). 1939. Dir. Carl Boese. Germany.

Heroes in Spain (*Helden in Spanien/España heroica*). 1938. Dir. Fritz C. Mauch et al. Germany/Spain.

Hindenburg. 1934. Germany.

Hitler Youth Quex (*Hitlerjunge Quex*). 1933. Dir. Hans Steinhoff. Germany.

Homecoming (*Heimkehr*). 1941. Dir. Gustav Ucicky. Germany.

I Accuse (*Ich klage an*). 1941. Dir. Wolfgang Liebeneiner. Germany.

I'll Be Back in a Minute (*Ich bin gleich wieder da*). 1939. Dir. Peter Paul Brauer. Germany.

I Love You (*Ich liebe Dich*). 1938. Dir. Herbert Selpin. Germany.

In Battle against the World Enemy: German Volunteers in Spain (*Im Kampf gegen den Weltfeind: Deutsche Freiwillige in Spanien*). 1939. Karl Ritter. Germany.

Jakko. 1941. Dir. Fritz Peter Buch. Germany.

Jew Süss (*Jud Süß*). 1940. Dir. Veit Harlan. Germany.

Jew Suss: Rise and Fall (*Jud Süß – Film ohne Gewissen*). 2010. Dir. Oskar Roehler. Germany.

Jews Unmasked (*Juden ohne Maske*). 1937. Dir. Walter Böttcher and Leo von der Schmiede. Germany.

King Kong. 1933. Dir. Merian C. Cooper and Ernest B. Schoedsack.

Kolberg. 1945. Dir. Veit Harlan. Germany.

Leave on Word of Honour (*Urlaub auf Ehrenwort*). 1938. Dir. Karl Ritter. Germany.

Life Can Be So Wonderful (*Das Leben kann so schön sein*). 1938. Dir. Rolf Hansen. Germany.

Life Goes On (*Das Leben geht weiter*). Unfinished. Dir. Wolfgang Liebeneiner. Germany.

Linen from Ireland (*Leinen aus Irland*). 1939. Dir. Heinz Helbig. Germany.

Little County Court (*Kleines Bezirksgericht*). 1938. Dir. Alwin Elling. Germany.

Lowlands (*Tiefland*). 1954. Dir. Leni Riefenstahl. Germany.

M. 1931. Dir. Fritz Lang. Germany.

Mad Girl (*Quelle drôle de gosse*). 1935. Dir. Léo Joannon. France.
Mario. 1936. Italy.
Masquerade (*Maskerade*). 1934. Dir. Willi Forst. Germany.
Mazurka. 1935. Dir. Willi Forst. Germany.
Meiseken. 1937. Dir. Hans Deppe. Germany.
Mirror of Life (*Spiegel des Lebens*). 1938. Dir. Géza von Bolváry. Germany.
Monte Carlo Madness (*Bomben auf Monte Carlo*). 1931. Dir. Hanns Schwarz. Germany.
Moscow–Shanghai (*Der Weg nach Shanghai*). 1936. Dir. Paul Wegener. Germany.
Mother and Child (*Mutter und Kind*). 1924. Dir. Carl Froelich. Germany.
Mother and Child (*Mutter und Kind*). 1934. Dir. Hans Steinhoff. Germany.
Mother Love (*Mutterliebe*). 1939. Dir. Gustav Ucicky. Germany.
My Life for Ireland (*Mein Leben für Irland*). 1941. Dir. Max W. Kimmich. Germany.
Nights in Andalusia (*Andalusische Nächte*). 1938. Dir. Herbert Maisch. Germany.
Now and Forever. 1936. Dir. Henry Hathaway. United States.
Old Heart Goes on a Journey (*Altes Herz geht auf die Reise*). 1938. Dir. Carl Junghans.
Olympia. 1938. Dir. Leni Riefenstahl. Germany.
Onward Spain (*Arriba España*). 1938. Germany
Operation Michael (*Unternehmen Michael*). 1937. Dir. Karl Ritter. Germany.
Our Führer (*Unser Führer*). 1934. Germany.
Paracelsus. 1943. Dir. G.W. Pabst. Germany.
Pettersson & Bendel. 1933. Dir. Per-Axel Branner. Sweden.
Pour le Mérite. 1938. Dir. Karl Ritter. Germany.
Princess Sissy (*Prinzessin Sissy*). 1938. Dir. Fritz Thiery. Austria.
Prosperity Crooks (*Konjunkturritter,* or *Geld wie Heu*). 1934. Dir. Fritz Kampers. Germany.
Refugees (*Flüchtlinge*). 1933. Dir. Gustav Ucicky. Germany.
Rembrandt. 1942. Dir. Hans Steinhoff. Germany.
Request Concert (*Wunschkonzert*). 1940. Dir. Eduard von Borsody. Germany.
Robert and Bertram (*Robert und Bertram*). 1939. Dir. Hans Zerlett. Germany.
Robert Koch (*Robert Koch, der Bekämpfer des Todes*). 1939. Dir. Hans Steinhoff. Germany.
Robin Hood of El Dorado. 1936. Dir. William A. Wellmann. United States.
Sacrifice of Honour (*Veille d'armes*). 1935. Dir. Marcel L'Herbier. France.
Samson. 1936. Dir. Maurice Tourneur. France.
Scipio Africanus (*Scipione l'africano*). 1937. Dir. Carmine Gallone. Italy.
Shock Troop 1917 (*Stoßtrupp 1917*). 1934. Dir. Hans Zöberlein and Ludwig Schmid-Wildy.
  Germany.
Snow White and the Seven Dwarfs. 1937. Dir. David Hand et al. United States.
So Red the Rose. 1935. Dir. King Vidor. United States.
SOS Iceberg (*SOS Eisberg*). 1933. Dir. Arnold Fanck. Germany.
Storm over Mont Blanc (*Stürme über dem Mont Blanc*). 1930. Dir. Arnold Fanck. Germany.
Storm Trooper Brand (*S.A.-Mann Brand*). 1933. Dir. Franz Seitz. Germany.
Stormy. 1935. Dir. Louis Friedlander. United States.
Strong Hearts (*Starke Herzen*). 1937. Dir. Herbert Maisch. Germany.
Such a Rascal (*So ein Flegel*). 1934. Dir. Robert A. Stemmle. Germany.
Swiss Miss. 1938. Dir. John G. Blystone. United States.
Tabu: A Story of the South Seas. 1931. Dir. F.W. Murnau. United States.
The Atlantic Wall (*Atlantik-Wall*). 1944. Dir. Arnold Fanck. Germany.
The Blue Angel (*Der blaue Engel*). 1930. Dir. Josef von Sternberg. Germany.
The Blue Light (*Das blaue Licht*). 1932. Dir. Leni Riefenstahl and Béla Balázs. Germany.
The Book of the Germans (*Das Buch der Deutschen*). 1936. Dir. Richard Skowronnek. Germany.
The Brighton Twins (*Les Jumeaux de Brighton*). 1936. Dir. Claude Heymann. France.
The Broken Jug (*Der zerbrochene Krug*). 1937. Dir. Gustav Ucicky. Germany.
The Dark Angel. 1935. Dir. Sidney Franklin. United States.

The Dismissal (*Die Entlassung*). 1942. Dir. Wolfgang Liebeneiner. Germany.

The Dreamer (*Traumulus*). 1936. Dir. Carl Froelich. Germany.

The Eternal Jew (*Der ewige Jude*). 1940. Dir. Fritz Hippler. Germany.

The Eternal Mask (*Die ewige Maske*). 1935. Dir. Werner Hochbaum. Germany.

The Fathers' Sins (*Die Sünden der Väter*). 1935. Dir. Rassenpolitisches Amt der NSDAP. Germany.

The Fire-Devil (*Feuerteufel*). 1940. Dir. Luis Trenker. Germany.

The Florentine Hat (*Der Florentiner Hut*). 1939. Dir. Wolfgang Liebeneiner. Germany.

The Flute Concert of Sans-Souci (*Das Flötenkonzert von Sans-Souci*). 1930. Dir. Gustav Ucicky. Germany.

The Fox of Glenarvon (*Der Fuchs von Glenarvon*). 1940. Dir. Max W. Kimmich. Germany.

The Führer Builds his Reich Capital (*Der Führer baut seine Hauptstadt*). Unfinished. Dir. Leni Riefenstahl. Germany.

The Führer Gifts the Jews a Town (*Der Führer schenkt den Juden eine Stadt*). 1944. Dir. Kurt Gerron. Germany. (Also known as *Theresienstadt: A Documentary Film of the Jewish Resettlement*.)

The Gambler (*Der Spieler*). 1938. Dir. Gerhard Lamprecht. Germany.

The German East (*Ostraum – Deutscher Raum*). Dir. Werner Buhre. 1940. Germany.

The Golem: How He Came into the World (*Der Golem, wie er in die Welt kam*). 1920. Dir. Paul Wegener and Carl Boese. Germany.

The Great Dictator. 1940. Dir. Charlie Chaplin. United States.

The Great Gambini. 1937. Dir. Charles Vidor. United States.

The Great King (*Der Große König*). 1942. Dir. Veit Harlan. Germany.

The Great Leap (*Der große Sprung*). 1927. Dir. Arnold Fanck. Germany.

The Great Love (*Die große Liebe*). 1942. Dir. Rolf Hansen. Germany.

The Great Time (*Die große Zeit*). 1938. Dir. Carl Junghans, Gert Stegemann. Germany.

The Heart of the Queen (*Das Herz der Königin*). 1940. Dir. Carl Froelich. Germany.

The Hereditary Defective (*Erbkrank*). 1936. Dir. Herbert Gerdes. Germany.

The Higher Order (*Der höhere Befehl*). 1935. Dir. Gerhard Lamprecht. Germany.

The Holy Mountain (*Der heilige Berg*). 1926. Dir. Arnold Fanck. Germany.

The Hound of the Baskervilles (*Der Hund von Baskerville*). 1937. Dir. Carl Lamac. Germany.

The Hound of the Baskervilles. 1939. Dir. Sidney Lanfield. United States.

The Immortal Heart (*Das unsterbliche Herz*). 1939. Dir. Veit Harlan. Germany.

The Inheritance (*Das Erbe*). 1935. Dir. Harold Mayer. Germany.

The Jungle Princess. 1936. Dir. Wilhelm Thiele. United States.

The Lion Has Wings. 1939. Dir. Michael Powell et al. United Kingdom.

The Love Nest. 1933. Dir. Thomas Bentley. United Kingdom.

The Nibelungs (*Die Nibelungen*). 1924. Dir. Fritz Lang. Germany.

The Old and the Young King (*Der alte und der junge König*). 1935. Dir. Hans Steinhoff. Germany.

The Plainsman. 1936. Dir. Cecil B. DeMille. United States.

The Punch Bowl (*Die Feuerzangenbowle*). 1944. Dir. Helmut Weiss. Germany.

The Red Terror (*G.P.U.*). 1942. Dir. Karl Ritter. Germany.

Theresienstadt: A Documentary Film of the Jewish Resettlement (*Theresienstadt: Ein Dokumentarfilm aus dem jüdischen Siedlungsgebiet*). 1944. Dir. Kurt Gerron. Germany. (Also known as *The Führer Gifts the Jews a Town*.)

The Return of Sophie Lang. 1936. Dir. George Archainbaud. United States.

The Rider on the White Horse (*Der Schimmelreiter*). 1934. Dir. Hans Deppe and Curt Oertel. Germany.

The Rothschilds (*Die Rothschilds*). 1940. Dir. Erich Waschneck. Germany.

The Ruler (*Der Herrscher*). 1937. Dir. Veit Harlan. Germany.

The Scourge of the World (*Die Geißel der Welt*). 1936. Dir. Hans Weidemann and Carl Junghans. Germany.

The Siege of the Alcazar (*L'Assedio dell'Alcazar*). 1940. Dir. Augusto Genina. Italy.

The Stars of Variety (*Menschen vom Varieté*). 1939. Dir. Josef von Báky. Germany.

The Testament of Dr. Mabuse (*Das Testament des Dr. Mabuse*). 1933. Dir. Fritz Lang. Germany.

The West Wall (*Der Westwall*). 1939. Dir. Fritz Hippler. Germany.

The White Ecstasy (*Der Weiße Rausch*). 1931. Dir. Arnold Fanck. Germany.

The Young Forest (*Młody Las*). 1934. Dir. Józef Lejtes. Poland.

Tip-Off Girls. 1938. Dir. Louis King. United States.

Togger. 1937. Dir. Jürgen von Alten. Germany.

Traitors (*Verräter*). 1936. Dir. Karl Ritter. Germany.

Triumph of the Will (*Triumph des Willens*). 1935. Dir. Leni Riefenstahl. Germany.

U Boats Westwards (*U-Boote westwärts*). 1941. Dir. Günther Rittau. Germany.

Uncle Krüger (*Ohm Krüger*). 1941. Dir. Hans Steinhoff. Germany.

Unworthy Life (*Unwertes Leben*). 1939. Dir. Rassenpolitisches Amt der NSDAP. Germany.

Victims of the Past (*Opfer der Vergangenheit*). 1937. Dir. Gernot Bock-Stieber. Germany.

Victory in the West (*Sieg im Westen*). 1941. Dir. Svend Noldan, Werner Kortwich, Edmund Smith, Fritz Brunsch. Germany.

Victory of Faith (*Sieg des Glaubens*). 1933. Dir. Leni Riefenstahl. Germany.

Victory over Versailles (*Sieg über Versailles*). 1939. Dir. Wilhelm Stöppler. Germany.

Volga Boatmen (*Bateliers de la Volga*). 1936. Dir. Vladimir Strizhevsky. France.

Walpurgis Night (*Valborgsmässoafton*). 1935. Dir. Gustaf Edgren. Sweden.

Way Out West. 1937. Dir. James W. Horne. United States.

We Make Music (*Wir machen Musik*). 1942. Dir. Helmut Käutner. Germany.

White Slaves (*Weiße Sklaven*). 1937. Dir. Karl Anton. Germany.

Wife vs. Secretary. 1936. Dir. Clarence Brown. United States.

Woman at the Wheel (*Frau am Steuer*). 1939. Dir. Paul Martin, Germany.

Woman Comes to the Tropics (*Eine Frau kommt in die Tropen*). 1938. Dir. Harald Paulsen. Germany.

Women Are the Better Diplomats (*Frauen sind doch bessere Diplomaten*). 1941. Dir. Georg Jacoby. Germany.

Word and Deed (*Wort und Tat*). 1938. Dir. Fritz Hippler. Germany.

Years of Decision (*Jahre der Entscheidung*). 1939. Dir. Hans Weidemann and Carl Junghans. Germany.

Yesterday and Today (*Gestern und Heute*). 1938. Dir. Hans Steinhoff and Ben Keim. Germany.

Youth of the World (*Jugend der Welt*). 1936. Dir. Herbert Brieger and Carl Junghans. Germany.

Index